Physical Education & Activity for Elementary Classroom Teachers

Kim C. Graber
University of Illinois

Amelia Mays Woods
University of Illinois

PHYSICAL EDUCATION & ACTIVITY FOR ELEMENTARY CLASSROOM TEACHERS

Published by McGraw-Hill, a business unit of The McGraw-Hill Companies, Inc., 1221 Avenue of the Americas, New York, NY 10020. Copyright © 2013 by The McGraw-Hill Companies, Inc. All rights reserved. Printed in the United States of America. No part of this publication may be reproduced or distributed in any form or by any means, or stored in a database or retrieval system, without the prior written consent of The McGraw-Hill Companies, Inc., including, but not limited to, in any network or other electronic storage or transmission, or broadcast for distance learning.

Some ancillaries, including electronic and print components, may not be available to customers outside the United States.

This book is printed on recycled, acid-free paper containing 10% postconsumer waste.

1 2 3 4 5 6 7 8 9 0 QDB/QDB 1 0 9 8 7 6 5 4 3 2

ISBN 978-0-7674-1277-3
MHID 0-7674-1277-X

Vice President & Editor-in-Chief: *Mike Ryan*
Vice President & Director of Specialized Publishing: *Janice M. Roerig-Blong*
Publisher: *David Patterson*
Marketing Coordinator: *Colleen Havens*
Development Editor: *Darlene M. Schueller*
Project Manager: *Erin Melloy*
Design Coordinator: *Margarite Reynolds*
Cover Designer: *Studio Montage, St. Louis, Missouri*
Cover Image: *Jon Dessen/Illini Studio, Champaign, IL*
Buyer: *Louis Swaim*
Media Project Manager: *Sridevi Palani*
Compositor: *Aptara®, Inc.*
Typeface: *10/12 Times*
Printer: *Quad/Graphics*

All credits appearing on page or at the end of the book are considered to be an extension of the copyright page.

Library of Congress Cataloging-in-Publication Data
Graber, Kim C.
  Physical education and activity for elementary classroom teachers / Kim C. Graber, Amelia Mays Woods.
    p. cm.
  ISBN 978-0-7674-1277-3
  1. Physical education for children—Study and teaching (Elementary) 2. Physical education for children—Curricula. 3. Movement education—Study and teaching (Elementary) 4. Education, Elementary—Activity programs. I. Woods, Amelia Mays. II. Title.
  GV443.G7 2012
  372.86′044—dc23
                                                                                    2011040787

This book is written in loving honor of my incredible mother, Helene, whose children always came first, and Larry, whose mentorship made my career a possibility.

K.C.G.

This book is lovingly dedicated to my husband, Jeff, and children, Jack and Mary Elizabeth.

A.M.W.

Brief Contents

Contents

About the Authors

Kim C. Graber *University of Illinois*

Dr. Graber is an associate professor and associate head in the Department of Kinesiology and Community Health at the University of Illinois in Urbana-Champaign. She also is the director of the Teaching Academy in the College of Applied Health Sciences. She received her bachelor's degree from the University of Iowa, her master's from Teachers College Columbia University, and her doctorate from the University of Massachusetts at Amherst. Her research focuses on children's wellness, teacher education, and the scholarship of teaching and learning. She has served as president of the National Association for Sport and Physical Education, chair of the Curriculum and Instruction Academy, secretary of the Research Consortium, and member of the task force that wrote the national physical education assessments. At the University of Illinois she serves on the Faculty Senate Executive Committee, Teaching Advancement Board, and Leadership Coordinating Committee. She has published numerous articles in peer-refereed journals and books and has presented her work at dozens of national and international conferences, including an invited keynote address at the Healthy Schools Summit in Washington, DC. She was recently named a University of Illinois Distinguished Teacher Scholar and received the Campus Award for Excellence in Undergraduate Teaching.

Amelia Mays Woods *University of Illinois*

Dr. Woods is an Associate Professor of Kinesiology and Community Health at the University of Illinois, Urbana-Champaign. She holds a PhD from the University of South Carolina and also studied at the University of Tennessee and Winthrop University. She taught in Newberry, SC public schools. Dr. Woods's research interests center upon physical educators' movement through their career cycles. Specifics include studies of the supports necessary to sustain innovative practices; factors contributing increased teacher credibility within schools, and on traits and motivators of enthusiastic and growing teachers, including National Board Certified Physical Educators. Woods is also interested in children's school-based physical activity. Her work is published in *Journal of Teaching in Physical Education, Research Quarterly for Exercise and Sport,* and *Journal of Human Movement Studies.* She is a Fellow in the Research Consortium of the American Alliance for Health, Physical Education, Recreation and Dance, was named Indiana State University's Howard Richardson Outstanding Researcher, and received the Winthrop University Distinguished Alumna Award and Illinois Association Physical Education, Recreation and Dance Past Presidents Scholar Award. She repeatedly appears on the University of Illinois' Chancellor's List of Instructors Ranked as Excellent.

Preface

Several years ago, when we began searching for a physical education methods textbook written specifically for undergraduate students who intended to become classroom teachers, we were struck by the lack of appropriate books for this target audience. A number of excellent books had been written for physical education majors, but none that we believed adequately addressed the needs of the classroom teacher. Some books were written for an audience that already had advanced knowledge of the subject matter in the areas of motor learning, exercise physiology, physical fitness, anatomy, and professional activity courses (e.g., fitness, dance, gymnastics, racket sports, team sports). Others, since they targeted physical education majors, were written with the assumption that future teachers had advanced skill levels themselves and were eager to teach children about the psychomotor domain. As a result, we were forced to select a textbook that never felt comfortable to us or our students.

We quickly decided that if we were to continue preparing classroom teachers for the exciting opportunity to teach children about physical education and activity, we needed a book dedicated specifically to the needs of the elementary *classroom* teacher. Although we believe that the gymnasium also constitutes a classroom, we recognize that there are significant differences between the physical educator and the elementary-grade-level teacher who is most often referred to as the classroom teacher. First, the classroom teacher often has limited knowledge of the subject matter of physical education. Second, many have little interest or experience in teaching physical education. Third, some classroom teachers themselves have encountered unpleasant physical education experiences that resulted in their lack of desire to teach children about movement.

While we recognized that a lack of relevant resources existed for the classroom teacher, we also acknowledged the need for the classroom teachers to teach children about physical education and activity. Reports from the Surgeon General and Centers for Disease Control, along with recent legislation related to children's wellness, clearly indicate that physical activity is one of the most important components of a child's education. Although we *strongly* encourage all schools throughout the United States to employ a certified physical education specialist, we realize that classroom teachers are increasingly expected to serve as the primary physical education teacher, to supplement physical education on days when children are not exposed to a hired physical education specialist, to supervise students during recess, or to introduce them to physical activity breaks spaced periodically throughout the school day. Therefore, we decided to write a textbook that would sufficiently prepare classroom teachers to successfully and effectively engage students in physical education and physical activity at a basic level and in a safely constructed environment—in the gymnasium, on the playground, and in the classroom.

Since many colleges and universities divide a physical education methods course for classroom teachers into separate lecture and laboratory sections, this text is divided into two primary sections. The first section is written to address topics that are covered during lectures in a university classroom. The second is written to address activities covered during laboratory experiences in a gymnasium. Each section contains 12 relatively brief chapters that cover in adequate detail the most important points of the chapter's focus. The reason for brevity is to avoid inundating future classroom teachers with too much information and to facilitate retention of the most important aspects of the chapter. It is anticipated that this approach will enable future classroom teachers to easily read one chapter per week from each of the two sections (one lecture and one lab).

The thematic element that is woven throughout the text is one that encourages individuals to develop an appreciation for the subject matter of physical education. Regardless of previous experiences in physical education or sport settings, prospective classroom teachers will be exposed to a philosophic orientation that encourages the enjoyment of physical activity and acquisition of skills and knowledge that promote participation throughout the lifespan. The book clearly emphasizes that the purpose of physical education and activity is to engage children in maximum levels of activity throughout the school day. The instructional strategies and curricula that are presented are prioritized with this goal clearly in mind. Overall, the book is designed to be a primary reference for future classroom teachers and a valuable resource for certified classroom teachers.

The following elements have been incorporated into the book to help readers remember the most important concepts from each chapter and encourage thoughtful reflection about the material in each chapter.

HIGHLIGHTS OF LECTURE CHAPTERS

Key Points
All lecture chapters have key points that emphasize the most important elements of the text that learners should retain.

Thinking Challenge
Each chapter contains a series of thinking challenges that require readers to contemplate what they have read and subsequently complete a learning activity.

Do/Don't List
The Do/Don't checklist at the end of each chapter includes a list of behaviors or attitudes that classroom teachers should strive to implement and achieve and those they should avoid.

Boxes
Most chapters contain one or more boxes with information readers may find particularly interesting or instructive. Some boxes introduce new concepts while others invite readers to complete a specific task or observation.

Chapter Summary
The end of each chapter includes a brief summary to facilitate readers' reflection on the overall content introduced in the chapter.

Review Activities
Every chapter includes review activities that learners can complete independently or during class instruction.

Photos
Interesting photos have been selected to emphasize important points and make the textbook reader-friendly.

HIGHLIGHTS OF LAB CHAPTERS

Developmental Levels
Many chapters include information about the different phases that learners experience while acquiring motor skills.

Learning Cues
Chapters include key teaching points that classroom teachers can utilize when introducing students to different skills and activities.

Common Difficulties
Since learners often experience similar difficulties when learning new skills, a list of common difficulties is included so the classroom teacher knows what he or she might expect to observe.

Activities
All chapters include appropriate, fun, and challenging learning experiences that are designed to positively influence student acquisition of skills while simultaneously keeping children physically engaged throughout the lesson.

Modifications

Since learners acquire new skills and knowledge at different rates, and since some face special challenges, chapters include suggestions for how to modify activities to meet the individual needs of all learners.

Assessments

Suggestions for how teachers can assess student learning are provided at the end of chapters.

RESOURCES

Instructor resources are available on the website at www.mhhe.com/graber. Check it out!

McGraw-Hill Create™

Craft your teaching resources to match the way you teach! With McGraw-Hill Create, you can easily rearrange chapters, combine material from other content sources, and quickly upload content you have written like your course syllabus or teaching notes. Find the content you need in Create by searching through thousands of leading McGraw-Hill textbooks. Arrange your book to fit your teaching style. Create even allows you to personalize your book's appearance by selecting the cover and adding your name, school, and course information. Order a Create book and you'll receive a complimentary print review copy in 3–5 business days or a complimentary electronic review copy (eComp) via email in minutes. Go to www.mcgrawhillcreate.com today and register to experience how McGraw-Hill Create empowers you to teach *your* students *your* way.

Electronic Textbook Option

This text is offered through CourseSmart for both instructors and students. CourseSmart is an online resource where students can purchase the complete text online at almost half the cost of a traditional text. Purchasing the eTextbook allows students to take advantage of CourseSmart's web tools for learning, which include full text search, notes and highlighting, and email tools for sharing notes between classmates. To learn more about CourseSmart options, contact your sales representative or visit www.CourseSmart.com.

Acknowledgments

Writing a textbook involves more individuals than those whose names are listed on the cover of the text. We are enormously grateful to those listed below.

- Gary O'Brien, our editor at McGraw-Hill, who provided much needed encouragement, valuable advice, and mentorship from the first to the last draft of the book.
- Christopher Johnson, Executive Editor at McGraw-Hill, who made publication of this book possible.
- The incredible staff at McGraw-Hill: Janice Roerig-Blong, Vice President and Director; Erin Melloy, Project Manager; Darlene Schueller, Developmental Editor; Colleen Havens, Marketing Coordinator; Margarite Reynolds, Designer; Susan Norton, Copy Editor; and Anna Hoppman, Digital Asset Librarian.
- Our graduate students at the University of Illinois: David Daum, Timothy Kahle, Jenny Linker, and Jung Hwan Oh, who helped coordinate the photographic process.
- Our photographer, Jon Dessen at Illini Studio, who skillfully captured beautiful photographs of children engaged in movement.
- Chuck Hillman, Bonnie Hemrick, and the FIT Kids staff and participants who allowed us photographic access.
- The reviewers who provided valuable insights and advice that enabled us to improve the clarity and comprehensiveness of the text.

Dianne Busch
Southwestern Oklahoma State University

Judy Potter Chandler
Central Michigan University

Kay Daigle
Southeastern Oklahoma State University

Joel Dering
Cameron University

Joyce Ellis
Fort Hayes State University

Ripley Marston
University of Northern Iowa

Arthur "Tucker" Miller
The University of Montana

Betty Rust
Worcester State College

Shannon Siegel
California State University—San Bernardino

Ann-Catherine Sullivan
Otterbein University

- Our family and friends who provided much needed encouragement and an open ear throughout all stages of the writing process (and whose names can be found in our examples throughout the text): Helene Graber; Bob, Liz, Robert, and Peter Schmidt; Stu, Jenn, Tara, and Tessa Graber; Larry Locke; Jane McMullen; Jeff, Jack, and Mary Elizabeth Woods; Jerie Weasmer; Susan Lynn; and Patsy and Everett Mays.

Chapter **One**

Developing an Appreciation for Physical Education

Once you become employed as an elementary classroom teacher you will likely be required to undertake many more tasks than you currently imagine. In addition to teaching children how to read, write, spell, and master simple arithmetic, you also may be asked to supervise students at recess, in the lunchroom, or boarding the school bus. You will be faced with responsibilities such as constructing bulletin boards, designing homework assignments, planning special class events, and creating a lively classroom atmosphere. Some classroom teachers also will be asked to assume the unexpected task of planning and conducting daily physical education classes for children.

Many school districts throughout the nation either do not have adequate financial resources or have decided not to employ a trained physical education specialist for their elementary schools. This is unfortunate because trained physical education teachers have received specialized preparation that enables them to design appropriate curriculum, diagnose and assess incorrect movement patterns, provide proper feedback to learners, and teach motor activities that are appropriate for a child's level of development.

If you are employed in a school without a physical education specialist, it will most likely be your responsibility to provide the children in your classes with instruction in the subject matter. You are currently enrolled in an exciting course where you will have an opportunity to learn how to competently teach a variety of physical education activities. You will also learn how to integrate physical activity into other lessons that you teach such as reading and social studies. Although one course or textbook cannot provide all of the information about the field, if you are committed to learning about the subject matter, you can acquire a sufficient degree of knowledge that will enable you to provide competent physical education lessons to your students. Complete Thinking Challenge 1.1.

THINKING CHALLENGE 1.1	As a classroom teacher you will be asked to juggle multiple responsibilities. In many cases you will be required to complete tasks that you never anticipated and teach subjects for which you have had minimal preparation. How will you respond to these different challenges?

There are a few terms that you should be familiar with as you proceed through this textbook. Each emphasizes movement, but each has a different meaning in relation to how children participate in movement:

- *Physical education* includes structured movement experiences that are taught by a knowledgeable instructor. Activities are progressive, developmentally appropriate, and facilitated by a formal curriculum. When a physical education teacher shows children a series of dance sequences that are accompanied by music, they are participating in physical education.

- *Physical activity* refers to exercises and activities that children engage in independently or during physical education class. These activities, however, can be spontaneous and unstructured. Playing tag with friends during recess is one example of physical activity.

- *Recess* is a period of time in which children can engage in adult-supervised activities that occur primarily on a playground, playing field, or gymnasium. This period is designed to give children a break during the school day. Although most recess is unstructured, some schools are progressing toward more structured recess activities in order to engage students in physical activity. Talking with classmates (sedentary) and playing soccer with a group of friends (active) are examples of two types of activities in which children might participate during recess.

PROCESS AND CONTENT OF TEACHING PHYSICAL EDUCATION

The purpose of this text is twofold. First, you will be introduced to strategies that will teach you about the *process of teaching physical education,* or what is sometimes referred to as the *pedagogy* of teaching physical education. This is the information that is necessary to help you learn how to develop curriculum and teach the subject. In other words, process refers to the behaviors a teacher employs in order to help children learn about physical education. It encompasses such acts as establishing an effective learning environment, designing lessons, managing students, and providing instruction. If you are currently enrolled in a physical education methods class designed for the classroom teacher, these responsibilities will be discussed by the instructor during lectures and perhaps be modeled for you in the gymnasium. Although you also will learn how to teach from methods courses and textbooks that are specific to your home classroom, the physical activity setting (gymnasium, playing field, multipurpose area) is also a classroom that requires a special set of skills. Some instructional strategies that are effective in the students' home classroom can be transferred to and employed in the physical activity classroom. Some instructional strategies that are effective in the physical activity setting also can be applied in the home classroom. The intent of this text is not to duplicate information that you may acquire from other methods courses, but to provide you with the specific skills that will enable you to confidently teach the subject matter of physical education.

The second purpose of this text is to help you become familiar with the *content of physical education.* This includes learning about: (a) the basic content of the field, (b) the instructional activities that are appropriate for teaching basic content, and (c) the curriculum that organizes the instructional activities in developmentally appropriate ways. While physical education majors take individual courses to learn how to teach fitness, dance, gymnastics, outdoor education, team sports, and individual sports, you will not have adequate time in your undergraduate curriculum to learn about all of the activities that you might like to teach (see Box 1.1). Although this is unfortunate, it does not mean that you cannot provide competent instruction.

This text is designed to provide you with a basic understanding of the most important components of the subject matter. Hopefully, you will have had other physical activity experiences that will enable you to supplement the information you acquire here. Regardless of your experience, however, after reading this text you should have acquired sufficient knowledge about the process of teaching and content of physical education to enable you to enter a physical activity setting with some degree of confidence.

Prior Experiences in Physical Education

Physical education is often referred to by elementary students as their favorite subject in the overall school curriculum. Students enter the physical activity setting with a natural desire to be active and a tremendous enthusiasm for learning new skills and activities. That may be surprising if your most recent memory of physical education consists of less than appealing experiences in high school. Fortunately, teachers at the elementary level typically have the advantage of eager clientele.

Box 1.1

A certified physical education teacher has some knowledge of most of the content areas listed below and is proficient in several of them. Which of the following activities would you feel most comfortable teaching to elementary-aged students? How might you acquire additional knowledge that would enable you to teach in those areas in which you feel unprepared?

TEAM SPORTS	INDIVIDUAL SPORTS	FITNESS	OTHER
Basketball	Badminton	Aerobics	Adventure Education
Field Hockey	Gymnastics	Circuit Training	Aquatics
Floor Hockey	Martial Arts	Cycling	Basic Motor Skills
Football	Pickle Ball	Jogging	Bowling
Soccer	Racquet Ball	Rollerblading	Ballroom Dance
Softball	Track and Field	Weight Training	Creative Dance
Tennis			Folk/Square Dance
Volleyball			Hiking
			Locomotor Skills
			Non-locomotor Skills
			Modern Dance
			Outdoor Pursuits
			Rhythms

Try to recall experiences from physical education that you encountered at the elementary level by completing Thinking Challenge 1.2. Perhaps you remember physical education as an enjoyable subject in which you received an adequate number of learning trials, were exposed to an interesting curriculum, and had ample opportunities to be successful. These positive experiences may have enhanced your enthusiasm for the subject matter. You may, of course, have entered elementary school physical education with a positive attitude for the subject because your parents had already exposed you to physical activities at a young age. They may have enrolled you in t-ball or youth soccer, or invited you to accompany them during activities such as bike riding, jogging, swimming, or throwing and catching a ball. If you had that kind of opportune background, you may be excited by the possibility of being able to teach physical education.

THINKING CHALLENGE 1.2	When you recall your elementary physical education experiences, what are the first five things that you remember?
	1.
	2.
	3.
	4.
	5.

Fortunately, many school programs at the elementary level are regarded as effective, that is, children acquire motor skills and enjoy the subject. There are, however, elementary physical education programs, taught either by physical education specialists or classroom teachers, that are less than ideal. These can be characterized as classes in which students are allowed to choose teams (stigmatizing those who are last to be selected) and to ridicule others who have less ability, and in which teachers engage students in inappropriate activities. If you encountered such a program, it is probable that you have negative feelings about the

Parental modeling is important for instilling appropriate values in children about the significance of physical activity.

subject and will be less than enthusiastic about having to teach physical education to your students. Let's explore some of the consequences of inappropriate physical education.

Some teachers believe that students enjoy picking teams. This, however, is an ineffective instructional practice. Not only does it waste valuable learning time, but also those students who are low skilled or unpopular are inevitably the last to be chosen. When children consistently experience such humiliation their self-esteem is eroded and some develop a dislike for the subject. They are placed into a situation where they are encouraged to reflect on their own performance in relation to their classmates.

Teachers also can design learning activities that are well intentioned but have the same negative outcome as having students select their own teams (see Key Point 1-1). For example, teachers often incorporate relay races into their daily instructional plans. They do this with the belief that students will enjoy the activity and have an opportunity to improve their motor skills. This, however, is a fallacy. First, students rarely perform a skill correctly when they are being rushed. If students are asked to dribble a basketball to one end of the gymnasium and back during a race, they often sacrifice proper form in order to increase speed and win the race. Second, if teams are structured evenly so that all skill levels are represented on a team, those students who are slower or low skilled are often ridiculed by their high-skilled teammates. Although teachers may warn students that ridiculing other students will not be tolerated, teachers often are not privy to the many negative verbal and non-verbal messages that students communicate to one another.

Key Point 1-1

Even teachers who are well intentioned sometimes design learning experiences that have negative outcomes. It is always wise to consider the consequence of all activities before you incorporate them into the curriculum.

Teachers must structure the physical education curriculum carefully if learning is to occur. Interestingly, teachers often select their curriculum not because it promotes student learning but because students appear to enjoy particular kinds of learning activities. Do you remember participating in activities such as "Duck, Duck, Goose," "Musical Chairs," and "Steal the Bacon"? Unfortunately, these activities have relatively no learning value. Their only assets are that they are easy to plan and most children are eager participants.

If these activities did not promote learning, why were they incorporated into the physical education curriculum? On the one hand, your teacher may have been well intentioned but was untrained in how to develop appropriate learning activities. On the other hand, you may have been one of the unfortunate individuals to experience a curriculum that was designed by a lazy or uninspired teacher.

Let's explore one popular activity that almost all students throughout the United States have encountered. Can you guess what this activity may be? For many students it represented their favorite activity in physical education. For others, however, it became a source of shame, brutality, and dread. If you answered correctly, you know that this activity is referred to as "Dodge Ball," "Poison Ball," or "Bombardment." Although some students

Activities like "Musical Chairs" should be played at birthday parties, not in physical education. Too many children are eliminated, and physical activity is minimal.

were highly skilled participants and eagerly welcomed the opportunity to participate in what is most commonly called "Dodge Ball," there also were an equal number of students who encountered an entirely opposite experience. If you are fairly high skilled you may be rolling your eyes and thinking, "Give me a break. Dodge ball is a great learning activity. It was the activity I enjoyed most, and I do not understand why it should not be played in physical education." If you are like those students, your thinking is understandable. You probably were one of the last eliminated and enjoyed the opportunity to demonstrate your athletic prowess to your classmates. As a teacher, however, it is important that you consider the emotions of ALL students enrolled in your class. Begin by trying to answer the following questions: What was the purpose of playing Dodge Ball? What motor skills did you acquire by participating in this game? What unintended messages did lower-skilled students receive? If you answered that Dodge Ball has little academic purpose, does not encourage the development of motor skills, and has the potential to create negative feelings in students, you are correct. It is the type of game in which low-skilled players who require the most opportunity to practice basic ball handling, catching and throwing skills are eliminated first. Not only does it facilitate a violent environment because children are encouraged to hit other children forcefully with playground balls that can cause injury, it also has little academic value. Complete Thinking Challenge 1.3.

THINKING CHALLENGE 1.3	Write down three negative experiences that you or your classmates encountered in elementary school physical education. Do not use the samples that are discussed in the the text. In addition, write down three positive experiences that you or your classmates encountered. For the latter, consider how your teacher(s) may have taken precautions to insure that the planned learning experiences were positive for all learners.

Negative Experiences
1.
2.
3.

Positive Experiences
1.
2.
3.

You may wonder why some teachers incorporate either inappropriate learning activities into the curriculum or engage in ineffective instructional practices. This can easily be explained. Prior to entering a college or university, you spent approximately 13,000 hours in the public schools (Lortie, 1975). During this period of time, often referred to as pre-training, you had many opportunities to observe the teaching process, and you probably experienced many types of curricula. The result of this experience was that you developed strong beliefs about how to teach and what you intended to include in your curriculum. If you liked a particular teacher, you will be inclined to emulate that person. If you enjoyed a particular activity, you will be inclined to include that activity in the curriculum you design. The problem is that it is not wise to rely solely upon past experience. Instead, effective teachers carefully examine all of their practices. They determine how to teach and what to teach based on what they learned during teacher education, and they continue to learn and improve by availing themselves of training opportunities and good resource materials.

As a classroom teacher, you can bring many assets to the physical education setting. You probably have a love for children and a strong desire to help them succeed. You also have knowledge about the individual children in your classes and will know which children might be more physically skilled than others, which ones are more likely to cause behavioral disruptions, and which ones will listen attentively to your instructions. If you also enjoy physical activity or played on a youth sport team, those experiences will give you confidence.

SIGNIFICANCE OF THE SUBJECT MATTER IN TODAY'S WORLD

At no other point in time has physical education been better positioned to have an impact on students. Not only have the virtues of a physically active lifestyle been extolled in the media, but also a landmark report from the Surgeon General of the United States (U. S. Department of Health and Human Services [USDHHS]; 1996) that firmly emphasized the benefits obtained from participation in modest to vigorous physical activity dramatically changed the public's perception about the significance of physical education. In addition, statistics, such as those below have been used to justify the relevance of the subject matter in today's society:

- Since 1980, the number of overweight children in the United States has tripled, and 60 percent of those children have cardiovascular disease risk factors (National Association for Sport and Physical Education [NASPE] & American Heart Association [AHA], 2006).
- Activities such as playing video games and watching television are linked to obesity and low levels of physical activity (Clocksin, Watson, & Ransdell, 2002).
- Given the physical state of the nation's children, it is likely that this generation will have a shorter life expectancy than that of their parents (Olshansky et al., 2005).
- Only about one-half of young people in the United States exercise regularly or participate in vigorous physical activity (Griffith, 2001; USDHHS, 2000).
- As children increase in age, their participation in physical activity declines drastically (USDHHS, 1996).
- Approximately 50 percent of individuals between 12-21 are not vigorously active on a regular basis (USDHHS, 1996).

Surprisingly, despite the findings listed above the general population remains ignorant to or unconcerned about physical activity in youth. Consider these additional findings:

- Physical education is "the best hope for the shape of our nation" (NASPE & AHA, 2010, p. 4).
- Increasing evidence shows a strong connection between participation in physical activity and improved academic performance (U.S. Centers for Disease Control and Prevention, 2010).
- Ninety one percent of parents believe that there should be more physical education in school (Harvard School of Public Health, 2003).

The National Association for Sport and Physical Education (NASPE) recommends that:

- Schools should deliver comprehensive health and quality physical education programs that are taught by a certified physical education specialist (NASPE & AHA, 2006, 2010).
- Children at the elementary level should receive at least 150 minutes per week of physical education (NASPE & AHA, 2006, 2010).

Considering that the excerpts above represent only a fraction of the overwhelming evidence to support daily physical activity, it is astonishing that many elementary-aged children do not receive physical education in their curriculum. Even if you teach in a school that employs a certified physical education teacher, students would significantly benefit from a classroom teacher who supplements the physical education curriculum with appropriate activities during recess or regular physical activity breaks. Students would return to the classroom refreshed and ready for other academic activities. Most important, your actions would demonstrate to students the importance of physical activity (see Key Point 1-2).

Key Point 1-2

Model the significance of physical activity by maintaining an active lifestyle and incorporating physical education activities into the overall school curriculum whenever possible. If possible, try to allocate a minimum of 30-60 minutes per day for appropriate physical activities, particularly on those days in which students do not receive instruction from a certified physical education teacher.

STANDARDS-BASED PHYSICAL EDUCATION

During the latter part of the last century, reform efforts began to sweep the nation in all educational areas. The result was the development of learning standards that outlined what children at different grade levels should know and be able to do. In the case of physical education, a panel of experts was assembled by NASPE to develop learning standards that states could use or modify (NASPE, 1995). Revised in 2004, the six standards are visible in the curriculum guides and lesson plans of thousands of physical education professionals throughout the United States. The standards describe what students should learn from physical education; they will be presented and discussed in greater detail in Chapter 2.

PURPOSE OF PHYSICAL EDUCATION

The purpose of physical education has not changed significantly within the past few decades. Although experts may disagree on which specific activities should be emphasized, most would agree that it is a subject in which students should:

- develop and refine basic motor skills
- experience creativity through dance and gymnastics
- be exposed to a variety of developmentally appropriate activities and sports
- have opportunities to learn about and acquire a commitment to health-related fitness
- acquire an understanding of movement principles, strategies, concepts, and tactics
- experience enjoyment
- learn to work with others.

What has changed within the past few decades, however, is the significance placed on keeping students actively involved in moderate to vigorous physical activity for a substantial portion of the class period. Yes, there are classes in which students can be observed waiting in long lines for a turn. Certainly, these classes could not be characterized as effective. Instead, the effective class is one in which students are continuously learning and frequently moving. It is difficult to ignore the results of the statistics cited earlier. Therefore, regardless of the specific learning activities that you may decide to emphasize in your lessons, it is important that they include many opportunities for an extended period of physical activity.

Interestingly, physical education is one of the few subjects in which students are educated in three different domains. First, the *psychomotor domain* emphasizes learning specific skills that allow individuals to competently participate in games, small-sided sports, fitness, dance, and other activities that require movement. Second, the *cognitive domain* includes knowledge students acquire about the rules, strategies, and techniques of different activities. It also emphasizes learning about how one's body functions. Third, the *affective domain* emphasizes learning about one's feelings, attitudes, values, and beliefs about movement and the different physical activities that one performs. Let's take fitness as an example. When students engage in aerobics they are learning in the psychomotor domain by acquiring knowledge of how to complete a routine to music. They learn in the cognitive domain by monitoring their pulse to determine heart rate. They also learn in the affective domain when they reflect on their feelings about their performance in a written journal. Although a primary purpose of physical education is to educate students in the psychomotor domain, the cognitive and affective domains are equally important considerations when planning and implementing lessons. If you believe in educating the whole child, it will be important for you to include learning experiences in the curriculum that reflect an awareness of all three domains. Complete Thinking Challenge 1.4.

THINKING CHALLENGE 1.4	Think of one physical activity that you feel competent performing. List three elements from each of the domains that you would emphasize if you were designing an appropriate and purposeful curriculum. For example:

Unit Name   Basketball

PSYCHOMOTOR	**COGNITIVE**	**AFFECTIVE**
1. Dribble while moving in general space	1. Remember to push ball with fingertips, not palm	1. Enjoy the activity

Unit Name

PSYCHOMOTOR	**COGNITIVE**	**AFFECTIVE**
1.	1.	1.
2.	2.	2.
3.	3.	3.

Appropriate and Purposeful Physical Education

As discussed earlier, one course or a textbook will not empower you to develop a curriculum with the same degree of depth or breadth as a trained physical education specialist. Nevertheless, it will be possible for you to design and implement perfectly credible lessons that children will enjoy and that will help them progress toward important educational goals. It will be your responsibility to take advantage of your strengths and gradually improve in areas where your knowledge and skills are less adequate. If you are a highly skilled individual who has participated in a variety of physical activities, it is likely that your curriculum will reflect your current assets. If you are a lower-skilled individual, you

Physical education emphasizes learning in the psychomotor, cognitive, and affective domains.

may not be able to incorporate the same variety of lessons into your curriculum as your more highly skilled counterparts. That should not, however, give you an excuse for developing inadequate lessons or implementing a poor curriculum. Instead, begin by incorporating those activities with which you feel comfortable and try to gradually add others as you learn more about the possibilities and gain confidence from experience. Even if you rarely participate in physical activity, perhaps because of a dislike for the subject or limitations imposed by your own physical conditioning, you can engage your students in an exciting curriculum from which everyone benefits—including you.

Appropriate and purposeful physical education can range from teaching students how to develop and refine motor skills to teaching students to develop an appreciation for maintaining an active lifestyle. Although developing and refining complex motor skills requires a teacher who has more advanced subject matter knowledge, all teachers can easily engage students in locomotor activities and simple drills related to less complex motor skill development. Interestingly, teachers with a high degree of physical ability are not necessarily the most effective. Instead, it sometimes is the less physically gifted teacher who is the most effective. This individual may spend a greater amount of time planning instruction and considering the needs of individual learners.

Developing a Lifelong Commitment to Physical Activity

One outcome of appropriate and purposeful physical education should be that students develop a commitment to engaging in physical activity throughout their lifespan. For some individuals this will include participating in extracurricular sports and engaging in vigorous physical activities such as mountain biking, running, weight training, or aerobics. For others, this might include brisk walking, leisurely swimming, or making a commitment to walk up a flight of stairs instead of waiting for an elevator.

A teacher's role in encouraging students to develop an appreciation for physical activity cannot be overemphasized. As a role model, you have the potential to influence the life patterns that children begin to establish at an early age. Therefore, it is critical that you design a curriculum in which all students can be successful and find enjoyment. Equally important will be your ability to implement that curriculum in a way in which learners will be eager to become involved and will have adequate opportunity to participate without fear of ridicule, embarrassment, or danger. As a teacher you are a person of privilege. Unlike those in many other professional positions, you have an opportunity to influence the future generation of our nation. Use that power wisely. Take the challenge. Consider the significance of physical activity for maintaining a long and healthy life. Challenge

These children made the right decision to use the stairs.

your students to become active participants in life. In the end, the benefits will have been worth the effort expended.

Summary

There is overwhelming evidence to indicate that physical activity is an important lifelong pursuit. Ideally, children should participate in moderate to vigorous physical activity for at least 60 minutes per day (U.S. Department of Health and Human Services, 2008). In some cases, children benefit from instruction that is provided on a regular basis by a certified physical education teacher. In other cases, classroom teachers are asked to teach this important subject. Regardless of your own previous experiences or knowledge of the subject, it is important to design a curriculum that is appropriate, emphasizes a lifelong commitment to engaging in regular physical activity, and facilitates success for all participants. See Box 1.2 for some dos and don'ts for helping students develop an appreciation for physical education.

DO AND DON'T CHECKLIST

Do	Don't
☐ insure that all learners receive an appropriate number of learning trials	☐ incorporate activities into the curriculum that are inappropriate
☐ keep learners active for the majority of the class period	☐ allow students to select their own teams
☐ consider the needs of all learners when planning and implementing instruction	☐ engage students in activities that have little curricular value
☐ engage students in appropriate and purposeful physical education	☐ ask students to participate in activities that could be humiliating
☐ model the importance of acquiring a physically active lifestyle.	☐ settle on a mediocre curriculum.

Review Activities

1. Define the process of teaching and the content of teaching physical education. Provide one example of each.
2. Describe your experiences in elementary physical education to a classmate.
3. Describe the ways in which you would like the physical education curriculum that you design to be both similar to and different from what you encountered as a pupil.
4. Discuss the degree to which you feel competent as a performer of physical activity and the degree to which you would feel comfortable teaching physical education.
5. Add to the items listed in Box 1-2.

References

Clocksin, B. D., Watson, D. L., & Ransdell, L. (2002). Understanding youth obesity and media use: Implications for future intervention programs. *Quest, 54*, 259–275.

Griffith, D. (2001, May). California Physical Education Health Project. *Schools fail to make the grade on health.* Retrieved December 21, 2005, from http://csmp.ucop.edu/cpehp/news/sftmtgoh.html

Harvard School of Public Health (2003). *Obesity as a public health issue: A look at solutions.* Boston: Author.

Lortie, D. C. (1975). *Schoolteacher: A sociological study.* Chicago: University of Chicago Press.

National Association for Sport and Physical Education. (1995). *Moving into the future: National standards for physical education: A guide to content and assessment.* Reston, VA: Author.

National Association for Sport and Physical Education. (2004). *Moving into the future: National standards for physical education* (2nd ed.). Reston, VA: Author.

National Association for Sport and Physical Education & American Heart Association (2006). *2006 Shape of the nation report. Status of physical education in the USA.* Reston, VA: National Association for Sport and Physical Education.

National Association for Sport and Physical Education & American Heart Association (2010). *2010 Shape of the nation report. Status of physical education in the USA.* Reston, VA: National Association for Sport and Physical Education.

Olshansky, S. J., et al. (2005). A potential decline in life expectancy in the United States in the 21st century. *New England Journal of Medicine, 352,* 1128–1145.

U.S. Centers for Disease Control and Prevention (2010). *The association between school-based physical activity, including physical education, and academic performance.* Atlanta, GA: U.S. Department of Health and Human Services.

U.S. Department of Health and Human Services (1996). *Physical activity and health: A report of the Surgeon General.* Atlanta, GA: U.S. Department of Health and Human Services, Centers for Disease Control and Prevention, National Center for Chronic Disease Prevention and Health Promotion.

U.S. Department of Health and Human Services (2000). *Healthy People 2010: Understanding and improving health.* Washington, DC: U.S. Government Printing Office, 22B, pp. 1–25.

U.S. Department of Health and Human Services (2008). *2008 Physical activity guidelines for Americans.* Washington, DC: Author.

Chapter **Two**

Curriculum Planning

As a classroom teacher, you will be responsible for designing a yearly curriculum that includes learning goals and appropriate educational activities. In addition to planning your curriculum for the teaching of reading, science, math, and social studies, you also may be required to integrate physical education into the overall curriculum for the grade level you are teaching. Our goal is to provide you with the skills necessary to successfully design that portion of your curriculum which relates to physical education. We also hope that the skills and knowledge you acquire from this chapter will assist you in developing other aspects of your classroom curriculum.

Although you will gain valuable knowledge from reading this text and completing a methods course related to teaching physical education, it is likely that you will need some assistance in planning an appropriate curriculum for your students. While the lab chapters are designed to provide you with a broad spectrum of developmental activities, you will also need to do some legwork. If a physical education specialist is assigned to your school, and you are writing a curriculum to supplement the curriculum taught by the specialist, it is likely that you will find a good friend in him or her. In almost all cases, that individual will welcome your interest in physical education and be happy to help you design an appropriate supplemental curriculum that provides children with increased opportunities to be active throughout the school day. By working with the specialist, you are participating in *collaboration,* an event that occurs when two or more individuals work together for a common purpose.

Unfortunately, many classroom teachers do not have an opportunity to collaborate with a physical education teacher because their school does not employ a certified specialist. If this is the case in your school, it would be wise to seek help from physical educators who might be employed in other schools within your district. You also can generate additional

Collaborating with other teachers from the school community is enjoyable and refreshing, and the result is a stronger curriculum.

ideas about teaching physical education by speaking with experts in your community who are employed as community recreation directors, fitness specialists, and outdoor adventure guides. At a minimum, it would be wise to seek the advice of other classroom teachers in your school, particularly those who have successfully incorporated physical education into the curriculum. Once you have acquired adequate knowledge about curriculum development and have accessed the appropriate resources, such as textbooks and journal articles, you can begin designing a physical education curriculum for your class. Complete Thinking Challenge 2.1.

THINKING CHALLENGE 2.1	List those individuals with whom you could collaborate when developing a physical education curriculum. In addition, state why that person would be particularly helpful.

One of the more difficult aspects of planning a physical education curriculum is finding enough time in the school day to accomplish everything that you might like to teach. Although teachers often have good intentions, they sometimes try to accomplish too much. Instead of trying to teach children every conceivable skill or concept that teachers might believe is important for them to learn, it is better for them to learn fewer skills very well.

If you are responsible for teaching physical education, try to maximize the amount of time that you allocate to the subject matter. Although you also need to worry about having adequate time to teach subjects like reading and science, remember that participating in physical activity and physical education can actually help improve academic performance in your home classroom (U.S. Centers for Disease Control and Prevention, 2010).

The National Association for Sport and Physical Education (NASPE) recommends that children at the elementary level receive at least 150 minutes of physical education every week. This means that at least 30 minutes per day should be set aside to engage students in meaningful, sequenced, and appropriate physical education activities (National Association for Sport and Physical Education [NASPE] & American Heart Association [AHA], 2010). In addition, teachers can also contribute to the recommended 60 minutes of physical activity per day that children receive by incorporating meaningful physical activity opportunities when teaching other subject areas (U.S. Department of Health and Human Services, 2008). Teachers can even give children brief physical activity breaks in the home classroom that enable them to run in place or stretch their muscles. Remember, for some children, school is the only place where they have an opportunity to participate in physical activity during the day. Planning a meaningful physical education curriculum and including frequent bouts of physical activity during the school day will make an important contribution to children's health and even their academic performance.

CURRICULUM DEFINED

In all probability, you can provide a definition for the term "curriculum." In fact, you would probably agree with most educational scholars who state that a curriculum is an aggregate of courses and learning experiences that are offered to students at a school, college, or university. At minimum, a curriculum is a yearly guide of the goals and activities that students will achieve. It can also be an extended longitudinal guide, whereby teachers plan goals and activities for the duration of a child's enrollment at an individual school. It is unlikely that classroom teachers assigned to a particular grade level would plan a longitudinal curriculum for physical education unless they were on a collaborative school planning committee; it is more common that a physical education teacher would be responsible for planning an extended, longitudinal curriculum. Since the specialist is responsible for teaching students in all grade levels, he or she must consider what students will learn as they progress through the grade levels. Since classroom teachers are typically only responsible for students during a one-year span of time, curriculum as it is described in this text will be considered a one-year plan. Although you will not need to plan what children learn from one year to the next, you will want to consider planning a sequenced curriculum, where children gradually build upon the different skills they are learning.

This chapter is designed to give you advice concerning the selection of developmentally appropriate goals and learning activities for your students. In Lecture Chapter 3, you will learn how to take these goals and incorporate them more specifically into daily lesson plans. Whereas a curriculum is broad and general, lesson plans are narrow and specific. In order to effectively plan the latter, a teacher must first consider the former—developing a broad and general curriculum to meet the needs of learners at a particular stage of development.

NATIONAL STANDARDS FOR PHYSICAL EDUCATION

Regardless of academic subject area, the past two decades have been considered a period of educational reform. Beginning with the release of *A Nation At Risk* (National Commission on Excellence in Education, 1983), a report that resulted in the development of national educational goals because American students had fallen short of their international counterparts in areas such as math and science, teachers were increasingly mandated to demonstrate student achievement in their classes. In the area of physical education, NASPE responded to reform efforts by appointing the Standards and Assessment Task Force to develop national content standards for physical education. Simultaneously, standards were rapidly being developed by other professional organizations for their area of disciplinary specialization. Since the publication of the first physical education standards (NASPE, 1995), and subsequent revision (NASPE, 2004), the standards have served to ground the curriculum of physical education in many schools throughout the nation. At present, 48 states (92 percent) have also developed state standards, and the six NASPE national standards are typically addressed within the state standards (NASPE & AHA, 2010).

The six physical education content standards listed in Box 2.1 inform teachers about what students should know and be able to accomplish at the end of each grade level. When developing a physical education curriculum, all six should be reflected in your goals and activities. Standard 1 relates to motor skill competency within the psychomotor domain, and includes locomotor (running, jumping, sliding), non-manipulative (stretching, transferring weight, twisting), and manipulative (throwing, catching, striking) skills. In earlier grades, when children are at the initial stages of development, teachers focus on teaching basic motor skill development. As students progress upward in grade level and developmental stages of learning, they begin to incorporate fundamental skills into partner and small-sided games that are a precursor to later participation in more competitive activities

Box 2.1

NASPE National Physical Education Content Standards (NASPE, 2004)

A physically educated person:

Standard 1: Demonstrates competency in motor skills and movement patterns needed to perform a variety of physical activities.

Standard 2: Demonstrates understanding of movement concepts, principles, strategies, and tactics as they apply to the learning and performance of physical activities.

Standard 3: Participates regularly in physical activity.

Standard 4: Achieves and maintains a health-enhancing level of physical fitness.

Standard 5: Exhibits responsible personal and social behavior that respects self and others in physical activity settings.

Standard 6: Values physical activity for health, enjoyment, challenge, self-expression, and/or social interaction.

When students participate in meaningful locomotor, non-manipulative, and manipulative curricular activities, they are working to achieve NASPE Standard 1.

and sports. Of the states that have state standards, 98 percent address NASPE Standard 1 (NASPE & AHA, 2010).

Standard 2 emphasizes knowledge development related to the cognitive domain. It was designed to ensure that students understand the tactics, strategies, and principles of movement along with the rules and history of different sports and activities.

Standards 3 and 4 correspond to the psychomotor domain, but to physical activity participation and fitness acquisition, not skill development. They were written to encourage the development of health-related fitness and commitment to engaging in physical activity throughout the lifespan.

Finally, Standards 5 and 6 are compatible with the affective domain. Standard 5 promotes respect for self and others, such as appreciation of diversity and special needs in the physical activity environment. Standard 6 encourages children to value physical activity for the sake of personal health, self-expression, social interaction, and for the challenges it provides.

The NASPE task force wrote the physical education standards in a format that matched standards associated with other academic subjects such as reading and math. In the majority of cases, the standards were written to address what students should know and be able to achieve in the grade level ranges of K-2, 3-5, 6-8, and 9-12. In order to determine if children are able to achieve the standards at the end of each grade level range (2, 5, 8, and 12), the task force also developed sample performance outcomes, some of which are described in Box 2.2.

For classroom teachers, the national standards and suggested outcomes are an important resource for planning curriculum goals and activities that are developmentally appropriate and achievable for students in the lower-level grade ranges of K-2 and upper-level ranges of 3-5. Although some may be more easily achieved than others, with effective instruction and appropriate developmental learning activities, children who are considered physically

Physical education class offers opportunities for students to learn to cooperate and appreciate difference in others.

Sample NASPE performance outcomes (NASPE, 2004)   Box 2.2

GRADES K-2
Standard 1:

- Drops a ball and catches it at the peak of the bounce.
- Performs a simple dance step in keeping with a specific tempo (e.g., slow-slow-fast-fast-fast).

Standard 2:

- Identifies correctly various body parts (e.g., knee, foot, arm, palm).
- States the short-term effects of physical activity on the heart and lungs.

Standard 3:

- Participates in chasing and fleeing activities outside of school.
- Engages in moderate to vigorous physical activity on an intermittent basis.

Standard 4:

- Participates in a variety of games that increase breathing and heart rate.
- Increases arm and shoulder strength by traveling hand-over-hand along a horizontal ladder (i.e., monkey bars).

Standard 5:

- Shows compassion for others by helping them.
- Honestly reports the results of work.

Standard 6:

- Continues to participate when not successful on the first try.
- Identifies several activities that are enjoyable.

Grades 3-5
Standard 1:

- Demonstrates good posture while lifting and carrying an object.
- Dribbles then passes a basketball to a moving receiver.

Standard 2:

- Explains how appropriate practice improves performance.
- Designs a new game incorporating at least two motor skills, rules, and strategies.

Standard 3:

- Participates in organized sport activities provided through local community programs.
- Participates in an intramural sports program provided by the school.

Standard 4:

- Maintains heart rate within the target heart rate zone for a specified length of time during an aerobic activity.
- Runs the equivalent of two laps around a regulation track.

Standard 5:

- Regularly encourages others and refrains from put-down statements.
- Cooperates with all class members by taking turns and sharing equipment.

Standard 6:

- Chooses to participate in group physical activities.
- Defends the benefits of physical activity.

educated should be able to achieve the standards at some point within their respective grade level range. Complete Thinking Challenge 2.2.

THINKING CHALLENGE 2.2   Select the grade level that you are most interested in teaching, and list one learning activity that you believe would be appropriate for accomplishing each of the performance outcomes listed in Box 2.2.

DESIGNING A DEVELOPMENTAL CURRICULUM

Now that you have learned about the NASPE Standards and performance outcomes that apply to the elementary grades of K-2 and 3-5, you can begin to think about the type of curriculum that you would like to develop. As you learn more from the lab chapters about the content of physical education and developmental levels of children, your curriculum will become increasingly refined. These chapters will also help to acquaint you with how to properly sequence your activities.

Developmental Stages

Physical education specialists are required to take courses that vary from motor development and control to physical activity and instructional methods. They spend countless hours receiving information and completing courses designed to teach them about the content area, curriculum construction, and how to diagnose and assess the developmental levels of learners. Unfortunately, the classroom teacher will not have the same extensive opportunities. You will gain some fundamental knowledge from the course in which you are now enrolled; however, it would be unrealistic to expect you to acquire the same depth of information related to distinguishing developmental differences in children as that of a physical education major. Instead of attempting to teach you specifics about children's development when performing locomotor, non-manipulative, and manipulative movement activities, you will learn to assess a child's level of development by matching it to one of three basic stages.

Stage I.

The first level of development is synonymous to a beginning or unrefined level of performance. Stage I refers to students who are only beginning to learn and perform a skill. They have little control of their movements and tend to make numerous mistakes. Below are some examples of what you might see during Stage I.

- When jumping forward, Amanda loses her balance and falls.
- Robert keeps his arms held stiff and outright when trying to catch a ball.
- When attempting to skip, Peter has difficulty remembering that he must pause to hop.
- During a lesson in which students are supposed to use the palm of their hand to consecutively hit a ball upward, Tonisha cannot consistently make contact.
- Although Jose appears to enjoy kicking, the ball is pushed forward only a few feet.

While these examples tend to be more characteristic of children in the lower grade range (K-2), it also is possible to encounter Stage I learners in the upper grades. For example, overhand throwing is a difficult skill to acquire. If a child has not had some form of instruction, it is possible to observe a 5th grade student who is at the Stage I level of development.

Stage II.

The next stage of development, which is synonymous with an intermediate level of performance, is referred to as Stage II. Children at this level have acquired some degree of skill in executing a particular movement. They will demonstrate greater consistency and easily perform the skill in an *invariant* environment, one that is stable and unchanging. For example, children will be able to control a ball when dribbling alone. At this level, however, learners are not yet ready to integrate skills they are acquiring into complex games that resemble regulation sports. Instead, they need additional practice in increasingly complex activities. They are ready to integrate skills into simple partner and small group activities, but not into large group activities that require the child to adjust to an ever-changing or *dynamic* environment. Below are some examples of students you might observe at the Stage II level of development.

- Antonio and his partner can overhand volley a beach ball back and forth for five consecutive trials.
- Lydia can integrate three skills (twisting, curling, and transferring weight) and three concepts (high, strong, and alongside) into a repetitive creative movement routine.
- Running down the length of the gym, George can throw a ball back and forth to a partner without missing.
- Gordon is able to complete a pike and straddle forward roll in succession.

Although it is tempting to plan increasingly advanced activities once a child has reached Stage II, it is important to create an environment in which he or she can be successful. This

Students who achieve some success while consecutively volleying a beach ball back and forth are probably at the Stage II level of development.

necessitates that the teacher develop activities for an environment that falls somewhere between invariant and dynamic. This is difficult for any teacher, regardless of whether or not he or she is a physical education specialist. With observation and practice, however, the classroom teacher will learn to create activities that are appropriate for this level of development.

Stage III.

An increasingly advanced level of development, Stage III, will generally not be witnessed in students who are in the lower grades (K-2) unless activities are basic and easily achievable. For example, many students should be able to competently perform locomotor skills by the end of 2nd grade, but activities that require greater skill, such as volleying, catching, and throwing, will not be refined unless the child has received adequate instructional opportunities outside of school. In the 3-5 grade range, however, teachers can expect to see students advance to Stage III for an increased number of activities such as dribbling, kicking, and chasing. Teachers may begin to observe students who can achieve the following:

- Brittany can successfully rebound a basketball and immediately pass it to a team member when playing 3-on-3 basketball.
- During a class demonstration, Larry and Sam perform a one-minute gymnastics routine that flows smoothly, integrates complex concepts, and can be explained to others.
- Benjamin and Helene play a modified game of badminton in which they must keep the shuttlecock in motion for 10 consecutive volleys back and forth across the net.
- Paige and her two teammates are able to effectively integrate both offensive and defensive strategies during a 4-on-4 game of soccer.

Remember, children will not necessarily be at the same level of development for all skills and activities that they are learning. If they are just learning how to skip in 4th grade, they will be at Stage I. At the same time, however, they may be at Stage III in kicking. Those who have had more opportunities to learn a skill and practice it appropriately will be at a higher level of development. Therefore, you will need to structure your physical education curriculum to meet the different needs of students in the same way that you would structure your reading curriculum. Not all activities you present will be appropriate for all children. As a result, the activities you introduce will need to be varied. Further, you will need to use caution to sequence your activities so they are introduced to children at an appropriate level and gradually increased in difficulty as students improve and can handle more challenging activities. The lab chapters will help you to make wise decisions about selecting and sequencing activities. See Key Point 2-1 for what you can anticipate when teaching physical education.

Key Point 2-1

A teacher who understands different stages of learning knows that:

1. It is possible to be at Stage III in kicking but Stage I in throwing.
2. As students progress upward in grade level, differences in skill level will become more apparent.
3. Some children may regress, particularly without frequent practice. For example, they might demonstrate Stage II characteristics of catching in October but regress to Stage I in January if they have not received practice or instructional activities in the interim.

Developing Realistic Curricular Goals

Before developing a new curriculum, you will want to evaluate any pre-existing curricular documents. If previous plans are not available, you will need to start planning from scratch. Do your homework by following those suggestions that were provided earlier in the chapter. That is, speak with the physical education teacher in your school, or if a specialist is not employed, speak with other physical education teachers in the district. Talk to physical activity specialists in the community. Ask students what they would like to learn in physical education. Involve your principal and school nurse, asking his or her input concerning what they hope can be achieved from the curriculum. Collaborate with other classroom teachers and acquire a variety of resources that include books, the National Standards (NASPE, 2004), and information about how much time per day is allocated for teaching physical education and where that instruction will occur.

Once you have accomplished the basics as described above, you are ready to think about what goals you would like to accomplish throughout the year. In order to develop realistic and attainable goals, you will want to follow three basic procedures.

Procedure #1.

As part of determining how much you can accomplish, you will need to know how many instructional days are available throughout the year. You can easily calculate this by multiplying the number of days per week in which you will teach physical education by the number of weeks in the school year. Subtract from this total the number of days in which physical education will be cancelled due to special events like field trips. Although some schools meet year round, most are scheduled to convene for 180 days per year, which equates to 36 weeks of instruction in physical education. For example:

> 2 days per week assigned to physical education $\times$ 36 weeks = 72 days
> 72 days − 6 days of special events = 66 days of instruction in physical education
> 66 days $\times$ 30 minutes of instruction = 1,980 minutes (1,980 ÷ 60 minutes = 33 hours)
> Grand total of *66 class days or 33 hours* of physical education per year

You might be surprised how little time is available during the year for physical education. Complete Thinking Challenge 2.3 to see if you can creatively find ways to increase this amount of time.

THINKING CHALLENGE 2.3	List five ways in which you can increase the amount of time allocated to physical education without reducing time in any of the other content areas you will be required to address.

Procedure #2.

List all of the goals that you would like to achieve. Be extravagant and think big. Brainstorm every form of knowledge and skill you believe students should acquire by the end of the year for the grade level that you will be teaching. Once you have generated this list, you will quickly realize that little can be accomplished in only 33 hours of time. Perhaps you will increase your instructional time by restructuring recess into purposeful physical education. Regardless, you will need to reduce your list to encompass only those goals that are achievable in 33 hours. You might reduce the list by eliminating activities you would have difficulty teaching because you have limited knowledge and do not wish to teach incorrect concepts, introduce inappropriate learning activities, or create an unsafe environment. You might further reduce the list because you do not have facilities and equipment, such as a swimming pool, that would allow you to teach some activities.

As you refine your list of goals, ask yourself two important questions: (1) Are my activities consistent with the NASPE Standards (or your state standards), and (2) Are they achievable given the amount of available instructional time? As emphasized in Key Point 2-2, at this point it is far better to think small and achieve your desired goals than to think large and have students participate in too many activities for which they have not yet developed the necessary prerequisite skills.

Key Point 2-2

It is better to successfully achieve a smaller number of goals than to achieve none because you have set an unrealistic number.

Procedure #3.

Now that you know what goals you wish to achieve, formally integrate them into the curriculum by writing them in sentence format. It will be very important that you write clear and achievable goals because your objectives and learning activities will be grounded in your goal statements. That is, for every goal you should have an appropriate learning activity. On the flip side, for every learning activity you should have an achievable goal.

Specifically, goals are broad statements concerning the skills and knowledge you anticipate students will acquire. Goals are not lists of specific activities that students will perform or statements concerning how they will be evaluated. They are much more general and less inclusive, and they address learning outcomes. Curriculum goals might appear as follows:

- Students will be able to perform locomotor skills.
- Students will throw and catch at different levels and with force.
- Students will perform gymnastic routines that incorporate different concepts.
- Students will understand the concept of force and be able to integrate it into a variety of manipulative activities.
- Students will understand the different components of basic motor skills.
- Students will develop an appropriate degree of cardiovascular endurance and engage in cardiovascular activities on a regular basis outside of physical education class.
- Students will enjoy themselves while participating in creative activities like dance.

Equipment and Facilities

It is much easier to write a curriculum when you have an unlimited amount of equipment and excellent learning facilities. If a physical education specialist is employed at your school, there will likely be a wide variety of equipment available. If the physical education teacher, however, is unwilling to share the equipment for fear of loss or damage, you will need to be creative. Although you might find his or her perspective on equipment sharing unreasonable, try to understand that the physical education teacher receives one of the lowest budgets in the school for purchasing some of the most expensive equipment. If a specialist is not employed at your school, again you will probably have access to limited equipment. In either of the less optimistic scenarios above, it is possible to acquire excellent equipment by being resourceful and proactive. See Box 2.3 for creative ways to acquire equipment.

Box 2.3

CREATIVE WAYS TO ACQUIRE EQUIPMENT

1. Ask parent volunteers to construct homemade equipment like beanbags.
2. Think of creative ways to use everyday products that would otherwise be disposed (e.g., paper towel holders as batons, milk cartons as objects to kick, sealed potato chip canisters with dried peas as musical instruments, or oatmeal containers as cones).
3. Request tennis instructors at park districts and country clubs to save balls that they would otherwise discard.
4. Fundraise for new equipment by hosting a school walk-a-thon.

Despite the obvious fact that your curriculum will, to a large extent, be influenced by the equipment and facilities available to you, try to think of ways to teach the activities you deem important within the environmental constraints you encounter. Of course, if you do not have access to mats, it will be more difficult, perhaps impossible, to teach basic gymnastics, and you may have to remove that content area from your intended curriculum. Despite periodic setbacks, such as inadequate equipment, if you demonstrate to your principal that you have developed a quality physical education program, he or she might be willing to help establish a small equipment fund to purchase necessary items like balls.

Once you know what equipment and facilities are available, list them under a major heading in your curriculum plan. Of course, as you develop individual learning activities, this list will be modified. It does, however, provide you with a place to begin. This section of your curriculum is typically preceded by your goals. Finally, be sure to consider how you will respond to inclement weather on occasions when you plan to be outdoors.

Planning for the Year

The next component of curriculum development is likely to require the most thought, ingenuity, effort, and resources. It also can be the most enjoyable aspect of planning. Now that you have listed appropriate goals and have a general sense of the equipment and facilities available to you, it is time to begin planning what activities you will teach during each day of the academic year. This process involves two primary steps.

Most classroom teachers must be creative if they are to acquire an adequate amount of equipment to meet the curricular needs of their students.

Sample Block Calendar   Box 2.4

TUESDAY, SEPTEMBER 1

Warm-up: Freeze Tag (3 minutes)

Activity: Locomotor skills & pathways (22 minutes)

Review: Reiterate components of each skill while stretching (5 minutes)

TUESDAY, SEPTEMBER 8

Warm-up: Throwing a ball against the wall (2 minutes)

Activity: Throwing a ball with a partner from different distances (15 minutes)

Throwing the ball up in the air alone and at different levels (10 minutes)

Review: Discuss components of an overhand throw (3 minutes)

THURSDAY, SEPTEMBER 3

Warm-up: Dance freely to music (5 minutes)

Activity: Develop a repetitive and creative movement routine to music integrating flow and pathways (22 minutes)

Review: Select two groups to demonstrate while students stretch (3 minutes)

THURSDAY, SEPTEMBER 10

Warm-up: Seal tag (3 minutes)

Activity: Focus on upper body strength:

Crab soccer in groups of 5 (12 minutes)

Different balancing poses with weight primarily supported by arms (12 minutes)

Review: Discussion of how to achieve upper-body strength while stretching upper-body muscles (3 minutes)

Determining Time for Individual Activities

Let's use the example previously given and say that you have 66 days of instructional time at your disposal. At this stage in curriculum development, you must consider how much time you will spend on achieving each goal. Obviously, you will make adjustments to your goals, deleting some and adding others, as you consider how much time will be needed to accomplish each. If you determine that 10 percent of your year should be devoted to teaching locomotor activities, you will devote 6.6 days to achieving that goal. If one of your goals states that students will understand the concept of force and be able to integrate it into a variety of manipulative activities, you might devote 5 percent or 3.3 days of instruction to teaching force as it relates to kicking, throwing, and volleying. In addition, there will be days during the year that you can emphasize force, even though that might not the primary goal of the lesson for that day.

Once you complete this process, the sum of time allocated to individual goals should total 100 percent. In order to make things easier, if you determine that 9.8 days will be devoted to creative movement, you might adjust that figure upward to 10 instructional days. This, of course, will require that you also adjust other days downward in order to retain the figure of 100 percent.

Developing a Block Calendar

After determining what percentage of time will be spent on each goal, you are ready to consider what activities you will teach to match your goals. In addition, you will enter those activities into a block calendar that corresponds to the academic year for your school. See Box 2.4 as an example. If you are assigned to teach only on Tuesdays and Thursdays, develop a table that includes only those two days. If you are strongly committed to the importance of physical education, you may decide to develop a block calendar for every day of the year. On those days in which you will be formally teaching physical education, you will be very specific. On non-physical education days, you may wish to state how you will incorporate physical activity into your lesson by using time during recess or providing children with short activity breaks after each hour of instruction to engage them in physical activities for two to three minutes. Complete Thinking Challenge 2-4.

THINKING CHALLENGE 2.4

Think of five different ways in which you could incorporate physical activity into your classroom activities.

Classroom teachers who are committed to physical activity have creative solutions for keeping children active throughout the school day.

You will notice that each day of instruction in the block calendar illustrated in Box 2.4 is divided into three sections. The first, *warm-up*, is geared toward engaging children in vigorous activities that directly relate to the lesson focus for the day. These activities should be engaging and enjoyable, not the traditional kind in which you may have been asked to participate as a child (e.g., push-ups, sit-ups, running laps). The second section, *activity*, briefly describes one or more activities that will achieve a particular goal(s) and provide the major focus for the lesson. These activities should be sequenced so they become increasingly more challenging as students acquire skill. The third, *review,* is a brief period of time in which students cool down while reviewing major concepts taught during the lesson. Although time considerations are more typically addressed in individual lesson plans (see Chapter 3), some teachers also like to include a time dimension within their block calendar.

A component of planning the block calendar includes knowing when to cluster activities so children acquire success before moving further. This requires some knowledge and experience. As your knowledge of physical education matures, you will learn which activities require greater curricular emphasis. You also will learn that it is important to return to more challenging activities periodically during the year so that students do not regress in their performance or forget important elements of the skill. For example, overhead volleying, one of the more difficult skills for students to acquire, may be best taught over a span of three consecutive days and then reviewed at two other points throughout the school year.

EVALUATING THE CURRICULUM

An important aspect of curriculum development includes evaluation. As a novice teacher, you will make many mistakes during your induction years. Never chastise yourself for imperfection. Some of the greatest ideas that we have today have been born as a result of human error. When particular activities fail, do not immediately abandon them without reflecting on why they were unsuccessful. Make modifications and attempt the activity again in the future. If you determine that an activity was far too simple, not enjoyable, or void of learning value, make a note in your block calendar to include a different activity in subsequent years.

Although it is unlikely that you will be asked to evaluate the physical education curriculum that has been developed by a specialist, it is incumbent on you to evaluate the physical education curriculum that you develop for your students. As curriculum experts, we recommend that you thoroughly evaluate your curriculum every three to five years. Once you have developed a strong curriculum, it is unlikely that you will need to re-develop an entire curriculum from scratch; instead you will revise what you have already developed in light of new information and in order to remain current. Below are some evaluation techniques you may choose to employ:

- Invite physical education teachers or classroom colleagues to comment on your current plan.
- Incorporate new goals and activities that reflect knowledge of current research.
- Ask students to comment on those learning activities they found most and least desirable.
- Periodically assess student performance to determine if your curriculum is appropriately challenging.
- Determine whether or not you have adequate facilities and equipment to address what students should be learning.

In some cases you may be provided with a prepared curriculum for physical education and asked to introduce pre-planned lessons that you believe students would enjoy or you feel comfortable teaching. If this is the case, you still have responsibility for evaluating what is successful and what requires improvement. Make notes about which activities were too easy or too difficult, which were more enjoyable than others, and which seemed to result in the most student learning. Based on your evaluation, you can modify the curriculum for the future so that it best meets the needs of your individual students.

Summary

This chapter was designed to introduce you to concepts of curriculum development and acquaint you with the process of developing a yearly plan. Most important, classroom teachers need to become aware of the NASPE Standards and understand how they can be achieved throughout the K-2 and 3-5 grade range and in consideration of the different stages of learning (I, II, and III). The most successful curriculum plans result from teachers who initially and carefully develop goals that reflect the NASPE Standards and are not limited by the facilities and equipment immediately available to them. In order to most effectively translate the curriculum into daily lesson plans, teachers are encouraged to develop a block calendar of activities that reflect individual learning goals. Finally, good curriculum requires periodic reflection and revision, particularly as related to the individual needs of students and the idiosyncrasies of the learning community in which the teacher resides. For dos and don'ts on curriculum planning see Box 2.5.

DO AND DON'T CHECKLIST

Do	Don't
☐ collaborate with other teachers when developing a curriculum and generate ideas from experts who reside in your community	☐ develop a curriculum in isolation
☐ design a curriculum that addresses all six NASPE Standards	☐ plan activities unless they can accomplish one or more of the NASPE Standards
☐ be conscious of the three Stages of development when designing learning activities	☐ assume that all students learn at the same rate
☐ think creatively for how to acquire an adequate amount of equipment for teaching different curricular activities	☐ assume that the physical education teacher is insensitive if he/she is unwilling to share equipment
☐ adjust your goals as you begin to realize what you can accomplish.	☐ plan activities without considering whether or not they are achieving an important learning goal.

Review Activities

1. In a small group with your classmates, brainstorm all of the skills and knowledge you believe children should acquire during 3rd grade. Now narrow that list to include only those skills that are achievable in 33 hours of instruction per year. Match the list to the NASPE Standards to determine if you have addressed all six. Write at least ten curricular goals that match what you intend students will learn. Finally, complete a one-month block calendar by using the goal statements you developed above.

2. Think of five examples where you can combine two or more of the NASPE Standards into one learning activity.

3. With a partner, brainstorm five different types of equipment that you could construct for your classroom at no cost.

4. Write a mock letter to parents describing the physical education curriculum you will emphasize during the year and what they can anticipate their child will learn.

5. Discuss with the class those aspects of curriculum development that you find most challenging.

References

National Association for Sport and Physical Education. (1995). *Moving into the future: National standards for physical education*. Boston: McGraw Hill.

National Association for Sport and Physical Education. (2004). *Moving into the future: National standards for physical education* (2nd ed.). Reston, VA: Author.

National Association for Sport and Physical Education & American Heart Association (2010). *2010 Shape of the nation report. Status of physical education in the USA*. Reston, VA: National Association for Sport and Physical Education.

National Commission on Excellence in Education. (1983). *A nation at risk: The imperative for educational reform*. Washington, DC: U.S. Government Printing Office.

U.S. Centers for Disease Control and Prevention (2010). *The association between school-based physical activity, including physical education, and academic performance*. Atlanta, GA: U.S. department of Health and Human Services.

U.S. Department of Health and Human Services (2008). *2008 Physical activity guidelines for Americans*. Washington, DC: Author.

Chapter **Three**

Lesson Planning

On average, the amount of instructional time allocated for physical education at the elementary level will be approximately 30 minutes twice per week. In some schools, students are fortunate to have physical education scheduled five times per week. This usually occurs in schools located in states such as Illinois, where there is a legislative mandate that students must receive daily physical education. Other states, such as Alabama, Florida, and Louisiana, require that students receive the national recommendation of 150+ minutes of physical education per week (National Association for Sport and Physical Education & American Heart Association, 2010).

Although it is preferable for students to receive daily physical education from a trained specialist, in those states where the mandate is less strict, classroom teachers are allowed to plan lessons in which students receive some form of physical activity. This less rigid mandate results in some classroom teachers who are committed to teaching high-quality physical education and others who simply allow students to engage in unstructured play in the gymnasium or on the playground. Those in the former group understand the significance of physical activity to children's health. Those in the latter group are satisfied if children are quietly playing in the sandbox or talking to friends.

In Lab Chapters 9 and 10, you will learn more about the obesity epidemic and why it is important to engage students in physical activities that promote health-related fitness. Today it is more important than ever to plan lessons that optimize the small amount of time that is allocated for physical education. Whereas you may have been able to ride your bike to school or play on the playground after class, children today are increasingly bussed or driven to school. This appears to be the result of parents who are worried about increasing traffic patterns that make it less safe to walk or bike to school or who work and cannot allow their children to stay after school and play on the playground. Instead, children return home and either watch TV or play computer games. For those students who are exposed to physical activity only within the school, because they cannot participate in extracurricular activities such as Little League for financial or logistical reasons, structured physical education is critical to their physical development and health.

As emphasized in Key Point 3-1, classroom teachers who understand the importance of physical activity for all individuals plan lessons that are carefully structured. They are concerned that students acquire motor skills that will facilitate their ability to be active throughout the lifespan. They also are concerned about planning activities that enhance a student's ability to achieve health-related fitness. The purpose of this chapter is to provide you with information about how to plan lessons that are carefully structured and optimize learning time.

Key Point 3-1

Teachers who understand the importance of physical education plan lessons that optimize available learning time.

The most effective teachers write lesson plans to guide their instruction.

LESSONS FROM RESEARCH

Teachers often consider planning to be an arduous process that is time consuming and far less satisfying than interacting with children. It is important to note, however, that executing instruction is far more enjoyable if children are learning from and engaged in the lesson. Strong lessons, however, do not occur by accident. Instead, they require thoughtful planning.

The research literature in physical education highlights four important findings (Graber, 2001). First, although experienced teachers demonstrate more awareness of the contingencies that may occur in lessons (Griffey & Housner, 1991), as they gain experience they spend less time actively planning lessons. For example, in a classic study it was discovered that experienced teachers spent greater time mentally planning lessons than constructing them in written form (Placek, 1984). Second, some teachers are primarily concerned about keeping students "busy, happy, and good" (Placek, 1983). This is unfortunate if it results in teachers who plan lessons primarily with the goal of keeping students happy and well-behaved as opposed to engaged in educational learning tasks. Third, teachers who carefully plan lessons have students who are off-task less frequently, spend less time waiting in line for a turn, and make better use of instructional time (Byra & Coulon, 1994). This equates to greater opportunities for students to learn about the subject matter and be engaged in activities associated with health-related fitness. Finally, teachers who were characterized as particularly effective relied on written plans that contained learning objectives. These teachers were committed to student learning and appropriate motor performance (Stroot & Morton, 1989).

PLANNING CONSIDERATIONS

Fortunately, most elementary-aged students respond favorably to physical education. In many cases it is their favorite subject, and they look forward to the opportunity to play and exercise. Therefore, it is incumbent upon the instructor to plan lessons that are engaging and challenging, and that maximize the natural desire within children to be active. For classroom teachers who have not received formal training in the subject matter of physical education, planning will be more difficult than for trained specialists. It will be more challenging to develop creative lessons that enable children to learn and receive adequate time

PE Central Website   Box 3.1

There are many resources that the classroom teacher can easily access for planning purposes. One reference that is frequently used by classroom teachers is the PE Central Website. This site, which was originally developed by faculty at Virginia Tech University, is designed to provide K-12 teachers with information on planning lessons, assessing student performance, creating a positive learning environment, accessing instructional resources such as books and music, and designing lessons for children with disabilities. The Web address is: http://www.pecentral.org/

engaged in physical activity. On the bright side, this textbook is designed to provide the classroom teacher with a variety of activities that will engage children in appropriate physical activity. There also are many other resources that are easily accessible and can assist you in planning (see Box 3.1).

As you begin to consider which activities you intend to teach during a particular day of instruction, it is important to reflect on the overall goals that you developed when planning your yearly curriculum. Remember, you will want your goals to match your activities and your activities to match your goals. You also will want to align your daily lesson plan with the block calendar you developed to ensure that your annual goals are met. The following is intended to serve as a checklist for determining whether or not the learning activities that you are planning are appropriate and will enhance the opportunity for children to learn basic skills and develop health-related fitness:

- Before considering the specific activities you would like to teach, first consider your learning objectives (which will be discussed in the next section of this chapter). That is, what do you want students to specifically learn from the lesson that you have planned? Be sure these goals align with those you have developed for the year.

- Determine whether or not you have adequate equipment to keep all students engaged throughout the lesson. If you plan to teach dribbling in basketball, but you have access to only 10 basketballs, ask yourself how you will keep all students engaged. You may decide that you also can use playground balls. This will ensure that every student has his or her own ball and can practice dribbling throughout the lesson.

- Be sure that you engage all students in physical activity. Avoid games in which students are eliminated or have to wait in line for a turn.

- Develop lessons where all students can experience success. Avoid activities such as relay races where students who are less skilled can be ridiculed or where the majority of time is spent waiting in line for a turn.

- Ensure that students have adequate time to develop skill in the activity that you are teaching. For example, learning how to set and bump a volleyball takes weeks of practice. Do not teach skills where you give students a limited number of practice trials (10 sets, 10 bumps) before progressing to a game-like activity. Instead, spend several lessons teaching the set and bump pass using a variety of interesting and challenging activities until students learn the skills. In cases of difficult skills like these, it can take months of practice before students become proficient.

- Determine whether or not students are developmentally ready to learn certain skills. If your intention is to teach students to shoot a basket in 3rd grade, the task will likely be too difficult for them to experience success. You will need to lower the height of the basketball hoops and provide students with balls that are appropriately sized for their developmental level.

- Avoid the temptation to include only games in the curriculum. In order for students to develop skill, they need to participate in learning activities and drills that will later

If you have limited access to equipment, be creative. Different kinds of balls, for example, can accomplish the same objectives—teaching students to dribble, throw, or kick.

enable them to successfully participate in a game situation. In some cases, you can make drills into challenging mini-games. For example, ask students to count how many times they can volley a ball in the air without letting it drop within one minute.

- Carefully scrutinize all aspects of your lesson plan to ensure that it is safe. For example, if students are throwing a ball back and forth with a partner, be sure that all students are throwing in the same direction. There is nothing more important than safety! If the activity is unsafe, the playing area contains hazards, or you do not have adequate skill to safely teach an activity, select something else to teach. Complete Thinking Challenge 3.1.

THINKING CHALLENGE 3.1

List at least two additional guidelines that will help to ensure that the lessons you are planning will keep students actively engaged, provide for maximal success, and produce student learning.

1.

2.

DOMAIN SPECIFIC OBJECTIVES

The first consideration in planning is to determine the specific objectives that you hope students will accomplish as a result of your lesson. When we teach future physical education majors how to write lesson objectives, they are asked to consider three factors:

1. *What* will students *learn* and be able to accomplish as a result of the lesson? This is often referred to as addressing the *performance* expected of the learner.

2. *How* will students accomplish the instructional task? This relates to the *condition* under which the performance will occur.

3. *When* will you be able to determine that students have learned? This addresses the *criteria for mastery* that will determine if the objective was accomplished.

As you may have noticed, the primary goal in planning a lesson is to ensure that students have learned something from the lesson. As emphasized in Key Point 3-2, it is not until after the teacher determines the lesson objectives that he or she considers what activities will be incorporated into the lesson.

Key Point 3-2

It is not until after the teacher determines the lesson objectives that he or she considers what activities will be incorporated into the lesson.

In all areas of education, there are three domains in which learning can occur. In physical education, more than any other subject area in the school, all domains are emphasized. As you might remember from Lecture Chapter 1, the first domain, *psychomotor,* relates to movement. In this domain the student learns about how to move appropriately (e.g., proper form when throwing a ball, how to pass a ball to a teammate who is running in general space, how to develop a creative dance). The second domain, *cognitive,* relates to knowledge that students acquire in physical education (e.g., rules, strategies, tactics, principles of fitness). The third domain, *affective,* is associated with teamwork, cooperation, and student feelings (e.g., working effectively with a partner, becoming a leader, developing good feelings about movement). Although the psychomotor domain is a primary focus in a physical education class, the teacher also must consider the cognitive and affective domains.

The following sample objectives were designed to assist you in learning how to write appropriate lesson objectives that focus on student learning in each of the three domains:

Psychomotor Domain

- Students will be able to bump a volleyball with good technique (*what*) to a partner who is standing 10 feet away (*how*) on five out of six trials (*when*).
- Students will be able to perform a creative dance (*what*) that is three minutes in length and incorporates the concepts of high, medium, and low (*how*) without any breaks in the movement while demonstrating good aesthetic quality (*when*).

Cognitive Domain

- Students will demonstrate their knowledge of the correct throwing pattern (*what*) by telling another classmate about the elements of proper form (*how*) and correctly identifying at least four elements (*when*).
- Students will demonstrate their understanding of the rules of badminton (*what*) on a written exam (*how*) by correctly responding to nine out of ten questions (*when*).

Affective Domain

- Students will demonstrate cooperation (*what*) when playing in a three-sided game of soccer (*how*) by passing the ball to a teammate who is less skilled (*when*).
- Students will demonstrate positive feelings about health-related fitness (*what*) by developing a collage of health-related fitness activities (*how*) and clearly describing to the teacher why those activities promote good feelings (*when*).

Complete Thinking Challenge 3.2.

THINKING CHALLENGE 3.2

Write one behavioral objective related to health-related fitness in each of the following domains. Distinguish the *what, how,* and *when*.

Cognitive:
-

Psychomotor:
-

Affective:
-

Please note that the objectives listed here are designed for writing daily lesson plans, where improvement may sometimes be only minimally noticeable. If, however, you are interested in writing an objective to determine mastery of a skill at the end of a unit, you will need to more carefully address *when* or the *criteria for mastery* of the skill. For example, if you are focusing on *mastery,* your objective might be:

Box 3.2

PSYCHOMOTOR VERBS
Run
Jump
Twist
Slide
Leap
Turn
Throw
Dribble
Kick
Catch
Roll
Gallop
Toss
Dismount
Strike

COGNITIVE VERBS
Understand
Know
State
List
Comprehend
Interpret
Explain
Diagram
Define
Discuss

AFFECTIVE VERBS
Share
Participate
Enjoy
Cooperate
Follow rules
Help others
Encourage
Appreciate

- At the end of a unit in track and field, students will be able to complete a mile run in 10 minutes or less without stopping at any point.
- At the end of a unit in hand dribbling, students will be able to dribble the ball from one end of the gym to the other within 15 seconds and without tripping, stopping, or palming the ball, and while keeping their eyes forward and not on the ball.

In order to help you write objectives for the *what* (*performance*) component of objectives, we are including several verbs in Box 3.2 that you might find useful. They are action words that describe what students should accomplish during the unit. There are many more verbs that would be appropriate for a physical education class than are listed here. Can you add to the list? You might notice that it is easier to generate verbs for the psychomotor domain than it is for the cognitive or affective domains.

Designing Developmentally Appropriate Activities: Procedures

After determining which objectives you intend to achieve in a lesson, it is now time to consider what activities are best suited for accomplishing those objectives. Again, it is imperative that you consider what you intend for students to learn prior to determining what activities are most appropriate. You will be tempted to first consider the activity. For example, if students respond well to a particular activity, you may be inclined to incorporate that activity into your physical education curriculum more regularly. Although it is easy to understand your intentions for wanting to include that activity, you will be doing your students a disservice. Given the limited amount of time available for physical education in the elementary school curriculum, you must capitalize on every opportunity for student learning to occur. The result will be greater exposure to different activities that promote new and interesting challenges.

At this point, you also must consider the developmental levels of your students (see Chapter 2 for a description of the three stages). Similar to classroom instruction, you will encounter students with a wide range of abilities. Just as you would not expose all students in your classroom to a book that was far too easy or too difficult for them to read, you also must not expose students to activities that are far too easy or too difficult for them to achieve. Planning developmentally appropriate activities for all students, however, is challenging even for the most experienced and well-trained teacher.

One very important aspect of planning developmentally appropriate activities requires the teacher to adequately and carefully explain the activity in written form on the lesson plan. All teachers, particularly novices, benefit from having a plan that carefully addresses all aspects of an activity and all elements of a lesson. Not only will careful explanations enhance the likelihood that the lesson will be successful, but it will also be possible for you to assemble the plans that you have created into a notebook that can be used as a reference from one year to the next. It is far more difficult to plan new lessons day after day and year after year than to initially take time to plan careful lessons that can be used in subsequent years.

When lessons proceed smoothly and students appear to learn from your instruction, make a notation on the lesson plan indicating that the plan worked well. When a particular plan is not successful, write down a few notes explaining how the lesson needs to be modified in the future. Remember, not even the most experienced teachers have lessons that are successful all of the time. The most effective teachers learn from their mistakes, reflect on why the lesson did not proceed as planned, and take notes to ensure that the lesson will proceed more smoothly in the future.

When considering the type of detail to initially include in a lesson, ask yourself whether or not a substitute teacher could teach the exact lesson that you intend. Although the plan may be clear to you, someone else may have difficulty understanding how particular activities should be executed. It is sometimes helpful to ask a friend or colleague to review your lesson plan and ask them to either teach the activity to you or verbally explain the activity. If they leave out important details or show confusion, it is a signal that you need to incorporate greater detail into the lesson plan. Hopefully, you will have an opportunity to plan several lessons and receive feedback on those lessons prior to encountering a class of students. See the sample lesson plan in Box 3.3.

Sample Lesson Plan for Health-Related Fitness · Box 3.3

Lesson Focus: Health-related Fitness (Station Training)
4th Grade (25 Students)
30-minute class period

LESSON OBJECTIVES:

1. Students will be able to complete two fitness circuits by spending two minutes at each circuit and without stopping or resting throughout the 20-minute duration of the activity. (Psychomotor)

2. Students will understand the concept of endurance training by answering questions asked by the teacher without any incorrect responses. (Cognitive)

3. Students will encourage classmates to remain engaged in the activities by providing encouraging comments to classmates on at least three occasions. (Affective)

NASPE STANDARDS:

Standard #2: Demonstrates understanding of movement concepts, principles, strategies, and tactics as they apply to the learning and performance of physical activities. (Lesson Objective #2)

Standard #4: Achieves and maintains a health-enhancing level of physical fitness. (Lesson Objective #1)

Standard #5: Exhibits responsible personal and social behavior that respects self and others in physical activity settings. (Lesson Objective #3)

PROCEDURE #1: ANTICIPATORY SET (3 MINUTES)

1. Students will enter the gymnasium and sit in the assigned location as usual.

2. Students will be informed that the purpose of the lesson is to teach them about principles of endurance and to encourage them to achieve a health-enhancing level of fitness.

   a. In order to improve how your heart functions, it is important to engage in regular physical activity in which your heart reaches the target rate for at least 20-30 minutes per day on five to six days of the week.

   b. You have practiced taking your pulse on many occasions. Take your resting heart rate. Ready, go. (Students take their pulse while teacher keeps time.)

   c. Remember the number of your resting pulse rate. Today we are going to see how much your heart works after we engage in some exciting physical activity. Try to get your heart to beat at least 126–168 beats per minute.

TEACHING POINTS #1:

1. Exercise vigorously five to six days per week.

2. Try to get your heart to beat 126–168 beats per minute when exercising.

continued

Sammple Lesson Plan for Health-Related Fitness (continued)   Box 3.3

FORMATION #1: (DRAW DIAGRAM OF STUDENTS SITTING IN AN ARC AROUND THE TEACHER.)

PROCEDURE #2: ACTIVITIES (23 MINUTES— 3 MINUTES EXPLANATION, 20 MINUTES AT STATIONS, 2 MINUTES PULSE)

1. Inform students that they will be working at five different stations.
2. Students will spend two minutes at each station.
3. The teacher will play music. When the music stops, students will move in a clockwise direction to the next station.
4. Students will complete the circuit twice. At the end of each circuit they will take their pulse.
5. Stations:
   a. *Jump Rope*
      1. Jump in whatever manner you wish (forward, backward, with a partner)
      2. Continue to jump without stopping until the music stops
   b. *Marching*
      1. March in place using high steps
      2. Pretend that you are in a marching band
      3. Add arm movements if you would like
      4. Try mirroring and matching with a partner
   c. *Steps*
      a. Step onto the bench with your left leg and then bring your right leg up
      b. Stop for a moment at the top of the bench in a straight position
      c. Go backward off the bench one leg at a time
      d. Select whatever sized bench feels most comfortable to you
   d. *Steal the Beanbag*
      a. Start at a red hoop that is laying on the ground
      b. Run 20 yards to the green hoop at the end of the gym and pick up a beanbag
      c. Return the beanbag to your own hoop
      d. You can pick up only one beanbag at a time
      e. See how many beanbags you can collect in two minutes
   e. *Dance to the Music*
      a. Dance creatively to the beat of the music using high and low movements
6. Remind students to encourage classmates throughout the lesson
7. Quickly place students into groups of five at each station. Begin music.

TEACHING POINTS #2:
1. Station #1: Jump Rope
   a. Think of creative ways to jump
   b. Don't stop

2. Station #2: Marching
   a. High steps
   b. Don't stop
3. Station #3: Steps
   a. Stand straight
   b. You can select any size bench you want
4. Station #4: Steal the Beanbag
   a. Try to get as many beanbags as possible into your hoop
   b. Encourage your classmates
5. Station #5: Dance to the Music
   a. Remember to use high and low movements
   b. Don't stop until the music stops

FORMATION #2: (DRAW DIAGRAM OF THE GYMNASIUM WITH THE FIVE STATIONS)

PROCEDURE #3: CLOSURE (3 MINUTES)
1. After the activity ask students to again sit in a semi-circle.
2. Have students slowly stretch their arms and legs while you ask questions.
   a. Which activity did you enjoy the most?
   b. How often should you exercise?
   c. Why is it important to give our heart a workout?

TEACHING POINTS #3:
1. Stretch slowly and hold the stretch
2. Remember to try to exercise each day of the week for at least 30 minutes.

FORMATION #3: (DRAW DIAGRAM OF STUDENTS SITTING IN AN ARC AROUND THE TEACHER.)

SAFETY:
1. Remind children to stay clear of others who are jumping rope.
2. Remind students to be careful when running through general space.

REFLECTION:
1. Students had difficulty moving from the marching station to the step station. Next time either design a new station or place the steps after the "Steal the Beanbag" station.
2. A few students had difficulty remaining active for the entire class period. Reduce length of each station to 90 seconds and add an additional "rest" station.
3. Next time ask students if their personal scores improved from the first trial to the second trial.
4. Students received a high level of activity in this lesson.

Below is a checklist of items that you will want to consider when describing activities in your lesson plan:

- Where will students be sitting when you provide directions?
- Have you told students the purpose of the activity (what they will be learning)?
- What are the logistics of the lesson? For example, if students are working with a partner, how far apart will partners be from each other? If you are using targets, what size are the targets, where will they be placed, and where will students be standing?
- If you have lines, how can you reduce the amount of time that students spend waiting? For example, if you have six lines of students with five students in each line waiting to dribble a basketball down the gymnasium floor, allow the second person in line to begin dribbling as soon as the first person has reached the 10-foot line of the gymnasium. Ask the other students in line to dribble in place until it is their turn to begin moving across the floor.
- Have you explained all safety procedures to students? This is critical!
- How will you ensure that all students understand the procedures of the lesson before placing them into activity?
- Have you explained all rules that are necessary for successful participation in the activity?
- Will students understand your stop and start signals?
- How will equipment be distributed so that minimal time is lost when students obtain equipment or transition from one activity to the next?
- How will you review the lesson with students, and what questions will you ask?

In the procedural part of the lesson, there are usually three sections to the lesson plan. The first section is the introduction, or what is sometimes referred to as the *anticipatory set*. The second section addresses the learning activities that you have planned. The third section is a review of the lesson. Each section contains teaching points and diagrams that help the teacher to remember how the lesson is physically structured.

TEACHING POINTS

Within your lesson plan you should consider those special points you want to emphasize with students. Many teachers rely on teaching points to address such things as proper technique or to remind students of safety procedures. For example, if you are teaching throwing technique, students need to understand the importance of trunk rotation and stepping forward on the opposite side of the body as the throwing arm. If you are teaching students about cardiovascular endurance, you will want to emphasize that they should begin running at a modest speed, not at full force. If children are running throughout the gymnasium, you will want to make sure they understand that they need to be careful not to run into others.

Teaching points are learning cues that teachers emphasize when providing verbal instructions *while* students are actively engaged in an activity. Novice teachers often forget that students sometimes learn the most while receiving feedback during a performance. Most important, however, is that teachers should primarily provide feedback to students that relates to the focus of the lesson, or the teaching points that were emphasized during verbal instructions. This type of feedback is referred to as *congruent* (see Lecture Chapter 8 in this text; Graham, 2001).

Probably the most important aspect of developing teaching points is to avoid covering too much material at one time. Students at the elementary level do not want to sit for long periods of time while you lecture on the most important elements of appropriate kicking form. Instead, they want to engage in the activity and begin kicking the ball. They will not remember all of the points that you cover, and the result will be lost time in which students could have been engaged in activity. Remember, a primary purpose of physical education is to keep students actively engaged for the majority of the class period. An effective teacher understands the significance of brevity. If teaching students how to kick the ball with light force is the primary emphasis, then include in your teaching points words such as "tap" or "gently nudge." When students are engaged in an activity, concentrate on giving teaching points that relate to that aspect of the activity you are hoping they will learn.

The following teaching points are the kinds of things that you might hear effective teachers emphasizing to their students:

- Contact the ball only on the shoelaces.
- Include at least three concepts in your creative dance.
- Tuck your chin when rolling forward.
- Accuracy is more important than force when throwing to your partner.
- Stretch slowly and hold the stretch. Do not bounce.
- Don't worry about what other students are doing—you are competing against yourself.
- Heads up when running in general space so that you don't run into anyone else.

LESSON PLAN FORMAT

Many teachers we know use lesson plans like the one highlighted in Box 3.3. Others, however, prefer to write lesson plans that use a *column* format because it is easy to read. They resemble the one in Box 3.4. Finally, some prefer to use a plan that is referred to as

---

Abbreviated Column Lesson Sample Lesson Plan for Health-Related Fitness   Box 3.4

LESSON OBJECTIVE:
1. Students will be able to complete two fitness circuits by spending two minutes at each circuit and without stopping or resting throughout the 20-minute duration of the activity. (Psychomotor)

NASPE STANDARDS:
Standard #4: Achieves and maintains a health-enhancing level of physical fitness. (Lesson Objective #1)

PROCEDURES	DIAGRAM	TEACHING POINTS
Procedure #1: Anticipatory Set	X	
Students will enter the gym and sit in the assigned . . .	X X / X X	Hurry in quickly so that we can get started.
Procedure #2: Activity	X	
Students work for two minutes at five different stations.		
Station 1: Jump rope (forward, backward, or with a partner).	X X X	Be careful so the rope doesn't hit anyone.
Station 2: Marching . . .	X X X	Don't stop until the music stops.
Procedure #3: Closure	X	
Have students return to the center circle. Ask them to stretch while reviewing the lesson.	X X / X X / X X / X	Stretch your arms slowly and hold the stretch.

Abbreviated Scripted Lesson Sample Lesson Plan for Health-Related Fitness　Box 3.5

Lesson Focus: Health-related Fitness (Station Training)
4th Grade (25 Students)
30-minute class period

SAME OBJECTIVES AND NASPE STANDARDS AS BOX 3.3

PROCEDURE #1
(This is an abbreviated version)
"Good morning, students. Please enter the gym and have a seat on the circle." *Students will have a seat on the circle and instructions will be given.*

"Today we are going to learn about principles of endurance. I want to encourage you to achieve a health-enhancing level of fitness. Can anyone tell me what endurance means? In order to improve how your heart functions, it is important to engage in regular physical activity in which your heart reaches the target rate for at least 20–30 minutes per day for 5–6 days of the week. How many of you exercise this often during the week? Can somebody tell me what they do?"

PROCEDURE #2
"Today you will work at five different stations. You will spend two minutes at each station. While you are at each station, I will play music. Once the music stops, you will move to the next station. At the first station, you will jump rope. You can jump forward, backward, or with a partner. You must, however, keep jumping until the music stops. At the second station . . . "

PROCEDURE #3
"Everyone please come back and have a seat on the circle. Hurry up. I don't want to see anyone walking. Thank you for getting here so quickly. You are very fast. I hope that you liked the five stations we did today. I would like to ask you a few questions, but let's stretch while we talk. Remember, we always want to be moving in physical education class. Stretch your arms as high as you can, and hold the stretch. Johnny, can you please tell me which station you enjoyed most? Connie, what about you? Lower your arms. Now raise them and stretch slowly again. Beth, how often do you exercise at home? David, why is it important to give our hearts a workout? That's correct. I would like to thank you for participating so well in class today. Let's now go quietly back to our home classroom . . ."

scripted. This type of plan is particularly good for beginning teachers or those who have some anxiety about teaching physical education. In a scripted plan, teachers write complete sentences about what they will say to students during the lesson. Although many teachers prefer this type of plan, we find that they may be tempted to directly read from the lesson as opposed to talking directly to students. You, however, must decide which you prefer and which makes you a more effective instructor. See Box 3.5 for an abbreviated lesson plan using a scripted format.

INDIVIDUALIZING THE LESSON

As mentioned earlier, it is important to remember that students learn at different rates. It is unrealistic to believe that all students will enter the gymnasium with the same kinds of skills and will progress at the same rate. Therefore, it is incumbent upon the teacher to design lessons that will be challenging to all learners. Those who are less skilled will require more simple tasks, whereas those with a higher degree of skill level will require more challenging tasks.

In many cases, differences in skill levels can be attributed either to the number of practice opportunities given to a student or to societal expectations. Consider this sentence for a moment: "You throw like a girl." Do you believe that girls are incapable of learning to throw? If so, you may wish to attend a girls' or women's softball game. Some individuals, however, believe that females cannot throw using mature form. This is absolutely untrue. Unfortunately, females often receive fewer practice opportunities and less instruction than their male counterparts. They are no less capable of learning to throw using mature form than boys. In other cases, females have not learned to throw due to societal expectations. Their parents, for example, may believe that females should not be involved in physical activity. Fortunately, due to the advent of Title IX, which is a federal law that requires females to be offered the same types of educational activities as males, females are given more opportunities than ever before to engage in physical activity.

In a physical education class, you will encounter males who have not learned to use proper throwing form. You also will encounter males who have greater difficulty learning to jump rope for exactly the same reasons that females may not yet have mastered mature throwing form.

It also is important not to "type" students. In other words, if a student has difficulty learning in one area of the curriculum that does not necessarily mean that he or she will encounter difficulties in all areas of the curriculum. Some students may have difficulty engaging in manipulative activities (kicking, throwing, catching), but they will excel in activities that require creativity (dance, imagery, gymnastics).

When planning, try to keep these important lessons in mind. In many cases you may not know how quickly a student will grasp an instructional activity until you implement that activity with your students. As emphasized in Key Point 3-3, while observing individual performances, ask yourself how you can further individualize the lesson based on the developmental level of learners. Although all students may be performing the same activity, some will require that you provide them with increasingly difficult challenges. Throughout the different chapters of this book, you will find many suggestions for how you can individualize a lesson plan. Although we would like to give you many examples here, the purpose of this chapter is to teach you the mechanics of planning. As you read further, you will learn how to individualize your plans.

Key Point 3-3

When writing your lesson plan, it is important to address the needs of all learners. Therefore, you may wish to include a variety of activities that will be challenging for the different ability levels of students. You might even allow them to make some decisions. For example, if you provide students with different-sized balls or different types of rackets (long, short, lightweight), students can select the equipment that they believe best meets their individual ability level.

Refining Performance

When students initially learn a skill it is important, as discussed earlier, to provide only the necessary teaching points that enable them to begin achieving some degree of success. If students are learning how to hand dribble a basketball, you might concentrate on having them use their fingertips to make contact with the ball. You will use cues such as, "Use your fingertips. Don't slap at the ball." At this stage you may allow them to watch the ball as they dribble. Once they begin to experience success, you will want them to refine their performance. You will begin to say things like, "Don't watch the ball. Look forward. In a basketball game you can't look at the ball because you need to watch where you are running." Rink (2006) refers to this progression as *refining performance*. Some students, of course, will need to watch the ball for a longer period of time than others. Do not be concerned that these students will be unable to master the task. Instead, they need additional opportunities and constant reinforcement to "use the fingertips." Once they master the task, you can move forward to the next level.

Extending Performance

Once students have refined their performance, they are ready to advance. At this point you will invite students to attempt a more challenging task, or to *extend their performance*. For example, once students have mastered the appropriate hand dribbling technique, you may ask them to dribble while moving forward in a particular pathway or around obstacles. You may begin to challenge them by asking them to combine tasks—such as dribbling forward and passing the ball to a teammate. Again, you will be able to challenge some students with more complex tasks sooner than other students. In such instances, however, it is important never to make students feel that they are underachieving. An effective teacher can creatively implement a number of different activities in the classroom without drawing attention to the different developmental levels.

DEMONSTRATING

As you are likely aware, some students are visual learners whereas others benefit primarily from verbal directions. Overall, all students will benefit from demonstration. A good demonstration clarifies the learning task and enables students to clearly understand the contingencies of the activity that they will be asked to perform. Supplemented with appropriate teaching cues, demonstration can ensure that students will be less confused when they begin to engage in the instructional activity. Demonstration usually occurs early in the lesson, when instructions are being given, or when a new instructional task is presented. The lesson plan you write should reflect when demonstration will be given and the teaching cues that will accompany the demonstration.

When demonstrating, it is important to ask yourself the following questions:

- Are all students positioned so that they can clearly view the demonstration?
- If you are teaching outside, can students view the demonstration without the sun shining in their eyes? (It is preferable for the teacher to face the sun.)
- Are you providing only those teaching points that are necessary?
- Is the demonstration an accurate portrayal of the skill?
- Is the demonstration brief?

Some teachers are concerned because they do not have the skill level to accurately demonstrate the skill that they are teaching. In fact, most trained physical education teachers cannot demonstrate all of the skills that they might teach to students throughout the year. Those teachers who cannot demonstrate have several options. First, they can ask a student who has mastered the task to demonstrate. Second, they can show pictures of the task. Third, they can demonstrate those components of the task that they are able to execute. Fourth, they can use important teaching cues. Let's take the headstand as an example. If the teacher cannot demonstrate a headstand, they might ask a student to demonstrate. They can show a picture of an athlete performing a headstand. They can place their hands and head on a mat to illustrate body position without actually attempting to complete the headstand. Or, they can explain that the student should form a triangle with their head at the top of the triangle and hands at the sides.

A final consideration when demonstrating is to ask yourself whether or not you need to turn your back to students so that they can more effectively understand the task that they will be asked to perform. In some cases, you may want students to mimic your performance. This might require you to turn your back. For example, when teaching the throw, it may be easier for students to view your performance if they are watching you from behind. Although you rarely want to turn your back to students, there are times when it is necessary.

In order to clearly view a demonstration, there are times when it is appropriate to turn your back to students.

SAFETY

Each lesson plan should address safety. Some teachers make notes related to safety in the procedures section of the plan. Other teachers develop a separate section at the end. Regardless, there should be a designated section of your plan that describes safety procedures that will be used to avoid injury. (See Lecture Chapter 9 for an in-depth discussion of safety and liability.)

REFLECTION

Once you have implemented the lesson, it is time to reflect on what went well and what requires improvement. Therefore, it is important to save a place on your lesson plan to make notations about the learning activities that were implemented. Were they too easy or too difficult? Which aspects of the lesson did students have difficulty understanding? Did student learning occur as a result of the lesson? Were students engaged in the lesson?

In reflecting on the lesson be sure to ask students if they enjoyed the learning activities that were presented. Ask what important points they remembered from the lesson. If they cannot restate the teaching points that you emphasized, you probably need to be clearer in the future. If they remembered the key points, congratulate yourself on an effective lesson.

Reflection is one of the most important components of teaching effectiveness. Effective teachers review even their most successful lessons and ask how the lesson can be improved. Although you will have limited time to adequately reflect on your lesson, time in the long run is saved by making a few notes on the plan immediately after it is taught. This will ensure that you do not repeat the same mistakes in the future and that the most successful activities can be recycled for another group of eager students—not lost in your own memory.

Summary

The purpose of this chapter was to provide you with information on effective planning. If you are committed to effective physical education, you will benefit by creating a notebook of plans that can be used and modified from one year to the next. Lessons are more effective when they are carefully structured, when objectives are developed prior to instructional activities, when teaching points clearly summarize the main points of the lesson, when the lesson is individualized, when demonstrations are provided, and when the teacher reflects upon the overall lesson after it is implemented. Above all else, make sure that your lesson plans are safe for all learners! For some dos and don'ts for planning lessons review Box 3.6.

DO AND DON'T CHECKLIST

Do	Don't
☐ consider objectives prior to planning learning activities	☐ continue to teach the same activities with too much regularity
☐ consider how tasks can be refined and extended prior to entering the learning environment	☐ assume that all students learn at the same rate or are at the same ability level
☐ clearly describe all procedures within the lesson plan	☐ spend too much time providing instructions
☐ emphasize only key teaching points	☐ provide teaching points that do not relate to the lesson
☐ reflect on how the lesson can be improved (during and after instruction).	☐ store the lesson plan away without making a few notes concerning what worked and what did not.

Review Activities

1. What obstacles do you anticipate encountering when planning a physical education lesson?

2. In your own words, describe the psychomotor, cognitive, and affective domains to a classmate.

3. Describe to a classmate how you would use extending and refining tasks when teaching students how to jump rope.

4. Select an activity that you would feel comfortable teaching. Design an abbreviated lesson in which you (a) write one objective, (b) select one NASPE Standard that fits the lesson and matches the objective, and (c) detail three procedures that address the anticipatory set, activities, and closure. If you have time, include your teaching points, safety procedures, and diagrams for how the lesson will be physically structured.

5. List how you could acquire additional information about physical education content with which you are unfamiliar but would like to teach.

References

Byra, M., & Coulon, S. C. (1994). The effect of planning on the instructional behaviors of preservice teachers. *Journal of Teaching in Physical Education, 13,* 123–139.

Graber, K. C. (2001). Research on teaching in physical education. In V. Richardson (Ed.), *Handbook of research on teaching* (4th ed.) (pp. 491–519). Washington, DC: American Educational Research Association.

Graham, G. (2001). *Teaching children physical education: Becoming a master teacher* (2nd ed.). Champaign, IL: Human Kinetics Publishers.

Griffey, D. C., & Housner, L. D. (1991). Differences between experienced and inexperienced teachers' planning decisions, interactions, student engagement, and instructional climate. *Research Quarterly for Exercise and Sport, 62,* 196–204.

National Association for Sport and Physical Education (2010). *2010 Shape of the nation report: Status of physical education in the USA.* Reston, VA: National Association for Sport and Physical Education.

Placek, J. H. (1983). Conceptions of success in teaching: Busy, happy and good? In T. J. Templin & J. K. Olson (Eds.), *Teaching in physical education* (pp. 46–56). Champaign, IL: Human Kinetics.

Placek, J. H. (1984). A multi-case study of teacher planning in physical education. *Journal of Teaching in Physical Education, 4,* 39–49.

Rink, J. E. (2006). *Teaching Physical education for learning* (5th ed.). Boston: McGraw-Hill.

Stroot, S. A., & Morton, P. J. (1989). Blueprints for learning. *Journal of Teaching in Physical Education, 8,* 213–222.

Chapter **Four**

Using Curriculum to Develop an Inclusive Learning Environment

In Chapter 2 we discussed how to develop an overall physical education curriculum. You learned about the national standards that were developed by the National Association for Sport and Physical Education (1994) and the importance of addressing all six standards throughout the year. You also learned about designing a curriculum that is developmentally appropriate for the different ability levels of students and how to set realistic curricular goals. Finally, you learned how to plan for the year and regularly assess the effectiveness of your curriculum.

In Chapter 3, we discussed how to develop individual lesson plans that matched your yearly goals and covered the psychomotor, cognitive, and affective learning domains. You were reminded of the importance of planning developmentally appropriate individualized lessons. You also learned that effective teachers reflect on their lessons and learn from their successes and failures. When a planned learning activity fails, it is not automatically dismissed by the teacher as useless. Instead, effective teachers ask themselves why an activity failed and consider how to modify that activity in the future to make it more successful.

The things that you learned about curriculum and lesson planning in Chapters 2 and 3 may seem like common sense. That is, the notion of carefully planning prior to a lesson is something that you had almost certainly anticipated you would do as a teacher. Planning an effective curriculum, however, goes far beyond what you have learned to this point. It involves structuring an environment that is sensitive to the individual needs of learners and

Students in an inclusive learning environment have a better educational experience.

takes into account children's interests, needs, backgrounds, and abilities. In other words, it requires that teachers make special efforts to develop an inclusive learning environment. It entails more than simply teaching students about an activity; it involves awareness about everything that students could potentially learn from your lessons.

The first purpose of this chapter is to introduce you to four forms of curriculum and to emphasize the power that each has in determining what lessons children bring away from school. The second purpose is to provide you with knowledge that will enable you to develop a curriculum that is inclusive and individualized. Specifically, you will be introduced to information related to (a) student ability levels, (b) gender issues, (c) racial, ethnic, and cultural appreciation, (d) socioeconomic status, and (e) special needs students.

FOUR FORMS OF CURRICULUM

To begin this chapter, we would like for you to consider all of the different lessons that students potentially learn from the physical education curriculum. Complete Thinking Challenge 4.1 by being as thoughtful as possible, considering the broad types of knowledge that students acquire from physical education. Think back to your own experiences as a student. After that you will be asked to define the term "curriculum." Begin now.

THINKING CHALLENGE 4.1	Within 60 seconds, list all of the things that you learned from your elementary physical education curriculum. If you didn't have physical education as a child, try to imagine what you think a student might learn. After you have completed this task, spend another 60 seconds defining the term "curriculum."

When completing this thinking challenge, it is likely that you thought about broad curricular areas such as basketball, volleyball, fitness, and gymnastics. Maybe you remembered specific games like Steal the Bacon or specific skills such as dribbling, kicking, volleying, and striking. If you thought broadly about curriculum, you may also have considered things like cooperation, sharing, teamwork, and knowledge about rules and strategies.

When defining curriculum, you and most of your classmates probably thought of words such as planning, syllabus, goals, lesson plans, teaching styles, equipment, facilities, time, instructional cues, and objectives. Very few of your classmates likely defined curriculum as *everything that happens to students from which they learn.* Although most experts agree with the standard definition of curriculum as being a course of study, a series of organized experiences, and teacher-planned outcomes; according to Key Point 4-1, many also acknowledge that the definition of curriculum should be broadened to include everything that students learn during school.

Let's be more specific. The curriculum of physical education can appear in different ways. If, for example, you were teaching children how to dribble and volley different types of balls over a period of several days, it is likely they are learning about manipulative skills. If you were teaching about flexibility and cardiovascular endurance, they are probably learning about health-related fitness. Both reflect a curricular *focus.* That is, they represent physical education content that the teacher is trying to convey to children.

Key Point 4-1

The curriculum consists of everything that happens to students from which they learn. In some cases, students will learn what the teacher intended. In other cases, they will learn what was not intended.

Interestingly, however, what children might remember most from lessons is not about manipulative skills or health-related fitness outcomes—the primary focus of the *intended* lesson—but about their personal experiences when learning these skills or the social status they held within the class—the *unintended* focus of the lesson. As you will discover, what children actually learn in a physical education lesson (or from any experience during school) may be surprising to the teacher and have life-long implications for the student. What children learn may represent far more than what appears in a teacher's formal lesson plans or yearly curriculum guide. As you continue through this chapter, you may be surprised by the variety of factors teachers must consider when planning and the unintended consequences that can result from lessons.

Explicit Curriculum

As Key Point 4-2 emphasizes, the explicit curriculum is defined simply as everything a teacher deliberately teaches to students that is shared or open to them. It is either written or spoken. For example, when a teacher writes a curriculum guide that is accessible to parents, students, and/or colleagues, the teacher has made the curriculum explicit. It is intended, and it is openly shared with others. Regardless of whether a teacher verbalizes to students that they will be learning the waltz during a ballroom dance unit, uses a bulletin board to emphasize the importance of cooperation during a group wall climb, discusses with other teachers that children will be acquiring rescue skills during a swimming unit, or explains to parents during "Back to School Night" the different activities that will be taught during the semester, the teacher is making the *intended* curriculum *explicit*.

Key Point 4-2

The explicit curriculum is intended by teachers and openly shared with others.

Before reading further, complete Thinking Challenge 4.2. Were you able to reach the desired goal of five? Does your list contain any of the following forms of explicit curriculum that we brainstormed: curriculum guide, lesson plans, written syllabus, course outline, formal explanation to others, demonstration, bulletin board, index cards with daily activities, informal conversations, letter to parents, teacher's Web site, or presentation during an inservice workshop? How much of your list matches ours? Each of these represents an important form of the explicit curriculum that teachers may use to convey their intended lessons to others.

THINKING CHALLENGE 4.2

Fill in the numbers below by brainstorming the different ways in which an explicit curriculum may appear visible.

1.
2.
3.
4.
5.

Explicitly developing an inclusive learning environment.

The explicit curriculum represents one way in which teachers can intentionally make the learning environment more inclusive. It enables them to develop plans that address individual student needs that foster success regardless of ability, gender, race, or socioeconomic

A bulletin board represents one form of an explicit curriculum.

status. The list below provides a few important examples of how teachers may use the explicit curriculum to humanize learning.

- Deliberately include activities in lesson plans such as small-sided games that facilitate greater participation among all students regardless of ability. Inform students that they have been assigned to small groups because they will have greater chance to participate.
- Use language during demonstrations that is not sexist, racist, or excludes a particular class of students.
- Plan activities where all students can accomplish the learning objectives, and inform students that the learning activities have been structured to foster their success.
- Encourage students to appreciate difference by designing a bulletin board that emphasizes the accomplishments of students in the Special Olympics.
- Discuss with parents why it is important to develop an inclusive environment when teaching physical education.
- Talk to students about the terrible harm that is done by bullying others and why bullying is not tolerated in physical education class.

Implicit Curriculum

The explicit curriculum represents the most common way of thinking about curriculum. For example, if a parent asked you questions about your curriculum, you would immediately think about what is contained in your curriculum guide and lesson plans. You would refer to the intended lessons you hope children will acquire from your instruction. As curriculum experts have emphasized, however, the explicit curriculum represents only *some* of the knowledge and information that children acquire in school (Eisner, 1994). Let's contemplate another type of curriculum. While the explicit curriculum is intended and shared, the implicit (sometimes referred to as covert) curriculum is *deliberate but not shared*. Before reading further, complete Thinking Challenge 4.3.

THINKING CHALLENGE 4.3	Use the space below to list three reasons not cited in the chapter why a teacher may *not* wish to share his/her intentions for a lesson with others. 1. 2. 3.

Was this a difficult challenge? Were you able to list at least three reasons why a teacher would not share his or her curricular ideas with others? Once you begin considering all of the different reasons for why you may not want to explicitly share your curriculum, you should be able to quickly generate a lengthy list. Below are just a few skills that you may wish to teach implicitly:

- Sharing
- Cooperation
- Holding hands

- Leadership
- Exercise
- Fairness
- Responsibility

There is a rather well-known game, Knots (New Games Foundation, 1976), where a group of individuals is asked to stand in a tight circle and place their hands into the center of the group. They are then asked to hold the hands of two different people from the group. Once everyone is holding hands, they are asked to become untangled without dropping hands until they have completed the task. You might have a group of four students initially complete the task as a small group. Once they are successful, you may ask them to join another group of four; thus becoming a group of eight. You can continue enlarging the size of the circle until you believe it becomes too difficult for students to solve the task. The larger the group, the longer it will take to become untangled. Not only do students find this task challenging, they also have fun while completing the activity.

Students will generally believe that they participated in the game for whatever reason you choose to share with them. For example, you might tell them you selected the activity because it was fun or fostered communication. There may, however, be other reasons that you will keep private for explaining why you elected to include the game in your curriculum. Those reasons may range from emphasizing cooperation with a group of new students to helping students learn to hold hands. Your reasons may also have included fostering leadership skills in students who are low skilled, emphasizing the success of all students, or teaching students to listen to the suggestions of classmates. Whatever your reason, it is implicit if you do not share your intentions with them.

Teachers often elect not to explicitly share their curriculum because they believe it may be more powerful if students independently make a discovery. In the game of Knots, for instance, they may learn that holding someone else's hand isn't so bad. They also may learn to think about physical activity as being enjoyable and exhilarating, not painful and embarrassing. Those who are low skilled in other activities may shine as highly skilled when playing Knots.

Sometimes a teacher may engage students in fun activities like crab soccer (modified soccer while using one's arms and legs to move like a crab) or seal tag (engaging in a game of tag while using only one's arms to maneuver across a small space on the floor like a seal). While students may believe they are engaged in a fun activity that allows them to play soccer or tag, the teacher's primary intention may be to increase arm strength.

Students can learn many valuable lessons from a single activity.

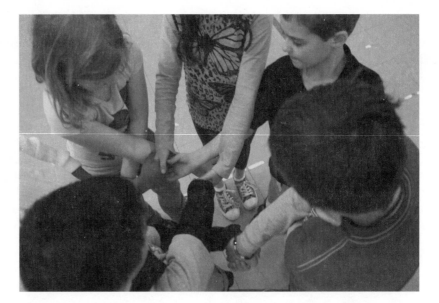

Implicitly developing an inclusive learning environment.

Similar to the explicit curriculum, there are many ways in which teachers can use the implicit curriculum as a mechanism for making the learning environment more inclusive. As emphasized in Key Point 4-3, the implicit curriculum may be the most effective means of teaching long-term lessons. As evidenced by the examples given above, students may learn more rapidly and effectively through implicit rather than explicit lessons about such things as leadership, cooperation, and sharing. Take, for example, the idea of teaching students to hold hands without complaint. By almost all accounts, physical educators find this one of the most difficult skills to teach. Students have learned to dislike hand holding because they believe it infers they "like" the person with whom they are holding hands. As a result, they become the butt of jokes that range from minor teasing about a budding boyfriend/girlfriend relationship to teasing that borders on homophobia. Using a well-liked activity to implicitly teach hand holding may make it easier for teachers to transfer that skill into activities like dance, which often raise objections to hand holding.

Key Point 4-3

The implicit curriculum may provide a more effective mechanism for encouraging long-term student learning than the explicit curriculum.

Hidden Curriculum

Often regarded as the most powerful form of curriculum, the hidden curriculum represents what students learn in school that was not intended to be taught and remains invisible to both the teacher and the learner. Once discovered, it is no longer considered to be hidden (Dodds, 1983). It often encompasses what students learn about the norms and values of the school environment (Posner, 2003).

Think about your fourth-grade classroom. If yours was like the classroom of many students, the desks and rigid chairs were probably placed closely together and assigned by the teacher to promote the least amount of disruption. Friends were separated, those with learning difficulties were placed closer to the front of the room, and disruptive students were often isolated from everyone else. Every 30 minutes a bell would ring to signify a transition from one activity like reading into another activity like art, lunch, or recess. Student work was placed neatly along the sides of the walls, with the most exceptional work, like a perfect score on a spelling test or neat handwriting, highlighted in a prominent location. There also were rules about leaving one's desk, eating in the classroom, getting in line to move to another location, raising one's hand before speaking, and submitting assignments.

Interestingly, you probably never thought much about what you actually learned from the scenario above. It is quite probable, however, that you learned a considerable amount about the routines, norms, and values that were promoted in the school and those that were not. Without formally recognizing the knowledge you acquired, you may have realized that learning occurs in an uncomfortable environment that discourages friendships, eating, leaving one's seat without permission, and talking out of turn but encourages regimented responses to signals and rigid compliance to rules. While excellence was promoted, the achievements of those who tried hard but were not at the top of the class were only marginally recognized. At a subconscious level you also learned not to raise your hand quite as high when you had not completed the homework but did not want the teacher to know that, or to raise your hand straight in the air, without waving it too wildly, when you wanted to be recognized.

The hidden curriculum may have taught some students that learning is highly structured.

As noted in Key Point 4-4, while the teacher may have wanted to create an orderly environment to promote learning, he/she probably did not intend for you to learn that classrooms can be uncomfortable and rigid environments that often favor gifted students. Despite the teacher's good intentions to optimize your opportunities to learn by creating structure, you may have developed negative memories about school. Although it is equally likely that you had a positive experience in school, as evidenced by your desire to become a teacher, there were students whose experiences were less than positive.

Key Point 4-4

What students learn from the hidden curriculum is unintended and tends to be more negative than positive.

After thinking for a moment about what you learned from the hidden curriculum in the classroom, complete Thinking Challenge 4.4. While most individuals who complete this task will have little difficulty brainstorming negative examples of what they learned from the hidden curriculum, there will be some who have greater difficulty because they were taught by a particularly effective and caring teacher who worked very hard so students would not learn negative lessons from the hidden curriculum. If you received only positive messages because you were exposed to thoughtful teachers, imagine what students might learn if they were taught by an insensitive teacher or someone who did not understand the power of the hidden curriculum.

Making the learning environment inclusive.

Since the hidden curriculum is considered to be hidden only when it is invisible to both the teacher and the student, think about what could potentially be a negative outcome of the hidden curriculum and turn that into something positive. Below are only a few examples of how to turn the potentially negative effects of the hidden curriculum into positive outcomes.

1. Elimination: Unfortunately, those who are least skilled and need the most practice are often the first ones to leave the activity in an elimination game. As a result, students learn that unskilled students are less worthy of participation. Instead of using elimination as a consequence, have eliminated students join the other team or ask them to serve

THINKING CHALLENGE 4.4

Think about what you learned from the hidden curriculum during elementary school physical education. If you did not have physical education, think about your experiences on the playground during recess. In the first column, briefly describe the experience from which you learned; in the second column describe what you learned. Place a + or − in the last column to summarize whether it was a positive or a negative learning experience. If you have difficulty completing this task, instead of reflecting on what you learned, imagine what others may have learned.

Describe the Experience	What You Learned	+ or −

in a capacity so they can stay involved. For example, if they are tagged out in a tag game, have them become one of the "its." Within a matter of minutes, the majority of students will be "its" chasing those who have yet to be tagged. Nobody will experience embarrassment and all will be involved.

2. Sexism: Instead of unintentionally reinforcing stereotypes by using language like "boys' push-ups" and "girls' push-ups," use terms like "straight leg" and "bent leg" push-ups. This will allow either gender to choose what they are most capable of performing without making females appear inferior. In the same vein, if you want girls to have an opportunity to participate, do not state that a female student must touch the ball before a goal can be scored. Instead, institute a rule that at least one male and one female must touch the ball. By using examples that are gender-neutral, students will learn that both genders are capable of performing.

3. Status: Students often learn that some classmates receive special recognition or favors from the teacher. These students are considered to have superordinate status. Those at the opposite end of the favoritism spectrum are relegated to subordinate status. Students frequently learn that a pecking order exists where athletes or highly skilled students have superordinate status. They learn this because these students are asked to demonstrate more frequently or allowed not to work as hard during game days. Status, however, can be equalized by teachers who carefully track to make sure all students are afforded the same opportunities to demonstrate or assume leadership positions.

Null Curriculum

The null curriculum refers to everything that is missing from the formal curriculum. The null curriculum in elementary physical education may include activities like swimming, gymnastics, golf, martial arts, archery, rock climbing, and skating. There are many good reasons why certain activities are not included in the curriculum so we will not spend much time discussing this subject. If, for instance, a pool or golf course was not available in a school setting, those activities would not be taught unless the appropriate facilities were accessible nearby. If a physical education teacher had no training in martial arts or gymnastics, those activities would also likely be excluded—and for very good reasons such as safety. As a classroom teacher, if you did not have access to a climbing wall or had never participated in a sport like soccer, there is a good chance that those activities would not be in your curriculum.

While there will *always* exist a null curriculum in every school—based on the simple fact that it would be impossible to teach every conceivable physical activity—negative consequences may emerge from the null curriculum so it is something to consider (see Key Point 4-5). For example, if a classroom teacher instructed students in basketball only because that was a favorite personal activity, or walking because it was the only activity the teacher could perform, students would acquire negative messages based on what was missing from their curriculum. They might learn that their teacher was lazy or in very poor physical condition.

By carefully thinking about what physical activities to include (or not include) in your curricular repertoire, think about those messages that you hope students will acquire from the formal curriculum. Games that are elimination oriented, require high amounts

Key Point 4-5

Although there are very good reasons why certain activities are not included in the elementary school physical education curriculum, teachers must carefully examine the null curriculum to determine if there are unintended and negative messages students may be receiving from what is missing.

of skill, or are potentially embarrassing to some, like relay races, might be activities best relegated to the null curriculum. Students who wish to participate in those activities can do so outside of school and not at the expense of their classmates. Activities that encourage cooperation, high levels of engagement, and maximize the success of all students should be encouraged.

PROMOTING AN INCLUSIVE LEARNING ENVIRONMENT

We would like to use snow as a metaphor for introducing the next section of this chapter. When you think about snow, certain things come to mind that are characteristic of all snowfalls; cold, white, freezing, and melting. Although these characteristics of snow can be generalized from one snowfall to the next, there also exists strong disagreement among different individuals about how snow is regarded. Some individuals, for example, believe that snow is beautiful, cleansing, and refreshing. Others would characterize it as ugly, dirty, and inconvenient. When all snowfalls during a year are accounted for as a collective group, we see them as being relatively similar. Often we forget that some snowfalls were short in duration while others lasted for days, some were heavy while others were light, and some were composed of large snowflakes while others had flakes that were barely visible. Overall, we rarely think of snow as composed of millions of individual flakes, each of which is uniquely different.

In a similar fashion, it is easy for teachers to forget when planning lessons that each child is uniquely different and beautiful in their own way. Since teachers by necessity tend to plan for all students as a collective group, they often forget that some are short and others are tall, some have lots of skill and others have little, some are overweight and others are underweight, some are female and others are male, some are black and others are white, some are rich and some are poor, and some have special needs and others have relatively few. We forget that students fall along a continuum of individual uniqueness; some lie at the extreme ends and others fall somewhere in between (see Key Point 4-6).

Key Point 4-6

Each child is uniquely different and should be appreciated for the differences that he/she brings to the learning environment.

Regardless of whether a teacher is planning a movement activity that will be shared explicitly with students or attempting to implicitly convey a learning objective like cooperation, he/she must always remain mindful of what *all* students in the class are learning. The teacher must make provisions to promote the success of each individual child. Learning how to individualize the environment, however, can be very difficult, particularly for new classroom teachers who may be struggling with the unfamiliar content of physical education or trying to establish themselves as leaders in the classroom. The purpose of this section is to acquaint you with the range of individuals who you are likely to encounter and provide you with strategies for insuring the success of these individuals when planning your curriculum. As you continue reading, we hope that you will always remember that students will learn from the example you set.

Ability

One of the most difficult challenges facing classroom teachers who teach physical education is the wide range of abilities with which they will be confronted. You might encounter a similar situation when teaching activities like reading and math, but nowhere is the ability gap wider than in physical education. Here you may have some students who participate on a travel soccer team while others have never touched a regulation soccer ball. Planning activities that challenge those who are skilled while introducing novices to the basics is more difficult than teachers anticipate. Try to complete Thinking Challenge 4.5. It may sound easier to complete than it is to achieve in reality.

THINKING CHALLENGE 4.5	Plan a brief 10-minute activity that will successfully engage 30 second-grade students in dribbling a soccer ball around an oncoming opponent. All students should be active simultaneously and have multiple opportunities to complete the task. The activity should challenge experienced students while providing success to beginners.

Regardless of skill level, most young elementary students simply enjoy the opportunity to participate and be active. They believe that if they try hard enough, they will achieve. At this stage in their development, they are unable to distinguish between effort and ability (Fry, 2001). As they progress through elementary school and begin to compare their performance to that of their peers, they begin to differentiate between the two and "develop beliefs about whether ability is fixed (innate) or malleable (acquired)" (Solmon, 2003, p. 158). As Solmon suggests, those individuals with a low perception of ability, and who believe that ability is fixed, may exert less effort than someone who believes they have low ability but can achieve with effort.

Scholars who study how children learn have suggested that a task-oriented learning climate that emphasizes individual skill development is more favorable than an environment that fosters high levels of competition where winning is emphasized. A task-oriented environment can be challenging for highly skilled students yet encourage effort in children who may be less skilled. Below are a few suggestions for how to challenge students of all abilities.

- Encourage students to consistently improve their own performance. For example, ask them to count how many times they can successfully dribble a ball within a 60-second period of time. Have students record their performance mentally and then repeat the task. Ask students if they have improved their individual score. Encourage students to practice the task at home and during class. Several days later, introduce the same task again to determine if there was improvement.

Children benefit when given the opportunity to improve their own performance as opposed to comparing their performance to others.

- Allow students to make decisions about their own performance. Some students will perform better with smaller or softer balls than others. Some will choose to stand closer to the target when throwing a ball than others. Help students to make wise decisions based on their own performance, not on the performance of their peers.
- Include activities in the curriculum that promote creativity and enable those who might not be skilled athletes to succeed during an expressive movement activity like creative dance. When appropriate, highlight their performance by asking them to demonstrate.
- Encourage students to complete a task by cooperating as a large group, not competing against each other. For example, challenge students to keep multiple balls rolling throughout the gym by tossing one new tennis ball into the activity area every five seconds. Continue the game until one of the balls stops rolling. Keep track of the number of balls that students kept rolling during the activity. Complete the task on several occasions to see if students can improve their performance as a group.

Gender

As emphasized in Key Point 4-7, prior to puberty there is little difference between the ability of boys and girls when performing motor tasks. In fact, it has been said that the two genders are more alike than they are different (Thomas & Thomas, 2008). Unfortunately, teachers often assume that female students are less skilled than their male counterparts even during the elementary years. Most likely, they have acquired this belief based on stereotypes about girls' abilities. Hearing statements such as, "You throw like a girl," does little to improve that perception. Both boys and girls progress through a series of stages when learning to throw. If girls do not progress as rapidly as boys, it is likely attributable to fewer practice opportunities and less instruction than it is to skill level. In the same vein, when boys are told they cannot jump rope, it is likely that they were not exposed to the same opportunities as girls. Both genders can learn to throw and both can learn to jump rope. It is a matter of opportunity, instruction, and societal expectations, not ability.

Key Point 4-7

Prior to puberty, the motor ability level of boys and girls is strikingly similar.

Although ability differences may begin to manifest as children enter the middle and high school grades, elementary classroom teachers should treat both genders equitably, expecting the same types of learning outcomes from each. Below are a few suggestions for minimizing the negative effects of gender stereotyping.

- Use gender-neutral language in the classroom. As mentioned earlier in this chapter, use phrases such as "bent leg" and "straight leg" push-ups as opposed to "boys " and girls' " push-ups. By carefully selecting your words, you will reduce the likelihood that expectations for one gender will be lower than for the other.

- Highlight both boys' and girls' accomplishments by asking them to demonstrate on an equitable basis. Use gender balancing so that both sexes equitably demonstrate during activities traditionally characterized as female (e.g., dance, gymnastics) and those commonly characterized as male (e.g., throwing, basketball).

- Implement rules so that both genders will have opportunities to participate on an equal basis.

- Organize activities by ability level, not gender. For example, you might organize four small-sided soccer games that range from highly competitive (very skilled) to non-competitive (less skilled). Allow students to choose on which team they would like to participate.

Race, Ethnicity, and Culture

The face of our nation's schools has changed from one that was predominantly Caucasian to one that is culturally diverse. In fact, in many schools throughout the nation, minority students now represent the majority of those enrolled (Tyson, 2003). Although the benefits of a multicultural society are numerous, there are challenges presented to teachers for which they are largely unprepared.

In many schools throughout the nation, teachers encounter students whose first language is not English. Attempting to convey subject matter and the norms of the classroom is very difficult. Different cultures also pose challenges to teachers of physical education. In some societies, female participation in physical activity is frowned upon, particularly if it induces sweating or encourages culturally perceived immodest attire (Randsdell et al., 2004). In other societies, female participation is desired and highly valued.

Regardless of the subject matter being taught, classroom teachers need to be aware of cultural norms and show respect to students who are different. Whereas difference used to be ridiculed, today it should be celebrated. Children learn more from those who are different from them than from those who are similar. Below are a few suggestions for ways in which teachers can celebrate difference and promote a positive learning environment for everyone. Once you have read these suggestions, complete Thinking Challenge 4.6.

THINKING CHALLENGE 4.6	Use the space below to list three additional strategies that you could use as a teacher to promote cultural sensitivity. 1. 2. 3.

- When possible, pair a non-English speaking student with a student who is multilingual or who speaks only English but is willing to assist through such means as demonstration. Another strategy is to use pictures to convey the activity you want the student to perform.

- Invite students from different cultures to share during class the different types of physical activities that are popular in their culture. Take time to participate in those activities.

- Implement rules and consequences that discourage racist behavior and intolerance.

- Model appropriate behavior. For example, do not laugh at racist jokes, even when told within the confines of the teachers' lounge; avoid using language from another culture simply to gain popularity with students from that culture; and apologize after making an error, as unintentional as it might be, that could be perceived as racist or insensitive.

- Implement physical education curriculum that is culturally sensitive.

Students learn from working with students who are different from them.

Socioeconomic Status

Although socioeconomic status will probably not play a major role in influencing your physical activity curriculum, it is important to be mindful that not all students will be able to afford the equipment or attire necessary for participating in particular types of activities. Some sports, such as ice hockey or figure skating, are difficult for parents of most socioeconomic levels to afford. Other activities like baseball, basketball, soccer, and volleyball will be affordable to most but not to everyone. Your job as a teacher is to introduce students to activities that can be enjoyed by all. Below are some strategies for reducing economic barriers for students from low-income backgrounds.

- Consistently emphasize to all students that they don't need the best equipment to enjoy physical activity participation. Basketball was invented by using peach baskets. Street ball was conceived by using an old broom handle and a rubber ball.

- Show students how they can design their own equipment. In fact, you may wish to hold a contest for the most creative piece of equipment that students can construct at no cost.

- Provide students with several pieces of interesting equipment such as (a) a cardboard box, (b) two paper plates, (c) a shovel, (d) four empty milk cartons, and (e) a broken hula hoop. Give students 15 minutes to create an activity where they must use all pieces of equipment and engage all students in physical activity for at least 50 percent of the class time. This will demonstrate how easy it is to brainstorm a fun activity with limited equipment. Take Thinking Challenge 4.7 to see how you perform on a similar task.

- Maintain a small slush fund for helping students with limited income to purchase items like gym shoes. Be sure to obtain permission from your principal because you will need to be careful not to offend parents or embarrass the student. Obviously, funding a necessary purchase for a needy individual must be done with the utmost of discretion.

- Allow students to participate in physical activity for as much of the school day as possible. Remember that there will always be some students who have no opportunities to engage in any form of physical activity outside of school because it is either unaffordable or unsafe. In the case of the latter, some students may not even have the freedom to walk from their home to school and back again because their neighborhood is riddled with crime or drug trafficking.

THINKING CHALLENGE 4.7	Within 10 minutes, design a game that involves all students in moderate physical activity for 75 percent of the time. You must use all of the following equipment: (a) paper bag, (b) old tire, (c) milk carton, (d) somewhat deflated playground ball, (d) 4 bath towels, and (e) medium-sized bucket.

Size

In Chapter One, we introduced you to statistics that relate to the obesity epidemic that plagues our nation and many others throughout the world. You will encounter some children who are in poor physical condition due to being overweight. Participating in physical education class can be especially traumatizing for these students, particularly if they are asked to wear clothing that accentuates their size. These children are often teased and severely bullied throughout the school day. Exposing them to a vulnerable learning environment like physical education can be damaging if not handled properly by the teacher.

As a classroom teacher, you will be familiar with those students who are overweight (and in some cases, underweight) in your class. We hope that you will have developed a culture where teasing and bullying are not accepted but where support and encouragement are expected. Although you will be challenged when working with students of different sizes, you also will be rewarded when they achieve. Below are some things to consider when working with children of different sizes.

- If an obese child is walking and not running, do not assume that person is not working hard. It takes far greater energy for an obese child to move quickly. Although that individual may be much slower in speed, that child's heart rate may actually be beating much faster than the quicker students in the class.
- Engage all students in activities where their performance cannot be compared to others. If, for example, students are running around a track, have them start from different locations so that slower runners will be less distinguishable from faster runners (Trout & Graber, 2009).
- Find activities where all children can be successful regardless of size (e.g., Frisbee golf).
- Allow children to select how they participate in an activity. For instance, you may let children select different sizes of equipment, determine where they stand when serving a ball, and decide if they will run or walk briskly during a soccer game.

Special Needs

In 1975, Public Law 94-142 was enacted to ensure the educational rights of students with disabilities and special needs. The education of these individuals should occur within the least restrictive environment possible, thus promoting the notion of mainstreaming special needs students into the regular classroom. Prior to 1975 the education of special needs students was often conducted in a separate classroom, which resulted in greater suspicion than understanding about children with special needs. Today special needs students are mainstreamed into the classroom where they can learn from others and where others can learn from them. Of course, there may be instances when children with special needs may also benefit from instruction in a special, self-contained classroom with a teacher who has special training in working with special needs students. When possible, however, it is critical to also include them in the traditional physical education classroom with their classmates.

An Individualized Education Program (IEP) is constructed for those students who require some form of assistance to participate in physical education (e.g., require an aide or special services) or when the curriculum requires modification to meet their needs. Although you will learn how to write IEPs in other education classes for which you will enroll, it is important to remember that if you are responsible for teaching physical education

Children with special needs should be mainstreamed into the classroom with other students.

in your school, in conjunction with a team of others, you will need to write short- and long-term goals and appropriate activities into the IEP.

If you are teaching a disabled student and have access to a physical education specialist at your school, it would be wise to ask for some curricular modification suggestions that are appropriate for the child's particular disability. Since there are so many types of special needs ranging from emotional to physical and from moderate to severe, it would be impossible to provide you with a list of curricular modifications that would work for everyone. Below are a few suggestions. You also will find additional ideas in the lab chapters of this text. As you take more education classes, you certainly will be provided with additional information about working with special needs students and writing IEPs.

- Modify the activity in ways that promote the success of the special needs student.
- Attend conferences and read teacher-oriented journals/books that provide you with ideas for appropriate curriculum for different types of disabilities.
- Partner special needs students with other children who are supportive and friendly.
- Become aware of the child's medical condition, familiarize yourself with the expectations of the child's parents, and work as a team with other teachers.
- Understand that there are a wide variety of conditions that require some form of special assistance. As Key Point 4-8 emphasizes, no single modification is suitable for every type of disability.
- Use creative thinking when planning a lesson for a child with a disability. For example, although a child in a wheelchair may not be able to kick a ball during soccer, that individual could be given a hockey stick for maneuvering the ball. In a rhythmic gymnastics unit that uses scarves as equipment, have students design a routine while everyone is sitting in a desk chair so that the child in a wheelchair feels less different from his or her peers during this activity.

Key Point 4-8

There are many types of disabilities that range from emotional to physical and from moderate to severe. Remember, no single modification is suitable for every type of special need.

Summary
Although we often think of the primary school curriculum as intended and written, students learn as much, if not more, from the unintended consequences of the unwritten and unspoken curriculum. In order to effectively humanize the learning environment, the explicit curriculum needs to account for the needs of all learners, regardless of ability, gender, race/ethnicity, socioeconomic status, size, or special needs. The implicit curriculum can serve as a valuable tool for teaching important lessons that are left untold because they are best discovered by students. The curriculum must be regularly evaluated and scrutinized to uncover potential negative consequences. Although the hidden curriculum can never be totally eliminated, its negative effects can be minimized by particularly skillful teachers. Finally, teachers should consider the null curriculum and what students learn from that which is missing.

As Box 4.1 illustrates, there are teacher behaviors that will increase the likelihood that you will be successful in achieving your intended curriculum and behaviors that will decrease that possibility. If you can remember that all children are unique, your chance of success will be enhanced. Like teachers, children bring baggage with them to school. In some cases, you will be privy to that baggage, which might make it easier to understand the circumstances of that child. In other cases, you will not have access to that baggage, and it will be more difficult to reach a particular individual. Regardless of the case, all children must be treated with sensitivity and as a unique and irreplaceable person.

DO AND DON'T CHECKLIST

Do	Don't
☐ carefully plan your intended curriculum with an eye toward making the learning environment inclusive	☐ assume that students learn only from the explicit curriculum
☐ use the implicit curriculum to promote student self-discovery	☐ expect that all students will receive the same messages from a lesson
☐ treat all students equitably	☐ ignore instances of intolerance
☐ carefully observe the learning environment for instances of intolerance	☐ assume that one activity will be successful and well-liked by all students
☐ plan lessons that encourage students from different cultures to work together	☐ be afraid that you will be unable to provide appropriate learning activities for students with special needs
☐ remember that society has become increasingly multicultural.	☐ stereotype your students.

Review Activities

1. Use your own words to define explicit, implicit, hidden, and null curriculums.
2. Give one example of each of the four forms of curriculum that are different from the examples given in this chapter.
3. Describe how you would respond to a student who did not want to participate in physical activity because of his/her low perceptions of personal ability.
4. Brainstorm three realistic strategies for encouraging students of different races, who have previously been reluctant to work together, to do so.
5. Discuss your primary concerns about planning appropriate lessons for children with special needs.

References

Dodds. P. (1983). Consciousness raising in curriculum: A teacher's model. In A. Jewett, M. Carnes, & M. Speakman (Eds.), *Proceedings of the third conference on curricula and theory in physical education* (pp. 213–234). Athens: University of Georgia Press.

Eisner, E. (1994). *The educational imagination: On the design and evaluation of school programs* (3rd ed.). New York: Macmillan College Publishing.

Fry, M. D. (2001). The development of motivation in children. In G. C. Roberts (Ed.), *Advances in motivation in sport and exercise* (pp. 51–78). Champaign, IL: Human Kinetics.

New Games Foundation. (1976). *The new games book*. Garden City, NY: Dolphin Books/ Doubleday & Company.

Posner, G. J. (2003). *Analyzing the curriculum* (3rd ed.). New York: McGraw-Hill.

Randsdell, L. B., Detling, L., Hildebrand, K., Lau, P., Moyer-Mileur, L., & Shultz, B. (2004). International perspectives: the influence of gender on lifetime physical activity participation. *The Journal of the Royal Society for the Promotion of Health, 124,* 12–14.

Solmon, M. A. (2003). Student issues in physical education classes: Attitudes, cognition, and motivation. In S. J. Silverman & C. D. Ennis (Eds.), *Student learning in physical education* (pp. 147–163). Champaign, IL: Human Kinetics.

Thomas, K. T., & Thomas, J. R. (2008). Principles of motor development for elementary school physical education. *Elementary School Journal, 108,* 181–195.

Trout, J., & Graber, K. C.(2009). Perceptions of overweight students concerning their experiences in physical education. *Journal of Teaching in Physical Education, 28,* 272–292.

Tyson, L. A. (2003). Context of schools. In S. J. Silverman & C. D. Ennis (Eds.), *Student learning in physical education* (pp. 43–66). Champaign, IL: Human Kinetics.

Chapter **Five**

Curriculum Models and Special Events

As you begin to formally plan your explicit and implicit curriculum, you will need to think seriously about your primary curricular focus and how best to convey it to students. In the lower elementary grades, units are relatively short in length. As mentioned in previous chapters, you might introduce an activity, like throwing or creative dance, for two or three consecutive days and then return to that skill periodically throughout the year. As children progress into the upper grades of elementary school, units become increasingly longer in duration.

The purpose of this chapter is to provide you with a sampling of different curricular models for elementary-aged students. Some options will be more appropriate for children in the lower grades while others are better suited for those in the upper grades. As a new teacher, it may initially be difficult for you to decide what type of physical education curriculum is best for your students. Despite this fact, it is wise to think well in advance of the beginning of school about the focus of your curriculum and to develop an overall plan for the entire academic year. In doing so, you will ensure that your students receive instruction in those skills and activities to which you believe they should be exposed, and you will be less likely to forget to teach an important activity. In contrast, planning on a piecemeal basis is generally ineffective and does not promote exposure to a well-rounded and thoughtful curriculum. As you read this chapter, contemplate whether you would want to promote only one curricular model in your yearly curriculum or introduce children to several different alternatives.

Deciding on a curricular focus is challenging but exciting.

BASIC MOVEMENT SKILLS

Movement can be characterized as locomotor, non-locomotor, and manipulative. These are the primary ways in which students can move their bodies. Developing skill in each of these areas will later assist the child in being able to successfully perform increasingly complex movements and participate in higher-order games and sports. Although you will find a brief description of each of the three forms of movement below, the lab chapters will provide more in-depth explanations of each and examples of how to effectively plan lessons addressing one or more forms of movement.

Locomotor

Activities that require students to move through space are considered locomotor. They require weight transfer to propel the body from one point to another. Primary examples of locomotor movements include the following:

- Walk: Always a period of foot contact with the ground
- Run: Brief period of non-contact with the ground
- Hop (through space): Take off on one foot, land on the same foot
- Jump (through space): Take off from both feet, land on both feet
- Skip: Step, hop; step, hop (alternate lead leg after each step, hop sequence)
- Gallop: Step forward with lead leg, bring legs together (same leg always leads)
- Slide: Step sideways with lead leg, bring legs together (same leg always leads)

Non-locomotor

Movement activities that are performed in self space and do not require the student to enter general space are referred to as non-locomotor. They form the foundation for many creative activities and are necessary when performing basic motor skills. A few examples are:

- Twist: One body part moves while another remains still or follows behind
- Turn: Change direction by rotating
- Reach: Extend part of the body to reach toward something else
- Stretch: Lengthen, widen, or extend the body
- Bend: Flex or bend part of the body

Many concepts such as twisting, reaching, force, flow, and level are associated with the movement activity of throwing.

Manipulative

When students use their hands, arms, legs, or another body part to receive or propel an object through space, they are engaged in a manipulative activity. Acquiring manipulative skills requires more practice and instruction than developing locomotor or non-locomotor skills. Below are a few examples of common manipulative activities.

- Throw: Propel an object through space usually with the hands
- Catch: Receive an object
- Strike: Hit or sharply contact an object
- Volley: Briefly contact an object multiple times to keep it airborne
- Dribble: Repeatedly and rapidly kick or bounce an object
- Kick/punt: Propel an object through space with the foot

CREATIVE MOVEMENT

Creative movement is a popular form of curriculum that is incorporated into the classes of many physical education teachers. It was influenced by the work of Rudolph Laban, a French artist and theorist who promoted Laban Movement Analysis in the early 1900s. Physical education teachers who emphasize creative movement in their curricular framework tend to believe that it is important to teach movement activities while introducing students to a wide variety of concepts that can later be transferred from one activity to another (see Key Point 5-1). Creative movement can serve as a highly beneficial framework, particularly for teaching movement to children in the elementary grades. It can be used by allowing students to explore how different pieces of equipment can be used or when teaching creative dance or gymnastics (see Lab Chapter 7).

Key Point 5-1

It is important for children to learn basic movement activities and concepts associated with those activities.

CONCEPTS COMBINED WITH BASIC AND CREATIVE MOVEMENT ACTIVITIES

Three primary concepts are outlined below to describe how different aspects of movement can be executed. The concepts of space, effort, and relationships, along with their respective sub-concepts, help students to understand the many ways in which they can move their bodies. As you read this section, try to complete Thinking Challenge 5.1.

THINKING CHALLENGE 5.1	In the space below, pair one locomotor, one nonlocomotor, and one manipulative skill with one concept that you could use when teaching creative movement.

1. Locomotor skill:
   Concept:
2. Non-locomotor skill:
   Concept:
3. Manipulative skill:
   Concept:

Space

The concept of space corresponds to how an object or the body moves through the environment. It includes a number of sub-concepts and is one of the most essential concepts to teach children. In fact, space is usually the first concept to be taught, particularly in relation to self- and general space. Below are several sub-concepts related to space and a few samples of how you they might be used within a lesson.

- Self-space
    1. Create your own self-space by sitting inside of a hula hoop
    2. Dribble the ball in your own self-space
- General space
    1. Create a dance in general space, but be careful not to touch anyone else
    2. Throw the ball through general space
- Direction (forward, sideways, upward, downward, backward, clockwise, counterclockwise)
    1. Slide sideways from one end of the gym to the other
    2. Hop upward, but not forward
- Pathways (zigzag, straight, curved)
    1. Leap through the gym in a straight pathway
    2. Dribble the ball in a zigzag pattern
- Levels (high, medium, low)
    1. Toss the beanbag at a high level, then a medium level, then a low level
    2. Dribble the ball at the lowest possible level without stopping
- Extensions (far, near)
    1. Create a dance where your hands consistently move far from and near to the rest of your body
    2. Hand dribble while keeping the ball near to your body and then far from your body to see which feels most comfortable

Effort

This concept refers to the amount of effort or muscular actions involved in particular movements. For example, a skip can be completed using fast or slow movements, depending on the mood or concept the child intends to convey.

- Time (fast, slow)
    1. Jump onto and off the platform as quickly as possible
    2. Avoid letting your opponent get the ball by quickly changing directions
    3. Slowly extend your arm as you perform the dance sequence
    4. Walk backward very slowly along the red line
- Force (strong, light)
    1. Show me how you might skip if one leg were stronger than the other
    2. Show your partner how your body would look if you were catching a light object
    3. Use strong force to throw the ball as far as possible
    4. Jump off this small wooden box landing lightly on your feet
    5. Lightly transfer your weight from one body part to another
- Flow (bound flow is easily stoppable and is controlled by the mover without difficulty; free flow is difficult to stop and more challenging to control)
    1. Move forward using a bound movement and quickly transition into free flow
    2. Walk down the beam using bound flow

3. Sequence three different movements together using free flow
4. Skip through the room using free flow

Relationships

The concept of relationships describes how students move their bodies in relation to objects and other students. It is important for children to understand the concept of relationships because there are many activities that require students to use equipment or work with others.

- With objects (between, inside, outside, around, through, over, under, above, etc.)
  1. Bounce a ball between and around your legs
  2. Jump over the box and climb under the pole
  3. Kick the ball around another person and through the goal
- With partners or others (lead, follow, mirror, match, meet, part)
  1. Try to mirror the movements that your partner is making
  2. Create a dance with your partner where you meet and part from each other at some point
  3. Lead the class in a creative movement using a ball

Movement Challenges in Lower Elementary Grades

When developing curriculum that is based on movement activities and concepts for children in the early elementary grades (grades K-1), initially introduce them to no more than one movement skill and concept combination at a time.

- Hop in self-space
- Skip quickly
- Reach high for the sky

As children begin to master individual skills and gain understanding of the concepts, you may begin to focus on grouping one or more movement activities and concepts together (grades 1-3). Below are a few examples.

- Quickly move sideways down the gym floor at a low level
- Bounce the ball using medium force, at a medium level, and using medium speed
- Move in a curved pathway through general space using free-flowing movements
- Kick the ball backward to your partner using light force
- Throw the ball upward at a medium level and lightly catch it in both hands
- Quickly dribble the ball down the field and then kick it with force toward the goal

Movement Challenges in Upper Elementary Grades

After children acquire basic motor skills and an understanding of the concepts that accompany those skills, usually by mid-third grade, they are ready to begin incorporating them into individual and small-sided games. Gradually the focus shifts from an emphasis on concepts to combining motor skills in increasingly complex situations. At this age of their development, children enjoy competing against themselves (to determine if they can improve their performance) or engaging with others to accomplish a task or play a low-organized game.

Although many teachers instruct their students in competitive games, at this point we strongly encourage a limited focus on competition. For example, activities that result in a strong emphasis on winning or losing, or that result in some children who would rather give up than participate because they are embarrassed by their skill level in relation to others, are inappropriate.

Creative dance and gymnastics are excellent activities for teaching students to combine multiple concepts.

The upper elementary grades are a time when students are best served with opportunities to improve their performance at basic motor skills. If they are to successfully engage in sports or other movement challenges at a later age, they will need to have acquired basic motor skills in order to be successful. Around grade 3, children are usually ready to engage in individual, partner, and small-sided games and activities. As they progress into grades 4 and 5, they are ready to participate with increasingly large groups of children. A few samples of appropriate activities for the upper elementary grades are listed below. As you read about these activities and others included in this chapter, remember that we are using grade level only as a guideline. The most important benchmark for determining if a child is ready to learn a more advanced activity should be determined primarily by that individual's developmental level (see Chapter 2).

- Count how many times you can keep the ball airborne at a medium level for 30 seconds (grades 3-4)
- Volley the ball back and forth with a partner and count how many consecutive contacts you make without letting the ball hit the ground (grades 4-5)
- Play a game of 3-on-3 soccer using two balls simultaneously and switching goalie positions every time you hear me clap (grades 4-5)
- Create a dance routine with a partner that includes (a) two balances, (b) a roll, (c) three different movement concepts, and (d) one-arm balance (grades 3-5)

FITNESS APPROACH

Throughout the past decade, particularly as a result of the emphasis on the obesity epidemic, a greater number of physical education teachers are stressing fitness in their lessons. This is witnessed predominantly at the middle and high school levels; however, some physical educators believe there also should be a strong fitness component at the elementary level. As highlighted in Key Point 5-2, teachers beliefs about fitness fall along a continuum that ranges from an exclusive focus on fitness at the left end of the continuum, to a modest emphasis in the middle, to almost no focus at the extreme right end.

Teachers at the extreme left end of the continuum tend to plan lessons that engage students in moderate to vigorous physical activity for the majority of the class period, emphasizing health-related fitness components such as flexibility, strength, and cardiovascular endurance. Teachers in the middle attempt to keep children actively engaged at

Key Point 5-2

Some teachers emphasize fitness above all other activities, some rarely incorporate fitness activities in their curriculum, and others fall somewhere in the middle. Although fitness is very important, it is equally important for children to learn basic skills and how to become creative movers.

a moderate to vigorous level when possible, but they also concentrate on other areas such as teaching basic motor skills and concepts. Finally, teachers at the extreme right have relatively no interest in fitness and are not concerned about including it in the curriculum. It should be noted that teachers on the right side of the continuum are relatively few in number.

As with most areas of controversy, there usually is a midpoint which is the most desirable for the largest number of people. As experts in physical education curriculum, we recommend that you teach fitness but not at the expense of neglecting to teach basic motor skills, movement concepts, or social skills such as sharing, cooperation, and teamwork. Below are some suggestions for ways in which you can successfully integrate fitness into the overall curriculum.

15-Minute Fitness Focus

The amount of time you have available to teach physical education or engage students in physical activity each day will determine what you are able to accomplish. Ideally, you will have 30 minutes of access to a gymnasium or safe playground area and ample equipment. In addition, another 15-minute period of uninterrupted time during the school day to focus on physical activity would be helpful. In one of these periods, we hope that you will be able to engage children in moderate to vigorous activity that will improve their strength or cardiovascular endurance. Although a large amount of space is preferable, fitness can also be enhanced within the confines of the classroom or during a brisk walk through the neighborhood. Your lab chapters provide you with many ideas for conducting fitness in the gymnasium during physical education or in the classroom during physical activity breaks. Here is a small sampling of activities that children would find fun and desirable. After reading these, try to complete Thinking Challenge 5.2.

- Play a non-elimination tag game that keeps children moving rapidly (running, jumping, seal tag)
- Take an active nature walk around the school yard
- Participate in a variety of jump rope activities
- March in place while engaging in a spelling bee
- Complete simple aerobic dance routines

Fitness and Motor Skill Development

In our opinion, there is no reason that you cannot simultaneously focus on teaching basic motor skills and movement concepts along with emphasizing fitness. There are many activities that teachers can plan that accomplish both goals. For teachers with only modest time allocated for physical education (e.g., 20 minutes per day), it will be important for them to carefully plan every second of instruction so that both goals can be achieved. Activities may include:

- Pass a ball back and forth with a partner while running down the field and back again
- Kick a ball around a large obstacle course (with all children moving simultaneously)

THINKING CHALLENGE 5.2

Pretend you are teaching 25 students in the 3rd grade. What activities would you include in your curriculum during a one-week period of time? Would you also concentrate on motor skill development? Jot down a few notes about activities you believe would be appropriate and enjoyable to children.

Monday

30 minutes of physical education

15 minutes of activity break

Tuesday

15 minutes of activity break

Wednesday

30 minutes of physical education

15 minutes of activity break

Thursday

15 minutes of activity break

Friday

30 minutes of physical education

15 minutes of activity break

- Throw a ball to a target, run to retrieve the ball, throw again (no stopping)
- Develop a continuous gymnastics floor routine
- Dribble a basketball around cones, shoot, retrieve ball, pass to the wall, catch, and begin again (with all children moving simultaneously)

Fitness and Game Play

Some games like soccer encourage running and vigorous movement. Other games like volleyball can result in large periods of inactivity. It is incumbent on the teacher to be creative. Whether someone is a certified physical education specialist or a classroom teacher, everyone has the ability to be creative by modifying or inventing games that encourage physical activity. Examples include:

- Volleyball: A beach ball is put into play with a toss over the net and both sides; see how many times they can rally the ball back and forth without dropping it—add two to three balls to the game to make it more challenging.
- Soccer: Everyone, including the goalie, must be continuously running, walking, or marching; if anyone stops, a point is scored by the other team.
- Softball: One person bats at a time while everyone else is in fielding position; after the ball is hit, fielders run to the person who catches the ball and form a line holding hands; the batter scores a point for each base touched before fielders get into position.

TRADITIONAL GAMES APPROACH

Although very few physical education teachers rely exclusively on game play to deliver the subject matter, some emphasize it more than anything else. Although we believe there certainly is a place for games in the curriculum, we frown on curriculum that predominantly emphasizes game play. Further, we believe some games are more worthy of inclusion in the curriculum than others. Games that neither teach skill nor develop health-related fitness—such as Musical Chairs, Duck-Duck-Goose, or Red Rover—are either inappropriate or belong only in settings like birthday parties. Other games like small-sided basketball, volleyball, soccer, floor hockey, and softball are appropriate only if children have adequately developed the basic motor skills required for successful participation and if all children are actively engaged in the activity.

Unfortunately, classroom teachers who rely primarily on games do so for a number of reasons. Some have little confidence in their ability to teach motor skills or fitness and thus rely on games they are familiar with from childhood or from recipe-like game books. Some classroom teachers do not believe in the importance of physical education and teach the subject matter only out of required obligation, with little concern for educating students in the psychomotor domain. Others allow children to play games because they are unable to resist the pressure placed upon them by their students or because they received no education in the curriculum of physical education.

As emphasized in Key Point 5-3, games are perfectly appropriate, but they must (a) have a purpose, (b) promote learning, (c) be developmentally appropriate, (d) encourage the success of all children, and (d) not serve as the primary curricular emphasis. Finally, students are best served by games that encourage engagement, sharing, success, and teamwork.

Key Point 5-3

Games are perfectly appropriate to include in the physical education curriculum, but they must (a) have a purpose, (b) promote learning, (c) be developmentally appropriate, (d) encourage the success of all children, and (d) not serve as the primary curricular emphasis.

TACTICAL GAMES APPROACH

In recent years, there has been increased focus on engaging children in games that increase their understanding of game concepts. Based on the premise that learning how to solve problems in one type of game transfers to other games, this approach focuses on raising students' cognitive ability to solve problems while simultaneously engaging them in sport-related activities. The benefits of this model are supported by empirical research and anecdotal evidence. Motivated classroom teachers who are interested in learning more about this approach should see the text by Mitchell, Oslin, and Griffin (2005) for ways in which to integrate this model into the curriculum in a developmentally appropriate manner.

NEW AND COOPERATIVE GAMES

As emphasized above, games that facilitate skill development and participation are appropriate in a balanced curriculum. Games that focus on developing social skills are also appropriate, particularly if they also promote psychomotor skills or fitness. As long as children receive adequate instruction in basic skills and are exposed to vigorous physical activity on a regular basis, it is highly desirable to sprinkle new and cooperative games into the curriculum.

New and cooperative games emphasize skills such as sharing, cooperation, and teamwork and eliminate competition that is unhealthy. In some cases, teachers can locate developmentally appropriate games from a series of texts that were published by the New Games Foundation (1976, 1981) or from numerous books written to encourage cooperation in indoor and outdoor settings. Some of the best games, however, are those that are teacher or child designed.

Teachers will find that students enjoy engaging in new and cooperative games. Similar to the other game models we discussed, teachers should, however, incorporate these into the curriculum only after children have acquired the appropriate skill level necessary for successful participation. Games should not represent the majority of the annual curriculum. Traditional, tactical, and new and cooperative games are all appropriate, but not as the entire annual curriculum.

TEACHER-DESIGNED GAMES

A moderately creative teacher can easily develop games that focus on social skill development. First, teachers should consider what aspects of social skills children need to learn (e.g., working with a partner, sharing equipment, achieving a common goal as a group). Second, the teacher should brainstorm activities that achieve the first goal while also engaging students in moderate to vigorous activity or problem solving. Third, the teacher should consider how to involve all students simultaneously in the game. Finally, student success should be a primary outcome. The teacher may also design games that encourage children who are less socially or physically skilled to actively participate in a challenge, even assuming a leadership role. For example, a cooperative game could engage students in discussion about how to move the entire group, including several pieces of equipment, safely from one end of the gym to the other without anyone's legs or feet touching the floor. Once children decide how to achieve the goal, it is attempted by everyone.

CHILD-DESIGNED GAMES

Some of the best, highly creative, and unique games are created by children. In this case, instead of the teacher establishing the rules for the game, he or she provides a framework for children to create their own game, boundaries, and rules. Lab Chapter 11 discusses child-designed games in greater detail and provides examples of how a teacher can successfully incorporate these types of learning experiences into the curriculum. Complete Thinking Challenge 5.3 to assess your feelings about the different games models.

THINKING CHALLENGE 5.3	Use the space below to list at least one advantage and one disadvantage of each of the following models:

Model	Advantage	Disadvantage
1. Traditional games		
2. Tactical games		
3. New and cooperative games		
4. Teacher-designed games		
5. Child-designed games		

After completing this exercise, which of the following models do you prefer and why?

ADVENTURE EDUCATION AND OUTDOOR PURSUITS

According to Key Point 5-4, adventure education refers to activities in which teachers create a learning environment, such as a climbing wall or a ropes course, whereas outdoor pursuits characterizes activities that are conducted in the natural environment, such as canoeing or hiking (Siedentop, Mand, & Taggart, 1986). Although few classroom teachers have the expertise or budget to construct something as complex as a climbing wall, many adventure education activities, such as challenging all students to cross a 4-foot "electric" fence without returning to the other side to help classmates, can be constructed with only a

Key Point 5-4

Adventure education refers to activities in which teachers create a human-constructed learning environment whereas outdoor pursuits characterizes activities that are conducted in the natural environment (Siedentop, Mand, & Taggart, 1986).

long jump rope tied to two trees. Classroom teachers who are interested in safely promoting adventure education activities, especially for students in the upper elementary grades, can enroll for any number of excellent courses after carefully conducting a Web search of potential options.

Engaging students in outdoor pursuits can also be challenging, particularly in urban environments, yet can be implemented in the curriculum by an enthusiastic teacher and a supportive principal. Many elementary schools, for example, offer weekend or week-long trips to children in the upper grades to engage them in activities like kayaking, orienteering, and hiking as a mechanism for teaching survival skills, cooperation, self-awareness, and team building. Students hold fundraisers throughout the year to earn money for the trip that is either supplemented by a financial contribution from parents or local company sponsorships. Of course, those teachers who teach in a rural environment and have greater access to outdoor open space are encouraged to engage children in outdoor pursuits on a more frequent basis.

The benefits of participation in unique activities like adventure education and outdoor pursuits have been demonstrated by research to promote cooperation, effort, risk taking, fun, trust, skill development, communication, and self-esteem (Dyson, 1995). Classroom teachers who have expertise in activities like camping and hiking may thoroughly enjoy exposing children to experiences such as these. Safety, of course, must be of the highest concern when planning adventure education or outdoor pursuits, but teachers can reduce risks by enrolling in appropriate courses at a community college or recreation center and soliciting an adequate number of qualified volunteers to help plan and execute the experience.

SPORT EDUCATION

Developed by scholars in the field as a mechanism for exposing children during physical education to the benefits of participation on a sport team, the sport education model encourages teamwork, positive sport experiences, and skill development regardless of ability level (Siedentop, Hastie, & van der Mars, 2004). The model is designed for children of all ages and developmental levels and has been supported through national and international research as an appropriate learning model (Hastie, 1996; Hastie & Sinelnikov, 2006). In addition, sport education and the alternative curricular models described above have demonstrated that they are highly enjoyable to children (complete Thinking Challenge 5.4).

THINKING CHALLENGE 5.4	List three reasons why you believe children would enjoy participating in adventure education, outdoor pursuits, and sport education.		
	Adventure Education	**Outdoor Pursuits**	**Sport Education**
	1.	1.	1.
	2.	2.	2.
	3.	3.	3.

The characteristics that make the model unique in traditional sport units are that students are assigned to a long-term team, participate over an extended season, and assume different roles such as coach, referee, record keeper, manager, and statistician. By remaining on the same team, they develop affiliation with a particular group of people and learn to help each other over a period of time. A culminating event, such as a competition or festival, concludes the unit. Although students may score tournament points by winning a game, they also may score by returning equipment to its appropriate location in good condition, supporting each other, or maintaining up-to-date records. Thus, a lower-skilled but more responsible team has the opportunity to win a competition. Activities included in sport education range from individual sports like tennis, golf, and gymnastics to team sports like basketball, volleyball, and rugby. Even activities like fitness can be applied to the model.

SPECIAL EVENTS

Spaced strategically throughout the year, or at the end of a unit, special events are something that children eagerly anticipate weeks in advance and remember throughout their lives. Although special events are *not* considered to be a curricular model, they should be integrated into your curriculum planning calendar well in advance of when they are scheduled. Some special events will include only the students from your classroom whereas others might combine your students with those from other classes of the same grade or from classes of several other grades.

If you are teaching in a parochial school, it is entirely appropriate to celebrate religious holidays within your curriculum. If, however, you are employed in the public schools, due to the separation of church and state, you can only teach about religious holidays, not celebrate them with students. Therefore, holidays such as Christmas, Yom Kippur, Easter, Rosh Hashanah, Kwanzaa, and Ramadan cannot legally be celebrated with parties or other organized events at the school. Even holidays like Halloween and Valentine's Day can cause problems for teachers because some parents and students do not celebrate these days. Although rules about not celebrating holidays may seem restrictive, after thinking more deeply about the issue, hopefully you can understand why it is not a good idea to mix church and state. Fortunately, there are many other events that lend themselves to celebration. Below are some examples of the special events you may wish to include.

Olympics

As a mechanism for either promoting or teaching a unit on the Olympics, incorporate Olympic-type events into the curriculum as part of a unit or special one-day event. You can host an opening ceremony, provide ribbons to all those who participate, and teach students about the history of the games and countries that have hosted the event (e.g., ancient Greece). Working in collaboration with other classroom teachers, you can promote the unit throughout the school and invite teachers of special subjects like art and music to participate and lend their expertise to the event. You may choose to promote physical activities that you have been practicing throughout the year, or introduce students to new activities to which they may not otherwise have exposure. Modification of physical activities is perfectly appropriate. Even adding silly physical activities like those below is appropriate:

- Have a contest to determine who can jump up and down for the longest period of time without laughing
- See who can blow a cotton ball down the gymnasium floor the most quickly using a straw
- Select the student who most creatively scores a basket

Track and Field Day

Some schools host end-of-the-year events like Track and Field Days. This special activity is usually offered only to students in the upper grades and serves as a culminating event after a unit on track and field. Children select two or three activities in which they would like to participate, and they assist as timekeepers, officials, and volunteers for other activities. Since several classes of teachers work together to organize and implement the event, several events can occur simultaneously. In addition, parents can be drafted to assist as volunteers.

Instead of presenting awards to only the winners of competitive events, each child should be provided with a ribbon or certificate as documentation of his or her participation in the event. Some activities may represent official track and field events whereas others may be incorporated into the event as a means of encouraging students to participate who are less skilled and more reluctant. Traditional activities can include events such as the 100-meter dash, softball throw (less dangerous than the shot putt at this age), long jump, and mile run. Other events might include:

- Contest to see which group of partners can toss and catch a water balloon the farthest without it breaking (have students bring extra clothes to school prior to this event and inform parents in advance)
- Challenge to determine which children can walk for the longest period of time around a modified track without stopping (this can occur throughout the day)
- Competitions to assess which students are most supportive of others during individual events

Dance Dance Revolution

You may have heard of an activity called Dance Dance Revolution. In fact, you may have seen children vigorously participating in the activity at a shopping mall or movie theater. Children stand on a platform and follow a pattern by moving their feet across different-colored arrows. The level of difficulty can be adjusted based on a child's level of ability. This activity is hugely popular throughout the world and is a fun and easy way to encourage children to be vigorously active.

Simulations of the activity are now available for teachers to use with students during school. Instead of a platform, electronic pads that record a child's score can be purchased. Although it is doubtful that teachers would have funds to purchase enough pads

Special events like Jump Rope for Heart promote physical activity and teach children the importance of giving back to the community.

for each child, it is possible to purchase a small number of pads and have other children follow by moving their feet across arrows marked on the floor with masking tape. The children rotate throughout the class so that everyone has an opportunity to participate on the electronic pad.

Jump Rope or Hoops for Heart

The American Cancer Society encourages teachers to raise money for heart and stroke research by hosting the Jump Rope for Heart (http://www.americanheart.org/presenter. jhtml?identifier=2360) or Hoops for Heart (http://www.americanheart.org/presenter. jhtml?identifier=2441) fundraising programs. Teachers can contact one of the Web sites above to download information related to organizing and implementing the event. Children throughout the nation participate on a regular basis by collecting pledges and subsequently participating in special jump rope or basketball activities. In addition to being an incentive that encourages students to acquire skill in these activities, it is a wonderful opportunity to teach children about giving back to society. Teachers receive complimentary jump ropes or a basketball and activity guide to help them implement the event, and students receive special prizes based on the amount of money they raise.

Fundraising

Similar to the special fundraising event described above, teachers can creatively design activities that accomplish the dual objectives of promoting physical activity while simultaneously raising money for special school projects like a weekend outdoor pursuits trip (described earlier in the chapter) or necessary physical activity equipment like ropes, balls, and mats. These events are relatively easy to plan and implement, and they are enjoyable to students. In fact, children will likely appreciate and take better care of equipment that they helped to purchase. Without events such as these, some teachers would not have access to adequate equipment for teaching physical education. With the support of the principal, and even other teachers, fundraising can become an annual event. After purchasing needed physical education equipment, surplus monies can be invested for long-term school initiatives that require a considerable amount of money like improving the school playground, adding a track, or purchasing gymnastics equipment. As highlighted in Key Point 5-5, it should be emphasized that any event that involves the collection of money should be endorsed by the principal or other appropriate administrator.

Key Point 5-5

Prior to any event that involves the collection of money, seek out the permission and support of the principal or other appropriate administrator.

Run/Walk-a-Thon.

This activity requires students to obtain pledges related to the number of times they run/ walk around the school track. For schools that do not have access to a track, a modified one can be constructed on the playground using cones as boundary markers, or students can keep track of the number of times they walk around the school. In order to encourage honesty, each time a child completes a lap, they are given a token by a volunteer parent or teacher to carry with them in a container or pouch strapped around their waist. Once they complete the event, the tokens are counted by students, the results are verified by teachers (which requires a signature), and students collect the money from their respective pledges.

Dance-a-Thon.

This is another fun activity where children raise money while concurrently participating in vigorous physical activity. Again, students obtain pledges based on the number of minutes (or hours) they can dance without stopping. Dance music can alternate from fast to slow and students can dance alone, with a partner, or with a group of friends. Although several brief mandated breaks are integrated throughout the event, once a student permanently stops dancing, their card is marked to indicate how long they danced, and they are then free to collect their pledge money.

Neighbor Assist.

In some cases, students can be asked to volunteer special physical activity services for a set amount of money. For example, they may agree to rake their neighbor's yard for $20, walk a dog for $5, or clean up trash for $7 per hour. With your guidance, children can develop a list of services and appropriate prices for the work they are willing to provide. They can ask relatives, friends, and neighbors if they would be interested in purchasing their services on one or two particular weekends during the year. During a pledge period prior to the event, teachers can construct a thermometer-like gauge posted on the bulletin board that rises higher based on the cumulative amount of donations pledged. The students and teacher might set a class goal. The amount that individual children raise does not need to be shared with other children; only the cumulative amount raised by the class is recorded. If it rains during the weekend in which activities were to occur, a rain date can be scheduled.

Summary

Although many new classroom teachers often express trepidation about teaching a subject for which they have limited knowledge, in all reality there are many ways that teachers can easily incorporate physical activity into the curriculum. If you are inexperienced, purchase activity guides that introduce you to activities that will result in appropriate student outcomes. Also, determine well in advance of the academic year your curricular focus and learning goals. Although many teachers will use a combination of the models described above, some teachers will be more comfortable focusing exclusively on only one or two. If this is the case, be sure that you are considering what is in the best needs of your students, not what is easiest for you to plan. See Box 5.1 for dos and don'ts to help you fit the needs of your students.

DO AND DON'T CHECKLIST

Do	Don't
☐ develop knowledge about the different types of curriculum models so you can be informed when selecting one or more that you will emphasize	☐ fall into the trap of teaching only those activities that are easy or familiar
☐ provide students with basic motor skills, an understanding of movement concepts, and exposure to different fitness activities	☐ focus only on one curricular emphasis throughout the year unless you can adequately justify what you have selected
☐ select games that are developmentally appropriate	☐ engage students in activities where they cannot successfully complete the movement challenge or understand the movement concept
☐ include special events in your curriculum	☐ focus strongly on competition during game play or special events
☐ provide students with appropriate equipment—fundraising if necessary to generate the necessary resources.	☐ lose the motivation to have an inspirational curriculum that includes exciting special events and challenges.

All students should have exposure to movement activities and concepts. They need to acquire basic motor skills and develop an understanding of concepts related to those skills. Without this foundation, it will be difficult for them to participate in complex activities that are introduced as they progress through the different grade levels. Students should also be exposed to fitness activities in the gymnasium (or playing field) *and* classroom. Although incorporating fitness into the curriculum is easier with a larger amount of space, brief activity breaks in the classroom can be more easily incorporated into the day than teachers might imagine.

Alternative curricular models such as adventure education, outdoor pursuits, and sport education are also appropriate but should not be the only models to which students are exposed. Instead, they will be more exciting and challenging to students if they are sporadically incorporated into the curriculum at appropriate times during children's development. For example, using a weekend hiking trip to encourage team building will have longer term profitability if it is offered during the beginning of an academic year as opposed to closer to the end.

Finally, special events are welcomed by children and create excitement about the subject matter of physical education. When executing these events, be mindful of soliciting an appropriate number of volunteers and recognizing all students for their individual accomplishments. Purchasing equipment necessary for the regular physical education curriculum and execution of special events is often costly, but funds can easily be generated by a creative and ambitious teacher who strives to provide his/her students with the best learning equipment possible. What unique fundraising activity could you plan? Complete Thinking Challenge 5.5.

THINKING CHALLENGE 5.5	Plan a fundraising event for additional physical education equipment that includes the following components: (a) Significantly engages students in physical activity (b) Raises a modest amount of money (c) Encourages students to work with a partner (d) Can be implemented within a two or three hour period of time (e) Requires a minimal amount of teacher time to plan and execute (f) Would be likely to be approved by the principal

Review Activities

1. Defend to others which curriculum model you believe would be most beneficial for the grade you hope to teach and state why.
2. Discuss how often games should be incorporated into the curriculum and why.
3. Explain how much competition you believe is appropriate to include in the physical education curriculum.
4. Work in a small group to develop a three-day hiking trip for students in the upper elementary grades. Consider everything you will need like transportation, meals, equipment, accommodations, and supervision. Compare your plans with those of other groups.
5. Discuss what a teacher would need to consider when planning a fundraising event.

References

Dyson, B. (1995). Students' voices in two alternative elementary physical education programs. *Journal of Teaching in Physical Education, 14,* 394–407.

Hastie, P. A. (1996). Student role involvement during a unit of sport education. *Journal of Teaching in Physical Education, 16,* 88–103.

Hastie, P. A., & Sinelnikov, O. A. (2006). Russian students' participation in and perceptions of a season of sport education. *European Physical Education Review, 12,* 131–150.

Mitchell, S. A., Oslin, J. L., & Griffin, L. L. (2005). *Teaching sport concepts and skills: A tactical games approach* (2nd ed.). Champaign, IL: Human Kinetics Publishers.

New Games Foundation. (1976). *The new games book.* Garden City, NY: Dolphin Books/ Doubleday & Company.

New Games Foundation. (1981). *More new games.* New York: Dolphin Books.

Siedentop, D., Hastie, P., & van der Mars, H. (2004). *A complete guide to sport education.* Champaign, IL: Human Kinetics Publishers.

Siedentop, D., Mand, C., & Taggart, A. (1986). *Physical education: Teaching and curriculum strategies for grades 5–12.* Palo Alto, CA: Mayfield.

Chapter **Six**

Teaching Styles

Throughout the previous chapters we have consistently emphasized that each child is unique. There is no single curriculum model, learning activity, or lesson plan that meets every child's distinct learning needs on every occasion. Therefore, it is critically important for teachers to vary not only the types of activities to which children are exposed but also the teaching styles used to present those activities.

As you are already aware, we all learn in different ways. You may be a visual learner who profits from demonstrations and lesson content that is conveyed through PowerPoint presentations, movies, or experiments. The person sitting to your right during class, however, may find this method of instruction boring and redundant. Perhaps this individual learns best through either listening or reading but does not require a demonstration or visual example. The individual sitting to your left may not find any of the techniques described above desirable. Perhaps this individual learns best through exploration or independent problem solving. Finally, the person in front of you may learn best in a participatory learning situation, where there are many opportunities to personally interact during the lecture or with the content being emphasized.

In relation to the individuals described above, who do you think is the most intelligent, quickest learner, or most promising student? If you answered, "You can't determine level of intelligence by analyzing someone's preferred learning style," you are correct. Some of the brightest individuals in our society are visual learners, whereas others are auditory or participatory. In fact, some of the nation's most successful contributors, like Walt Disney, Albert Einstein, Helen Keller, and George Patton, are said to have had some form of a learning disability that they were able to overcome (Independent Living Resource Center, n.d.). It is likely that they worked hard and were exposed to a supportive environment and knowledgeable teachers, ones who understood that all individuals have unique learning needs that are rarely met through one universal learning activity or style of instruction.

Children learn in different ways.

Although most children in your classroom will not require special accommodations, most will have a learning style preference. Whereas in the preceding chapters we primarily discussed the content of physical education and how to plan appropriate instructional activities, in this chapter we will address how to vary your instructional style to accommodate for the many learning style preferences that you will certainly encounter in your classroom.

SELECTING A STYLE

For a variety of reasons, many new teachers find it very difficult to incorporate a variety of different styles into their lesson. Even when observing the lessons of experienced teachers, it may seem that they rely predominantly on the same style of teaching. Interestingly, in the case of many teachers, their instructional style resembles the primary style(s) to which they had been exposed as children. Why do you think this occurs? After reading the potential reasons below, complete Thinking Challenge 6.1.

* Mr. Jones is *comfortable* with his current style of teaching and does not wish to try something new.
* Since Ms. Chu has 15 years of *experience* with her primary teaching style, she believes she has found the style that works best for her.
* After teaching for 25 years, Ms. Sinnett believes it is *too late* for her to change styles.
* Ms. Cardinali is a new teacher and is afraid to vary her instructional style for *fear* that it will not work.
* Mr. Yost *never learned* during teacher education that there were different styles that could guide his teaching.

THINKING CHALLENGE 6.1	Think about the style of teaching you will be most inclined to implement. In the column to the left, describe five characteristics of that style. In the column to the right, describe why those characteristics feel comfortable to you.
	List five characteristics of the style you will most likely implement / **Why are those characteristics comfortable to you?**
	1.
	2.
	3.
	4.
	5.

There are guidelines to consider when selecting which style is best. In some cases, decisions are based on how the majority of students in the class learn best. In other cases, choices are dictated by the content being introduced. In still other cases, decisions are grounded in a particular teaching philosophy or belief concerning how children should learn. Regardless, effective teachers use established guidelines, such as those below, for informing their decisions.

* Content being taught
* Children's previous experiences with the content
* Physical developmental level of students
* Social developmental level of students
* Lesson objectives

- Safety
- Size of class
- Available teaching space
- Amount and type of available equipment

In addition to these reasons, you will need to consider the time that it takes to implement a particular style and determine if it balances in a positive direction the drawbacks associated with having less available physical engagement time.

THE CONTINUUM OF STYLES

The preeminent scholar in physical education who has advocated for the significance of using multiple teaching styles to influence student learning is Muska Mosston. Although Mosston is unfortunately deceased, his longtime colleague, Sara Ashworth, continues to promote his vision. Mosston and Ashworth (2001) have employed the word "spectrum" to convey the wide range of styles to which a teacher has access. Placed on a continuum, teaching styles can range from being highly teacher directed at the left end to primarily student directed at the right. Several of the styles that have been advanced by them and other experts in the field, and which we believe could be relatively easily implemented by classroom teachers who do not have extensive training in physical education, are presented in this chapter.

As you will learn, selecting an appropriate style is an important consideration of every lesson. Key Point 6-1 stresses this fact. Some students, for example, require greater teacher direction than others. Some styles also lend themselves more readily to one particular activity than another. As you gain familiarity with the different styles, implementing them will become second nature. If, however, you are not provided with an opportunity to practice these styles during teacher education, or if you tend to give up when something is not immediately successful, the odds that you will incorporate multiple teaching styles into your instructional repertoire are drastically reduced. Therefore, we hope that you will have many opportunities to practice the different styles during this class and those in which you will be subsequently enrolled. Remember that when you initially learned to ride a bike, you likely fell off several times before you were consistently successful.

Key Point 6-1

Selecting an appropriate teaching style is just as important as selecting an appropriate curricular focus or lesson activity.

TEACHING STYLE FORMS

In this section we will introduce you to the primary styles that we believe you may wish to incorporate into your curriculum. Beginning with those styles that are the most teacher directed and progressing along the continuum, we will arrive at those that are the least teacher directed. Throughout the chapter, we will use the content of throwing to demonstrate how one skill can be taught multiple ways. The styles for teaching throwing, however, will differ based on the specific objectives of the lesson and instructional activities that are used to convey the skill of throwing. The examples provided represent the type of lesson to which a child with advanced beginner throwing skills in 3rd grade might be exposed.

As you progress through the chapter, consider if you believe one teaching style is best for teaching throwing or if multiple styles can be incorporated into a single lesson. Some experts insist that individual lessons should consist of only one style, whereas others advocate for blending several styles based on the activity being introduced and/or degree to which students are responsive to the style used. In total, nine different styles, as illustrated in Box 6.1, will be introduced. For additional information about many of these styles (and others), see the Mosston and Ashworth (2002) text.

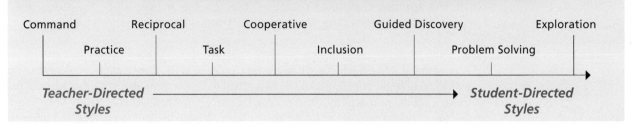

Teaching Style Continuum   Box 6.1

Command   Reciprocal   Cooperative   Guided Discovery   Exploration

        Practice   Task   Inclusion   Problem Solving

Teacher-Directed ————————————————→ *Student-Directed*
      Styles   *Styles*

Command

At some point or another in your experience, you were most likely the recipient of the command style of teaching. In this style, the teacher introduces commands and students follow. It is the most highly teacher directed of all of the styles. The steps in the style are as follows:

1. Teacher introduces an activity through demonstration and explanation
2. Students are told where to locate themselves and what task they will perform
3. Students begin performing the challenge on the teacher's command and stop on the teacher's command
4. Tasks may be repeated
5. Teacher observes and provides feedback
6. Teacher closes lesson with a brief review

Throwing example.

A teacher employing the command style would present a demonstration of and explanation about throwing form and the specific task that students were to practice. Students would be

All students are practicing the same task and throwing in the same direction.

told where to stand and given commands related to when to release and retrieve the ball. The throwing task is practiced repeatedly and students are provided with feedback about their performance and a brief review at the end of the lesson. As emphasized in Key Point 6-2, the teacher makes all of the decisions and students respond.

Key Point 6-2

In the command style of teaching, the teacher makes all of the decisions and students follow the teacher's directions upon command.

Almost any activity can be taught using the command style. For example, students can be told when to begin dribbling a soccer ball, when to kick it through a goal, and when to retrieve it for the next activity. Students can be instructed when to begin lightly volleying a balloon through space, when to use greater force to push the balloon higher, and when to move forward while volleying.

Advantages.

The command style is easy to plan and implement, and it makes good use of available learning time. If a teacher can effectively provide demonstration and instructions, students can be quickly engaged in physical activity and remain active for the majority of the class period. It also is effective with large groups of students because the teacher can interact with everyone simultaneously. In addition, safety is facilitated. For example, lessons like archery and shot putting can be safely instructed if all students are under the control of the teacher and engaged only when commanded. Finally, it can be highly effective when teaching structured activities like dance sequences, martial arts, or marching.

Disadvantages.

As with all styles, there are disadvantages. In fact, if you complete Thinking Challenge 6.2, you probably can brainstorm a few of your own. The primary disadvantages of the command style are that it is more difficult to individualize learning tasks and does not encourage creativity. For example, students are not given the freedom to design their own dance; they are told what steps to perform, how to perform them, and when to begin and end.

THINKING CHALLENGE 6.2	List two additional advantages and disadvantages to the command style that may not have been addressed in the text.

Advantages	Disadvantages
1.	1.
2.	2.

Practice

As stated in Key Point 6-3, one of the most popular teaching styles employed by physical education teachers is the practice style. In this style, the teacher provides students with the activity that they will complete and subsequently moves throughout the instructional

Key Point 6-3

The practice style is the most popular method of conveying content to students. It is easy to implement and very familiar to most classroom teachers.

The practice style is structured but enables students to make some decisions such as when they will begin executing a movement.

area providing feedback as students perform. The style is sequenced as follows:

1. Teacher provides a demonstration and explanation of the learning task
2. Teacher responds to student questions
3. Students begin practicing a movement task alone, with partners, or in a group
4. Teacher moves from one group of learners to the next, providing feedback and suggesting modifications
5. Teacher closes lesson with a brief review

Throwing example.

Similar to the command style, the throwing lesson would begin with a demonstration and explanation. Teachers might instruct children about the most important elements of the throw and then ask them to throw the ball back and forth with a partner. The teacher would provide feedback, encouragement, and modifications. Students would throw and catch at their own rate but would stop when asked and would participate in a review session at the end of the lesson.

Like the command style, almost any activity can be taught using the practice style. Students can volley a ball against a wall in the practice style and determine when to begin the task and even where to stand. They also can practice cartwheels or forward rolls independently while the teacher moves about the gym providing feedback. The number of different activities that can be taught using this style is almost limitless.

Advantages.

This style encourages maximal participation and is easy for a teacher to plan and implement. Most classroom teachers are familiar with this style so they have little difficulty putting it into practice in a physical education setting. It saves time and is effective with large groups. It also enables the teacher to interact individually with students and allows some student decision making.

Disadvantages.

Like the command style, the practice style can be more difficult for the teacher to individualize and does not promote creativity. All students are practicing the same task so it may be too easy for some yet too difficult for others. If the teacher is not actively supervising, or turns his/her back from students, individuals may become off-task.

Reciprocal

The first significant step away from a primarily teacher-directed lesson is represented by the reciprocal style. Students begin to assume responsibility for their own learning, and assisting their peers, by serving in a peer-teaching capacity. The characteristics of the style are as follows:

1. In advance of the lesson, the teacher prepares a task sheet that explains the roles of the peer teacher and learner and may include diagrams and key points about the task to be performed
2. Teacher describes the task sheet and roles of peer teacher and learner to the class
3. Teacher explains and demonstrates the learning activity
4. Children disperse through the gym or playing field, usually in pairs or groups of three

The reciprocal style encourages students to help each other.

5. One student serves in the role of peer teacher and the other(s) in the role of learner
6. Children complete the task sheet, with the peer teacher making the appropriate checks
7. The teacher moves from one group to another, providing feedback *primarily* to the peer teacher—suggesting how to improve the performance of the learner
8. Students switch roles
9. Teacher may provide a review and feedback to the group at the end of the lesson

Throwing example.

The teacher would disseminate and explain the task sheet, how to execute appropriate technique, and how to perform the activity correctly. In addition, the teacher would emphasize that students will be helping each other, serving in either the role of peer teacher or learner and then switching roles. Finally, the teacher would tell students that he/she will primarily be interacting with the peer teacher, providing suggestions for how to improve the performance of the learner. The task card may require students to throw a ball to the wall while being observed by a peer. Box 6.2 provides an example of a 3rd grade task card for throwing. Try to complete Thinking Challenge 6.3 by creating your own task card.

There are so many activities that can be taught using the reciprocal style. In particular, skills that require a specific technique are well suited for this style because the teaching peer can easily follow the task card to determine if the learner is correctly performing the task. Skills like throwing, kicking, catching, volleying, and striking can be easily taught with the reciprocal style.

Advantages.

Research has demonstrated that the reciprocal style is advantageous for children's cognitive development (Goldberger, 1995), probably because they encounter a task as both a teacher and a learner and have access to a task sheet where key points are constantly reinforced. This learning style also encourages cooperation and peer interaction and promotes responsibility.

Disadvantages.

Despite its many advantages, there are some drawbacks to the reciprocal style that need to be anticipated in advance. First, children need to have reading and social development skills that are advanced enough for understanding task sheets and successfully working with others. Second, peer teachers need to be carefully monitored to ensure that they are providing the

Throwing Task Sheet

Box 6.2

PEER TEACHER'S NAME _____

LEARNER'S NAME _____

DIRECTIONS:
Ask the learner to stand on the black line and use his or her best throwing form to throw the tennis ball overhand to the wall for five minutes. Observe and evaluate his or her throw using the checklist below. Switch places.

	ALWAYS	SOMETIMES	NEEDS WORK
1. Elbow of throwing arm is bent and faces away from target prior to throw			
2. Upper body turns as ball is thrown			
3. Steps forward on opposite foot of the throwing arm			
4. Ball held and thrown with fingers, not palm			
5. Throwing arm straightens as ball is released			

THINKING CHALLENGE 6.3 Develop a task sheet for teaching 5th grade students with moderate skill how to volley a ball with a paddle.

correct feedback to learners. Third, it takes more time than some of the other styles for teachers to plan and explain to students. Finally, students may acquire skill at a slower rate because they have fewer opportunities to participate (Goldberger, 1992). This last point, however, may be reversed by the positive advantages of cognitive learning that the model promotes.

Task

The task style of teaching can be presented to students in several ways. For example, it can entail taking an individual task and making it increasingly difficult for students to perform as they acquire greater skill, or it can involve providing students with a comprehensive list

The task style of teaching allows students to progress at their own rate.

of all the tasks that encompass a unit of instruction (like gymnastics) and asking them to try new skills as they master those that are more rudimentary. For purposes of the classroom teacher, the style would best be employed at a basic level to encourage individualization of a lesson. If used in this manner, the style would be sequenced as follows:

1. Teacher presents a task card to students
2. Teachers demonstrates those tasks listed on the card
3. Students are allowed to work independently, making decisions about starting/stopping and which tasks to perform
4. Teacher circulates throughout the activity area speaking to students about the choices they are making and their performance outcomes
5. Once students are able to adequately perform the task, it is checked off by the teacher, learner, or a peer observer

Throwing example.

After providing students with a task card that lists overhand throwing skills in increasingly difficult sequence (see Box 6.3), students are asked to practice different throwing skills and check them off once they have been achieved. Depending on level of trust, the student, a classmate, or the teacher will be responsible for signing the task card.

Advantages.

This style is individualized and increasingly gives the students some responsibility for their own learning. They determine when to begin and end a task and when they believe they have sufficient skill to advance to the next level on the task sheet. The style maximizes a

---

Overhand Throwing Task Sheet   Box 6.3

Name _____

Begin practicing the first task. Once you think you can successfully perform the skill, ask a classmate to observe your performance and provide his/her signature and date. Once you have a classmate's signature, you can move to the next task.

SKILL	APPROVAL	DATE
1. Hit red target on the wall 4 out of 5 times from a distance of 10 feet		
2. Hit red target on the wall 4 out of 5 times from a distance of 20 feet		
3. Hit red target on the wall 4 out of 5 times from a distance of 30 feet		
4. Hit black target on the wall 4 out of 5 times from a distance of 10 feet		
5. Hit black target on the wall 4 out of 5 times from a distance of 20 feet		
6. Hit black target on the wall 4 out of 5 times from a distance of 30 feet		
7. Throw a tennis ball back and forth 10 times in a row to a partner from a distance of 10 feet (no misses)		
8. Throw a tennis ball back and forth 10 times in a row to a partner from a distance of 20 feet (no misses)		
9. Throw a tennis ball back and forth 10 times in a row to a partner from a distance of 30 feet (no misses)		

teacher's ability to individually assist a greater number of students, and it makes good use of learning facilities.

Disadvantages.

This style requires more planning time than some of the other styles because teachers must design appropriate task sheets. Although all students were given the same task sheet in the throwing example above, some teachers actually design individual cards for everyone in their class (based on each child's developmental level). This latter technique is inordinately time consuming and, therefore, an unrealistic expectation for most teachers. Further, if the teacher is responsible for also evaluating individual performance and subsequently signing the task card, it can take considerable time that could be better spent engaged in other tasks. If students are allowed to sign their own cards or those of their peers, they need to be trusted to work independently and taught to fairly assess performance. Now that you are familiar with this style, try to complete Thinking Challenge 6.4.

THINKING CHALLENGE 6.4

Plan a comprehensive task sheet for a tumbling unit of instruction. We have started the task card for you, but there are many other skills that can be added to the task sheet other than the forward roll, backward roll, and cartwheel. Be as comprehensive as possible,

Tumbling Task Card

Name _____

Instructions:

Side roll	**Approval**	**Date**
1. Log roll		
2. Egg roll		

Forward roll

1. Forward roll on incline mat
2. Forward roll on level mat with appropriate form
3. Roll forward three times in a straight line on mat
4. Straddle forward roll
5. Dive roll over two mats

Backward roll

1.
2.
3.
4.
5.

Cartwheel

1.
2.
3.
4.
5.

Like the other styles, the task style can be incorporated into the teaching of many activities. Individual activities, like gymnastics, work particularly well because a child can advance at his or her own rate of progression.

Cooperative Learning

Similar to reciprocal learning, cooperative learning is designed to encourage team building, interdependence, and cooperation. In this form of teaching, students are typically placed onto teams of mixed ability. Although there is flexibility in relation to how this style is

Cooperative learning encourages students to work together to acquire new skills.

executed, usually pairs of students work together and then combine with another pair to assess performance, or individuals within a group become experts on one component of a skill and teach that component to their cohorts in the group. Characteristics of the style include:

1. Teacher explains the task, style, and student groupings to the class
2. Students are placed throughout the activity area and asked to practice and teach/assess each other in sets of two pairs or small groups, or they are asked to each learn a component of the task and teach that aspect to their team members (with or without a task sheet)
3. Students continue to practice and teach each other while the teacher moves throughout activity area observing and making mental notes

Throwing example.

The teacher would explain the throwing task to students, emphasizing how the task would be completed, how students should be partnered, and how they would work together to learn the skill. With or without a task sheet, students would throw a ball against a wall using appropriate form. Although there are many variances to how the style might be enacted, two are described here. In the first situation, pairs would practice together and then receive feedback from another pair about their performance. In the second situation, they might be placed into small groups. Each individual in the group would become an expert about one element of the throw and then teach that element to group members. Students would then practice throwing against the wall using appropriate form.

In addition to throwing, teachers may wish to use cooperative learning for a variety of activities that range from team to individuals sports. Although the style fits nicely with basic motor activities like throwing and kicking, it also can be used in a rhythmic gymnastics unit or when teaching creative dance.

Advantages.

Research has demonstrated that cooperative learning can result in higher achievement and be used successfully with highly diverse groups of individuals (Dotson, 2001). Although research on cooperative learning in physical education trails behind that of classroom research, it seems logical that this style promotes many of the same advantages as the reciprocal style.

Disadvantages.

The disadvantages of this style are also similar to those of the reciprocal style. Although children will likely benefit from the style in relation to cognitive growth, they will have fewer practice opportunities than with the command or practice styles and may be given incorrect information from peers. Therefore, as highlighted in Key Point 6-4, the teacher must be vigilant about observing what children are learning and careful about not using this style until students are developmentally and socially ready.

Key Point 6-4

Before exposing students to the cooperative style of teaching, it is particularly important to evaluate if they are developmentally ready and have the social maturity to successfully engage with their peers.

Inclusion

The inclusion style provides students with considerable decision-making responsibility and is the most individualized of all the styles presented to this point. In this style the learner is provided with a learning task and then allowed to make a large number of decisions related to the task. As stressed in Key Point 6-5, the inclusion style allows all children to experience success. Students are challenged to select the most appropriate equipment and means of completing a task in relation to their individual skill level. The procedures in the style are as follows:

1. Teacher presents the task to students and tells them that they will be able to make a number of decisions related to completing the task (task sheet may or may not be presented)
2. Students independently practice the task and make decisions
3. Teacher moves from one student to another assessing their performance and asking questions as a means of helping them to determine if they are making the appropriate decisions

---

Key Point 6-5

In the inclusion style of teaching, children are provided with a number of different choices related to how they will perform a physical task. As a result, more children are successfully included in the activity.

Throwing example.

After explaining the throwing task, the teacher provides students with a number of options. Students might be provided with different-sized balls that vary in weight and softness. If throwing at a target, they could decide where to throw. If throwing into the air, they could make a decision about the height at which the ball would be thrown. If throwing into a basketball hoop, they would decide how close to stand to the basket and at which basket height they would prefer to throw. The teacher would ask questions related to how well they were throwing as a means of indirectly helping them to make appropriate decisions about whether they were practicing a throwing skill that was either too easy or too difficult for their ability.

We believe that the inclusion style is one of the most important styles to use when teaching because it promotes individual success so nicely. In fact, it can be incorporated into almost every other style. When teaching the volleyball serve, for example, allow students to stand as close to the net as they need to experience success. Once they have some success, gradually encourage them to move closer to the end line. When teaching jump rope, allow students to select the type of rope they prefer (plastic or cloth) and let them decide how quickly, at what height, and with which style they will jump.

Advantages.

The inclusion style is highly individualized and allows children to makes choices based on perceptions they have about their own ability and what they believe they can achieve. It

The inclusion style gives students many choices about how they will perform an activity.

teaches children to work independently and encourages them to develop self-assessment skills. Further, all children have opportunities to experience success.

Disadvantages.

There are few disadvantages with this style. Students, however, need to be monitored to ensure that they are on task and making appropriate decisions about how to complete the task and what equipment to select. This can sometimes be tiring for a teacher because he or she must continually move throughout the activity area to make sure that students are challenging their current skill level, not simply settling for the activity at which they enjoy success.

Guided Discovery

This style of teaching entails asking students a series of questions and posing a succession of movement challenges that are designed to guide them to independently discover the correct solution to a challenge without being told by the teacher. It is assumed that when students arrive at an answer by themselves, that the lesson will be more memorable and have a more powerful effect than if the teacher were to provide the solution. The style would be implemented as follows:

1. Teacher poses a movement challenge/question to the class
2. Students practice the challenge and attempt to arrive at an answer
3. Teacher anticipates student responses and continues asking questions and providing movement challenges until students arrive at the desired response
4. Teacher does not provide the answer but continues asking questions until students generate the correct response

Throwing example.

The teacher (T) would pose a throwing-related movement challenge to the class and anticipate a student response (ASR) such as:

T: Stand on the red line and underhand throw the tennis ball to the target on the wall which is a distance of about 20 feet away. Remember to use only the underhand throwing position. What did you need to do to get the ball to reach the target?

ASR: Throw hard.

The guided discovery style encourages cognitive and psychomotor engagement in the activity being performed.

T: Good. Try throwing with different degrees of force to see how much you need in order to get the ball to the wall. Now that you have practiced several times, does the ball always hit the center of the target?

ASR: It usually hits the target but not always in the center.

T: Try different movements to see what you need to do to get the ball to hit the center of the target (student practice for several minutes). What worked best?

ASR: Throwing straight and watching the target are really important.

T: Good for you. You are correct. Both are very important. Keep trying. What other elements of the throw are important for helping the ball hit the center of the target?

ASR: Looking at the target for the entire throw.

T: Okay. Try throwing the ball to the right of the target and then to the left of the target. What did you do differently to make the ball go either right or left?

ASR: Following through to the target area is really important.

T: Yes, that is correct. You figured out the answer to the problem by yourself! What you want to remember is that the follow-through is one of the most important aspects of getting the ball to hit the target when using the underhand throwing motion. Now practice hitting the center of the target.

Although guided discovery is an excellent method for encouraging cognitive ability, we believe it is much easier to incorporate small segments of the guided discovery style into many different lessons as opposed to teaching lessons using only this style. In fact, many effective teachers incorporate elements of guided discovery into their lessons on a daily basis. They develop short segments of questions so that children discover the correct answer without being told.

Advantages.

The guided discovery style cognitively engages students in the movement task and theoretically helps them to transfer what they learned to other similar skills. It also encourages them to think about how they are performing particular skills.

Disadvantages.

This style presents the teacher with several challenges. First, the classroom teacher needs to have adequate knowledge about what he or she is teaching students. Second, the teacher must be willing to spend the necessary time to think about the questions/movement challenges that will be posed to students and the responses that they might provide. If students do not answer with the response the teacher anticipated, the teacher needs to think of additional questions on the spot. Third, it is difficult to use when there is great skill variability among students. Finally, the teacher must remember *not* to provide the correct answer to students. Instead, he or she must continue to refine the movement challenges posed or questions asked until students arrive at the correct response. Complete Thinking Challenge 6.5 by writing a series of questions and anticipated student responses for teaching students about balance.

THINKING CHALLENGE 6.5	Develop a series of at least five movement challenges and questions to which students would respond when teaching the concept of balance in a gymnastics unit.
	T:
	ASR:
	T:
	ASR
	T:
	ASR
	T:
	ASR:
	T:
	ASR:

Problem Solving

In this style of teaching, the teacher poses a series of problems to the students. Children are encouraged to be creative and arrive at as many solutions as possible. As highlighted in Key Point 6-6, there is no single correct solution to a problem. Instead, many solutions are supported. In this style, creativity is promoted. Children are encouraged to focus on developing their own solutions to the problem and not simply mimicking the responses of others. The style would appear as follows:

1. Teacher presents a series of movement challenges to the class
2. Students respond by using their bodies to solve the problems posed
3. New movement challenges are added based on students' previous responses

Key Point 6-6

In the problem-solving style, there is no single correct solution. Instead, the teacher encourages students to arrive at multiple solutions to a problem.

Throwing example.
In this style, the teacher would present a series of movement challenges that students would be expected to complete, such as those below.

- Can you show me five different ways to throw the ball into the basketball hoop?
- Can you show me several different ways to get the ball into the hoop without throwing forward?
- How about trying to get it through the hoop by using a different part of your body?
- Can you get it through the hoop while moving slowly? What about moving quickly?
- Can you incorporate the following elements into a single throw: (a) Throw sideways, (b) use your non-dominant hand, and (c) move quickly but toss slowly?

The problem-solving style of teaching encourages creativity.

Again, this style can be used for teaching almost any activity. We recommend using it when you want children to explore and come up with many solutions to a problem. For example, teachers can ask students to generate multiple solutions for how to hand dribble a ball, move a balloon through space, kick a ball to a target, maneuver over an obstacle, or leap through the air. It is, however, less effective when you want to teach students how to perform an activity using a specific technique like kicking a soccer ball through a goal area using the instep kick.

Advantages.

This style encourages a very high degree of cognitive functioning and causes students to think about multiple ways to solve problems. Creativity is encouraged and all students can be successful regardless of skill level.

Disadvantages.

Like guided discovery, the problem-solving style takes time to plan in advance. It requires a creative teacher, one who is willing to accept that there are often multiple solutions to a movement problem.

Exploration

This final style of teaching falls at the extreme right side of the continuum, representing the style that is the least teacher directed. It is best suited for younger children who are still exploring their bodies and how to use equipment. The style would be implemented as follows:

1. Teacher would consider what movements or pieces of equipment he or she wants students to explore
2. Teacher would provide students with parameters related to exploring, particularly in relation to ensuring a safe learning environment
3. The students would explore while being supervised by the teacher
4. Students would be given an opportunity to share their explorations with others

Throwing example.

For safety purposes, it would be difficult to teach throwing using an exploration style of teaching. Since different objects would be moving in different directions through space, it would be easy for someone to become injured. The teacher, however, might allow students to throw soft items like cotton or sponge balls into hula hoops, basketball hoops, buckets, small cans, and garbage cans. Students would be encouraged to throw in unique ways; perhaps even to music. Try to complete Thinking Challenge 6.6.

THINKING CHALLENGE 6.6   Plan an exploration activity that would encourage students to explore at least five new pieces of equipment while moving to music. Include a learning objective. Use no more than 100 words to describe the challenge and objective.

This style is best suited for creative activities. For example, a teacher could place various types of gymnastics equipment throughout the gym (e.g., mats, low balance beams, springboard, parallel bars) and allow the children to explore the different types of equipment. The teacher would, of course, need to set safety parameters (e.g., no flips).

Exploration allows children to creatively explore new activities and different types of equipment.

Advantages.

The style is an excellent means of introducing children to new equipment and promoting creativity. Interestingly, teachers often curtail creativity by informing students that there is an appropriate or "right" way of performing a motor task. By incorporating a mixture of styles into one's curriculum, such as guided discovery, problem solving, and exploration, creativity is encouraged and students are allowed to think about many different ways in which they can move.

Disadvantages

A teacher must be conscientious about supervision when implementing this style since children may be unaware that potential safety problems could arise if equipment is mishandled or used inappropriately (e.g., flip off a springboard onto a mat). Further, it can result in disruptive behavior if students are unaware of the behavior expectations of the classroom.

Summary

Since each child is unique, and most have learning style preferences, it is incumbent on classroom teachers to implement teaching styles that are well suited to the individual needs of students enrolled in their classes. Relying on only one or two styles because of an existing comfort level with a preferred style, lack of knowledge about implementing new styles, or inadequate time for planning are unacceptable excuses for not having a variety of styles at one's disposal. Whether teaching math in the classroom, science in the lab, music in the orchestra room, or physical education in the gymnasium, an effective teacher relies on multiple styles throughout the year to convey subject matter to students in ways that are comprehensible and understandable to everyone.

Teaching styles fall along a continuum and range from being highly teacher directed to primarily student directed. The style at the most teacher- directed end, command, requires the teacher to make all of the decisions about the lesson. The teacher plans the lesson, tells students what tasks to complete, informs them when to begin and end, and tells them when to move to a new task. The style at the most student-centered end of the continuum, exploration, requires the teacher to set parameters for the lesson and be conscious of safety factors, but the students make the majority of decisions related to when and how they will perform and how and in what ways they will use equipment. Those styles in the middle progress gradually from teacher to student directed.

Teachers should select styles based on a variety of factors that include such things as the activity being taught, developmental level of learners, lesson objectives, and available equipment and facilities. Interestingly, with the exception of the exploration style, which is best suited for younger children, student age is not related to progression along the continuum. The command style might be as appropriate for teaching throwing to 1st grade children as it is for teaching archery to college adults. The problem-solving style may be equally appropriate for teaching kindergarten children about gymnastics as it is for teaching advanced-level high school students to create new movements for a modern dance routine. Likewise, problem solving may be inappropriate for teaching swimming to both beginners and advanced-level athletes on the swim team. And, the reciprocal style may be inappropriate for both young children and adults who are learning about expressive movement.

Finally, if a teaching style does not work well initially during a lesson, do not abandon that style. The styles presented here were selected because they have been effective in

DO AND DON'T CHECKLIST

Do	Don't
□ challenge yourself to learn more about the teaching styles presented in this text	□ assume that all children learn in the same way
□ incorporate at least five of the styles into your lessons as a student teacher	□ give up on a style if it is not immediately successful with students
□ try to implement at least two different styles during an individual lesson	□ be dissuaded from using a particular style because of student pressure
□ select styles based on instructionally sound guidelines, not because you are unfamiliar with a style or rushed for time	□ forget to assess whether children are developmentally and socially ready for a particular style
□ carefully consider the safety implications when selecting a style.	□ assume that teaching styles will be as effective with one group of students as they were with another.

teaching students about physical activity. You will stumble. There will be styles that do not work as well with one type of subject matter as another or with one group of students as another. Instead, carefully assess why the style was not successful and how it could be modified for future lessons or used more successfully with other types of physical education content. See Box 6.4 for a few additional suggestions.

Review Activities

1. Select an activity you enjoy, and with a partner, plan one movement task for teaching that activity to 5th grade students using each of the nine styles presented in this chapter.
2. In a small group setting, describe which teaching style you prefer and why.
3. Discuss in a small group if some types of activities lend themselves to a particular style more than other types of activities.
4. Describe your preferred learning style to a partner and why that style facilitates your learning.
5. Which teaching style is your least favorite and why?

References

Dotson, J. M. (2001). Cooperative learning structures can increase student achievement. *Kagan Online Magazine.* Retrieved June 7, 2008, from http://www.kaganonline.com/KaganClub/FreeArticles/IncreaseAchievement.html

Goldberger, M. (1992). The spectrum of teaching styles: A perspective for research on teaching physical education. *Journal of Physical Education, Recreation & Dance, 63*(1), 42–46.

Goldberger, M. (1995). Research on the spectrum of teaching styles. In R. Lidor, E. Eldar, & I. Harari (Eds.), *Proceedings of the 1995 AIESEP World Congress* (429–435).

Wingate Institute, Israel: The Zinman College of Physical Education and Sport Sciences.

Independent Living Resource Center. (n.d.). *Famous people with disabilities.* Retrieved June 2, 2008, from http://www.independenceinc.org/trivia.htm

Mosston, M., & Ashworth, S. (2002). *Teaching physical education* (5th ed.). San Francisco: Benjamin Cummings.

Chapter **Seven**

Establishing an Effective Learning Environment

Research suggests that students enter teacher education programs at colleges and universities with the belief that they already know how to teach and have little more to learn (Lanier & Little, 1986). This belief is likely the result of having spent approximately 13,000 hours as a student in public or parochial schools (Lortie, 1975). During this time future teachers have observed how their teachers implemented lessons, disciplined students, provided feedback, and organized the class. Although these experiences do provide a good foundation for understanding the process of teaching, they also are limited. For example, did you ever have an opportunity to observe a teacher writing lesson plans? Have you ever asked a teacher why he or she distributed equipment in a particular manner? Do you understand why teachers organized class activities similarly from one day to the next?

Think for a moment about those teachers you encountered during elementary, middle, and high school. In particular, what characteristics distinguished teachers you perceived as "good" from those you perceived as "poor"? Also, think about some of your more memorable physical education teachers, both those whom you would characterize as good and those whom you would characterize as poor. Do similarities exist among them?

In all likelihood, the teachers you characterized as good not only cared deeply about students, but they also structured the learning environment so as to promote maximal opportunity for student learning to occur. These teachers are individuals who implemented knowledge about effective teaching that they had acquired from teacher education courses, in-service teacher workshops, by observing other effective teachers, and by remaining actively committed to acquiring new knowledge as they continued to proceed through their professional career (see Key Point 7-1).

Key Point 7-1

Effective teachers do not believe that they have learned everything they need to know about teaching. Their success is built on a foundation of knowledge acquired during teacher education and supplemented with experience, observation, and on-going learning by reading professional journals, speaking with other teachers, and attending professional conferences.

As a new teacher, you will make mistakes. This is to be expected. Initially, you will be more focused on examining your own instructional behaviors than whether or not pupils are learning from the lessons that you have designed. As you gain experience, however, it is likely that you will become increasingly concerned with *teacher effectiveness*. Although effective teachers continue to reflect on their own instructional behaviors, they do so in light of what their students are learning from lessons. Whereas beginning teachers might reflect on their lesson and state, "My instructions were too long. I should have planned additional activities because students appeared bored. I was glad when the lesson ended," more experienced teachers would reflect differently. They might evaluate the lesson by emphasizing, "I provided students with too much information during the instructional part of the lesson. This resulted in some students who stopped paying attention and others who could not remember the primary points that I wanted to emphasize. Students became bored during the activity because it was too challenging for some and not challenging enough for others. Once I observed student boredom and the misbehavior that resulted, I should have immediately stopped the class and re-organized the activity at a level that would account for the differences in student ability level. Now, I want to restructure the lesson and try it again in the near future."

Effective teaching entails making a series of decisions that promote the opportunity for student learning to occur. Interestingly, almost every decision that a teacher makes has direct influence on the type of learning environment that will be established. Throughout this text, "effective teaching" will be a term commonly employed. You will read about how to effectively implement instruction, evaluate learning, and reflect on your teaching practices. As a future teacher you have two choices. On the one hand, you can either believe that you have learned all there is to know about teaching and have relatively little more to learn. On the other hand, you can become an active consumer of research-based knowledge about effective teaching. Although some of the information that you acquire will reinforce what you already believe to be true about teaching, other information will contradict what you currently believe. Instead of dismissing information that feels uncomfortable or unfamiliar, consider that the material introduced in this text is based on the efforts of many professionals who have dedicated their careers to learning about the most effective ways in which to teach students about physical education.

THE PHYSICAL EDUCATION ENVIRONMENT

The physical education environment is both significantly similar to and different from the elementary classroom. Both environments are structured to foster student learning. Observers to both environments would witness teachers providing instructions, monitoring for learning, and providing feedback to pupils. They would observe students listening to directions, interacting with classmates, working independently, and moving from one learning activity to another. The differences in both environments, however, are striking. First, there exists greater potential for physical injury in the physical activity setting than in the classroom. Therefore, teachers must be vigilant observers; anticipating potential dangers, monitoring for unsafe practices, and maintaining an instructional space that is devoid of

Teaching in a gymnasium poses new challenges to the classroom teacher.

potential safety hazards. Second, it is more difficult to gain pupils' attention in the physical activity setting than in the classroom. Whereas the classroom is a relatively small and quiet space, the physical activity setting is a large and noisy setting (particularly when children are engaged in drills and game play). Third, while children in a classroom are often contained within a particular space (such as at their desk or at a learning station), children in the physical activity setting are constantly moving and changing directions. Complete Thinking Challenge 7.1.

THINKING CHALLENGE 7.1

Add to the following list of similarities and differences:
Similarities *between the home classroom and physical activity areas*

Classrooms	**Physical Activity Environments**
1. Bulletin boards showcase student work	1. Gymnasium walls showcase work
2. Certified teacher leads instruction	2. Certified teacher leads instruction
3. Equipment aids instruction (e.g., books, pens)	3. Equipment aids instruction (e.g., balls, mats)
4.	4.
5.	5.
6.	6.

Differences *between the home classroom and physical activity areas*

Classrooms	**Physical Activity Environments**
1. Relatively safe environment	1. Potentially dangerous environment
2. Small, quiet space	2. Large, noisy space
4.	4.
5.	5.
6.	6.

As a teacher education student, you will acquire knowledge about how to effectively organize the classroom in ways that optimize learning. Although some of this knowledge can easily be transferred to the gymnasium, there is knowledge that remains unique to the specialized environment in which physical activity transpires. In other words, there are instructional behaviors that you can learn, grounded in findings from research on effective teaching, which will improve your opportunity for success as a teacher. If you can discover how to successfully implement these behaviors in the physical activity setting you will decrease the likelihood of injury, create an environment ripe for student learning, and increase your enjoyment as a teacher of physical activity.

Although a multipurpose room is more self-contained than a gymnasium, it also poses challenges for a teacher who requires high ceilings for teaching activities like volleying.

A large outside area enables children to move freely.

The majority of classroom teachers who are assigned to teach physical education will have access to a gymnasium, cafeteria, or multipurpose room. Some of these environments, particularly a gymnasium with high ceilings, are ideal locations for instructing students about fitness, sports, games, and dance. Students have ample space to run, throw balls, manipulate objects, and move without restriction. Other spaces, particularly those that must serve other functions (e.g., cafeteria, multipurpose room), pose limitations that inhibit movement and increase the potential for injury to occur. Teachers who have access to basketball hoops, mats, and a wide variety of equipment can plan activities with less difficulty than teachers with greater space restrictions and less access to equipment.

Some elementary teachers who reside in the southern and western regions of the United States will not have access to an indoor facility. In a large percentage of schools in these regions, even physical education teachers do not have access to a gymnasium or multipurpose room. Instead, physical education is taught on a grassy playing field or on the paved surface of a playground. When it rains, these teachers often conduct class in the hallway or in another multiple-use space that is not designed for physical activity.

Regardless of where you may be assigned to teach, whether the environment is optimal or less than ideal, you can implement an effective physical education program. Interestingly, it is sometimes those individuals who teach under the worst of conditions who make delicious lemonade from the most bitter of lemons.

DEVELOPING PROTOCOLS

If you expect that students will learn as a result of your instruction, it is imperative that you organize the environment in ways that foster opportunities for learning. Without structure and organization, chaos will inevitably ensue. This is particularly true for teachers who are instructing in large or unconfined environments such as a gymnasium or playing field.

The first instructional task that effective teachers implement when initially meeting pupils is to introduce them to *protocols*. These are the routines and rules of the classroom. In this chapter, we will focus on *routines,* or the procedures of the physical education class. In Chapter 10, we will continue our discussion of routines, and we will also introduce you to important *rules* that guide the teacher's expectations for student behavior.

Routines are simple tasks that students consistently perform on an everyday basis. They are designed to provide structure and organization, to optimize learning time, and to reduce the potential for injury. As emphasized in Key Point 7-2, they are practiced regularly during the initial weeks of school and reviewed throughout the year. After students

Key Point 7-2

Routines should be introduced and practiced regularly during the initial weeks of school. They should be reviewed throughout the year and reinforced with praise.

learn to engage in routines, the behaviors become integrated in students' thought processing to such an extreme degree that they are not questioned or rarely deviated from. For example, fire drills represent a routine that is universally practiced in all schools throughout the United States. When the alarm bell sounds, students line up at the door and quietly proceed outside to a specific area. In some cases, a designated student holds the outside door open while classmates walk to a safe area. In other cases, a student may be responsible for closing all of the windows in the classroom prior to leaving the building. Regardless of the specifics, this routine consists of a set of operating procedures that have been implemented for a specific purpose–insuring that students exit the building safely and without incident.

In physical education class, routines are particularly important because they enable a teacher to retain control of a large group of students not confined to a particular location, reduce the potential for injury, and significantly lessen discipline problems. Interestingly, during an investigation of seven effective elementary physical education teachers, it was discovered that routines were taught as a regular part of the physical education curriculum (Fink & Siedentop, 1989). That is, routines were introduced, practiced, and reinforced with praise or a gentle reprimand–using the same instructional strategies teachers employ when helping students learn physical skills. Even the novice teachers who participated in the study had little difficulty with classroom management because they quickly established routines in their classes that they had learned during teacher education.

In order for routines to be optimally successful, they must be established during the first weeks of the school year. Although routines can be taught at any time throughout the year, teachers who establish routines early will more quickly establish an environment conducive to learning. Before reading further, what types of routines do you remember as an elementary school pupil? How were those routines taught and reinforced? Think back to your characterization of good and poor teachers. Did those teachers you characterized as good establish routines? Why do you believe they selected those particular routines? A few of the more important routines are discussed below. Complete Thinking Challenge 7.2.

THINKING CHALLENGE 7.2	Before reading further, what three routines do you believe are most critical to teach during the initial days of the school year?

Entering and Leaving the Physical Activity Area

As a classroom teacher you are both disadvantaged and advantaged with regard to your ability to effectively structure the physical activity learning environment. On the one hand, it is unlikely that you will be able to arrive at the gymnasium or playing field prior to your students, which enables you to set out equipment in advance and ensure that no safety hazards are present. On the other hand, it is likely that you will be able to lead your students to the physical activity learning area. This will ensure that students enter the area quickly and without incident. In some cases, when a trained physical education teacher teaches physical education, students walk to the activity area without being accompanied by an adult. By the time they arrive they are anxious to participate in physical activity and, as a result, have the potential to become wild and inattentive. They may enter the gymnasium yelling, pushing, and without listening to the physical education teacher. The end result is problematic. Before the teacher can begin instruction, he or she must first calm the students to the degree that they pay attention and follow directions appropriately.

Most elementary students eagerly anticipate the opportunity to be active. They enjoy moving and look forward to participating in a wide range of activities. Although all teachers of physical activity welcome this enthusiasm, this automatically increases the likelihood that students will not behave appropriately. Therefore, as a teacher it is your responsibility to make certain that students enter the physical activity setting as they

A seating arrangement such as the one highlighted in this picture ensures that all students can observe the teacher when instructions are given.

would any other classroom. There are routines that can be taught and reinforced for purposes of enhancing student attention. You may wish to select from some of the following options.

Circle time.

Immediately upon entering the activity area, students are asked to sit in a circle (or semicircle) in the center of the gymnasium or activity field. This formation ensures that all students have a clear and unobstructed view of you, the teacher. If you have a difficult class of learners, where it becomes problematic when groups of friends sit together, you can assign students to a particular location in which they remain throughout the duration of the year. This can easily be accomplished by having students line up in a prescribed order prior to leaving their regular classroom. They are expected to walk from the classroom to the physical activity area without changing their order in line. Once they reach the gymnasium, they walk in a line until they are appropriately placed in a circle. In addition, by asking students to sit, you reduce the kinds of behavioral problems that transpire when students are standing (e.g., pushing, not paying attention). As a time saver, you may request that students sit in alphabetical order for the entire year. This ensures that students are always in a particular order, and you can easily detect if students are not in their appropriate location. If you have a class of learners who are generally not disruptive, you may not need to be concerned about the order in which they sit in the circle.

Circle time not only assists teachers in quickly establishing order at the beginning class, but it also should be used at regular intervals throughout class. For example, instead of trying to explain a new activity to students who are spread throughout the physical activity area, students return to the circle for new instructions or a review. This formation again facilitates instruction because all students can clearly observe demonstrations and listen to directions from a teacher who does not have to substantially raise the level of his or her voice in order to be heard. Prior to leaving the physical activity area, students return to the circle and one person is designated as the leader. This student leads the class from the physical activity area to the regular classroom by having students immediately to the leader's right follow him or her out the door in the order in which they are seated in the circle.

Line time.

As an alternative to circle time, some teachers prefer having students sit on a clearly marked line in the gymnasium or on the playing field. For example, students might be asked to sit along the sideline of a basketball court or on a line that divides a concrete surface from the grassy area of a playing field. In some cases, teachers place numbers on small pieces of tape that are permanently affixed to the gymnasium floor. Students are assigned a number and asked to sit in this location throughout the year. Although both circle time and line time are effective, students sometimes have a more obstructed view of the teacher when sitting on a straight line rather than in a circle or semi-circle. Complete Thinking Challenge 7.3.

THINKING CHALLENGE 7.3	Imagine that you are outside on a sunny day providing students with instruction about a new activity. How should students be seated in order to clearly hear your instructions and observe your demonstrations?

Squads.

Another effective way of having children sit in the physical activity area is in the form of squads. This technique involves placing students in small groups of five or six. Squads are pre-assigned and students know to enter the gym and sit in a row with their other squad members. From one week to another, students take turns as squad leaders. These individuals sit at the head of the row and are responsible for helping you to distribute equipment and perform other tasks that you deem appropriate.

Ideally, you should have an even number of squads so that it is also an easy way of forming teams. For example, squads 1, 3, and 5 would be one team, and squads 2, 4, and 6 would be another. On a different day you may wish to put squads 1, 2, and 3 together and 4, 5, and 6 together. For tasks that require students to work in small groups, they will already be assigned to a squad. Periodically throughout the year, you may regroup squads so students have opportunities to work with different classmates.

Signaling Students

A critical issue to which teachers must attend is immediately gaining the attention of students. In a physical activity environment this is significantly more difficult than in a classroom. Therefore, it is essential that teachers spend ample time during the initial days of school instructing students when to stop performing. This routine requires substantial practice during the first few weeks of school and needs to be reinforced throughout the year. Students are generally quite receptive to learning this routine after teachers inform them that it is designed to gain their attention in cases of emergency and enable them to receive further instructions from a teacher who does not have to raise his or her voice to an unreasonable level.

There are a number of different signals that you may wish to use. Some signals may have different purposes than others. A number of signals are suggested in the text that follows. As emphasized, however, in Key Point 7-3, it is good to have one signal that is commonly used from one class to the next. This does not mean that other signals cannot also be used, but in cases of emergency, or when you need to gain students attention quickly, it is good to have one signal that can be quickly implemented and which results in an immediate student response. Our suggestion to you is to use the same signal, when possible, in both the home classroom and physical activity setting. This will allow carry over from the home classroom to the physical activity classroom.

Key Point 7-3

As a general rule, it is good to have one verbal signal for gaining students' attention that is commonly used from one physical education class to the next.

Signals such as freeze are important for gaining students' attention.

Freeze.

This signal is commonly used in elementary school classrooms and physical activity areas throughout the United States. Upon the teacher's command to "freeze," students are expected to immediately stop performing or interacting with classmates and listen to the teacher. When teaching students to use this signal it is important that you not yell. By raising your voice you are teaching students that they do not have to listen closely. Instead, be assertive when using this word, but do not raise your voice beyond what you would reasonably need to do in order to be heard in a relatively quiet environment. Teach students that they need to always listen for your voice, even when they are talking to other students or engaged in game play.

It also is important to teach students that "freeze" is a signal that requires them to immediately listen *and* stop. When they hear "freeze" they are not allowed to take three additional steps and then freeze. Instead, they are expected to freeze their body in the position it was in at the time the signal was given and to remain silent. Once you have the attention of all students, you can tell them that they can relax, have a seat, or return to the circle.

A useful technique for teaching this activity is to engage students in activities in which they are moving throughout the gymnasium. For example, during the first days of school focus on teaching locomotor, non-locomotor, and non-manipulative activities. At various intervals use the "freeze" signal to praise students for appropriate behavior ("You are doing a great job of avoiding contact with your classmates"), to modify the activity ("This time try jumping instead of hopping"), or to offer corrective feedback ("Don't forget to use your arms for momentum"). Interestingly, students will not realize that the implicit objective of the activity is to practice their listening skills. At periodic intervals, however, particularly if they freeze quickly, praise them for attending to the signal. On those occasions when they do not freeze and listen as quickly as you would prefer, remind students of the signal and emphasize that they will need to practice using the signal at more frequent intervals if they do not respond more quickly.

Freeze is a signal that works well with both older and younger elementary-aged students. In fact, it is not unusual to observe teachers at the middle and high school levels who also use this signal. There are differences, however, in how the signal should be introduced with different age groups of students. When introducing this signal to younger students, incorporate it into a variety of teacher-designed games. For example, ask students to skip throughout the activity area. Inform students that the first person observed to freeze upon hearing the command gets to select the next locomotor or non-locomotor activity that classmates will perform. Students will enjoy this game, and you will observe students freeze into very interesting shapes. When introducing the signal to older students, you can simply state that freeze is a classroom rule, and upon hearing the signal students are to immediately stop working and listen for further instructions. If students do not pay attention to the signal, a verbal warning is given. If students continue to disregard the signal, other consequences will result.

Word of the day.

In addition to using freeze as a primary signal, many teachers also are beginning to incorporate a word of the day or word of the week into the lesson as an additional means of gaining students' attention. In a physical activity environment, you should select words

Some teachers clap their hands when students are expected to stop moving and listen.

that are appropriate to that environment. For example, you may wish to teach students the names of different muscles. If you are unaware of different muscle groupings, you can choose words that suitably match lesson content such as "locomotor," "non-manipulative," or "fitness." When students hear these words, they are expected to stop and listen. You may even wish to use the same word in the home classroom so that there is carry over from the physical activity setting.

Music.

Students often enjoy listening to music while they perform. As a classroom teacher, you will likely incorporate music into the curriculum at various times, such as when teaching a history unit or when students are working at different learning stations. Although you will integrate music into the physical activity curriculum when teaching dance, it also can be incorporated into other components of the curriculum. For example, when students are engaged in locomotor, non-locomotor, and non-manipulative activities, background music can nicely accompany the lesson and further motivate students. As you have certainly observed, many individuals wear headphones and listen to music while running. Most runners have elected to do so because they perform better, are distracted from thinking about any physical discomfort that they may be experiencing, and find it motivating. As long as students make appropriate selections, you may even allow them to bring their favorite music to class.

Equally important, however, is that music can be an excellent means of providing signals to students. For example, you may establish a routine in which students are provided with five minutes of free time prior to instruction. Music is played while they engage in three or four different activities that you deem are appropriate to your learning objectives (e.g., throwing a ball with a partner, practicing a dance routine, shooting a basketball, engaging in different fitness activities). Once the music stops, students are expected to immediately freeze and listen for further instructions. Again, this routine should be practiced and reinforced, particularly at the beginning of the year.

Other signals.

There also are other devices that you may utilize in order to gain students' attention, particularly if you have difficulty projecting your voice. Some teachers use tambourines. When the teacher shakes the tambourine, students are expected to stop and listen. Other teachers use drums or simply clap their hands three times. Historically, physical education teachers have used whistles (which would not work well in the classroom). In fact, you have likely encountered one or two of these individuals. Although whistles are an excellent means of signaling students, they also bring to mind the stereotypical physical education teacher who was more interested in keeping order than providing students with a good experience while learning about physical activity. Therefore, it may behoove you to use a whistle only as a last resort.

Obtaining and Returning Equipment

As a classroom teacher, you will develop routines for distributing equipment, disseminating assignments, and returning homework. Such established routines enable you to

Teaching routines saves time and develops self-responsibility.

minimize organization time and optimize learning time. In the gymnasium, these routines are equally important. Therefore, during the initial days of the school year, it is important to carefully describe to students how they are expected to retrieve and return equipment. Be specific in your instructions and practice these routines with students. In many cases, it is beneficial to also demonstrate how equipment should be retrieved and returned. For example, if students are returning jump ropes to a hook in an equipment closet, show students how the ropes should hang from the hooks. Teach them to bend the rope in half so that both handles of the rope are at equal distances. Ask students to hang the middle section of the rope on the hook. This will ensure that ropes are neatly returned to the equipment closet and ready for the next class of students. There are a number of useful strategies for organizing equipment that will also be discussed in Lecture Chapter 9.

Personal Needs

Again, as a classroom teacher you will establish routines that are designed to accommodate students' personal needs. When teaching physical activity, the most frequent student request is for a drink of water. You will quickly notice, however, a domino effect in which multiple students will request a drink after observing their classmates at the water fountain. Therefore, your best strategy is to establish routines for such requests as water and bathroom breaks.

STRUCTURING THE LEARNING ENVIRONMENT

At this point it should be clear that an effective learning environment is structured and organized. Students learn best when they know what to expect from one class to the next. This is why routines are critical. In the same vein, teachers also benefit from a structured environment (see Key Point 7-4). Therefore, effective teachers often implement similar instructional procedures over an extended period of time. For example, classroom teachers follow a fairly regular routine of taking attendance, teaching specific instructional units during certain periods of the day, taking students to lunch, and overseeing students' departure from school. In the physical activity setting, it also is important to establish teacher routines. The following information is presented in order to assist you in understanding the significance of routines for both teachers and students.

Key Point 7-4

In the same way that students benefit from routines, teachers also benefit from routines.

Warm-ups

Physical education teachers often engage in a routine of taking attendance while students perform warm-up activities. As a classroom teacher it will be unnecessary for you to take attendance. You will already know who is present and who is absent. You may, however, be inclined to introduce traditional types of warm-ups as part of an instructional routine. Physical education teachers often ask students to stretch or complete fitness exercises while taking attendance. They implement warm-ups in their classes because this activity is something to which they were exposed for many years while they were students in the public schools. If you also were exposed to this routine, it is likely that you will expect students to engage in traditional warm-ups prior to instruction. Unfortunately, if you engage in this practice you may be wasting valuable learning time. For example, teachers often believe that stretching is necessary for avoiding muscular injury. Stretching prior to activity, however, is often less beneficial than stretching after one has completed an activity.

Did you enjoy running laps or performing sit-ups and push-ups? If so, you are one of the few. In fact, if you observe an on-going activity class in which students are exercising, you will notice that they immediately stop whenever the teacher's back is turned. This is not to suggest that placing students immediately into strenuous activity is a wise idea. Instead, spend the first few minutes of class by engaging students in enjoyable activities that fit the content of the lesson that will be introduced. For example, if students are going to play basketball, allow them to dribble or pass the basketball to each other for several minutes. If students are going to be engaged in brisk locomotor activities, allow them to engage in an activity in which they are required to walk briskly.

Further, as a classroom teacher you will need a few moments to get organized. You will need to retrieve equipment and place it in the appropriate location in the physical activity setting. During this period of time you can establish a routine in which students are engaged in warm-up activities that are fun, interesting, relevant to the lesson, and not reminiscent of the types of warm-ups to which you were likely exposed as a student. In general, you may wish to establish a routine in which the first five minutes of class are used for a purposeful introduction to the activity. If you are planning to teach soccer, quickly spread a large number of balls

Students can stretch while watching others demonstrate.

throughout the activity area and ask students to dribble the ball in a controlled fashion until you can finish organizing the remainder of equipment that will be used for class that day.

Closure

As introduced in Chapter 3, an effective way of ending class is to have students regroup in a circle for a brief review of the day's activities. You may wish to select two or three students to demonstrate something that they did especially well during class. If you use this technique, be sure to alternate among students so that all students have an opportunity to demonstrate over time. While you review the major points of the lesson, ask students to perform simple stretching exercises. Not only will this serve as an appropriate culminating activity, but students will also calm down prior to returning to the classroom. Finally, by returning to the circle, you can provide last-minute instructions prior to leaving the activity area. You may need to appoint a few extra students to help with equipment, or you might want to remind students to walk quietly through the hallway.

Making Notes

The last routine in which you will want to engage is to find a few moments during the day to briefly reflect on the success of the lesson and make a few notes on your lesson plan. This routine is the most difficult to complete because you will have so many other tasks that need attention. It is, however, an important routine for insuring that subsequent lessons proceed smoothly and are more successful. You should commit yourself to making notes in both the home and the physical activity classrooms.

Summary

The experiences that you encountered during the apprenticeship-of-observation will serve as a foundation for guiding your future teaching practices. In some cases, these experiences will enhance your opportunities for success. In other cases, however, the practices that you encountered as a pupil may be antithetical to effective teaching. Teachers who draw from knowledge acquired during teacher education, and who understand the significance of effective teaching, will build a stronger foundation of knowledge from which to draw—and will likely experience greater success at promoting student learning.

Regardless of the type of physical activity setting in which you may teach, effective teachers establish an environment that is conducive to learning. They have protocols that emphasize rules and routines. Routines are introduced early in the year and practiced at regular intervals. Students learn how to enter and leave class, when to stop and listen, and how to obtain and return equipment. In addition, teachers develop routines for themselves that provide structure to the lesson and decrease lesson disruptions (see Box 7.1).

DO AND DON'T CHECKLIST

Do	Don't
☐ be committed to learning about effective teaching	☐ believe that you already know how to teach and have relatively little more to learn
☐ make lemonade out of lemons if the physical activity setting is less than ideal	☐ give up if you do not have adequate space or equipment
☐ teach routines early in the school year and practice them throughout the year	☐ assume that students will know how to behave in the physical activity setting
☐ teach students signals that require them to stop and listen	☐ allow students to keep talking and moving when you signal them to stop and listen.
☐ develop teacher routines that enable you to be organized and effective.	

Review Activities

1. Explain to a classmate how you would teach pupils about the following routines:
   a. Entering and leaving the physical activity area
   b. Signaling students
   c. Obtaining and returning equipment

2. When teaching physical education, what teacher routines do you believe are important to establish that are not listed in this chapter?

3. Imagine that your students continue to disregard the freeze signal after you have introduced it to them over a period of weeks. What might you have done incorrectly? How can you regain their attention?

4. What difficulties might you encounter if you ask second-grade students to sit alphabetically in a circle? How might you remedy the problem?

5. How could you store equipment in your classroom if you have little available space?

References

Fink, J., & Siedentop, D. (1989). The development of routines, rules, and expectations at the start of the school year. *Journal of Teaching in Physical Education, 8,* 198–212.

Lanier, J. E., & Little, J. W. (1986). Research on teacher education. In M. C. Wittrock (Ed.), *Handbook of research on teaching* (3rd ed.), pp. 527–569. New York: Macmillan.

Lortie, D. C. (1975). *Schoolteacher.* Chicago: University of Chicago Press.

Chapter **Eight**

Effective Teaching

During the past two decades, researchers who study education have undertaken a number of investigations in which they have discovered which teaching behaviors are associated with an increased opportunity for student learning. In Lecture Chapter 7, strategies for structuring the learning environment in effective ways were discussed. For example, you learned that it is better to require students to sit in a semi-circle when you convey instructions than to have them standing in locations where they may not be able to hear what you are saying or see what you are demonstrating. In this chapter, you will learn about additional pedagogical techniques that may increase the opportunity for students to learn while they are engaged in activity.

These techniques, commonly referred to as *effective teaching behaviors,* are grounded in research findings in which investigators have spent thousands of hours observing how teachers structure learning tasks and how they interact with pupils. Based on these investigations, it is possible to provide teachers with knowledge about the ways in which they can most effectively execute their pedagogical responsibilities. Although many of the behaviors discussed in this chapter are similar to effective teaching behaviors that teachers employ in the classroom, many are distinct to the unique environment of the physical activity setting.

In some cases, effective teaching behaviors are relatively easy to implement and do not require much practice. In other cases, it takes many hours of practice before an instructor becomes comfortable and skilled at executing effective teaching behaviors. As emphasized throughout the text, beginning teachers sometimes make the mistake of abandoning strategies that are associated with effective teaching because they are not immediately successful when initially implemented. This, however, is a grave mistake. Prior to abandoning techniques that have promise, ask why a particular behavior may not have been successful. Discuss the unsuccessful strategy with a more experienced teacher, asking for specific strategies that may improve your chances for success. Remember, even expert teachers continue to learn from their own mistakes. Before reading further, complete Thinking Challenge 8.1.

THINKING CHALLENGE 8.1	What teaching behaviors do you believe are associated with effective teaching? Provide at least five descriptors.
	1.
	2.
	3.
	4.
	5.

HOW DOES GOOD TEACHING DIFFER FROM EFFECTIVE TEACHING?

When undergraduate students initially enter a teacher education class, they often explain that they elected the teaching profession because they were influenced by a particularly good teacher. Over the past two decades, when we have asked our students to define a good

As effective teacher can be well liked yet still promote student learning.

teacher, they consistently use descriptors such as kind, caring, fair, good listener, energetic, fun, good sense of humor, knowledgeable, enthusiastic, good role model, physically fit, and creative. They have never, however, defined a good teacher as someone who creates opportunities that promote learning.

Arguably, a good teacher has all of the characteristics listed above. Those descriptors are what distinguishes the teacher and makes him or her likable to students. An effective teacher often possesses the same characteristics you may have listed in Thinking Challenge 8.1; however, he or she also employs instructional behaviors that are associated with student learning (see Key Point 8-1). Despite a handful of teachers who are naturally effective, most become effective as a result of enrolling in classes, reading the literature, attending conferences, talking to colleagues, learning from mistakes, and practicing pedagogy on a daily basis. The purpose of this chapter is to introduce you to a variety of teaching behaviors that relate to effective teaching. In addition to introducing you to basic research that addresses effective pedagogy, we will attempt to provide real-world examples of how to become an effective classroom teacher who competently teaches physical education.

Key Point 8-1

Being described a good teacher is not synonymous with being effective.

KEEPING STUDENTS ACTIVELY ENGAGED

There are many teacher behaviors that correspond to effective teaching. One that has received a great amount of attention in the literature relates to keeping learners actively involved in appropriate activities. It may seem obvious to you, but you would be surprised by the number of physical education teachers who cannot achieve this in their classes. Children spend the majority of instructional time standing in lines, waiting for a turn, or sitting on the floor listening to instructions. Given the physical inactivity and obesity epidemic that characterizes youth of today, it is inexcusable to allow students to be inactive in physical education.

We hope that increasing your awareness of instructional time will encourage you to follow the same principle that guides teachers of quality physical education programs. That is, children must be actively engaged in moderate to vigorous physical activity (MVPA) for at least 50 percent of the class period (U.S. Department of Health and Human Services, 2000). Below is a discussion of the obstacles you may encounter in keeping students actively engaged and how they can successfully be overcome.

Equipment Constraints

Imagine teaching reading to a second-grade class. How would you engage learners in the activity? How would you convey directions? Based on your own experiences as a pupil in an elementary school, you may recall techniques that your teachers employed. It is probable that many of those techniques were based on effective practices. Imagine, however, teaching reading to a class of students with only one textbook. It would be impossible to individualize instruction and students would never have an opportunity to practice independently. Imagine if they had to wait in line for a turn before they could read. Since they would not be engaged, many would become distracted and eventually disruptive.

Physical education teachers are sometimes confronted with the dilemma of having inadequate equipment at their disposal. They are asked to teach dribbling with only eight balls, gymnastics with only three mats, or tennis with only two courts. The literature indicates that many teachers, particularly those in urban environments, are challenged by a lack of facilities and inappropriate amounts of equipment (Siedentop, Doutis, Tsangaridou, Ward, & Rauschenbach, 1994). Some teachers become frustrated with such challenges and elect to leave the teaching profession (Macdonald, 1995). Those who remain and are distinguished as effective have learned how to structure the environment so that all students can be engaged in appropriate learning activities.

Consider the teacher with the one textbook who was described above. If you were that teacher, how would you handle the challenge? Would you give up and enter a new profession, or would you try to create an effective learning environment despite the constraints under which you would be working? If you elected to remain, how could you insure that all students had an opportunity to learn? The proactive teacher would take students to the library, borrow books from other teachers, ask for donations from parents and other schools, and sponsor a book drive. Similarly, the creative teacher of physical education would engage in similar behaviors because he or she would understand that students must be involved in activity if they are to learn.

As a classroom teacher, there is a strong probability that you will have access to limited physical education equipment and facilities. If you have only a limited amount available, how might you structure the learning environment to keep all students activity engaged? Perhaps you might elect to do some of the following:

- Organize three learning stations: six students practice gymnastics (such as rolling) on three available mats, twelve participate in animal walks with the teacher, twelve develop a routine by pretending that the marked lines on the floor are a balance beam.

- If you have only limited access to a gymnasium or playground, take students on a brisk walk.

An effective teacher does not allow an inadequate amount of equipment to interfere with learning or the opportunity to be active.

- Consider creating your own homemade equipment. Ask students to help with the task. For example, plastic milk jugs filled with sand and sealed shut can make good cones that can be used to mark boundaries or serve as goal posts. Beanbags can be used to teach tossing skills. Paper towel holders stuffed with plastic garbage bags to ensure they are sturdy can serve as batons for teaching relays in a track and field unit.

- Emphasize MVPA by planning activities such as tag games and creative dance that do not require equipment but keep children moving.

- If you wish to teach dribbling but have only a limited number of basketballs, also use playground balls. Likewise, use beach balls instead of expensive volleyballs.

Variation in Skill Level

You will quickly notice, particularly as children progress upward in grade level, that there will be tremendous disparity in ability. Some students will quickly acquire new skills and expect to encounter increasingly difficult challenges. Others will have such low regard for their physical abilities that they give up before walking through the gymnasium door. Most, however, will fall in the range of intermediate level ability. As Key Point 8-2 emphasizes, this unfortunately is the only developmental level that most teachers address in their curriculum. For intermediate level students, they might do well in class and receive adequate practice and engagement. More advanced students, however, become bored while low-skilled learners become *competent bystanders* (Tousignant, 1981). These are non-disruptive individuals who skillfully fake involvement in the lesson activities. Do you remember pretending to participate so that the teacher thought you were engaged in the lesson?

Key Point 8-2

Teachers often focus their efforts on teaching to students at the intermediate grade level. The needs of students at the lower and higher ends of the skill ability continuum are often neglected.

Given the difficulty that physical education teachers sometimes have addressing disparate ability levels, it would not be surprising if you too would find this aspect of physical education challenging. In Lecture Chapter 6, you acquired knowledge related to different teaching styles. By incorporating a variety of styles into your lessons, you will be able to address the needs of a greater number of learners. In addition, the techniques below may be useful.

- Provide for variation and choice in activities. For example, provide greater challenge to highly skilled students (e.g., dribble and pass a basketball to a partner while advancing down the gym) and less difficult tasks to the lower skilled (e.g., dribble in place or in pathways). Allow students to choose a basketball or a playground ball for completing the task.

- Allow students to work at different stations, selecting what task they will perform. At a throwing station, they can elect to (1) underhand toss the ball to a box, (2) overhand toss to a partner, (3) overhand toss to a target on the wall, or (4) toss and catch the ball to self. In addition, they select the size and softness of the ball and distance from which they will throw.

- Encourage students to select a skill to perform based on their individual level of skill. In a tumbling unit, beginners can practice egg rolls, log rolls, and simple forward rolls. Intermediate students can add increasingly challenging tasks to the forward roll like starting from a straddle or pike position. Advanced students might be encouraged to incorporate rolls into a gymnastics routine that also employs other skills like handstands.

STRUCTURING AVAILABLE LEARNING TIME

As highlighted above, an effective teacher is conscious of providing students with appropriate levels of activity. Typically, children spend the majority of their time waiting or engaged in instructional tasks or managerial tasks. The teacher's role is to engage in behaviors that facilitate an effective environment for learning. When conveying information about how to perform a skill, the teacher engages in instructional tasks. When distributing equipment and placing students in groups, the teacher engages in managerial tasks. Although each has a place in the lesson, each has the potential to also create an environment devoid of learning.

Instructional Tasks

The period of time an instructor spends teaching children is often referred to as instructional task time. That is, learners are acquiring information about how to perform a skill, knowledge about a concept, or information about how to practice an activity. Generally, they are either sitting or standing while receiving instruction, or engaged in an activity after they have been released to practice. As Rink (1994, 2006) explains, teachers should use this time to provide direct instruction related to (a) set induction (describing what students should learn), (b) organizational conditions/procedures (how to organize for and practice the learning activity), and (c) goal of practice (communicating the purpose of the task). If executed appropriately, teachers succinctly progress through their explanations and quickly organize learners into activity. Unfortunately, research has demonstrated that teachers often have difficulty providing clear directions, and students spend from 15–30 percent of class time listening (Siedentop & Tannehill, 2000).

The strategies below may help you to decrease unnecessary instructional time while increasing the clarity of the directions you are providing. In short, you will accomplish more with less.

- Provide only that amount of information necessary for completing the task. Too often teachers attempt to convey information about every aspect of a skill to students. Students, however, will remember only a small portion of that information. Therefore, concentrate on making only one to three essential points during instruction. What you are unable to cover at one point can always be covered at another. For example, when teaching the skip, emphasize to children in 1st grade (a) that the motion is a step-hop-step-hop on alternating feet (briefly demonstrate) and (b) to carefully avoid contact with others as

Students can learn a skill only if they have ample opportunity to practice.

they practice while moving through general space. Let them begin practicing before providing unnecessary additional information.

- Consistent with the point above, it is better to have several short bouts of instruction as opposed to one long and extended period.

- Use a technique that Graham, Holt/Hale, and Parker (2004) refer to as *checks for understanding*. Ask simple questions to determine if students understand particular points of instruction. For instance, a teacher might ask, "What part of the hand is used to dribble the ball?" If students respond, "Fingertips," the teacher will know that students correctly understand the concept being conveyed. If some appear confused and others say, "Our palms," the teacher will know that students have yet to adequately understand the concept. In this latter case, further instruction is necessary.

- Avoid asking general questions like, "Does anyone have any comments or questions?" When working with elementary-aged children, a question like this only encourages children to think of something to say simply for the sake of contributing. Instead, get students into activity as quickly as possible. You will soon learn if students understand the directions or if further clarification is required.

- While performing, the teacher can provide additional instructions to individual students. This enables the teacher to individualize instruction that may not be relevant to everyone else. In the long run, valuable time is saved. Complete Thinking Challenge 8.2.

THINKING CHALLENGE 8.2	In addition to those listed, think of three additional strategies that you could implement to increase your clarity while decreasing instructional time. How much time would each save?
	1.
	2.
	3.

Managerial Tasks

In addition to providing clear instructions, teachers are responsible for managing and structuring the environment in a way that is conducive to learning. The managerial tasks for which they are responsible include grouping students, disseminating equipment, transitioning from one activity to another, and managing student behavior. While at first glance these behaviors may appear easy to execute, they actually take hundreds of practice hours to refine.

Managerial tasks are a fact of life in the gymnasium. They cannot be eliminated or ignored. They can, however, be practiced and refined. Effective teachers are cognizant that, on average, students spend 20–25 percent of the lesson engaged in managerial tasks and up to 50–70 percent in the most unproductive classes. Teachers who are concerned about learning attempt to reduce managerial time to no more than 5–10 percent of the lesson (Siedentop & Tannehill, 2000).

Grouping students.

A large amount of class time in physical education has traditionally been devoted to grouping students into teams or assigning them to a partner. Arguably, grouping unnecessarily consumes substantial portions of the lesson and robs children of countless hours of engaged time. Lecture Chapter 9 will address ways in which to minimize time spent in this activity.

Disseminating equipment.

Another managerial task that consumes unnecessary time is distributing equipment to students. Again, Lecture Chapter 9 will provide strategies for reducing time in this area. If, however, a lesson requires equipment, some portion of time must be devoted to disseminating it efficiently. Once a teacher acquires different strategies for effective distribution, time spent in this activity can be reduced.

Transitioning.

Skillful teachers have developed ways for quickly transitioning from one activity to another. One strategy you read about in the previous chapter entailed asking students to sit in a circle or semi-circle during instructions. If instructions need to be provided, developing the student routine of sitting in the semi-circle can save time that would otherwise be spent trying to convey instructions to students who were spread throughout the instructional area and unable to hear.

Managing behavior.

The most important strategy for saving time is related to introducing students to protocols. By engaging students in routines and consistently enforcing rules, countless hours of class time will not be wasted. When students understand the expectations of the learning environment, and the consequences of not meeting them, the teacher has reduced the potential for misbehavior.

Engagement

The third component of time relates to that portion of class which is devoted to engaging students in practice tasks. Prior to the late 1970s, little information existed that described the ways in which physical education teachers used their time. With the advent of an instrument for measuring time, Active Learning Time—Physical Education (ALT-PE), teachers were able to obtain insight into how time was spent in the gymnasium (see Box 8.1). A series of studies, initially undertaken at The Ohio State University (e.g., Metzler, 1979; Siedentop, Birdwell, & Metzler, 1979), and later by scholars throughout the nation, resulted in such increased awareness of learning time that effective teachers could no longer ignore students who were not engaged. What might seem like common sense—that students must be active to learn—was not previously a pressing concern of teachers. Scholars in both physical education and those in general education were beginning to understand the importance of how class time is spent.

Box 8.1

Instructional time can be diagramed as a pie, apportioned by teachers according to their priorities and knowledge concerning how to use time most effectively. A traditional class, with a well-intentioned but misinformed teacher, might resemble the pie on the left, whereas an effective environment would be characterized by the pie on the right.

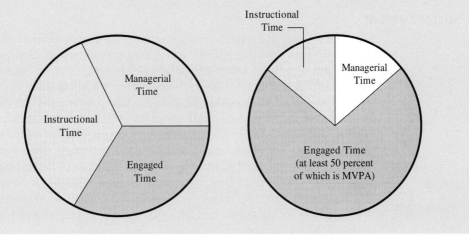

APPROPRIATE PRACTICE

For many years it was assumed that if students were engaged in an activity, they would learn. It became evident, however, that some students could be engaged for great amounts of time yet not acquire skill. Acknowledging this led to the realization that in order for students to learn, they must be engaged in appropriate practice (Silverman, 1985). It makes sense that if students are going to learn how to add, they must be practicing appropriately. Regardless of the number of hours spent practicing, they will not arrive at a correct sum unless they know when it was necessary to carry over from one column to the next when adding. The same rule of thumb holds true for physical education. Complete Thinking Challenge 8.3.

THINKING CHALLENGE 8.3	If student achievement is correlated with appropriate practice, how would you account for the success of an individual like Tiger Woods, who might swing his club using form that experts would characterize as not entirely correct? Are there occasions when exceptions to the appropriate practice rule may exist? Does that mean the rule should be ignored? During your next class, ask your instructor his or her opinion.

If you are required to teach physical education, and there are activities that you do not feel qualified to teach, it would be far better to focus on what you do well and leave unfamiliar content to someone else. Although this is not an ideal situation, we believe it is far better than teaching incorrect techniques—which become increasingly difficult to modify as students grow older. There is more than enough content related to physical education that you certainly could develop a one year curriculum—even if your curriculum primarily consisted of brisk walking, appropriate tag games, and practice trials at basic tasks.

Further, we hope that you will adhere to a general rule that physical education teachers try to follow. That is, provide opportunities whereby students can be successful during 80 percent of their attempts. While there exist occasions where this is unrealistic, such as successfully shooting a free throw in basketball (which some professional players cannot execute with 80 percent success), the majority of activities you design should be individualized to the degree that all students experience high degrees of success.

STUDENT INFLUENCE ON ENGAGEMENT TIME

Although most teachers believe that they control the learning environment, it is students who often determine how time is spent. The student social system is a powerful mechanism that influences how much time children are appropriately engaged in activity.

Student Social System

The instructional and managerial task systems were introduced by Doyle (1979, 1981) around the same time that ALT-PE was gaining prominence. A third task system, the student social, became evident during Allen's (1986) study of the classroom in which he observed the degree to which students pursue their own agendas when they are expected to be otherwise engaged. In physical education, Siedentop & Tannehill (2000) comment on the degree to which the student social system can overpower the instructional task system. That is, students can become so involved in socializing that they stop engaging in instructional activities. You might remember engaging in the student social system. Do you recall when you were supposed to be volleying with a partner or developing a creative dance routine with your friends? There were probably many occasions when you stopped practicing and instead altered the activity or engaged in conversation. Although some less disruptive behaviors are sometimes best left ignored, those that create an environment devoid of learning must be addressed.

As a classroom teacher, you will become familiar with those students in your classroom who are more likely than others to cause disruption. As emphasized in Key Point 8-3, the less contained area of the gymnasium or playground, however, may make it somewhat more difficult to control the student social system than the more contained area of the home classroom. When students begin engaging in behaviors that are either disruptive to the learning of others, or produce an unsafe environment, it is the responsibility of the teacher to quickly intervene.

Key Point 8-3

Without continuous supervision, students will begin to modify tasks and potentially become more disruptive. This is particularly true of the less constrained environment in which physical activity occurs. It is very important to supervise at all times. Disruption may be the fault of an ineffective or lazy teacher.

Monitoring

Closely observing students as they practice instructional tasks is an essential behavior of anyone responsible for teaching physical education. Research demonstrates that teachers who monitor closely greatly reduce the opportunity for the more damaging aspects of the student social system to emerge (Hastie & Saunders, 1990). Therefore, it is incumbent on the teacher to supervise all aspects of physical education instruction. While monitoring, teachers have an opportunity to provide individual feedback and determine if students are competently learning the skills introduced in the lesson. It also is an opportunity to determine if students are receiving adequate amounts of successful practice.

Negotiation

Another student behavior that has the potential to reduce learning is negotiation within the task system. This behavior is described as "any attempt by students to change tasks, to change the conditions under which tasks are performed, or to change the performance standards by which task completion is judged" (Siedentop & Tannehill, 2000, p. 47). In some cases students negotiate tasks because they are bored with the activity and desire a more challenging pursuit. For example, a student who plays on the community soccer team may not be challenged by kicking a ball to a partner with light force. That student may modify the task, standing farther away from the partner and kicking with much greater force than instructed. The teacher may choose to modify the task in order to meet the needs of this particular student. Or, if the teacher believes the student is kicking harder than necessary merely to be disruptive, he or she may intervene to stop the behavior. Regardless of students' intentions for negotiating tasks, it is the teacher's responsibility to determine when task negotiation is appropriate and when it is inappropriate or disruptive.

Students who are carefully supervised have less tendency to engage in off-task, disruptive behaviors.

ASSUMING EFFECTIVE PERSONAL BEHAVIORS

In addition to creating opportunities for students to be engaged, clearly understand instruction, and be adequately challenged, an effective teacher can employ personal behaviors that also have the potential to influence learning. These range from demonstrating enthusiasm for the lesson to proper positioning to engaging in with-it-ness.

Enthusiasm

Although there is only cursory evidence, from studies conducted over two decades ago, that correlates enthusiasm with student learning (Carlisle & Phillips, 1984; Rolider, Siedentop, & Van Houten, 1984), common sense dictates that teachers who are enthusiastic and energetic convey vibrancy that is contagious. As you might recall, learning is less exciting from a boring and unenthusiastic teacher than from one who is vibrant and alive. Students who observe teachers who are uninterested may question the relevance of the subject matter and have greater difficulty becoming enthusiastic about what they are learning. If we are to convince students that lifelong physical activity is important, we must demonstrate enthusiasm that draws them toward the subject as opposed to pushing them away.

As a classroom teacher who may be mandated to teach physical education, it is our hope that you will be able to convey enthusiasm to your students. If you were an unsuccessful mover, this may be more difficult. Therefore, we encourage you to evaluate those activities that you do enjoy (walking, biking, hiking, yoga) and engage students in activities that convey excitement.

Positioning

Effective teachers clearly understand that positioning is a basic behavior associated with sound instruction. Consider the example of a classroom teacher who has the habit of consistently standing in front of the overhead projector so that students have difficulty viewing the screen. Amazingly, this is not an unusual behavior—it can be witnessed in the elementary classroom and even with university teacher education professors. At the most fundamental level, it demonstrates a lack of awareness about the learning environment.

In the physical education environment, Graham and his colleagues (Graham, Holt/Hale, and Parker, 2004) recommend a strategy called *back-to-the-wall*. This technique requires that the teacher move about the perimeter of the learning area without turning his or her back on students. Not only does this technique convey a message that the teacher is there to prevent off-task behavior, but it also promotes safety. Further, the teacher is able to observe the individual progress of all students and whether or not an activity is too simple or difficult. The only time when you may need to turn your back is during a demonstration so that students can view from behind exactly how to perform a skill.

With-it-ness

The term "with-it-ness" refers to teachers who students perceive as aware and perceptive. They are quick on their feet and respond swiftly and appropriately. Initially used as a descriptor for perceptive classroom teachers (Kounin, 1970), with-it-ness has increasingly been considered a characteristic of an effective physical education teacher who has greater student compliance (Johnson, 1995). Again, think about those teachers who allowed for little disruption as opposed to those whose classes were characterized as chaotic. It is likely that the teachers in the less disruptive classrooms employed with-it-ness behaviors.

PROVIDING EFFECTIVE FEEDBACK

Although the research literature is unclear concerning the effectiveness of teacher feedback in physical education (Graber, 2001), most educators believe that providing appropriate feedback is critical to the improvement of skill (Graham, 2001). There are several types of feedback that teachers can choose to employ, some of which is more useful than others.

For example, feedback can be positive or negative, general or specific, congruent or not congruent. In many cases, feedback is a combination of two of the above.

Positive Feedback

Statements given by the teacher about a student's behavior or performance, such as "good job" or "great throw," describe positive feedback. For some odd reason, perhaps as a means of encouraging students, physical education teachers often provide positive feedback even when a performance is unworthy of praise. For example, it is not unusual to hear a teacher shout, "Good job," to a student who runs to execute a volleyball bump and sends the ball to the ceiling. Although it is important to be supportive, positive feedback that is related to performance should be provided only on occasions when it is warranted. Otherwise, it tends to become less meaningful over time. Instead of saying "Good job" when the ball hits the ceiling, say, "Nice try getting to the ball before it hit the ground."

Negative Feedback

Phrases such as "horrible effort" or "terrible volley" refer to feedback that is primarily negative. With regard to performance, it would be inappropriate to provide negative feedback that could be destructive to a child's self-esteem. Instead, tell a student who missed a catch, "Next time, be sure to keep your eye on the ball." In terms of behavior, simply state, "This is your first warning; please do not kick the volleyball again."

General Feedback

This form of feedback describes some of the examples given above, such as "good job." It is usually so general that it does not provide any meaningful information to students concerning what was good or poor about their behavior or performance.

Specific Feedback

When teachers specifically address components of a student's behavior or performance, he or she is receiving specific feedback. The sentence, "John, you pointed your feet nicely during the forward roll," or "Karen, you need to listen to instructions because I asked you to use a soccer ball, not a playground ball," are examples of specific feedback. In the case of the former, the statement is specific and positive. In the case of the latter, it is specific and negative. Below are specific feedback statements that could be helpful to learners.

- "Eric, you are using too much force when kicking the ball. Remember to only tap or nudge the ball forward."
- "Karen, please keep the ball below knee level when kicking. If you are going to continue to kick in a dangerous manner, you will need to take a time-out."
- "I thought that the class did an outstanding job of quickly returning to the circle when asked. Thank you. This saves valuable learning time."
- James, remember to keep your eyes forward when dribbling. If you look down, you won't be able to see where you are going or where you might want to pass the ball."
- "Connie, don't forget to tuck your chin when completing the forward roll. You might want to pretend that your chin is glued to your neck."

Feedback is an important component of being an effective teacher, but it is sometimes difficult to determine when to provide it to learners. For example, when learning a new skill, students will experience some failure. This is part of the learning cycle, and it would be inappropriate to barrage the learner with feedback after every unsuccessful attempt. There is a point, however, at which it is critical for the teacher to intervene so the child does not learn inappropriate technique or become discouraged and give up. With practice, you will learn when is the appropriate point at which to facilitate the progress of the student by providing feedback that is necessary for further progress. Try completing the activities in Box 8.2.

Box 8.2

Read each feedback statement and characterize it using the code below (there may be instances when two types of feedback are given in one statement):

P = POSITIVE   **N = NEGATIVE**   **G = GENERAL**   **S = SPECIFIC**

1. Be sure to watch the ball as you make contact with the racket. _____
2. That's not very good. _____
3. What a great try. _____
4. Please stop throwing so forcefully. _____
5. I like how you are pointing your toes. _____
6. That's right. Reach, reach, reach. _____
7. Cool dance. It looks creative. _____
8. Remember to rotate your trunk. _____
9. Yes, you keep watching the target. _____
10. Step, hop, step, hop. _____
11. You are a star. _____
12. Don't stop. Keep going. You can do it. _____
13. Your behavior is very disruptive to others. _____
14. Don't forget to use your arms. _____
15. You should be able to do it correctly on your next try. _____

Congruent Feedback

Educators believe that congruent feedback is the most meaningful to improvement in student performance. It addresses only those components of a skill or behavior that a teacher has just emphasized (Graham, 2001). If, for instance, a teacher stated during instruction to dribble using fingertips, subsequent feedback should address that point. The teacher would say, "Hailey, remember to use your finger pads, not the palm of your hand." Incongruent feedback would appear in the form of a statement like, "Hailey, keep your head up." If the teacher is focusing on teaching the follow-through when throwing, then feedback should emphasize that element of the skill, not whether the student is watching the ball. If the lesson focus is on extending one's limbs during a creative dance routine, feedback should be specific to that element of the routine, not whether the student is bending his or her legs. Try completing the activity described in Box 8.3.

Box 8.3

Observe a teacher for approximately 10 minutes, using the codes below to record the type of feedback he or she is providing (you may have instances where teachers combine two forms of feedback). Use an asterisk to designate if the feedback is congruent. What percentage of statements are positive, negative, general, or specific? What percentage is congruent?

P = POSITIVE   **N = NEGATIVE**   **G = GENERAL**   **S = SPECIFIC**

1.   11.
2.   12.
3.   13.
4.   14.
5.   15.
6.   16.
7.   17.
8.   18.
9.   19.
10.   20.

Evaluation: How would you evaluate the observed teacher with regard to the frequency and type of feedback that he or she provided?

Summary

The purpose of this chapter was to introduce you to behaviors that are associated with effective teaching. We hope you will begin to distinguish between teachers who are perceived to be good, or characterized as popular, and those who are considered to be effective. Effective teachers distinguish themselves by keeping students actively engaged in appropriate learning tasks for the majority of the class period. They provide quick instructions, disseminate equipment effectively, and swiftly transition from one activity to another. They understand that students have a tendency to socialize during practice and respond by carefully monitoring, using techniques such as back-to-the-wall. They are enthusiastic about their subject matter and demonstrate with-it-ness by responding to situations quickly and effectively. They understand the individual needs of learners and provide feedback accordingly, using specific statements that are congruent with subject matter recently taught. Most important, students in their classes learn from their instruction.

Now that you have been introduced to effective teaching behaviors, it is unlikely that you will be able to observe a teacher without considering the degree to which he or she is engaging in effective techniques. Regardless of whether you are teaching math in the classroom, or dance in the gymnasium, we encourage you to become the effective teacher we know you have the potential to be. (See Box 8.4.)

DO AND DON'T CHECKLIST

Do	Don't
☐ practice behaviors associated with effective teaching	☐ think that because you are a popular teacher you also are effective
☐ keep instructions and managerial tasks to a minimum	☐ provide instruction on every aspect of a skill during one session
☐ provide opportunities where students are appropriately practicing a skill	☐ assume that because students are engaged they also are acquiring skill
☐ closely monitor the class for off-task behavior	☐ address every instance of off-task behavior without understanding why it is occurring
☐ demonstrate enthusiastic behavior	☐ provide activities that are appropriately challenging as a means of reducing the opportunity for the student social system or task negotiation to emerge
☐ use with-it-ness to convince students you are aware of what is happening in the learning environment	☐ expect students to recognize their own mistakes.
☐ provide frequent congruent feedback on a regular basis.	

Review Activities

1. Is it possible to be a good teacher without creating opportunities for student learning? Can you be an effective teacher without being considered good by students? Defend your position on these issues.
2. If you have access to only six playground balls, discuss how you could keep everyone actively engaged for three days of developmentally appropriate instruction. State your goals and describe your learning activities.
3. Recall the behaviors of a physical education teacher you would characterize as effective. Describe a typical class. How much MVPA did you receive?

4. What types of student social system behaviors might you expect to see from fifth-grade students? How about students enrolled in kindergarten?

5. List five behaviors you associate with effective teaching and state why you selected each.

References

Allen, J. D. (1986). Classroom management: Students' perspectives, goals, and strategies. *American Educational Research Journal, 23,* 437–459.

Carlisle, C., & Phillips, D. A. (1984). The effects of enthusiasm training on selected teacher and student behaviors in preservice physical education teachers. *Journal of Teaching in Physical Education, 4,* 64–75.

Doyle, W. (1979). Classroom tasks and students' abilities. In P. L. Peterson & H. J. Walberg (Eds.), *Research on teaching: Concepts, findings and implications* (pp. 183–209). Berkeley, CA: McCutchan.

Doyle, W. (1981). Research on classroom contexts. *Journal of Teacher Education, 32*(6), 3–6.

Graber, K. C. (2001). Research on teaching in physical education. In V. Richardson (Ed.), *Handbook of research on teaching* (4th ed.), pp. 491–519. Washington, DC: American Educational Research Association.

Graham, G. (2001). *Teaching children physical education* (2nd ed.). Champaign, IL: Human Kinetics.

Graham, G., Holt/Hale, S. A., & Parker, M. (2004). *Children moving* (4th ed.). Boston: McGraw Hill.

Hastie, P. A., & Saunders, J. E. (1990). A case study of monitoring in secondary school physical education classes. *Journal of Classroom Interaction, 25*(1 & 2), 47–54.

Johnson, B. D. (1995). "Withitness": Real or fictional? *The Physical Educator, 52,* 22–28.

Kounin, J. S. (1970). *Discipline and group management in classrooms.* New York: Holt, Rinehart and Winston.

Macdonald, D. (1995). The role of proletarianization in physical education teacher attrition. *Research Quarterly for Exercise and Sport, 66,* 129–141.

Metzler, M. W. (1979). *The measurement of academic learning time in physical education.* (Unpublished doctoral dissertation). The Ohio State University, Columbus, OH.

Rink, J. E. (1994). Task presentation in pedagogy. *Quest, 46,* 270–280.

Rink, J. E. (2006). *Teaching physical education for learning* (5th ed.). Boston: McGraw Hill.

Rolider, A., Siedentop, D., & Van Houten, R. (1984). Effects of enthusiasm training on subsequent teacher enthusiastic behavior. *Journal of Teaching in Physical Education, 3*(2), 47–59.

Siedentop, D., Birdwell, D., & Metzler, M. (1979, March). *A process approach to measuring teaching effectiveness in physical education.* Paper presented at the annual meeting of the American Alliance of Health, Physical Education, Recreation and Dance, New Orleans, LA.

Siedentop, D., Doutis, P., Tsangaridou, N., Ward, P., & Rauschenbach, J. (1994). Don't sweat gym! An analysis of curriculum and instruction. *Journal of Teaching in Physical Education, 13,* 375–394.

Siedentop, D., & Tannehill, D. (2000). *Developing teaching skills in physical education* (4th ed.). Mountain View, CA: Mayfield.

Silverman, S. (1985). Relationship of engagement and practice trials to student achievement. *Journal of Teaching in Physical Education, 5,* 13–21.

Tousignant, M. (1981). *A qualitative analysis of task structures in required physical education.* (Unpublished doctoral dissertation). The Ohio State University, Columbus, OH.

U.S. Department of Health and Human Services. (2000). *School health index for physical activity and healthy eating: A self-assessment planning guide for elementary school.* Atlanta, GA: Centers for Disease Control.

Chapter **Nine**

Class Organization and Management

Learning how to effectively organize and manage the classroom is an essential skill for teachers who are concerned about promoting maximal learning and high amounts of engagement time. To this point, you have learned that teaching organizational routines to students and carefully structuring learning time may positively influence what you are able to accomplish as a teacher and what students ultimately learn from your instruction. The purpose of this chapter is to build on what you have already learned about creating an effective learning environment. Specifically, you will acquire additional knowledge about how to maximize instructional time by minimizing time spent organizing and managing the class. In addition, you will learn how to establish a safe learning environment.

As you learned in Chapter 8, students in physical education spend their time engaged in one of four primary activities (Siedentop & Tannehill, 2000). First, some of their time is spent waiting. Usually this involves waiting in line for a turn, but it could also entail waiting to gain the teacher's attention or for instruction to begin. Second, their time is spent engaged in managerial activities such as choosing teams, selecting captains, obtaining equipment, and transitioning from one activity to another. Third, they spend some time in instruction where they receive directions related to the skill they are learning and the task they will perform. Finally, they spend time engaged in physical activity. Ideally, the majority of student time should be spent in this latter category. We hope that this chapter on class organization will provide you with information for how to eliminate waiting time, minimize organizational time, and maximize engagement time.

TIME MANAGEMENT

In Chapter 2, you learned that time devoted to instruction in physical education is limited. Although the National Association for Sport and Physical Education (National Association for Sport and Physical Education [NASPE] & American Heart Association [AHA], 2010) and government agencies (Centers for Disease Control and Prevention, 1997) advocate that elementary school children should receive at least 150 minutes per week of physical education (see Key Point 9-1), the reality is that children in most schools receive considerably less time.

Key Point 9-1

Professional and organizational agencies recommend that elementary-aged children receive physical education for at least 150 minutes per week.

If you are fortunate enough to have some mandated time allocated for instruction in physical education, you need to make the most out of every minute that is allocated. For

Effective teachers are conscious about how time is spent.

example, if you are located in a school that offers physical education for 30 minutes twice per week, that is only 33 hours of available instruction time per year. Although you will not have any wiggle room in which time can be wasted, you can develop strategies for maximizing the modest amount of time you do have at your disposal.

Thoughtful physical education *and* classroom teachers can easily engage an elementary child in activity for the majority of the class period by planning in advance and being conscientious about how time is spent. If you are motivated to become an effective time manager, by practicing and implementing some of the strategies you acquire from this text, we believe that you can maximize student engagement time in physical education by effectively organizing the learning environment.

ORGANIZING CLASS BY GROUPING STUDENTS

What do you recall about how you were assigned to a partner, small groups, or a team? Based on our own memories, we recall being able to select whom we wanted to partner with. While choosing partners and small groups was typically done quickly and relatively harmlessly, selecting teams was much more complicated and often resulted in hurt feelings. We remember having teachers who appointed two captains. These individuals were responsible for taking turns while picking individuals for their respective teams. Those individuals who were either highly skilled or close friends of the captains were always selected immediately. Those with average skills or who had less acquaintance with the captains were selected next. Finally, students who were low skilled and unpopular were always selected last.

The example above may seem outdated by today's educational standards, but when we were in elementary school, it was the strategy teachers most often employed for selecting teams. Imagine, however, the number of rules of effective pedagogy that were broken by this practice and the amount of unnecessary class time that was wasted. As Key Point 9-2 stresses, do not waste class time on relatively unimportant matters like selecting teams.

Key Point 9-2

Maximize class time by thinking in advance how you will select teams and group students.

When progressing from having students work by themselves to working with others, we suggest that you begin gradually. Initially, introduce the concept of cooperation by having students work with a partner. Once they have grasped how to effectively work with another person, place them into small groups where they must interact, share, and cooperate. Finally, you can place them in larger groups or teams that require more advanced social skills. Below are some examples of how to effectively organize students into partners, small groups, and teams.

Partners

Selecting partners is a relatively easy pedagogical strategy to learn. Teachers who are thoughtful can quickly pair students rather easily. Many of these same strategies can be used when asking students to work in groups of three. In fact, there will be instances when one student is left without a partner. The teacher can quickly place that student with an existing pair to create a group of three. Sometimes teachers assume the role of partner when one child is left without anyone with whom to work, but this strategy prevents the teacher from providing feedback to other students and is not a good use of his or her time.

Proximity.
This entails asking students to pair with the individual standing most closely to them.

Equal size.
This strategy requires students to locate an individual of approximately the same size to serve in the role of partner.

Self-selection.
On occasion, teachers may allow students to select their own partner. This technique, however, should be used only if friends can work together effectively and not become disruptive.

Assigned partner.
In some cases, a teacher might pre-plan how students will be partnered and may even elect to keep students with that partner for a set amount of time (e.g., week or unit of instruction).

Small groups

Strategies similar to those used for partnering students may also be appropriate for placing students into small groups. Additional techniques are suggested below.

Two-pair proximity.
This strategy requires one student to partner with the student standing closest, and then this group joins with another pair standing nearby.

Deck of cards.
Each student receives one playing card from a deck of cards. Those students holding the same card form a small group of four. For example, those holding a "10" would form a group as would those holding a "Queen." Remember, that there are 52 cards in a playing deck. Therefore, some cards (such as the face cards) may need to be removed from the deck before they are distributed. Otherwise, there would be more cards than students available. Teachers can also manipulate the deck to include only three cards of a particular value if the goal is to have them work in groups of three. Similarly, teachers can use card suits for dividing students into teams.

Squads.
Depending on the overall size of the class, teachers often assign students to semi-permanent squads. These squads become a useful mechanism because the teacher does not have to spend time during class grouping students. The composition of squads is considered in

advance of class so that each is balanced by ability and gender. Squads work together as small groups for several weeks, throughout a unit of instruction, or until the teacher decides to change the composition of the squads.

Numbers.

Assign numbers to students at the beginning of the year. This is a wonderful mechanism for grouping students. For example, if you want small groups of students, you can have numbers 4, 8, 12, 16, and 20 work together; or you may have students 1, 2, 3, 4, and 5 work together. By using numbers, you are easily able to maneuver the composition of small groups.

Teams.

We believe that physical education teachers spend far too much time worrying about and assigning students to teams. We hope that classroom teachers will not make the same mistake. The strategies suggested below can be implemented within a period of seconds and are just as likely to be equitable as those teams that take much longer to determine.

Divided partners.

When students are asked to locate a partner, they often search for their friends or someone of equal ability. Therefore, one easy means of assigning equitable teams is to ask students to quickly get with a partner. One of the partners is subsequently asked to sit down. The individuals who are standing are asked to move to one location of the activity area as Team #1 and those who are sitting are asked to move to another area as Team #2. By using this technique, friends are separated and teams are equalized. Another useful strategy is to ask students to find a partner who is approximately the same size (or even the same gender). Once the students are divided you will have two teams of equal size and/or gender.

Squads.

If you pre-assign students to permanent or semi-permanent squads, be sure to have an even number of squads. Doing so will allow you to group squads into teams. For example, squads 1, 2, and 3 might become one team and squads 3, 4, and 5 another team. The composition of teams is periodically modified so that each squad has an opportunity to team with all other squads.

Eyeballing.

Using this technique, teachers simply eyeball the class and explain to students that it will be divided into two halves. They might point to George and state, "All students between George and Alicia are on one team and everyone else is on the other team."

Deck of cards.

As students enter the gym, each receives a playing card. One team of students can be composed of students who selected red cards and another team who selected black cards. Another option would be to have students with hearts and spades work together and those with clubs and diamonds work together.

Numbers.

If students have been assigned a number at the beginning of the year, this will be helpful for selecting teams. Similar to using numbers for placing students into small groups, use numbers for grouping students into large groups or teams. On one day, numbers 1–12 form one team and numbers 13–24 another team. On another day, you might have students with even numbers work together and those with odd numbers work together.

We hope that this section of the chapter has provided you with an adequate number of strategies for grouping students into partners, small groups, and teams. If you notice large

There are many ways to quickly select teams that are equally balanced.

imbalances in ability, you can always be discrete and make minor adjustments to existing teams or small groups. There are many other strategies that teachers can easily invent and incorporate into their practice. We also encourage you to develop your own techniques by completing Thinking Challenge 9.1.

THINKING CHALLENGE 9.1	Describe two strategies for *quickly* selecting partners, small groups, and teams that you believe would be pedagogically appropriate and have not been discussed in this chapter.	
	Strategy #1	**Strategy #2**
Partners		
Small Groups		
Teams		

SELECTING CAPTAINS

Many teachers continue to believe that students acquire leadership abilities as a result of serving in the role of team captain. Although we will not dispute that the practice may have merit, we will advocate that there are some techniques for selecting and using captains that are more appropriate than others.

First, if captains are used, all children should have equal opportunities to be a captain. The teacher, for instance, could select two new captains each week who remain in that role for the duration of the week. By the end of the year, all students will have had an opportunity to be a captain.

Second, the captain should be given leadership responsibilities such as distributing equipment or assisting others. The captain should *not* be allowed to select teams or tell others what to do unless it is in a helping capacity.

Finally, utilize captains to maximize instructional time. This might involve asking captains to set up equipment or help move it from one location to another during transitions. They can even be used as instructional aids. They should not, however, be allowed access to student records or asked to serve in a capacity that might infringe on another student's right to privacy. For example, it would be inappropriate to ask them to record student scores on a fitness test or ask them to return exams.

ORGANIZING EQUIPMENT

An activity that tends to waste an inordinate amount of time is equipment distribution. Although Chapter 7 provided you with information about teaching students routines for obtaining and returning equipment, you have yet to learn how to organize the learning environment so that equipment distribution is safe and expedient. We hope that after reading this chapter, you will understand how much time is wasted on equipment distribution and be confident enough to begin developing your own strategies and shortcuts.

Equipment distribution is something that cannot be avoided, but it can be conducted efficiently. Do you remember how equipment was distributed in your elementary school? We remember waiting in line to obtain a red playground ball. It was a slow process and those at the end of the line usually received those balls that were in the worst condition. Interestingly, the students at the end of the line usually were those who were the lowest skilled and most in need of good equipment.

Advance Preparation

As with most aspects of teaching, when you have planned carefully in advance, you will usually be more effective. In relation to equipment, consider how it can be quickly disseminated to students without having them wait. For certified physical education teachers who teach multiple back-to-back classes, they must often transition from a first-grade class on throwing, to a fifth-grade class on floor hockey, to a kindergarten class on tumbling. This makes equipment distribution difficult, and they must learn to be creative in order to save time. In the case of the classroom teacher, you will not have to teach back-to-back physical education classes, but you will likely be required to share equipment with other teachers. Thus, you may never be entirely sure what equipment will be available when needed and in what condition. If you have access to your own equipment, you will be fortunate. Ask the principal for his/her assistance in locating a safe place for storage. If the only available storage space is in your classroom, ask parents to construct large bags for balls or to donate storage bins for objects like beanbags, small-sized balls, or poly spots.

Dissemination

Stations help make distribution of equipment orderly and quick.

A common mistake made by teachers is that they assume the entire responsibility for equipment distribution and collection. For example, the teacher hurries out to the field to set up the goals for a soccer game. He or she then places students on teams and quickly runs to put the soccer ball into play. At the end of class, students quickly leave the playing field while the teacher hurriedly retrieves the goals and soccer ball. As emphasized in Key Point 9-3, students should be taught to assume responsibility for the equipment they use. This involves assisting the teacher with equipment set-up, distribution, and take down.

Another common mistake is related to the manner in which equipment is distributed. Students are either asked to stand in line and take one piece of equipment at a time, or the teacher disseminates individual pieces of equipment to each student in the class. Below are some options for reducing organization time and increasing engagement time. Can you think of three additional suggestions by completing Thinking Challenge 9.2?

Key Point 9-3

Teachers can help students learn responsibility by asking them to assist with such things as equipment set-up and distribution. This also maximizes available learning time for others.

THINKING CHALLENGE 9.2

List three strategies not mentioned in the chapter for quickly distributing equipment to students.

1.

2.

3.

Captains.

If you utilize the technique described above of selecting weekly captains, they can assist with equipment. If greater numbers of students are needed to help, you can ask for volunteers or assign students. Most will be eager to serve in the capacity of assistant. You will be teaching students to assume responsibility while not becoming resentful for being overly burdened.

Dump and roll.

This simple procedure entails taking a basket or bag of balls and simply dumping them across the length of the floor for students to retrieve as they roll by. The procedure is quick and fair to all students.

Distribute in advance.

Prior to asking students to begin an activity, and preferably before class or while students are engaged in another activity, the teacher strategically places equipment throughout the gym. There may be one bag of balls at each corner of the gymnasium or balls may be placed individually across the length of the gymnasium floor.

Squad distribution.

This strategy involves asking the squad leader or captain to obtain and distribute equipment to his/her squad. It also could entail having individual squads obtain equipment from different locations in the gymnasium or on the playing field. Squad #1 might be assigned to the east corner to retrieve equipment while Squad #2 is assigned to the west corner.

30-second rule.

When students are asked to obtain or return equipment, they usually do so relatively slowly. Most elementary students, however, are eager to become involved in activity and are willing to obtain and return equipment more rapidly if encouraged. In our own teaching, we have used something called the 30-second rule (which can be modified to as little as 10 seconds or to 40 or more seconds depending upon what needs to be accomplished). On the teacher's signal to begin, students quickly obtain or return equipment to its appropriate locations within the time limit specified by the teacher. The teacher counts each number aloud or signals students at key points, such as every 5 or 10 seconds. If equipment is not returned within the desired time, it is redistributed throughout the playing area until students are successfully able to return it within the specified time limit. This activity saves tremendous class time and is enjoyable to most students. It does, however, have to be occasionally practiced such as when students are obtaining or returning equipment more slowly than you might like.

Parent aides.

In many schools where we have observed, one or more parents serve in the role of physical education aides throughout the year. Willing parents arrive at the school prior to physical education class and help the classroom teacher distribute equipment and work with students. Ideally, the same parents serve throughout the entire year so that they learn the routines of the class and how best to help the teachers with tasks like equipment distribution.

Maintenance

Similar to assuming responsibility for the set-up and take-down of equipment, students should also learn to assist with equipment maintenance. Again, captains can be asked to clean off balls or check on a weekly basis to determine if they need to be re-inflated. Individual students can also be asked to report equipment problems to the teacher, such as torn mats, inadequately inflated balls, or leaking beanbags. On occasion, the teacher might ask for volunteers willing to give up free time or stay after school for purposes of periodic equipment maintenance or the cleaning of the equipment room. Most children appreciate the opportunity to spend extra time with the teacher outside of the classroom. Finally, to facilitate engagement time, equipment maintenance should be conducted outside of structured class time.

LESSON TRANSITIONS

Most teachers include several different activity tasks within an individual period of instruction. Although we encourage this practice, particularly because students become bored practicing the same task without additional challenges, it is important to learn how to transition from one activity to another effectively. Great amounts of engaged time are lost when teachers do not have adequate skill for understanding how best to move from an activity like throwing at a target to throwing in pairs. We hope to provide you with some skills for gaining expertise in this instructional behavior.

First, plan in advance. Like every topic covered in this chapter, and as emphasized in Key Point 9-4, planning in advance how to transition from one activity to another is absolutely critical if you intend to reduce time spent in class management. You need to anticipate where students will be located when receiving the next set of instructions, how they will switch equipment, and how they will move from one location to another. If you plan to have them move from an individual activity to a team event, plan in advance how you will appoint teams.

Key Point 9-4

Planning in advance is essential for good time management. Since lesson transitions are a form of management, consider in advance how you can reduce wasted time during transitions.

Second, make sure that students can hear your instructions. Although it seems like common sense, not all teachers are cognizant about whether or not students can hear them. If students do not understand what is expected, such as how to transition to a new activity, they will slow down the entire class. A strategy we have found successful is to give all students five seconds to return to the center circle on the gymnasium floor and to have a seat. This practice ensures that all students are in a location to see and hear the next set of instructions.

Third, avoid equipment distractions. Another problem that slows instruction and transitions is that students become sidetracked by the equipment they may be holding. When we supervise student teachers, we often notice that they will ask students to freeze while they provide instructions necessary for engagement in the next activity. When students are allowed to hold onto basketballs, rackets, or other types of equipment, they are distracted. Equipment accidentally falls from their hands, they are inclined to continue bouncing a

Effective teachers have learned how to transition quickly from one activity to the next.

ball, or they play with the strings of their racket. Even when instructed by teachers not to bounce a ball, several students cannot resist the temptation. Therefore, we have developed strategies for reducing problems in this area. If equipment is not needed for a subsequent activity, students should be given a few seconds to return the equipment to its proper location and quickly have a seat on the center circle. If the equipment is needed for the next activity, students can be asked to leave it in place and return to the circle or to place it on the floor at least two feet behind their back. This ensures that they hear the next set of instructions without distraction.

Fourth, engage in effective teaching behaviors. Activity transitions represent a period of time when students can easily become off-task. They may begin talking to others or playing with equipment in ways that you had not anticipated. Therefore, maintain a back-to-the-wall position so you can observe all students in the class and correct those not transitioning appropriately. Exhibit with-it-ness behaviors so students know you are monitoring their behavior and expect compliance with the established rules for transitioning.

Finally, be aware of the time. It is easy to become distracted when giving instructions. Teachers sometimes encourage unnecessary student questions or spend far too long providing instructions. Students can remember only a limited amount of information, so set and adhere to a time limit for how long you will speak and how much time you will spend in transition. Move students into activity quickly, even if you think they may still have questions. In the majority of cases, their questions will be answered as they become involved in activity. If they still seem confused, briefly stop the activity and quickly clarify the instructions.

SAFETY AND LIABILITY

The most important role of a teacher, in any setting, is to protect students from injury. By taking proactive measures, many potential injuries can be avoided, and children will be more inclined to move because they will not fear for their safety. This section of the chapter will teach you how to establish a safe learning environment, avoid litigation, and respond appropriately when an injury occurs.

Establishing a Safe Learning Environment

Effective teachers recognize how easily injuries can occur and do everything within their power to create a safe environment that is free of potential safety hazards. Many have learned to be cautious as a result of witnessing student injuries or hearing stories from colleagues who were teaching when an injury occurred. Although minor injuries can happen in almost any setting, the nature of physical education and equipment used increases the possibility of injury.

No matter how hard you may try to create a safe environment, some minor injuries are inevitable. For example, it is easy to sprain an ankle when landing after executing a jump shot in basketball, to bump one's head during a collision while running with others in general space, or to incur a minor bruise as a result of sliding into home plate. Further, children are more prone to injuries than adults because they are less cautious when moving. They do not anticipate dangerous situations in advance or have the same instincts as adults for avoiding an unsafe situation. Therefore, since the teacher is more knowledgeable about potential safety hazards, it is the teacher's responsibility to be proactive and create a safe environment. What follows are suggestions that we hope will reduce the possibility of both major and minor injury.

Anticipate dangerous situations in advance.

As adults, we have learned which environmental situations are likely to be unsafe. For this reason, parents often forbid children from jumping on furniture, wrestling in the house, using knives, or running through the yard with sharp objects like sticks. As Key Point 9-5 illustrates, as a teacher you are responsible for ensuring the safety of those you have been

Key Point 9-5

Teachers are accountable for the safety of the children in their classes and responsible for keeping them from harm.

charged to educate. You assume the role of protector while children are in your custody. It is your obligation to anticipate potential safety hazards and prevent injury from those hazards. Below are a few guidelines:

- Teach children to act in a safe manner while engaged in activity. For example, remind them that they need to be aware of others who are also moving in general space. Tell them to use caution when landing so they don't step on another child's foot or a ball that might be rolling across the floor. Frequently remind them to use caution when engaged in activity.
- Ask children to immediately inform you of any situation they believe could be unsafe.
- Have discussions about safety and teach children to anticipate danger.
- Once you discover an unsafe situation, immediately stop the activity or remove the safety hazard.
- Do not allow children to engage in activities where severe injuries are known to occur. For this reason, many schools have banned equipment like trampolines and do not permit students to execute flips during gymnastics. In fact, many school districts throughout the nation have outlawed activities like traditional dodge ball because of the safety hazards associated with being injured by playground balls that are forcefully thrown at human targets.

Establish and firmly reinforce safety rules.

Children become excited when engaged in activity and often forget about safety. In order to prevent injuries, teachers need to provide rules that are strictly reinforced. A few suggestions for developing rules include:

- Prior to allowing students to engage in activity, review the safety rules of that activity.
- If children do not follow safety rules, there needs to be an immediate consequence such as removal from the activity.

- Teach rules related to particular activities.
- Select a teaching style that promotes safety when teaching dangerous activities.

Complete Thinking Challenge 9.3 by listing the specific safety rules you would enforce in your classroom.

THINKING CHALLENGE 9.3	Describe three specific safety rules you would enforce when teaching each of the following activities:

Tag Games
1.
2.
3.

Tumbling
1.
2.
3.

Floor Hockey
1.
2.
3.

Soccer
1.
2.
3.

Provide and require students to wear protective equipment.

There are some activities that have such strong potential for danger that children should be allowed to engage in them only when wearing protective gear. Below are a few examples of rules you may wish to enforce:

- Helmets are required when riding a bike.
- Children must wear shoes *and* socks when engaged in activity. Also encourage them to wear appropriate clothing like pants or shorts under skirts to class. (Since most elementary schools do not have areas for children to change clothes, they will wear the same outfit for physical education as they wear in the home classroom.)
- Helmets are required for batters and catchers when playing baseball or softball.
- Knee pads are encouraged when playing volleyball.
- Life jackets are necessary when canoeing while on a class camping trip.

Conduct regular safety inspections.

Not only do teachers need to learn how to anticipate hazards, they also need to regularly inspect equipment and facilities to ensure safety. By engaging in preventive measures such as those described here, the likelihood of injury will be reduced.

- Inspect playing field for glass, potholes, and unsafe debris.
- Be sure that gymnastics and other similar equipment are tightly locked in place (e.g., parallel bars and legs on the balance beam need to be tightly locked so they do not collapse). Mats should be placed in and around potentially dangerous areas such as underneath a balance beam *and* around the leg supports.

Teachers must carefully examine the physical environment in which children participate. A dangerous situation that may not be present on one day may make itself visible the next.

- Inspect equipment like gymnastic mats to be sure they are not torn.
- Make sure the gymnasium floor is clean and free of dirt and debris.
- Keep equipment in good working condition by conducting periodic maintenance repairs and discarding unsafe equipment like cracked bats.

Create a safe environment.

Although children will gradually learn to be cautious, the teacher must assume that they do not have the skill to foresee danger and should proactively create a safe environment in anticipation of injury. A few guidelines include:

- When teaching dangerous activities like batting or swinging a golf club, require students to perform in a particular location in the activity area that other students are not allowed to enter. For example, designate one area of the playing field for practice of that activity. Allow only a handful of students to practice dangerous skills while you actively supervise. Other students can be engaged in safer activities like throwing and catching until it is their turn.
- Discourage students from standing in unsafe locations such as under a basketball hoop while others are shooting baskets.
- Allow children to throw and catch in one direction only.
- Establish rules related to swinging objects. For example, do not allow children to swing floor hockey sticks above knee level when engaged in game play.

Avoid Litigation

Compared to other nations, the United States is a relatively litigious society. In other words, individuals in our society are inclined to sue for monetary compensation if they have been injured and believe others are responsible or could have prevented the injury. In the case of a parent suing a teacher or school, the teacher is disadvantaged because jurors tend to sympathize with injured children and may believe that school districts carry adequate insurance coverage. Although teachers should be legally protected by the district in which they are employed, we recommend that you purchase supplementary liability coverage that is affordable and usually offered by professional teacher associations. This additional coverage will help to protect your personal assets from being taken in the unfortunate case of losing a lawsuit. Again, the liability coverage and legal expenses provided by most districts should be sufficient, but in order to protect oneself against a catastrophic injury that involves negligence, we recommend additional coverage.

There are guidelines which expert witnesses in physical education have used as a means of determining negligence. Knowledge of these guidelines can assist teachers in planning safe activities and help them to avoid future litigation. Below are a few useful guidelines (Gray, 1995; Hart & Ritson, 2002):

1. The activity should have a "legitimate" educational purpose.
2. The activity should not be inherently dangerous (e.g., running on a wet outdoor surface).
3. Participants should be appropriately matched for such things as size, weight, and skill level.
4. Students should have the physical and emotional maturity to participate in the activity.
5. Children should be warned about potential risks and how to avoid injury.
6. Correct instruction should be provided.
7. The teacher should have taught the physical skills necessary for engagement in the activity.
8. The student should be properly supervised.
9. The equipment and facilities should be safe and in good condition.

Responding to an Injury

Learning how to appropriately respond to an injury is important, and we encourage all future teachers to enroll in first aid and CPR courses offered through your university, YMCA, local fire department, or the American Red Cross.

Serious versus minor injuries.

Because children in elementary school have a tendency to cry when physically or emotionally injured, it is sometimes difficult for a teacher to accurately assess whether an injury occurred or if a child is crying because his or her feelings were bruised. If in doubt, always act as though an injury was serious. We also would recommend that in the beginning of the year, when you are teaching students the rules and routines of the classroom, you teach them how to accurately report the degree to which they have been injured. Encourage them to be honest with you about whether an injury is physical or primarily emotional. For some children, this will be difficult. They will react the same way when they experience a minor injury as they do when they are embarrassed or emotionally hurt. For others, you may need to be particularly observant after they are injured because they may not want to report their injury to you for fear of being withdrawn from the activity.

All teachers should have training in first aid and CPR.

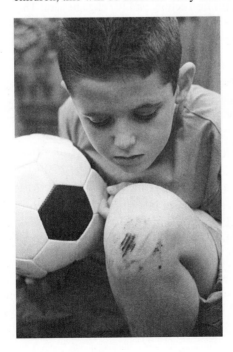

Responding to minor injuries.

Most teachers will learn to quickly distinguish between injuries that are minor and those that are more serious. When you initially begin teaching, you will have the tendency to stop instructing and immediately tend to the needs of anyone who is crying or has been injured. As you gain experience, you will learn that you can be empathetic and manage a minor injury without disrupting the lesson. If, for instance, a child has fallen or collided with a classmate, they may immediately begin to cry. After a quick assessment you should be able to determine the degree to which they have been injured. If they are crying, but you believe the injury is minor, simply tell them you are sorry this happened to them and invite them to sit down until they are feeling better. In the majority of cases, students will sit for a few moments and then quickly become re-engaged in activity. If a child does not wish to reenter the class, you may need to assess whether the injury may be more serious than you initially anticipated and take the appropriate action (see Key Point 9-6).

Key Point 9-6

In the case of a serious emergency, immediately call 911 and begin care for the injured person. Enroll in an American Red Cross course to learn appropriate first-aid and CPR procedures. This training will benefit you in both your professional and personal lives.

Responding to serious injuries.
When an injury is serious, immediately call 911 and begin care for the victim. When teaching students routines at the beginning of the year, one routine they should learn is how to respond in case of an emergency. This may mean that they discontinue all activity and remain silent until they receive further instructions from you. Your school should also have procedures in place for how to respond to emergencies and situations that involve blood. Talk to your principal about these procedures. If you have the luxury of having an intercom, phone system, or walkie talkie at your disposal, you may need to use these tools to obtain assistance. Complete Thinking Challenge 9.4.

THINKING CHALLENGE 9.4	Write a brief paragraph that you could use as a script for instructing children in your class about how they should respond when a classmate becomes injured.

Summary

Class time in physical education can be divided into the four components of (a) waiting, (b) management, (c) instruction, and (d) engagement. This chapter focused on providing you with information for reducing waiting and management time and increasing engagement time (see Box 9.1). Children who are not waiting in line for a turn are less likely to

DO AND DON'T CHECKLIST

Do	Don't
☐ eliminate wait time	☐ allow children to develop bad habits such as returning equipment slowly
☐ reduce time spent managing students	
☐ allow all students to assume leadership positions throughout the year	☐ permit children to select their own teams
☐ be proactive in relation to safety	☐ allow students to always work with the same partner
☐ become educated about treating injury and administering CPR by enrolling for a course sponsored by the American Red Cross.	☐ let children play with equipment while you are giving directions
	☐ assume a child who is not crying may not be seriously injured.

become disruptive and will have greater opportunity to learn because they are engaged in activity. Further, if teachers acquire techniques that facilitate quickly placing students into groups, effectively disseminating and returning equipment, and quickly transitioning from one activity to another, students will have greater likelihood of meeting the federal guidelines for being physically active.

Finally, teachers are responsible for providing students with safe movement activities, a hazard-free learning environment, adequate equipment, and protective gear. Those who fail to adequately instruct students about safety, who introduce students to an activity before they are ready, or who allow them to engage in unsafe behaviors, expose their students to injury and themselves to litigation.

Review Activities

1. Select a strategy and defend why you believe it is the most effective means of grouping students.
2. List the ways in which you would use captains in your classroom.
3. Brainstorm with a partner all safety procedures you would take when teaching students how to swing a bat.
4. Discuss the challenges you may encounter when trying to transition from one activity to another.
5. List five ways you would defend yourself if you were sued after a child was injured during a game of tag.
6. Describe your beliefs concerning how a teacher should respond to a child who consistently cries every time he or she falls.

References

Centers for Disease Control and Prevention (1997). Guidelines for school and community programs to promote lifelong physical activity among young people. *Morbidity and Mortality Weekly Report, 46* (No. RR-6), 1–36.

Gray, G. R. (1995). Safety tips from the expert witness. *Journal of Physical Education, Recreation and Dance, 66*(1), 18–21.

Hart, J. E., & Ritson, R. J. (2002). *Liability and safety in physical education and sport* (2nd ed.). Reston, VA: National Association for Sport and Physical Education.

National Association for Sport and Physical Education & American Heart Association (2010). *2010 Shape of the nation report: Status of physical education in the USA.* Reston, VA: National Association for Sport and Physical Education.

Siedentop, D., & Tannehill, D. (2000). *Developing teaching skills in physical education* (4th ed.). Mountain View, CA: Mayfield.

U.S. Department of Health and Human Services. (2000). *School health index for physical activity and healthy eating: A self-assessment and planning guide for elementary school.* Atlanta, GA: Centers for Disease Control.

Chapter **Ten**

Preventive Class Management and Discipline

The primary concern of most new teachers relates to establishing a respectful class climate that is relatively free of discipline problems. This concern stems from the simple fact that novice teachers feel unprepared for entering the classroom and dealing with unruly students. Since the exact nature of discipline problems cannot be anticipated in advance, new teachers are apprehensive about what they might encounter and which discipline techniques are most likely to be effective for solving the immediate problem and avoiding similar future situations. They worry, and rightly so, that failure to create a respectful learning environment early in the year does not bode well for what they might encounter during the remainder of the year.

The purpose of this chapter is to provide you with strategies for preventing the emergence of disciplinary infractions and techniques for appropriately addressing them when they do occur. You will learn about those problems that you are most likely to encounter and which strategies have the greatest probability of success. Although it would be impossible to prepare you for every situation you might experience, we hope you will acquire basic principles to guide you in determining how to respond. Some of the most useful knowledge, however, will be the result of experiencing real life situations. Until you enter the classroom as a teacher, any hypothetical situations that you discuss during teacher education will feel like insufficient preparation. We encourage you, however, not to worry too

Most children enjoy physical education and are eager to follow the rules.

much. Very few teachers leave the profession out of an inability to manage students. If you can remember the basic principles introduced here, and acquire some useful practical experience under the supervision of an effective cooperating teacher, we have confidence in your ability to effectively confront whatever situations might arise.

As you read this chapter, we hope that you will keep in mind that effectively handling discipline problems at the elementary level is usually much simpler than at the middle and high school levels. Although the content matter of physical education and the environment in which it is conducted will produce challenges that you may not experience in the smaller confines of your classroom, remember that physical education is a favorite subject of many elementary students. Therefore, students will typically be more eager to become involved in an activity than they will to cause problems. Those that do arise are often the result of children's excitement. That is not a bad problem to have!

PREVENTIVE CLASS MANAGEMENT

Preventive class management and discipline enforcement are considered to be managerial tasks of the teacher. The best weapon against misbehavior is to anticipate potential problems in advance and act decisively to prevent their emergence. Establishing class routines, setting and enforcing rules, holding high expectations for a positive class climate, and positive reinforcement will increase the likelihood that you will be successful. Complete Thinking Challenge 10.1.

THINKING CHALLENGE 10.1	What are five techniques you can use to create a positive class climate in both the home classroom and gymnasium?
	1.
	2.
	3.
	4.
	5.

A primary reason for using preventive strategies and immediately stopping inappropriate behavior when it initially emerges is that once one student breaks the rules or becomes overly rambunctious, other students will have a tendency to follow this child's lead (see Key Point 10-1). It is better to quickly stop the inappropriate actions of one than to have to manage an entire class of misbehaving students. Interestingly, however, many new teachers are reluctant to clearly emphasize their expectations and enforce the rules of the classroom. They are concerned that if they are perceived by students to be strict, that they will be unpopular and disliked. Think back, however, on your own experience as a student. Were the teachers who had orderly classrooms actually those who were disliked? Contrary to what you may think at the moment, it is likely that those teachers who were firm but fair were some of the most respected individuals in the school. Those who conceded control of the classroom to students were probably laughed at behind their backs and not respected. In all probability, you did not learn as much from them as from those who effectively managed the classroom.

Key Point 10-1

Once a student breaks the rules or becomes overly rambunctious, other students will have a tendency to engage in similar behaviors. It is very important to stop individual instances of misbehavior before other students also begin acting inappropriately.

Ask yourself if being a friend to students is what teaching is about. Friendship, in our opinion, is a give and take situation where two or more parties equally contribute to a relationship. Can an elementary child effectively serve the teacher in this role? The answer is an unequivocal, "No." Can teachers be friendly and kind to students? "Absolutely yes." In fact, you will be expected by children, parents, and administrators to demonstrate behaviors that are perceived as kind, friendly, warm, engaging, and caring. Those behaviors are what often distinguish teachers as particularly exceptional. You will, however, also be expected to maintain a professional relationship that will require you to set expectations and enforce rules even when it might be difficult. You are not a friend, you are a teacher.

If you hope to minimize discipline problems, your best strategy is to engage in preventive class management. When students know the routines of the classroom, understand the rules, consistently experience consequences when rules are broken, and are held to high behavioral standards, the potential for discipline problems to emerge is reduced. Therefore, develop protocols for your classroom.

Establishing Routines

In Chapter 7 you learned that effective teachers establish routines in their classroom. These include such things as teaching children how to enter and exit the activity area, how to obtain and return equipment, and how to respond to start and stop signals. Since that topic has already been covered extensively, we will not be redundant and repeat that information. Nevertheless, we must reinforce the criticality of routines for reducing discipline problems. Without routines, expect to spend a considerable amount of time engaged in managerial tasks.

Setting and Enforcing Rules

As highlighted in Key Point 10-2, in order to function well in society, individuals need to understand cultural norms and the boundaries that guide behavior. Similarly, children need to understand teacher expectations and limits of behavior. Do you remember the rules that you were expected to follow in elementary school? Were those rules unique to the individual classroom, or were they the same throughout the entire school?

Key Point 10-2

In order to function well in society, individuals need to understand cultural norms and the boundaries that guide behavior. Similarly, children need to understand teacher expectations and limits of behavior.

School-wide discipline

An increasing number of schools throughout the United States have implemented a system whereby all students in the school are expected to adhere to the same rules. They follow the same rules in the classroom as they do in the lunch room, gymnasium, art room, and on the school bus. The rules are clearly communicated in both written and oral form, are posted in individual classrooms and throughout the school, and are reinforced by teachers in the classroom, during announcements, and even during school assemblies.

In the case of many schools, there is a universal set of consequences for breaking the rules. Of course, variances in consequences often exist between the upper and lower elementary grades and among individual teachers. For example, teachers may be more patient with younger children than they are with those who are older. One teacher may be more lenient in allowing students to deviate from the rules than another teacher.

Rules should be clearly posted in all areas of the school.

The primary advantage to a school-wide system is that all students understand the rules and consequences. They do not need to learn a new set of rules as they progress from one grade level to the next or move from one subject area like physical education to another like art. The rules are also clearly communicated to parents.

Establishing rules.

Although school-wide discipline is popular, there are probably an equal number of schools throughout the country where individual teachers set the rules for their individual classrooms. It is acknowledged in these schools that teachers should have the ultimate decision-making authority for their classrooms and that some subject matter areas, like physical education, art, and music, may require special rules. Although there may be a few common school rules, teachers are given the responsibility for establishing the particular rules for their classroom. Complete Thinking Challenge 10.2.

THINKING CHALLENGE 10.2	Use the space below to develop a set of rules for teaching physical education that could be used with all elementary-aged students. 1. 2. 3. 4. 5.

When establishing rules, there are a few important guidelines to follow. By adhering to these principles, you are likely to have greater student compliance.

- Rules should be succinct. In fact, five or fewer rules are best. It is difficult for elementary-aged children to remember a lengthy list of complex behavioral rules. As a means of reduction, collapse a variety of similar rules into only one rule. For example, a simple rule like, "Respect yourself, others, and the equipment" is easy to remember and covers a number of different categories. See Box 10.1 for an example of rules you may wish to

Physical Education Rules   Box 10.1

1. Respect yourself, others, and the equipment
2. Demonstrate courtesy by listening when someone else is talking
3. Stop when you hear the signal
4. Try your best
5. Always remember to be safe

implement when teaching physical education. Compare this list to the one you created in Thinking Challenge 10.2.

- Clearly post the rules in the classroom.
- Regularly remind students of the rules during the initial days of class and periodically repeat them throughout the year, particularly when you begin to notice increasing incidents of student misbehavior.
- Positively reinforce instances when students are adhering to the rules, especially in the beginning of the year.
- Use positive language when stating rules.

Provide examples.

As you explain the basic rules to students, provide them with examples. Since multiple rules may have been collapsed into a single category, be sure that students understand the breadth of expectation covered by a single rule. For example when introducing students to the rule "Respect yourself, others, and the equipment," inform them that this requires them to:

1. Be patient with themselves
2. Treat others with kindness (no fighting or bullying)
3. Take good care of equipment (no sitting on playground balls, no kicking volleyballs, no intentionally throwing equipment onto the gymnasium rafters)

Enforcing rules.

In the next section of this chapter you will be provided with sample consequences for breaking the rules. The most important element for maintaining a well-behaved classroom is that rules must be consistently enforced with a consequence. If a teacher, for example, states that he or she will enforce a consequence if a rule is broken, that consequence *must* be immediately and consistently enforced.

Think back to your childhood and the rules that were established by your parents or the parents of friends. There probably were instances when you were able to maneuver around the rules in order to get what you wanted. Perhaps you cried, screamed, or pleaded until your parents gave in to your wishes. If they threatened to punish you but did not follow through, you learned that you could execute power and push the limits of the rules by engaging in certain behaviors that caused your parents to concede to your desires.

As a teacher, you do not have the time or energy to allow students to massage the rules to meet their desires. If, however, you resort to leniency because you dislike enforcing consequences, children will learn that you can be manipulated. Children are extremely intelligent and quickly learn how to gain control. If you desire an orderly classroom yet do not consistently enforce the rules, you will probably have a less enjoyable teaching experience than you otherwise might. Remember, enforcing rules can be one means of demonstrating that you care about your students.

Adhere to the "five C's" of behavior management.

In a useful article, it is suggested that teaching appropriate behavior can be encouraged by a simple five-step plan (Almeida, 1995). Specifically, teachers are encouraged to:

- Be *clear* about expectations
- Enforce *consequences* for breaking rules
- Be *consistent*
- Demonstrate *caring* toward all children
- Demonstrate a willingness to *change* by modifying curriculum and routines when necessary

Expectations for a Positive Class Climate

Teachers often tell students that their classroom is designed to promote a positive environment for everyone. In reality, however, students learn quickly through the hidden curriculum that school is an environment that favors children who are popular and skilled. When teachers inform students that kindness and respect are expected but do not enforce that expectation, they learn that behaviors such as bullying are tolerable.

The vast majority of teachers are concerned about promoting a fair and equitable learning environment for everyone. It is impossible for them to observe and detect every instance of name calling, disrespect, or intolerance. The fact, however, remains that schools are rife with incidents of bullying and peer pressure to conform. While many students experience success and enjoyment while engaged in physical education or recess, others struggle to maintain their composure until they can return to the smaller confines of the classroom that they perceive to be better supervised.

Bullying in the United States is a problem plaguing every state and most schools. In fact, as Key Point 10-3 indicates, it has been estimated that up to 50 percent of all children have been bullied at some point in time during school and that 10 percent experience it on a regular basis (American Academy of Child & Adolescent Psychiatry, 2008). Unfortunately, the negative effects of bullying are witnessed regularly in news reports of massive school slayings and have long-term consequences for those who experience its negative effects (Leff, Power, & Goldstein, 2004).

Key Point 10-3

Up to 50 percent of all children have been bullied at some point in time during school and 10 percent experience it on a regular basis (American Academy of Child & Adolescent Psychiatry, 2008).

Given the often competitive nature of physical education, it is an environment that is conducive to intolerance and bullying. Although children can be incredibly gentle and caring individuals, they also can be mean spirited and unkind to others. During relay races, for example, those students who are high skilled sometimes become so frustrated with those who have lower abilities that they begin to name call and make fun of the person they believe caused their team to lose. Over time, hostility and frustration builds up in other environments. Eventually, the individual experiences regular instances of bullying-type behaviors from classmates.

Students need to be taught how to exhibit acts of kindness in a physical activity environment.

Again, we recognize that it would be very difficult to prevent all forms of name calling and bullying. We remember only too well instances of bullying that we observed on the playground and in the gymnasium as children. Teachers, however, must make every reasonable effort to ensure that bullying does not occur in their classroom or under their supervision. In addition, we strongly encourage teachers to become increasingly responsible for proactively establishing environments where bullying and intolerance become impossible to implement. Below are a few examples for how to create a positive class climate for everyone:

- Publicly praise students for acts of kindness
- Insist that everyone deserves to be treated with respect and that instances of cruel behavior toward others will have negative consequences
- Plan special events that encourage kindness (such as a day when students must exhibit acts of kindness to five people they know and five whom they do not know)
- Carefully observe students when supervising them in the classroom, gymnasium, and on the playing field by maintaining back-to-the-wall posture and with-it-ness
- Teach students to discourage others from bullying-type behaviors by asking them to intervene when classmates are being treated unkindly
- Do not group students together who have especially adversarial relationships
- Avoid planning events, such as relay races, that are likely to promote bullying

Finally, do not ignore instances of bullying because you believe a child deserves to be bullied. Stay in touch with resources that relate to bullying and may help reduce its emergence. Many states, like Massachusetts, maintain statistics about bullying and other health risks that you may find interesting: http://www.doe.mass.edu/cnp/hprograms/yrbs. As incomprehensible as it may seem, there are teachers who subtly encourage acts of bullying toward some children by turning their back when they are being teased or harassed. Remember, all children deserve to be treated fairly. They are little people who will eventually become adults. They need to learn to function in a society that is composed of many different types of people. How they are regarded today certainly will have an impact on how they behave and perceive themselves tomorrow. Complete Thinking Challenge 10.3.

THINKING CHALLENGE 10.3	Describe how you would reduce incidents of bullying in each of the following environments:
	Classroom during a physical activity break
	1.
	2.
	3.
	Gymnasium during physical education
	1.
	2.
	3.
	Playground during recess
	1.
	2.
	3.

Positive Reinforcement

A technique used by effective teachers is to positively reinforce good behavior when it is observed. It is believed that children have a desire to please. In most cases, positive reinforcement helps children to feel good about their performance and creates a desire in them to continue to please the teacher. Interestingly, some children need attention so badly from the teacher that they act inappropriately in order to be noticed. The theory behind using positive reinforcement is that students who need attention will be just as likely to respond to positive attention from the teacher as they do to negative attention. By praising students for appropriate behavior, they will be less inclined to engage in negative behavior (Graham, Holt/Hale, & Parker, 2004; Siedentop & Tannehill, 2000). A few strategies for positively reinforcing students are described below.

School-wide reinforcement.

Those schools that utilize a school-wide discipline approach sometimes offer incentives to all children in the school. This facilitates school cohesion and encourages students to work together toward a common goal. When individuals or an entire class of students behave particularly well, they are given a token, such as a strip of paper that they can link with strips of paper received by other students. Once linked, the individual strips form a paper chain. The chain begins slowly at one end of the school with the goal of reaching the other end of the school within a specified period of time. Once children accomplish the goal, they are rewarded. In the case of one school, the principal offered to shave his head and host a school-wide pizza party when the chain made its way across the school. He kept his promise!

Any host of small incentives can be used to reach a goal. For example, students can be awarded some type of token, like a marble, that they place in a large jug. When the marbles reach the top of the jug, everyone receives a reward.

Some schools remove a specified number of tokens for inappropriate behavior. For example, strips of paper would be removed from the paper chain or marbles would be taken from the jug. Although this technique can be effective, we have also seen its negative effects and, therefore, recommend that the allotting of tokens be used exclusively to reward students, not to punish them.

Individual reinforcement.

Similar to the school-wide approach, teachers can reward individual students for good behavior. In some cases, students may be given a special privilege such as serving as line leader or captain. In other cases, students are given a material item such as a jump rope. In still other cases, students receive tokens that they can save to "purchase" a special item like a playground ball from the teacher.

Teach internal motivation.

Since accumulated research overwhelmingly supports that intrinsic motivation, such as wanting to participate appropriately in physical education for the pure sense of enjoyment, not for purposes of receiving a reward, is the preferred method of motivation, it is recommended that children learn to be internally motivated (Standage, Duda, & Ntoumanis, 2005). As stressed in Key Point 10-4, although rewards may prove to be effective for initially establishing good behavior and full participation in the gymnasium, teachers are encouraged to gradually wean students from external rewards and help them to participate appropriately because it feels right, not because they earn a material object.

Key Point 10-4

Teachers are encouraged to gradually wean students from external rewards and help them learn to be intrinsically motivated.

Non-verbal praise can be highly effective at promoting appropriate behavior.

Verbal and non-verbal praise.

When children do something right, particularly in the beginning of the year, and especially if it involves a behavior the teacher is working hard to promote, verbal or non-verbal recognition is highly appropriate. In some cases, teachers may wish to praise a student publicly, thus reinforcing to everyone the appropriate behavior. In other cases, the teacher may believe it is more appropriate to praise the child individually. In either case, simple gestures such as a handshake, nod of the head, or wink of the eye can be tremendously rewarding to students. Words of praise such as, "Great job," "Way to go," "Does everyone see how nicely Tanisha and Roy are sharing," can be equally rewarding.

Individual teacher time.

Since most students enjoy the opportunity to spend individual time with the teacher, students can be rewarded with an opportunity to help a teacher create a bulletin board, serve as an assistant, or eat lunch together. Rewards such as this are free, enable a teacher and student to develop a closer bond, and help teachers to understand their students better. There also are some students who receive relatively little attention at home. Behaving appropriately in order to spend additional time with the teacher may be a tremendous incentive for a child who requires greater individual attention. In fact, we have personally observed a situation where a child with severe emotional difficulties was provided with extra one-on-one teacher time and was ultimately invited to serve as an assistant to the teacher. The change in his behavior was drastic. He received the attention he desperately needed, but in a positive way, while simultaneously improving his behavior. Complete Thinking Challenge 10.4.

THINKING CHALLENGE 10.4	List one positive and one negative reaction that you have about each of the following techniques:		
	Technique	**Positive Reaction**	**Negative Reaction**
	School-wide Reinforcement		
	Individual Reinforcement		
	Teach Internal Motivation		
	Verbal and Non-verbal Praise		
	Individual Teacher Time		

DISCIPLINE

As previously mentioned, inexperienced teachers often struggle with discipline. They find it very difficult to reprimand and punish students. This is largely due to a personal need to be perceived favorably, not as a result of educational research that demonstrates it is inappropriate to discipline students. It is unfortunate when teachers do not discipline because they fear that they will no longer be liked. Remember, those who are most respected are often those who have orderly classrooms.

Although the vast majority of new teachers have an awakening at some point in the year where they ultimately recognize the need for discipline, it is much easier when they can begin the year by clearly communicating rules and enforcing consequences. It is confusing to children when they receive mixed messages. Ultimately, they are much better served when they learn the rules and norms of the classroom immediately from the first day of school. Changing the rules mid-way through the year is difficult for both teachers and students.

This next section of the chapter will address how to establish and implement appropriate consequences. Before you read further, think about those consequences that you believe are most appropriate for elementary-aged children and complete Thinking Challenge 10.5.

THINKING CHALLENGE 10.5	Develop a progressive list of consequences that you would employ when students break the rules. Ideally, the consequences that you implement in the gymnasium or on the playing field should be the same as those you employ in the classroom. 1. 2. 3. 4. 5.

Establishing Consequences

As emphasized in Key Point 10-5, children are best served when the consequences for rule infractions are clearly established and consistently enforced. The guidelines below were developed to assist you in developing consequences that are fair, easy to implement, and effective in eliminating inappropriate behavior.

Key Point 10-5

Children will be better served and less confused when teachers clearly communicate the consequences for rule infractions and consistently enforce the rules.

Common consequences.

As emphasized already, children will be better behaved when they understand the rules and consequences of the learning environment. Although some consequences cannot be determined in advance, students profit from having a relatively clear understanding about what will happen if they break the rules. The following consequences have been proven to be effective for many teachers:

- *Warning*. When students misbehave, they should immediately be given a warning. Although we prefer to warn children privately, there are occasions when a public reprimand, either in the form of a verbal statement or non-verbal signal, is necessary. For example, if a student continues to talk while you are talking, you might need to remind

Sometimes a simple conversation with a student can stop disruptive behavior.

the child that only one person speaks at a time. If a child is engaged in dangerous behavior across the gym, you may need to quickly issue a loud verbal reprimand to prevent that child from becoming injured. If a child is getting overly rambunctious when working with a partner, you may need to look sternly at that individual.

- *Time-out.* If misbehavior continues after an initial warning, a child should be given an immediate time-out. The individual needs to leave the activity area and sit in a pre-determined location of the gymnasium or playing area where he or she will not interfere with other students and can think about their misbehavior. This is a highly effective consequence for elementary-aged students because they enjoy participating in physical activity. We recommend an initial time-out of five minutes. At the end of the five minutes, simply invite the student to re-enter the activity.

- *Additional time-out or removal.* Some children have a tendency to break the rules more often than others. If the same child has been given a previous warning and subsequent time-out, yet they continue to misbehave once they re-enter the activity area, you must decide whether to give them another time-out or to remove them from activity for the remainder of the class. If the second infraction is minor, and is not related to the first infraction, a second time-out may be appropriate. If the second infraction is more serious, or if the child continues to use the same inappropriate behavior that resulted in their initial removal from activity, you may wish to have that individual sit out for the remainder of the class.

- *Remove privileges.* When time-outs are not successful, teachers might find that taking away privileges is very effective. Taking away the opportunity to attend a special event or to participate in a highly regarded class activity may prove effective. We would, however, caution teachers against taking away physical education opportunities when the child's misbehavior occurred while engaged in another subject like science, reading, or math. Physical education is equally as important as these other subjects, and removing a child's opportunity to learn in physical education because of misbehavior at some other point in the school day is wrong and has negative implications for maintaining good health.

- *Contact parents.* Children who continue to create a disruptive presence in the classroom interfere with their own learning and the learning of other students. If strategies such as warnings, time-outs, and removal of privileges are ineffective, parents need to be contacted and asked to intervene. Some teachers ask children to write a letter to their parents (that must be signed by them and returned to the teacher) describing what they did wrong. This works well because it forces children to contemplate their behavior and is a good writing exercise. Other teachers would prefer to call parents themselves to discuss the problem. In most cases, parents will be responsive when contacted by the teacher. If they are not helpful, however, you will save yourself time and aggravation by not complaining about their lack of support but by trying to locate another strategy that will work with that child.

- *Conference with parents.* Asking parents to schedule an appointment to discuss their child's behavior is another effective technique. Many parents are disturbed that their child's behavior warrants a conference, and, as a result, they will take a more proactive role in promoting positive behavior from that child in the future. Once you have an opportunity to speak individually with parents, and if you believe that you have their support, you may invite the child to attend the last portion of the conference. Please note, however, that since both parents work in many families, a conference may need to be scheduled after work hours.

- *Meeting with the principal.* As a last resort, you may need to discuss a child's inappropriate behavior with the principal. You can either send the child to the principal to explain his or her behavior, or you can meet with the principal individually to strategize how to solve the problem. We suggest the principal as a last resort for two primary reasons. First, you do not want the child to fear the principal but to perceive that individual as someone who facilitates the educational environment of the school. Second, you do not want to send the message to the child or the principal that you are incapable of handling problems that occur in your classroom. The principal is an incredibly busy individual and should be asked to intervene only when other strategies have failed.

Implementing Consequences

Every behavior that a teacher exhibits sends a message to students. Before a teacher acts, he or she needs to consider the likely outcome of the action. As you gain experience, you will develop a repertoire of reactions to situations that become second nature. By contemplating the guidelines below in advance of a discipline problem, you will have better odds of responding in the most appropriate way.

Don't spend excessive time addressing misbehavior.

Inexperienced teachers have a tendency to spend too much time addressing a behavioral infraction during class. In doing so, they are providing attention to the misbehaving student while simultaneously taking away from the learning time of those who are adhering to the rules. It is better to quickly address the misbehavior and ignore the student until they are either effectively re-integrated into the activity after a time-out or until you can personally speak with that individual outside of class.

Always maintain a calm demeanor.

There will be occasions when you will be confronted with situations that are particularly troublesome. On some days you may have less patience than usual, or a student may irritate you to the point where you believe that you will lose your composure. Not only will you later regret having done so, but you will also be sending a message to that student and others in class that you probably do not want to send. If you believe that you are close to losing your temper, take a deep breath or walk away from the situation for a few moments. Another strategy is to tell the student that you will handle the situation at the end of class.

Inform the student what he or she did wrong.

Before or after disciplining children, always inform them of what they did incorrectly. If you fail to do so, there will be occasions when they will be confused as to why they are being punished. In some cases, children will actually believe they are being punished for something other than what you believe they did wrong.

Catch good behavior.

After a child has been disciplined, try to observe their performance for instances of good behavior that you can reinforce and praise. You do not want them to perceive that they receive more negative reinforcement from you than they do positive.

After a child has been punished, praise him or her for subsequent good behavior.

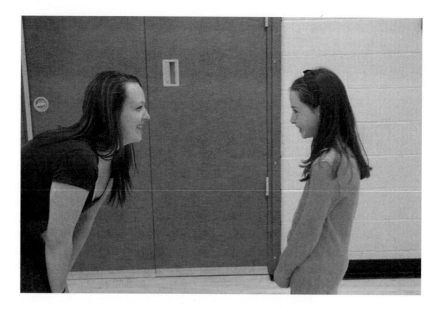

For every negative situation, create a positive one.

Teachers in some schools are confronted with discipline problems more than teachers in others. While those in the latter group are fortunate, those in the former can quickly experience burnout. One strategy for remaining positive about your job is to recognize good behavior just as frequently as you correct poor behavior. For example, for every negative phone call to a parent, make a positive one to another parent.

Avoid public embarrassment.

Just as you do not like to be publicly embarrassed, no child wants to be publicly corrected. Whenever possible, communicate a warning to a child quietly and in a manner that cannot be overheard by others. The misbehaving child will appreciate this strategy and may be more inclined to meet your expectations in the future. Of course, this is not always possible or even desirable. There might be instances when you must publicly correct a child. When you have an opportunity to be discrete, however, we encourage you to do so.

Do not punish the class for the actions of one.

Some teachers use peer pressure as an effective strategy for reducing misbehavior. They might punish the entire class for the actions of only one or a handful of children. This truly is not fair to those children who are behaving appropriately, and we highly recommend that you do not employ this strategy in your teaching. Children who behave properly resent this teacher behavior, and rightly so!

Make the punishment fit the crime.

Those consequences that are most effective are usually those that are designed to fit the crime. If, for example, children are abusing the equipment, an appropriate consequence is to have them remain after school to help inflate the balls or clean the equipment room. If children are throwing trash, an appropriate consequence is to have them remove trash from the playground. If they are unkind to other children, ask them to write a paper about the negative outcomes of treating other children poorly. Children will learn more from consequences that fit the crime than from those that do not.

Never physically harm a child.

There is no reason for a teacher to engage in corporal punishment by hitting or physically harming a child. If you become angered to the point of considering physical punishment, immediately remove yourself from the situation. Walk to the other end of the gym or ask another teacher to supervise your class until you calm down. Corporal punishment is a missed opportunity to educate and will not make a situation better. In some states, you also will lose your job!

Do Not Use Physical Exercise As Punishment.

Not using exercise or physical activity as a consequence is more important than any other guideline that has been presented in this chapter. Children need to be encouraged to move and become physically active, not to dislike activity or perceive it as a punishment. Although asking children to run laps or perform push-ups is a highly effective consequence, it sends an inappropriate message to students. In reality, you are teaching them through the hidden curriculum that exercise is negative. There are an abundance of strategies, such as those suggested above, that are equally or more effective. As emphasized in Key Point 10-6, there simply is no excuse for using physical activity as a consequence.

Key Point 10-6

Physical activity should *never* be used as a punishment!

Selecting a System that Works for You

Two types of discipline systems have received considerable attention in the literature. The first, *assertive discipline,* is associated with Lee Canter who believes that educators have the right to teach and misbehavior in the classroom should not be tolerated. He encourages teachers to develop a series of simple rules that should be firmly but positively enforced. When students are engaged appropriately, they should be recognized and rewarded. When they are misbehaving, there should be an immediate consequence (Canter & Canter, 1992). It is one of the most widely used discipline systems, but it is sometimes criticized for teaching children that if they behave, they will receive a reward.

Another popular system, particularly in the field of physical education, is Don Hellison's *personal social responsibility model* (Hellison, 2011). The model was initially implemented in urban schools where he was working with children who had limited self-control. Contrary to Canter, Hellison believes that students should be taught to behave appropriately not to receive extrinsic rewards but for the intrinsic good feelings that come from practicing self-responsibility. The model has five levels: Level 0: Irresponsibility, Level 1: Self-control, Level 2: Involvement, Level 3: Self-responsibility, and Level 4: Caring. Teachers assist students to gradually assume greater responsibility and assess their own level of performance with the ultimate goal of reaching Level 4 where they begin focusing less on themselves and more on helping others.

Summary

The purpose of this chapter was to provide you with information related to preventive class management and discipline. Although first-hand, real world experience is preferable, teachers can learn techniques for promoting good behavior and enforcing consequences by carefully anticipating what they are likely to encounter and how best to respond. By anticipating in advance, it is likely that you will respond more effectively in the future (complete Thinking Challenge 10.6).

Those teachers who are most effective work diligently to create a positive class climate and proactively promote good behavior. They establish routines, set and enforce thoughtful rules, have high expectations for positive behavior, and positively reinforce good behavior such as exhibiting kindness toward others. While they are firm and consistent, they also are

THINKING CHALLENGE 10.6

The scenarios below were written by future teachers in anticipation of discipline problems they perceived they might encounter. How would you respond?

Case Study 1:
It is about a month into the school year and a 5th grade teacher is having trouble with her students abusing the equipment. She has caught her students hitting things with their rackets, as well as throwing the rackets and intentionally dropping them. This activity has happened on countless occasions and with more than just one student.

Case Study 2:
The end of the first semester is getting close. A 4th grade teacher is getting frustrated with his students' constant arguing over rules to various games that they have been playing throughout the year. In every unit, there appears to be several students who do not seem to agree with the rules that are being used in class. The students are continually arguing with one another and with the teacher.

Case Study 3:
A 2nd grade student constantly tattles on other children in class. Students are becoming increasingly annoyed at this individual and you have overheard them calling her names. You are irritated that she constantly tattles, but you also do not condone the negative behavior of other students toward her.

Case Study 4:
A 3rd grade class is in the middle of a floor hockey unit. The class has just begun a game. As the game progresses, Joe accidentally hits Tom in the leg with his stick, but Tom feels it was done intentionally. The two begin exchanging words, which quickly progresses to pushing. Before the teacher is able to intervene, the two students begin hitting each other.

caring and considerate of student feelings. They publicly praise good behavior and, when necessary, use appropriate rewards as reinforcement.

Effective teachers do not enjoy disciplining students but understand that it is a necessary element of an orderly classroom. Consequences should be known by students, fairly and consistently enforced, not meant to publicly embarrass children, and appropriate for the infraction that occurred. Although effective teachers understand that some consequences may be more effective than others, they also are unwilling to use exercise, physical activity, or other equally inappropriate measures as consequences.

DO AND DON'T CHECKLIST

Do	Don't
☐ establish high expectations for an orderly learning environment	☐ expect that you will become friends with students
☐ consistently enforce consequences when rules are broken	☐ ignore instances of inappropriate behavior
☐ expect children to treat each other with kindness	☐ tolerate instance of bullying
☐ implement strategies for proactively encouraging appropriate behavior	☐ punish everyone for the actions of a few
☐ select consequences that are appropriate to the infraction that occurred.	☐ embarrass students by needlessly punishing students publicly
	☐ use physical activity or exercise as punishment.

Review Activities

1. In a small group, develop a school-wide discipline system that you believe would promote appropriate behavior.
2. Discuss how teachers can reduce instances of bullying.
3. Debate with others whether or not material rewards are appropriate for encouraging positive behavior.
4. Discuss how you would respond if parents were unreceptive after you contacted them to report a discipline problem.
5. Debate whether or not it is appropriate to punish everyone for the actions of a few.

References

Almeida, D. A. (1995). Behavior management and "The Five C's." *Teaching K-8, 26,* 88–89.

American Academy of Child & Adolescent Psychiatry. (2008). *Facts for families: Bullying.* Retrieved June 11, 2008 from http://www.aacap.org/cs/root/facts_for_families/bullying

Canter, L., & Canter, M. (1992). *Assertive discipline: Positive behavior management for today's classroom.* Santa Monica, CA: Canter and Associates.

Graham, G., Holt/Hale, S. A., & Parker, M. (2004). *Children moving: A reflective approach to teaching physical education* (6th ed.). New York, NY: McGraw Hill.

Hellison, D. (2011). *Teaching personal and social responsibility through physical activity* (3rd ed.). Champaign, IL: Human Kinetics.

Leff, S. S., Power, T. J., & Goldstein, A. B. (2004). Outcome measures to assess the effectiveness of bullying prevention programs in the schools. In D. L. Espelage & S. M. Swearer (Eds.), *Bullying in American schools* (pp. 269–295). Mahwah, NJ: Erlbaum.

Siedentop, D., & Tannehill, D. (2000). *Developing teaching skills in physical education* (4th ed.).Mountain View, CA: Mayfield.

Standage, M., Duda, J. L., & Ntoumanis, N. (2005). A test of self-determination theory in school physical education. *British Journal of Educational Psychology, 75,* 411–433.

Chapter **Eleven**

Assessment and Evaluation

This chapter addresses the purposes of assessment, how children have traditionally been evaluated, alternative methods of assessment, and guidelines that classroom teachers might find useful when conducting assessments. Since many elementary schools do not have certified physical education specialists, classroom teachers are responsible for conducting assessments. Although we encourage classroom teachers to create their own assessments that meet the particular needs of children in their class and the specific subject matter being presented, it is important to emphasize that physical education assessments have recently been published for elementary-aged children by NASPE (National Association for Sport and Physical Education, 2010). These assessments were written by experts in the field, relate to what experts believe children should know and be able to accomplish at the end of specific grade levels, and have been demonstrated to be valid and reliable. They also were written to address the six national standards that were introduced in Lecture Chapter 2. We urge classroom teachers to obtain copies of these assessments.

Assessment and evaluation are very important responsibilities of the teacher because they convey information to others about a child's performance. In some states, like South Carolina, legislators have instituted state-mandated testing (Rink & Mitchell, 2003). Schools are required to list students' scores on a state report card. This enables parents, legislators, and others to compare and contrast individual schools. The result of this process has been greater school accountability for student learning.

PURPOSES OF ASSESSMENT

Before progressing further, it is important for you to understand the difference between the terms "assessment" and "evaluation." Although each is used to provide information about a student's performance, each has a slightly different definition. As Key Point 11-1 explains, *assessment* refers to a diagnostic process whereby teachers receive information about students' performance or progress toward a goal. *Evaluation* is product oriented and provides a comparative judgment about how students have achieved the goal. Assessment is primarily *formative*. It is used to provide information to students about their overall progress. Evaluation, however, is summative. It is "used to judge the quality of a performance or work product against a standard" (Parker, Fleming, Beyerlein, Apple, & Krumsieg, 2001, p. T3A-1).

Key Point 11-1

Assessment refers to a diagnostic process whereby teachers receive information about students' performance or progress toward a goal. *Evaluation* is product-oriented and provides a comparative judgment about how students have achieved the goal.

Classroom teachers can learn to appropriately assess and evaluate student performance.

The NASPE assessment text described above can be used by teachers to *formatively assess* students' *progress* toward achievement of the national standards and as a mechanism to *summatively evaluate* their performance at the end of a grade level in relation to the national standards. It is an ideal tool for helping teachers determine what children should know and be able to accomplish and can be used as a guide in the development of an annual curriculum. In addition to this tool, classroom teachers can also develop their own tools for assessing and evaluating, or they can seek out any number of other useful references for ideas (e.g., Holt/Hale, 1999; Lambert, 1999; Lund, 2000; Melograno, 2000; O'Sullivan & Henninger, 2000).

Try to recall your own experiences in elementary physical education class. Before reading further, complete Thinking Challenge 11.1. What do you remember? Are those memories positive or negative?

THINKING CHALLENGE 11.1

List those techniques teachers employed in elementary physical education for assessing and evaluating your performance.

Assessment	Evaluation
1.	1.
2.	2.
3.	3.
4.	4.
5.	5.

Teachers assess and evaluate for a variety of reasons. Based on class time available throughout the year, and contingent on their professional beliefs about assessment and evaluation, they may elect to do so regularly or only periodically. Below are a few purposes for *assessing* students:

- Classify students by ability for purposes such as grouping
- Inform students about their improvement
- Motivate students to work hard
- Diagnose performance difficulties
- Predict future ability level
- Enable the teacher to evaluate his or her effectiveness
- Inform the teacher about the success of a lesson, unit, or curriculum

Below are a few purposes for *evaluating* students:

- Determine if students have achieved an outcome
- Establish if students can meet the national standards
- Report a student's status at the end of a unit of instruction
- Determine if children have achieved the objectives of a unit

TRADITIONAL ASSESSMENT AND EVALUATION

In our experience, physical education teachers have spent more time evaluating students than assessing them. Although we cannot attest to how classroom teachers might behave, evaluation has been conducted primarily for purposes of grading. In the majority of elementary schools, grades convey whether children are **O**utstanding, **S**atisfactory, or **U**nsatisfactory. In a few schools, children receive either a lengthy statement written by the teacher, or a traditional letter grade of **A, B, C, D, or F.** Whatever system is used, the final report provides information about students' status to (a) themselves, (b) parents, (c) teachers, and (d) other schools, such as private elementary schools, to which students might later apply. Although students are sometimes asked to write a self-evaluation, or participate in peer evaluation, the vast majority of evaluations in elementary schools are conducted predominately by the teacher. Before reading further, complete Thinking Challenge 11.2.

THINKING CHALLENGE 11.2	List one advantage and one disadvantage for each of the grading systems below that are not discussed in this chapter.		
	Grading System	**Advantage**	**Disadvantage**
	O, S, U System		
	A, B, C, D, F System		
	Written Report		

Each type of grading system has advantages and disadvantages. Traditional letter grades are advantageous because they can be quickly and easily completed by teachers and convey to students and parents information about children's performance that is easy to interpret. They do not, however, provide specific information for those areas in which a student's performance is strong or weak. For example, if a child receives a "C" in physical education, that individual may have been outstanding in creative activities such as gymnastics and dance but lacking in basic motor skills such as throwing and catching. The "C" conveys that a child's performance is average, but it does not describe why.

Although written reports are exceptionally useful to parents and children, they take an inordinately long time to complete. They consume time that could be used by the teacher to prepare new or improve current lesson plans.

Ideally, parents have an opportunity to meet individually with their child's teacher on several occasions throughout the semester. This allows parents to obtain a better understanding of their child's performance while enabling the teacher to convey a great deal of information that would be extremely time consuming to express in writing. Written reports, however, are an important mechanism for informing future teachers about a child's past performance and are critical when children relocate from one school to another. Box 11.1 contains a sample report card that could be used in elementary school by classroom teachers. It contains letter grades and also enables a teacher to insert comments related to the specific topics covered each quarter. If professionally printed, multiple pages can be affixed together. The top portion of the forms can use a carbon-type paper so that grades entered first semester will be visible when completing the report for subsequent terms. The lower portion of the form, however, would not use the carbon paper so that new comments can be inserted each quarter.

Physical Education Report Card
Grades K-5

Box 11.1

Student Name _____

Grade _____

Teacher Name _____

Date _____

KEY

O = Outstanding

P = Consistent Progress

I = Needs Improvement

(+ or − values may be added to the grade)

AREA OF EVALUATION	Quarter			
	1	2	3	4
Basic Motor Skills Comments:				
Creative Movement Comments:				
Fitness Comments:				
Knowledge Comments:				
Teamwork and Cooperation Comments:				
Attitude Comments:				
Overall Performance Comments:				

Students are typically evaluated in the three domains discussed earlier in the text: psychomotor, cognitive, and affective. Interestingly, as emphasized in Key Point 11-2, students in physical education are often assessed primarily on the affective domain, not psychomotor. Teachers want children in physical education to behave and participate. They believe that it is unfair to penalize a child with a poor grade because that individual is lacking in

Key Point 11-2

Children in physical education are sometimes assessed more in the affective domain than they are in the psychomotor domain. They should, however, be assessed primarily on their motor performance.

coordination. As long as the student "tries hard," that individual can receive the highest grade possible—even if that person is the least skilled in the class. Is this fair? Does this accurately convey a student's progress to the child and his or her parents? Consider how you as a classroom teacher would assess and evaluate students as you continue reading.

Psychomotor Domain

It would seem logical that children in physical education would primarily be assessed based on their motor performance. Oddly, this area is often the most overlooked for those reasons described above. Assigning an outstanding grade, however, to a student in physical education who has not demonstrated exceptional performance in the psychomotor domain demonstrates inappropriate pedagogy. It is no different than assigning a grade of "A" in reading to a student because he or she consistently remembers to bring a book to class and tries hard, yet cannot read.

Teachers are hired to objectively assess and evaluate performance. Being generous because you like the student or believe that he or she exerts tremendous effort does a disservice to you, the child, and the parents. It does not portray an accurate picture of progress and may actually result in great harm to the child if he or she is later assigned to a higher level class than he or she can actually handle.

Report cards, such as the one highlighted in Box 11.1, are useful because they enable a teacher to comment on different areas related to children's performance. If a child is strong in areas like basic motor skills and fitness but weak in performing creative activities, that information can be accurately conveyed. Parents learn that their child is skilled and fit but may need to be registered in an after-school program to assist in developing his or her creative talents.

Teachers employ appropriate skills and fitness tests to assess in the psychomotor area. Many assessments, such as those recently produced by NASPE (2010) are valid, reliable, and easy for physical education and classroom teachers to utilize. Instruments such as checklists, task cards, assessment sheets, and visual analysis are useful for assessing students in this domain.

The psychomotor area encompasses all activities in which a child is asked to physically perform. Examples include:

- Basic motor skills
- Health-related fitness
- Creative movement
- Performance in individual, partner, and team activities

Basic motor skills entail such things as throwing, catching, kicking, striking, dodging, landing, running, turning, twisting, and so forth. They include those skills that a child needs to learn in order to be able to participate effectively in other activities. They are initially taught individually and later combined into complex movements. Valid and reliable assessments have been developed by the NASPE Assessment Task Force (2010) and can also be obtained from other professional texts.

Health-related fitness includes cardiovascular endurance, body composition, and muscular strength, endurance, and flexibility. Children's fitness levels should be regularly assessed in all grade levels. Assessments like the FITNESSGRAM that are frequently utilized by certified physical education specialists can also be used by classroom teachers (Welk & Blair, 2008; Welk & Meredith, 2008). To assess aerobic capacity, children complete the (a) PACER test, (b) one-mile run/walk, and (c) walk test (for children 13 and over). For the most recent information on the FITNESSGRAM go to: http://www.cooperinstitute.org/ourkidshealth/fitnessgram/documents/FITNESSGRAM_ReferenceGuide.pdf. Another Internet site you may wish to visit is the President's Challenge: http://www.presidentschallenge.org/. This program also promotes fitness testing and enables teachers to purchase awards for children who meet the requirements of the challenge.

To assess body composition, percent of body fat or body mass index can be calculated. Although a variety of mechanisms have been used to assess body composition, the most

Fitness assessments can provide important information about whether or not a child is in the Healthy Fitness Zone.

common measures include using skinfold calipers or simple calculators that are available on credible Web sites such as U.S. Department of Health and Human Services: http://www. nhlbisupport.com/bmi/.

Finally, to determine muscular strength, endurance, and flexibility, teachers can assess (a) abdominal strength and endurance (curl ups), (b) trunk extensor strength and endurance (trunk lift), (c) upper-body strength and endurance (push-up, pull-up or flexed arm hang), and (d) flexibility (sit-and-reach or shoulder stretch). Teachers can learn to design appropriate health-related fitness units using the multiple products that come with the FITNESS-GRAM, and they can determine if children fall within the Healthy Fitness Zone (see http://www.fitnessgram.net/home/).

Creative movement should be taught in all grade levels. Some children will excel in the area of basic motor skills whereas others perform more competently in the area of creative movements. Still others may be competent in both areas. Children who perform well creatively tend to do well in gymnastics and dance units. They use their bodies to express themselves and may even enjoy connecting movements to music. NASPE offers multiple assessments for evaluating creative movement (2010).

Performance in individual, partner, and team activities is emphasized once children begin to acquire expertise in basic motor skills. Teachers assess student skills such as passing to others, catching while running, and successfully completing offensive and defensive strategies during game play. Valid and reliable assessments in this area are also available from NASPE (2010).

Cognitive Domain

Another important area in which children in physical education need to be assessed is the cognitive domain. This includes testing students and using assignments to assess such things as (a) cognitive understanding and processing (e.g., rules, strategies, safety factors, history of games, problem solving); (b) ability to apply knowledge, and (c) understanding of principles and mechanics of movement (e.g., force production, use of levers, conditioning). Without a class in biomechanics or principles of conditioning, assessing children in some cognitive areas will be difficult for the classroom teacher. There are, however, resources like the NASPE assessments where teachers can obtain cognitive tests that are valid and reliable (NASPE, 2010). In addition, you may also assess cognitive performance using instruments you develop such as quizzes, written tests, and interviews to assess students in those areas that you have expertise and feel most comfortable.

Teaching the rules and history of certain activities will prove to be easier than trying to learn complex principles related to areas like biomechanics. You are, of course, encouraged to accumulate knowledge in order to help children understand how their body functions, how concepts can be applied in a physical activity setting, and how different strategies can be used in game-like situations. Further, as emphasized in Key Point 11-3, it is important to spend the majority of time engaging students in physical activity. Therefore, if you can carve out a period of time in the home classroom for children to take cognitive exams about what they are learning in physical education, you will have more time to keep them active during time assigned to physical education.

Key Point 11-3

Although assessing in the cognitive domain is important, classroom teachers should use the majority of physical education time to keep children moving, not completing written assignments.

If you do attempt to develop written quizzes or exams, they can either be objective or subjective in nature. You will learn about test construction as you progress through your teacher education program. Therefore, we will not spend much time covering how to write questions other than to emphasize that written assessments can either be objective or subjective. *Objective* exams use multiple choice and true/false questions. There is a definite correct answer. *Subjective* exams include short-answer and essay-type questions that are more difficult to grade because a clear-cut answer does not always exist. A teacher's bias for or against a particular child can sometimes influence how that individual is evaluated on a subjective assessment. Therefore, it is important to remind yourself to be fair and equitable when assessing subjectively.

Another means of cognitively assessing students includes asking them to complete assignments during class or as homework. We encourage teachers to use assignments and homework because they promote learning and provide another source for assessing cognitive understanding.

Affective Domain

Assessing children in all three domains is important.

The third area in which children can be evaluated is the affective domain. This includes assessing students on their ability to cooperate, share, work with others, and exhibit appropriate conduct during a game. It also involves effort. Interestingly, most physical education teachers put more emphasis on the affective domain than they do on the psychomotor or cognitive domains. They rely on measures such as attendance, appropriate dress, and attitude when assessing in this area. Although their intent to reward students who try hard is commendable, it sends an incorrect message about students' actual capabilities to themselves and their parents.

Despite the inappropriate imbalance in favor of primarily assessing in the affective domain, it is an area that cannot be ignored. Children should be assessed to determine if they are making appropriate progress in the areas of personal and social skill development. It is important to understand if they have acquired skills that promote cooperation, sportspersonship, and tolerance of others who are different. Assessing primarily in this domain at the expense of the psychomotor and cognitive domains is, however, inappropriate.

Assessing in the affective area is difficult because most assessments are entirely subjective. It is, for example, difficult to determine if a child is trying hard. It may appear that they are trying because they follow the rules, perform when asked, and smile when communicating with the teacher. They may, however, possess the skills of a competent bystander, thus fooling the teacher about their actual level of engagement.

The NASPE Assessment Task Force has written assessment questions that will test students to determine if they understand concepts like cooperation, sharing, effort, and tolerance. These questions are a valid and reliable means of testing what students have learned in the affective domain. Complete Thinking Challenge 11.3.

THINKING CHALLENGE 11.3	Develop an assessment for evaluating student performance in the affective domain that is not subjective and does not require them to complete a written exam.

ALTERNATIVE ASSESSMENT

Increasingly, physical education teachers throughout the nation are substituting traditional evaluation with alternative assessment. This form of assessment, sometimes referred to as *authentic assessment,* has the following characteristics (Doolittle & Fay, 2002; Graham, 2001):

- Designed to be more meaningful than traditional assessments like paper and pencil exams
- Developmentally appropriate for children
- Conducted in authentic settings such as during complex game play
- May require complex thinking skills while performing an activity
- Intended to assess the actual curriculum being taught by the teacher
- May become public
- Can be used to assess the psychomotor, cognitive, and affective domains

Analyzing student performance during complex game play is one form of an authentic assessment.

Hand Dribbling Assessment   Box 11.2

Ask students to dribble in a 5′ by 5′ area while keeping control of the ball. After scoring students using the rubric below, total the points and then average the score.

4 = Performs the skill expertly and without error
3 = Acceptable performance
2 = Sometimes performs the skill correctly
1 = Rarely performs the skill correctly

Student Name	Does Not Watch Ball	Uses Fingertips	Slight Knee Bend	Total Points	Average Score
Betty					
Charlene					
Mike					
Stewart					
Julie					
Juanita					
Keisha					
Patricia					
Katrina					
Greg					

Alternative assessments at the elementary level may require teachers to use a checklist of rubrics for evaluating a student's skill level while engaged in game play (see Box 11.2).

Both teachers and students often find these types of assessments to be meaningful because they assess real-world learning (see Morrow, Jackson, Disch, & Mood, 2005). For example, a teacher might observe a student's play in a game situation or during a simple drill (see Box 11.2). Many alternative assessments are developed by individual teachers, and although they have not been tested for validity and reliability, they can be a valuable mechanism for testing what students are learning in authentic situations. Some assessments can be completed as homework while others are completed during class. Below are some examples of alternative assessments that students can be asked to complete that focus on the three learning domains.

- Maintain a portfolio related to what students learn during a unit of instruction in physical education (see Box 11.3)
- Write an individualized health-related fitness plan
- Construct a poster that describes the principles of conditioning that are most important to personal health
- Create a collage that depicts how you feel about physical education
- Maintain a food diary of everything you ate during the past week and list which food group corresponds to the individual items you ate
- Write a written test that you could give to your classmates about the official rules of lacrosse and include an answer sheet

5th Grade Unit Portfolio - 50 points   Box 11.3

You are being asked to develop a portfolio that contains information related to everything you will learn during the (*fill in the name of the unit*) that we will be completing during the next six weeks. Your portfolio should include the following:

1. Handout of the rules that you could share with classmates

2. 500-word essay that describes the history of the unit and its impact on society

3. One-page essay describing the ways in which you tried to improve your performance in the unit outside of class

4. Daily diary entry of at least 25 words that states how you felt about your performance during class

5. All class handouts

6. A test containing 20 questions that you could give to your classmates about the unit (10 true/false questions and 10 multiple choice questions)

7. Additional information that you believe is relevant to include

Your portfolio should be typed and presented in an attractive format. It should contain pictures and other graphics.

- Develop a rubric for assessing a gymnastics routine and evaluate your own routine using the rubric
- Write a paper describing your most memorable performance in physical education during the past unit
- While participating in a volleyball game shout out which strategies you are electing to use
- Develop a creative dance that expresses how you feel about movement

ASSESSMENT GUIDELINES

As you develop and implement assessments, it is important to consider a number of different factors. These factors will determine the success that you have at implementing the assessments and student feelings toward the assessment process.

Increasing the Success of the Assessment Process

When you plan your assessments it is important to follow appropriate assessment procedures and to accurately report the results of the assessment. It also is important to keep in mind how the assessment will be administered to the student being tested and what other students will be doing during the assessment.

Frequency of evaluation.

Remember that you have limited time allocated for the instruction of physical education. Therefore, be cautious as to how your time is spent conducting assessments. Ideally, students can be engaged in physical activity and moving while they are being assessed. As long as students are physically active during psychomotor assessments, you will not be taking away from engagement time. If, however, they are being tested with a paper and pencil exam or written assignment, they will not be moving and engagement time will decrease. As a classroom teacher, be conscious about periodically testing students, but do not become extreme. When possible, administer assessments quickly. For example, in the assessment described in Box 11.2, you can assess a number of students simultaneously, and the assessment should take no longer than a few minutes to conduct.

Pre- and post-testing.

Assessments are designed to provide information about student progress. If you have not taught an activity, there is no need to assess progress toward achievement in that activity.

For example, if you do not plan to emphasize health-related fitness in your curriculum, there is less need to pre- and post-test unless you want to know the fitness levels of children in your class or believe it would be beneficial for them to have this information. Pre-testing is intended to assess a child's current capability whereas post-testing is designed to assess their performance after instruction and practice.

In relation to health-related fitness, we would encourage taking time to conduct a pre-test in all areas of the FITNESSGRAM at the inception of the school year. Children should be challenged to increase their fitness levels throughout the year, and teachers should provide them with appropriate activities for doing so. If fitness was emphasized, it should be post-tested at a later date to determine if students have made progress toward reaching the Healthy Fitness Zone.

Match assessment to your instructional activities.

As emphasized in Key Point 11-4, you should assess only what you have taught. If you have not instructed children in volleyball, and do not intend to do so in the future, there is no need for an assessment. If, however, you do include a volleyball unit in the curriculum, it is absolutely appropriate to assess those skills on which you instructed. If you emphasized the bump and set passes, those skills should be assessed. If you discussed the rules of volleyball, you may wish to develop a volleyball quiz. If you emphasized cooperation, you should observe to see if students exhibit cooperative skills.

Key Point 11-4

Teachers should assess only those activities that they have taught.

Check for understanding prior to and during an assessment.

Throughout a unit of instruction, regularly ask students questions and observe their performance to ensure that they understand your instructions. If, for example, they continue to use their palm, not fingertips, to hand dribble a basketball, there is a chance that they misunderstood your instructions and thought they should use their palm. When they take the assessment, they would likely use their palm, thinking that is what they were taught. In reality, they might be able to dribble with their fingertips but did not know this is what was expected.

If you administer an assessment that all students fail, there is a strong likelihood that they may not have understood the assessment instructions. If you believe this to be the case, you may need to restate the instructions and re-administer the assessment.

Homework.

It is perfectly reasonable to give students homework in physical education. Since the amount of time allocated for physical education instruction during school is so brief, supplemental instruction through homework can be quite useful. Homework can consist of asking children to learn the rules for particular activities, to gather information about the history of a sport, to develop a personalized fitness plan, to wear a pedometer over the weekend to track the number of steps taken, or to maintain a food diary of everything eaten over the period of a week. Ideally, written homework can supplement what they are learning in the classroom. If, for example, you are emphasizing vocabulary, assign words for them to learn that are related to physical activity. Finally, homework can require their participation in physical activity outside of the school day. Children can be asked to engage in particular activities or to select their own. Parents can be asked to verify their participation by simply signing a log. In the long run, homework should be designed so that it results in an elevated level of student performance on assessments. Complete Thinking Challenge 11.4 by creating your own homework assignment.

THINKING
CHALLENGE 11.4

Create a homework assignment that would engage students in physical activity *and* require them to demonstrate cognitive knowledge of health-related fitness.

Don't make claims you can't back up.

Physical education teachers sometimes have a tendency to make claims about student learning that are inaccurate. For example, it is not unusual to overhear a physical education teacher stating that his or her class makes students physically fit. Although physical education should result in improved fitness levels, the amount of time available during the day in most schools cannot result in dramatic fitness gains unless children engage in supplementary physical activity outside of school. Some improvement in fitness may be related to physical education, but it also may be related to participation in other activities. If you develop a program that you believe is strong, you have every right to boast about its success. If that program emphasizes fitness for an appropriate amount of time during school and encourages children to be active outside of school by requiring physical activity homework, you should use improved fitness scores to justify your program to parents and administrators.

Keep all students active during assessments.

Some teachers have more difficulty conducting assessments than others. They find it easier to have the majority of the class sitting down while only a few are assessed. This is a mistake for many reasons. First, it does not respect a student's privacy. Second, it results in large amounts of time where children are waiting. They are not learning, nor are they physically engaged in activity. This results in an incredible waste of learning time.

If you are overwhelmed when conducting assessments, ask for parent volunteers to help you record scores so that multiple children can be simultaneously assessed, or assign them to engage those children not being tested in similar or alternative activities. If you are unable to obtain assistance, test one or a handful of students while you engage the remainder in safe activity. As you gain experience, you should be able to observe multiple events at one time by strategically placing yourself in a location in the gymnasium where you can observe everyone.

Increasing Positive Student Feelings Toward Assessments

Classroom and physical education teachers share the common problem of engaging students in assessments that many dislike and even come to resent. Those who exert effort and do not perform well begin to believe that they are incapable. Others believe that a poor score indicates that they are unintelligent or unskilled. Fortunately, some of the damage caused during assessments is preventable.

Assessments should be conducted privately and while other students are engaged in activity.

Inform students on what they will be tested.

In one study that examined elementary school fitness testing, students lacked the ability to explain the purpose of the mile-run test and did not understand why they were being tested (Hopple & Graham (1995). In this case, it is likely that the teacher did not clearly instruct students during the year about why engaging in the mile-run was important and why they were being subsequently tested. In other cases, teachers sometimes ask students to complete an assessment but forget to inform them of the criteria on which they will be assessed. This results in student confusion and may result in a poor performance that could otherwise have been acceptable. In fact, you can probably recount many instances of when you studied hard for an exam or assessment and did not perform well because you thought that you were going to be tested on something else.

Create a positive assessment experience.

As emphasized in Key Point 11-5, many children suffer great anxiety when completing an assessment. Some cannot concentrate and are easily distracted. Others forget what they learned or are incapable of performing under the stressful conditions of assessment. Teachers should exert every effort to create a positive environment that does not put undue pressure on any student. Some children may need longer to take an exam than others. If the exam is not time-sensitive, there is no harm in providing extra time. Some physical education teachers try to reduce the stressful conditions of assessment by allowing children to take an assessment twice but record only their best score. When appropriate, we would encourage classroom teachers to do the same.

Key Point 11-5

Many children suffer great anxiety when completing an assessment. Therefore, teachers should attempt to make the assessment environment as positive as possible.

Create a private environment.

Unfortunately, many assessments in physical education are conducted publicly. Whereas students taking an exam in the classroom cannot observe the performance of others, testing in physical education is often highly visible. The problem is exacerbated by teachers who have one child perform at a time while others sit and watch. This is a cruel practice and has resulted in traumatic experiences for many children, particularly those who are low skilled.

Effective teachers understand the necessity of making testing private and implement techniques that make it more difficult for students to compare their performance to others. Either all children are being tested simultaneously or teachers engage those students not being tested in alternative activities that keep them busy and unable to observe those being assessed. Additional strategies include never publicly announcing scores or the time that it took to complete an assessment like the mile-run.

Due to the childhood obesity epidemic, some states have recently mandated that children be weighed at school. This controversial requirement has resulted in many public debates about both the benefits and the harm that can be caused by this practice. Although the purpose of this chapter is not to debate the requirement, if you are asked to assist in weighing students, we would strongly urge you take every measure to guarantee that the procedure is conducted in a private room away from other students and to keep measurements in a secure location.

TEACHER ASSESSMENT

One additional topic that we would briefly like to address is teacher assessment. Although physical education teachers are trained to thoughtfully reflect on the quality of their lessons and to implement advanced coding procedures to assess such things as student engagement time in relation to instruction provided, we do not expect classroom teachers to demonstrate the same degree of expertise in relation to teacher assessment. We would, however, encourage you to periodically assess your effectiveness in the gymnasium in the same way that you would in the classroom.

Understanding your behavior as a teacher is critical if you wish to improve. By coding things like the amount of feedback you provide, the number of interactions you have with different children, the types of positive and negative comments you make during class, and the amount of time that you spend in instruction can provide you with valuable data that can facilitate behavior change in a positive direction. Knowing how children spend their time is another vital area that classroom teachers should examine. Are they engaged in activity for the majority of the class, waiting in line for a turn, or listening to directions? By examining your behavior, you can determine if you need to make adjustments that favor keeping children involved in activity.

You can choose to create your own instruments for assessing your behavior (complete Thinking Challenge 11.5), or you may wish to purchase any number of teacher assessment books that are available. You can either video-record your lessons for later self-analysis or ask another teacher or student to code your performance. Please note, however, that in some schools, children are not allowed to be videotaped without parental consent—even for purposes of teacher self-assessment.

THINKING CHALLENGE 11.5	Develop an assessment that you believe would help you to improve your teaching ability in physical education.

Summary

Educational reform efforts have resulted in increasing pressure for schools to demonstrate student achievement and for professional associations to create assessments that are valid and reliable. In some states where mandated testing is required, there has been increased accountability for student learning. Although not all states require testing, reform efforts in physical education have resulted in the development of assessments that match the national standards and have been demonstrated to be valid and reliable.

Assessing students is critical because it provides information related to student progress and whether they can achieve at a level established by experts in the field. Although traditional assessments like skills tests and written exams continue to be a standard method for evaluating students, alternative assessments that are conducted in authentic settings are becoming increasingly popular. Both traditional and alternative assessments address the psychomotor, cognitive, and affective domains.

Finally, teachers need to consider whether they will conduct pre- and post-tests and how frequently. During the assessment process, it is important to inform students about the purpose of the assessment, describe the criteria being used, create a positive assessment environment, and conduct assessments as privately as possible. See Box 11.4.

DO AND DON'T CHECKLIST

Do	Don't
☐ conduct assessments that are valid and reliable	☐ conduct assessments at the expense of engaging students in physical activity
☐ employ both formative and summative assessments in the curriculum	☐ forget to inform students about the criteria on which they are being assessed
☐ select assessments that match the physical education content standards	☐ assess only in the affective domain
☐ enlist the help of parents when conducting assessments	☐ publicly share the results of assessments with other students
☐ periodically assess your own teaching.	☐ make claims about your curriculum unless they can be supported with assessments.

Review Activities

1. In your own words, describe the difference between formative assessment and summative evaluation.

2. Discuss how you were tested in the psychomotor, cognitive, and affective domains. Describe how you felt about those tests.

3. Discuss whether or not students in physical education should receive a good grade if they try but are unable to achieve in the psychomotor area.

4. Design a report card for physical education that you would like to use with your students.

5. Discuss procedures you would implement to ensure that fitness testing was not embarrassing.

References

Doolittle, S., & Fay, T. (2002). *Authentic assessment of physical activity for high school students.* Reston, VA: National Association for Sport and Physical Education.

Graham, G. (2001). *Teaching children physical education* (2nd ed.). Champaign, IL: Human Kinetics.

Holt/Hale, S. A. (1999). *Assessing and improving fitness in elementary physical education.* Reston, VA: National Association for Sport and Physical Education.

Hopple, C., & Graham, G. (1995). What children think, feel, and know about physical fitness testing. *Journal of Teaching in Physical Education, 14,* 408–417.

Lambert, L. (1999). *Standards-based assessment of student learning: A comprehensive approach.* Reston, VA: National Association for Sport and Physical Education.

Lund, J. L. (2000). *Creating rubrics for physical education.* Reston, VA: National Association for Sport and Physical Education.

Melograno, V. J. (2000). *Portfolio assessment for K-12 physical education.* Reston, VA: National Association for Sport and Physical Education.

Morrow, J. R., Jackson, A.W., Disch, J. G., & Mood, D. P. (2005). *Measurement and evaluation in human performance* (3rd ed.). Champaign, IL: Human Kinetics.

National Association for Sport and Physical Education (2010). *PE metrics: Assessing national standards 1-6 in elementary school.* Reston, VA: Author.

O'Sullivan, M., & Henninger, M. (2000). *Assessing student responsibility and teamwork.* Reston, VA: National Association for Sport and Physical Education.

Parker, P. E., Fleming, P. D., Beyerlein, S., Apple, D., & Krumsieg, K. (2001, October). *Differentiating assessment from evaluation as continuous improvement tools.* Paper presented at the 31st ASEE/IEEE Frontiers in Education Conference, Reno, NV.

Rink, J., & Mitchell, M. (Eds.). (2003). State level assessment in physical education: The South Carolina experience [Monograph]. *Journal of Teaching in Physical Education, 22,* 471–588.

Welk, G. J., & Blair, S. N. (2008). Health benefits of physical activity and fitness in children. In G. J. Welk & M. D. Meredith (Eds.). *FITNESSGRAM /ACTIVITYGRAM reference guide* (3rd ed.) (pp. 40–51). Dallas, TX: The Cooper Institute.

Welk, G. J., & Meredith, M. D. (Eds). (2008). *FITNESSGRAM /ACTIVITYGRAM reference guide* (3rd ed.). Dallas, TX: The Cooper Institute.

Chapter **Twelve**

Integrating Movement Across the Curriculum

You might recall that in Chapter 1, we presented you with a number of different statistics that related to the obesity epidemic. For example, due to the sedentary lifestyle and unhealthy diet of many children, the number of overweight children aged 6 to 11 has more than tripled over the past three decades (U.S. Department of Health and Human Services, 2004), leading to predictions that today's children will be the first generation whose life expectancies will be shorter than those of their parents (Olshansky et al., 2005). For this reason, Congress passed the Child Nutrition and WIC Reauthorization Act (see http://www.fns.usda.gov/tn/healthy/108-265.pdf). The bill mandates the adoption of local wellness policies, including nutrition education, physical activity, and other school-based actions promoting student wellness.

As a result of the legislation, school personnel throughout the nation examined their current practices and addressed ways in which the overall school environment could be improved in order to facilitate better nutrition and additional opportunities for children to be physically active during the school day. In many cases, the school lunch program was improved to offer children a healthier variety of food and beverage options. In some cases, the amount of physical education children received was increased, or additional time for recess was incorporated into the daily schedule. The legislation also motivated many classroom teachers to begin offering physical activity opportunities to their students throughout the day. When classroom teachers incorporate movement into their home classroom activities, this is referred to as integrating movement across the curriculum. Complete Thinking Challenge 12.1.

THINKING CHALLENGE 12.1	School personnel are often reluctant to implement new policies because of the challenges they create, such as the need for additional financial resources in order to successfully implement the legislation. What are three additional barriers that school personnel may confront? 1. 2. 3.

BRAIN-BASED LEARNING

Another advantage for teachers eager to jump on the bandwagon to promote wellness is the current focus on brain-based education. Children learn at a much more rapid rate during their elementary years. Sousa (1998, p. 52) explains the impact of this "windows-of-opportunity" concept, whereby what the child learns between the ages of 2 and 11 "will strongly influence what is learned after the window closes." Further, emerging research has demonstrated that children who are physically active and fit have better academic

The Child Nutrition and WIC Reauthorization Act has led to healthier food and beverage options for children in many schools.

achievement, perform better in school, have fewer discipline problems, and do better on achievement exams (U.S. Center for Disease Control and Prevention, 2010).

Functions governing brain activity are directly tied to movement, benefiting not only the heart but the brain as well. When children are actively engaged, glucose and oxygen rush to the brain, increasing nerve connections that aid in learning. If student learning is enhanced by movement, there is a strong likelihood that retention will also increase. Thus, if a teacher wants students to review information, the best means of committing such data or ideas to memory is to keep them moving during the review. For example, prior to a spelling test, students may jump, run in place, or hop on one foot beside their desk while spelling words in unison.

When planning curricula, it is essential to consider these advantages and to schedule some kind of vigorous physical activity during every hour of the school day. When reviewing multiplication tables students may bend at the waist for the first number (4), crouch at the second (6), and spring into the air at the answer (24!). Engaging children in developing physical education content-related activities also increases their creativity and investment in their own learning. For children who have difficulty sitting still for long stretches of time, physical activity associated classroom learning affords a welcome relief and a much needed stimulus.

Participation in physical activity is linked with improved academic performance.

Rink, Hall, and Williams (2010) maintain that learning through movement contributes to academic success. In addition to promoting better health, physical activity also helps students perform better in school. For example, University of Illinois researchers found that after 20 minutes of walking, children scored "a full grade level higher in reading comprehension than after a period of rest" (Hillman, et al., 2009). Likewise, the Robert Wood Johnson Foundation (2007) determined that students who spent more time in PE or school-based physical activity "maintained or improved their grades and scores on standardized achievement tests," despite the reduction of classroom instructional time (see Key Point 12-1). Such data empowers teachers to build time for walking, jumping,

Key Point 12-1

Although children who participate in physical education spend less time in the home classroom, active and fit children tend to perform better academically and have fewer disruptive behaviors.

bending, and stretching into the curriculum. Although physical activity has typically occurred during physical education class or recess, classroom teachers who understand the cognitive benefits of physical activity are incorporating segments of physical activity into the curriculum at frequent intervals throughout the school day. Complete Thinking Challenge 12.2.

THINKING CHALLENGE 12.2

Describe one physical activity that you could integrate into the home classroom when teaching each of the activities listed below.

1. Activity for teaching reading:
2. Activity for teaching spelling:
3. Activity for teaching addition:
4. Activity for teaching social studies:
5. Activity for teaching cooperation:

BENEFITS OF INTEGRATING MOVEMENT

Certainly the field of education has advocated integrating curricula for decades, and evidence attests to the improved academic performance of children after engaging in physical activity (Fleshner, 2000; U.S. Centers for Disease Control and Prevention, 2010). Educators are also well aware of Bloom's taxonomy and recognize the importance of making connections across disciplines as a form of higher order thinking. Bandura (1998), a famed behavioral theorist, asserts that teachers' committing themselves to increasing daily activity can have a positive effect on children's health.

Jensen (2005) maintains that movement should play an integral role in school-day learning. He advocates periodic breaks whereby physical activity is integrated with academic content. "You can pour all the water you want from a jug into a glass," he emphasizes, "but the glass can only hold so much" (p. 34). Jensen offers seven reasons to have students move more to learn more:

1. *Circulation.* When children spend long periods in sedentary positions, it is essential to include time for them to stretch or move in place, increasing flexibility while sending

oxygen to key brain areas and relaxing the eyes. Not only does this interrupt musculo-skeletal tensions, but it also narrows focus upon return to seated learning.

2. *Episodic encoding.* Giving a new spatial reference on the room provides enhanced learning. After interrupting learning time with movement, students move to a new location in the room, changing their relationship to the scenery.

3. *A break from learning.* Brains learn best when exposed to bursts of information followed by time to reflect. The brain cannot learn an unlimited amount of content, and thus, teacher determination to cover too much material is a serious mistake.

4. *System maturation.* As a child's brain matures and grows, breaks are essential for cognitive remapping. Some areas expand in size whereas others shrink, necessitating the need for physical activity as a respite from learning.

5. *Good chemicals.* One's body produces a number of natural motivators, including noradrenalin (the hormone of risk or urgency) and dopamine (the neurotransmitter producing good feelings). Noradrenalin can be produced by having students set personal goals, like practicing multiplication tables while jumping rope, and striving to jump progressively faster, demonstrating increased mastery of the tables. Dopamine is generated through gross motor repetitive movements, such as preparing a gymnastics routine in rhythm with a poem learned in language arts.

6. *Too much sitting.* When a child spends more than ten minutes confined to a seat, he or she runs the risk of poor breathing, strained spinal column and lower back nerves, poor eyesight, and overall body fatigue. Pressure on the spinal discs increases while sitting rather than standing, creating fatigue, which inhibits learning. Likewise, in order to see, children often compensate by leaning forward with rounded backs, restricting internal organ function and reducing blood circulation and oxygen to the brain. Therefore, it is evident that integrating meaningful physical activity should play a major role in curriculum planning.

7. *Value of implicit learning.* Implicit learning is a procedural or skills-based learning typical in physical education or art classes. Thus, when physical activity is integrated, retention of content information increases.

Jensen's evidence on reasons why students should "get moving" offers strong rationale for integrating movement in curricula. Further, educators aware of the science behind learning cannot overlook the need for movement throughout the school day.

Children enjoy the opportunity to be physically active in the home classroom.

IDEAS FOR INTEGRATION OF MOVEMENT

Below are some ideas for incorporating physical education activities into the home classroom. They were designed to be successful for classroom teachers. Although the likelihood of achieving school-wide devotion to integrated learning is remote, individual teachers can empower themselves and their students by incorporating physical education lessons into their classrooms.

Imbedding Process

Woods and Weasmer (1999) tell a story of an Iowa track coach who repeatedly won state championships. The day before each competition he would direct his students to write in detail the procedure they would follow as they competed in the next day's meet. A sprinter, for example, would define precisely how he would spring out of the starting blocks, establish stride lengths, use arms for momentum, lean for corner rounding, and maintain his speed past the finish line. By visualizing and documenting the vision, the runner would imbed the process in his thinking, enabling him to enhance movement efficacy. At the outset of the warm-up, team members isolated themselves and read the descriptions they had composed the previous day, centering each athlete's focus on specific expectations for the event.

National Standards

This coach's strategy points toward ways physical educators can integrate language arts and movement in elementary schools. When students are pressed to connect their knowledge across disciplines, their critical thinking skills are enhanced. Education at its best is not fragmented. Ideally, prior learning blends with new information to form fresh perspectives. The National Association for Sport and Physical Education extols physical education as an important component of students' education from kindergarten through grade 12. The national physical education standards (National Association for Sport and Physical Education, 2004) were designed to reinforce what students learn across the curriculum. They demonstrate that physical education can also serve as a laboratory for application knowledge acquired in subjects such as math, science, and social studies. Classroom teachers who try to unite and overlap learning experiences offer students additional opportunities to develop skills and apply concepts. See Key Point 12-2.

Key Point 12-2

Physical education is a subject that is well-suited for integration. There are many physical activities that can be combined with lessons from other content matter areas such as math, reading, science, and art.

Models of Integration

Nichols identifies three formats for integrating curricula. In the *sequenced model* "each subject is taught separately but scheduled so that similar units coincide in several subject areas" (1994, p. 49). In a Civil War unit, for example, a history teacher may collaborate with a physical educator to introduce the Virginia Reel. In a *shared model,* disciplines are brought together into a single focus using overlapping concepts. When science classes are studying recycling, for instance, small groups can design and complete fitness challenge courses using recyclable materials. Finally, in the *webbed model* integration is taken one step further by establishing a school-wide goal focusing on a central

Activities like dance transfer easily to other units of instruction.

theme. A project employing this model might center for several weeks on Greece and would incorporate Greek plays in language arts classes, history in social studies classes, music in music classes, and Olympic events in physical education classes. All of these models offer teachers and students opportunities to integrate learning through rich contemporary practices.

Individual Initiative

Ideas for integrated learning can be generated from the ground up by a single individual willing to take action. Jack, a physical educator at a small-town elementary school, read in a professional journal about a school that had successfully adopted a webbed model focusing on transportation. He had a keen interest in marine life and believed an effective web could be formed with that theme. Because the school had a contract with the town council to use the city pool for the first five weeks of the fall semester, his students could work on swimming skills and apply the body dynamics of sea creatures to their own movements in the water. Note that in each of the lab chapters in this text, integrated learning activities were included. Such suggestions should serve as springboards for collaborative idea development among teachers.

Collaborative Initiative

Innovative activity spurred by creative teachers comfortably connects content area learning with fitness. In another example Alysson, an energetic and innovative physical educator, began teaching at a rural elementary school. At a professional conference she attended in the fall, she learned possibilities for integrated instruction and was eager to share the experience with her students. The three 4th grade teachers in her building had a good rapport with one another and seemed progressive, so she approached them with a proposal to integrate language arts with an upcoming unit she had planned on kicking and foot dribbling. To describe the process in writing, the students would need to reflect on and articulate the procedure, which would ensure understanding and aid retention. The 4th grade teachers were delighted at the opportunity to connect writing to physical education, a discipline in which many of their students excelled. The four teachers agreed that due to the limited amount of time spent in physical education, the experience should be incorporated as a classroom assignment. See Key Point 12-3.

Key Point 12-3

Since physical activity is enjoyed by most children, they may be more excited about learning when classroom teachers couple lessons in physical education with lessons from other subject matter areas.

Use of Surprise

Willis (2007) asserts that surprises enhance learning, making it more likely that the content presented with the surprise will be retained. Students may be particularly surprised when their teacher begins incorporating movement breaks into the curriculum immediately before progressing to a new classroom learning activity. When younger children are working with phonics, for example, they "pop up" beside their seats and use their bodies to form letters, and then, after exposure to a lesson on phonics, leap up at a cue from the teacher in response to a letter sound. Likewise, older children studying weather may first be asked to move in groups across an area, enacting a kind of storm front, such as a tornado, a hurricane, or a rainstorm. After studying weather patterns, however, they may explain each member's role as they demonstrate in a more explicit manner the way the front travels. Complete Thinking Challenge 12.3.

THINKING CHALLENGE 12.3	What are three obstacles that teachers may encounter when trying to incorporate physical activity into the home classroom? What are three advantages of incorporating physical activity?

Obstacles
1.
2.
3.

Advantages
1.
2.
3.

Providing Transitions

Because of the need for transitions from one content area to the next during the school day, seizing such opportunities for movement is in order. In applying the strategy called "Popcorn," described above for use with phonics, children can move from closing one session by "popping up" with summary words to start up ideas for the next activity. When some students fall behind completing an assignment, in order to instill a minor sense of urgency, engaging those who are done and restless in an organized physical activity should spark others to step up the pace toward completion so they may join the rest of the class.

Additional Resources

Multiple handbooks on integrating physical activity are available for teachers. *Take 10!,* for instance, is a program designed for children from kindergarten through 5th grade that integrates physical activity and diet within the traditional curriculum. It offers a collection of suggested activities to involve students in engagement with movement while learning content. Included are activity cards, worksheets, a video, and curriculum objectives offered by the International Life Sciences Institute (ILSI), an Atlanta-based non-profit foundation that focuses on health-related education.

Another program, *Active Academics,* offers ways of integrating physical activities with K-5 math, language arts, and health/nutrition. Likewise, *Brain Breaks* provides lessons that

Motivated classroom teachers can provide additional opportunities for children to engage in physical activity on days when they do not have physical education class.

can be incorporated in K-6 content area studies. Another resource, *Energizers,* integrates physical activities with academic concepts. If the teacher is interested in taking the students out of the classroom, *Winter Kids Outdoor Learning Curriculum* offers several possibilities. To take the concept even further, *Activity Bursts for the Classroom* demonstrates ways to restructure physical activity into multiple brief episodes repeatedly throughout the day.

Whole School Involvement

A successful school-wide approach to physical activity engagement was created by Roth (2005). The "Around the Clock" program requires students to meet with the physical education teacher for 30 minutes during their normally scheduled class, but on those days that physical education is not scheduled, their classroom teachers are responsible for physical education. Several goals are met through "Around the Clock PE." First, all students are encouraged to walk and run around the clock (i.e., throughout the day) and keep track of their time engaged in activity. Teachers take students outside for 10 minutes each day to walk or run and then record the total number of minutes they are active. Second, students engage in active play at recess, extending the program to "Recess Around the Clock." At the end of recess, they again record engagement time. Finally, as an extension of the programs described above, students participate in "Weekend Around the Clock" where they tabulate their individual physical activity levels. This encourages them to remain active while not in school. At the close of the program, the number of minutes of walking or running by all members of the school community is tabulated first by the individual, then by the class as a unit, then by the entire school.

In prioritizing physical activity as a viable component of every subject area and grade level, teachers acknowledge children's need to move to learn. The results benefit all students, especially those kinesthetic learners who often struggle with a traditional segmented curriculum. Ongoing physical activities integrated with content area studies can facilitate wellness while stimulating academic growth.

Summary

Increasing evidence has shown a strong linkage between participation in physical activity and improved classroom performance. Physically active and fit children tend to perform better on achievement tests and have fewer discipline problems. Given the alarming rise in obesity levels, coupled with insufficient exposure to physical activity opportunities, it makes sense for the classroom teacher to simultaneously emphasize physical activity and academic performance by introducing bouts of physical activity spaced throughout the school day into lessons that are occurring in the home classroom.

Motivated teachers who incorporate physical activity into their home classroom lessons may wish to assess the interest levels of other teachers in the school in order to facilitate a school-wide emphasis on integrating movement across the curriculum. There are many resources available that can guide interested teachers.

Review Activities

1. Discuss in a small group how you feel about incorporating physical activity into the home classroom. Is this something you support?
2. In a small group, discuss how you could use a webbed model to develop a curriculum theme that would integrate what students are learning in art, math, physical education, reading, and social studies.
3. How could you integrate a lesson on creative dance with another lesson you might be teaching on the same day in your home classroom?
4. Discuss why physical activity may help to reduce behavior management problems.
5. How would you convince a skeptical teacher to become involved in an integrated curriculum effort?

References

Bandura, A. (1998). Health promotion from the perspective of social cognitive theory. *Psychology and Health, 13,* 623–649.

Fleshner, M. (2000). Exercise and neuroendocrine regulation of antibody production: Protective effect of physical activity on stress-induced suppression of the specific antibody response. *International Journal of Sports Medicine, 21,* 14–19.

Hillman, C. H., Pontifex, M. B., Raine, L. B., Castelli, D. M., Hall, E. E., & Kramer, A. F. (2009). The effect of acute treadmill walking on cognitive control and academic achievement in preadolescent children. *Neuroscience, 159*(3), 1044–1054.

Jensen, E. (2005). *Teaching with the brain in mind* (2nd ed.). Association for Supervision and Curriculum Development. Alexandria, VA.

National Association for Sport and Physical Education. (2004). *Moving into the future: National standards for physical education* (2nd ed.). Reston, VA: Author.

Nichols, B. (1994). *Moving and Learning: The elementary physical education experience* (3rd ed.). Boston: McGraw Hill.

Olshansky, S. J., Passaro, D. J., Hershow, R. C., Layden, J., Carnes, B. A., & Bordy, J. (2005). A potential decline in life expectancy in the United States in the 21st century. *New England Journal of Medicine, 352,* 1138–1145.

Rink, J. E., Hall, T. J., & Williams, L. H. (2010). *Schoolwide physical activity: A comprehensive guide to designing and conducting programs.* Champaign, IL: Human Kinetics.

Robert Wood Johnson Foundation. (Fall 2007). Active education: Physical education, physical activity and academic performance. San Diego: Active Living Research.

Roth, J. F. (2005). *The role of teachers' self-efficacy in increasing children's physical activity.* (Unpublished doctoral dissertation). Louisiana State University, Baton Rouge.

Sousa, D. (1998). Is the fuss about brain research justified? *Education Week, 18*(16), 52+.

U.S. Department of Health and Human Services. (2004). *Steps to Healthier Women.* Retrieved October 25, 2006, from www.4woman.gov/pub/steps/Obesity.htm

U.S. Centers for Disease Control and Prevention (2010). *The association between school-based physical activity, including physical education, and academic performance.* Atlanta, GA: U.S. Department of Health and Human Services.

Willis, J. (2007). Brain-based teaching strategies for improving students' memory, learning, and test-taking success. *Childhood education, 85*(5), 310.

Woods, A. M., & Weasmer, J. R. (1999). Integrated learning: Greater than the sum of its parts. *Teaching Elementary Physical Education, 10*(1), 21–23.

Chapter **Thirteen**

Locomotor Skills: Fundamental Patterns

A two year old walks down the stairs, jumps off the last step, and races around the kitchen table chirping, "Look, Mom! I'm a good runner!" In her short life, she has developed from a sedentary infant to a toddling whirlwind. She is proud and confident of her ability to move and continuously seeks new motions to master. Most two year olds enjoy walking, running, and jumping, skills important to children exploring their world. The joy of discovery motivates youngsters to keep moving.

As children get older they master complex locomotor skills, such as hopping, leaping, skipping, and galloping. Though most children learn simple locomotor skills through trial and error, when they enter school they need guidance to perform more complicated skills. For example, some children will need to see skipping demonstrated and have time to practice before they master the movement. Once students have acquired these skills and learned the names of such movements, they can incorporate their new skills into more structured activities, such as sports, dance, and gymnastics.

Elementary teachers must ensure that children have mastered fundamental locomotor patterns efficiently. Children also need guidance in adapting the movements they have mastered to different environments and activities. By revisiting the basics of movement throughout the elementary years, teachers can help students further develop locomotor skills.

FUNDAMENTAL LOCOMOTOR PATTERNS

Transporting the body from one space to another requires locomotion. In order to advance or retreat, one's extremities unite in an effort toward a movement goal.

The legs and the arms sustain the bulk of the responsibility for such movement. Instruction on correct form can result in improved movement efficiency. Specific learning cues outline correct procedures for each skill. Common difficulties are also noted. Those locomotor skills requiring whole-body movement include the following:

Walking

At what age can a child first stand up? When does he or she take their first step? When can she or he cruise in circles around the coffee table? When can she or he finally walk independently, shuttling from one end of the room to the other? These movements are milestones for children during their first years. In elementary school years, the teacher's responsibility is to recognize and reinforce mature walking patterns. Such fundamental movements lay the groundwork for more refined demands that come later, such as dancing, gymnastics, and other sports.

Individuals walk in forward, backward, and sideways directions. In a forward gait, a person moves ahead while shifting weight evenly from one foot to another, always contacting the ground with one foot. The heel meets the ground first, followed by the middle of the foot, then the ball of the foot, finally pushing off with the toes. In efficient walking, the toes point forward and the feet are placed on the ground in an even line that divides the

Children enjoy moving through space with a variety of locomotor movements.

body in half vertically. The body is held in a straight posture with the head erect, each arm swinging forward and backward with the opposite foot.

Learning Cues
- Place foot "heel, ball, toe"
- Point toes forward
- Keep body erect with head held high
- Relax arms and move in opposition to legs

Common Difficulties
- Contacting with a flat foot
- Pointing toes inward
- Pointing toes outward
- Keeping arms stiff/rigid/held out for balance
- Crossing the midline of the body with arms
- Holding head forward, causing forward trunk position

Running

Participation in numerous elementary-aged activities utilizes a running pattern. Running uses all of the basic motions of walking, but because the speed is faster there is a brief moment between steps when neither foot is touching the ground. During running there is an increase in stride length, arm movement, forward body lean, and knee flexion. While jogging the foot meets the ground heel first as in a walk. When sprinting the child's feet push off the ground with the toes, and the heels do not make contact. As the leg swings back, the heel moves toward the buttocks; the arms, with the bend of the elbows creating a right angle, swing forward and backward with the opposite legs. See Figure 13.1.

Learning Cues
- Maintain a brief period of flight
- Place foot "heel, ball, toe" in a jog
- Place foot "ball, toe" in a run
- Bend and move arms in opposition to legs
- Lean body forward with head erect
- Open mouth and breathe naturally

FIGURE 13.1
Mature running.

Common Difficulties
- Swinging arm excessively
- Swinging arms incompletely
- Crossing midline of body with arms
- Contacting ground with flat feet
- Crossing midline of body with legs
- Swinging legs out from the body
- Closing mouth or inhibiting breathing

Jumping

Jumping is an exciting skill for children, who enjoy the thrill of leaving the ground to become momentarily airborne. As their jumping skills improve, children enjoy more challenging jumps. They may jump off stairs, porches, and even moving swings. Jumping is a common skill used in sports, dance, gymnastics, and individual play such as hopscotch and jumping rope.

Three different styles include jumping from two feet to two feet, from one foot to two feet, or from two feet to one foot. A jump can be modified to aim for vertical height or horizontal distance or to keep time rhythmically, as in jumping rope. An efficient jump demands coordination of all body movements.

When children are jumping vertically, their performance is improved if they are jumping to reach a target. For example, if a teacher places a balloon at a certain height, children may jump to touch it. Before jumping for height, a person crouches and bends the hips, knees, and ankles. In a burst of energy, the body springs with both feet, extending as the arms surge upward. At the height of the jump one arm drops to allow the reaching arm to extend farther. Eyes focus on the target, causing the head to tilt up. In the middle of the

FIGURE 13.2
Jumping for distance.

jump, the body is completely extended. As the jumper lands, the hips, knees, and ankles flex again to absorb the impact and maintain balance.

Learning Cues
- Crouch to prepare
- Tilt head and look at target
- Extend body fully
- Drop one arm at height of jump
- Bend legs during landing

Common Difficulties
- Taking off from an upright position
- Taking off with only one foot
- Extending incompletely
- Keeping head down
- Reaching with both arms at height of jump
- Landing with extended legs

When children are jumping for distance, they usually begin by taking a few running steps to gain momentum. Before jumping horizontally, the body crouches down and the arms swing back. As the arms swing in front of the body, the body springs forward off the ground and extends fully at a 45-degree angle. The legs reach in front of the body just before the jumper lands. As the jumper is landing, the balls of the feet contact the ground and the hips, knees, and ankles bend. The arms may be held in front of the body for balance. See Figure 13.2.

Learning Cues
- Crouch and swing arms back to prepare
- Swing arms forward
- Extend body fully
- Land on balls of feet with bent legs
- Balance with arms in front

Common Difficulties

- Taking off from an upright position
- Taking off with only one foot
- Extending incompletely
- Failing to move arms backward and forward
- Landing with extended legs

Hopping

On a hand-sketched chalk grid, a child bounces on the sidewalk, deftly switching from using one foot to two feet, reaching the end with a combination of these movements. While this game is called "hopscotch," it is really a mix of hopping and jumping. Though similar to jumping, one hops from a single foot and lands upon the same foot whether hopping in place or covering a distance. While one foot is hopping the other leg should be bent at a right angle as arms are used for balance and momentum. The hopping leg springs from and lands upon the ball of the foot. Hopping requires endurance and balance because the movement is concentrated on one foot. Teachers should have children practice hopping on one foot and then the other foot to even the strain on each leg.

Learning Cues

- Hop one foot to the same foot
- Contact the ground with ball of foot
- Bend inactive leg
- Use arms to increase balance and force
- Switch active leg often

Common Difficulties

- Contacting ground with flat foot
- Overusing arms
- Failing to control movement of hopping leg
- Extending inactive leg

Leaping

Leaping is common in dance and gymnastics and also in youth sports where children may leap to catch a baseball or shoot a basketball. Crossing a wooded field, children may leap over puddles, creeks, and ditches and then leap up to touch the leaves on a tree. Combining the skills of running with an upward spring, leaping sustains an airborne suspension while covering the distance from one foot to the other. In executing an efficient leap the leading leg extends fully and the body leans forward, as arms move in opposition to the legs, swinging upward from the body to gain height. At the completion of the leap the landing is on the balls of the feet.

Learning Cues

- Step out forcefully with leading leg
- Lean forward
- Use arms for balance and force
- Land on balls of feet

Common Difficulties

- Contacting with a flat foot
- Moving arms out of sync with legs
- Lacking height
- Lacking distance

Galloping and Sliding

The gallop is an uneven movement with the lead leg making the larger movement and the trailing leg closing the gap. As children attempt to replicate the movement of horses, one foot leads with a forward bouncing step and the other foot leaps to meet the lead foot without crossing. The trailing foot lands next to or behind the lead foot as the lead foot steps again, repeating the motion. Arms are not a critical part of the movement, though an arm swing may increase the speed and force of the gallop. Children can practice leading with one foot and then switching to lead with the other leg. Sliding uses similar movements in a sideways direction.

Learning Cues

- Lead with the same leg
- Take a long step with leading leg
- Close the gap with trailing leg

Common Difficulties

- Overemphasizing height, not forward movement
- Stepping too long or short
- Contacting following foot in front of lead foot
- Lacking dexterity in leading with both feet

Skipping

Skipping combines stepping and hopping while alternating the lead from one foot to the other. The skipping movement starts with a step forward on the ball of one foot, pushing off with the toes, and then a hop on the same foot. The skipper lands first on the toes of the foot. The other leg repeats the movement, and the skipper continues alternating lead legs. Arms move with the opposite legs and can be used to increase force or height. Skipping is a movement associated with happiness—a person skips gaily or joyfully. Once children learn this complex movement, they skip as an expression of joy, like when getting an ice cream cone or entering a park.

Learning Cues

- Step with one foot
- Hop on the same foot
- Repeat movement with other leg
- Move arms in opposition to legs

Common Difficulties

- Contacting with flat feet
- Stopping between steps and hops
- Lacking dexterity in leading with each foot
- Moving arms out of sync with legs
- Overemphasizing height; de-emphasizing forward movement

MOVEMENT EXPERIENCES

Monkey See; Monkey Do

Objectives

To enhance student awareness of mature walking, running, and jumping form

To improve students' dynamic balance

To encourage pleasurable movement learning

Targeted Age Group

K-2

Equipment

Lively music
CD player

Management

1. Designate a large activity area.
2. Divide class into groups of 4–5. Appoint a lead monkey for each troop and ask the other monkeys to form lines behind their leaders.

Pre-activity

As the teacher describes each movement, the lead monkeys demonstrate for the rest of the troops the correct form for walking.

Another representative from each troop models running, and a third demonstrates jumping maturely.

The teacher stresses that it is the lead monkey's responsibility to model correct walking, running, and jumping.

The teacher explains the advantages of efficient movement.

Activity

1. At the start of the music lead monkeys guide their troops to any location in the activity area while practicing efficient movement. When the leader runs the rest of the troop apes that action until the leader shifts to walking or jumping and the troop follows in kind.
2. When the music stops the lead monkey goes to the back of the line and the second monkey becomes the leader.
3. Continue the activity until all monkeys have had the opportunity to lead, modeling mature movement.

Modifications

- The tempo of the music can be varied to enliven or slow the pace of the children's movement.
- When students begin to master efficient foot/leg movements, they can add creative arm movements.
- The activity area can be divided into three segments using cones or polyspots. As groups cross into new areas, they begin the activity designated for that segment.
- Study monkeys and their habitat. Discover behavior and movement patterns.

Assessment

Are all students striving to improve locomotion efficiency?
Are students following rules and safety measures?
Are students enthusiastic about the activity?

Jumping Beans

Objectives

To work toward more efficient jumping skills
To encourage students to jump toward targets
To demonstrate enjoyable locomotion activities

Targeted Age Group

K-2

Equipment

10 balloons

10 polyspots or cones

Masking tape

15 long jump ropes

5 golf tees or other markers

CD player

Lively music

Management

1. Divide activity area into four quadrants.
2. Inflate 10 balloons and then in one quadrant adhere them to playground equipment, trees, or areas in the gym that are in varying heights above students' reach when their arms are extended.
3. In another quadrant situate five pairs of jump ropes in V shapes.
4. In a third quadrant lay out five jump ropes to serve as restraining lines. Place one tee or other marker beside each rope.
5. Assign students in equal numbers to four groups. Direct each group to a different quadrant.

Pre-activity

Students brainstorm sports and activities that require jumping.

As the teacher describes the procedure for distance jumping, a representative bean from each of the two groups assigned to distance jumping quadrants will demonstrate proper jumping form.

As the teacher outlines correct form for height jumping, a representative bean from each of the groups assigned to the quadrants for height jumping will demonstrate proper form.

Activity

As a signal from the teacher beans will switch quadrants.

First quadrant

Beans in this quadrant will leap up to touch balloons fastened to high objects in varying degrees beyond their reach. When they reach one or if they have tried unsuccessfully for three jumps, they move to another balloon.

Second quadrant

Beans will dart to and jump across the segment of the jump rope V. They may choose the narrowest spread or the widest portion of the V.

Third quadrant

Beans will dash across the quadrant until they reach the restraining ropes and then jump as far as they can past the rope, using a tee to mark their farthest jump.

Fourth quadrant

Beans will pair up and face each other. One bean pops up as high as she or he can, while the other drops down on her or his haunches ready to spring up as the partner bean drops down.

Modifications

- Beans can use boxes as platforms to jump up upon or down from.
- Beans can jump over or into hoops.
- Beans can use jump ropes, attempting to jump as high as they can with each jump.

Assessment

Are beans moving safely while jumping?

Are beans reaching challenging heights and distances?

Is each bean working to achieve correct jumping form?

Are beans enjoying the activity?

Jungle Safari

Objectives

To develop efficient locomotor skills

To increase enthusiasm for locomotor activities

Targeted Age Group

K-5

Equipment

CD player

Jungle music

Management

1. Safari participants divide into groups of five and scatter over a wide activity area.
2. Jungle boundaries are established.

Pre-activity

Students brainstorm what might be encountered in a jungle safari.

The students are told they are about to embark and will be traveling through a great jungle with challenging terrain, wild animals, and changing weather.

Activity

1. Each group of children led by their safari guide can travel anywhere in the designated area.
2. The teacher calls out an obstacle and each group follows the announced directions.

Examples

"An alligator has his jaws open and waits in the swamp ahead. Run fast and leap up and over the alligator."

"Oh no! Here comes a herd of wildebeests! Turn to your right and run to avoid being trampled!"

"Up ahead is a swinging footbridge. Carefully walk in correct form to ensure a safe crossing."

"Here is a big bed of coals a group of cannibals left behind. Skip across it as fast as you can to keep from burning your feet!"

"A long black snake is dangling from the baobab tree. Jump up, grab it, and put it in a sack."

"Here comes a heard of zebras! Join in with them and gallop across the jungle."

"Oh no! A wart hog has bitten the big toe on your right foot. Hop on your left foot in and out of the trees."

"Look at the giraffes grazing here! Jump up as high as you can to pat the tops of their heads."

"A group of hippopotamuses is sleeping in the water below us. Slide along the rocks quickly and quietly so as not to disturb them."

"A rhino is charging at us! Turn and run as fast as you can before he gets you with his sharp horn."

"Here is a lovely waterfall. Walk carefully behind it using proper form to be sure you can keep your balance. Extend your arms out for balance. Be sure that you don't get wet."

3. At a signal from the teacher the guide moves to the end of the line and the second participant leads the safari.

Modifications

- Couple this lesson with a unit on jungle life.
- Study about and create a similar activity in the Wild Wild West.
- At Halloween time use ghosts, haunted houses, witches on brooms, and black cats as obstacles.
- Study about and travel to a different planet to confront foreign obstructions.

Assessment

Have the students maximized the activity possibilities?

Are students demonstrating correct form?

Are all students enthusiastically engaged?

Wagon Wheel

Objectives

To encourage students to concentrate on modeling correct form

To develop locomotor skills

To enthuse students about locomotion activities

Targeted Age Group

3–5

Equipment

Signs that announce "Walking," "Running," "Hopping," "Leaping," "Jumping," "Galloping," "Sliding," and "Skipping"

Eight long jump ropes

CD player

Lively music

Management

1. Signs are posted around a wide activity area.
2. Jump ropes are extended as the staves of a wagon wheel to separate the areas.

Pre-activity

Children are divided into eight groups. Each group takes a position at one of the locomotor stations.

Activity

1. When the music starts the children perform the locomotor activity designated by the sign labeling their area.
2. When the music stops each group moves clockwise into the next area.
3. The teacher will periodically signal a change of direction, timing, and pathways, such as "Backward!" "Zigzag!" "To the right!" "To the left!" "Clockwise!" "Counterclockwise!" "Fast!" "Slow!"

Modifications

- The teacher can call out a child's name and the child then signals a change of direction, timing, and pathway.
- Perform the activity with a partner.
- Students can assume another persona such as a tin man, a soldier, a ballerina, a clown, or an animal and demonstrate the way such an individual might perform the locomotor activity.

Assessment

Are the children demonstrating proper locomotor form?

Are the students following directions and maintaining safe pathways?

Are the students enjoying the activity?

Chapter Fourteen

Manipulative Skills: Throwing and Catching

Brad glances out the window at his fourth graders enjoying their recess time. He smiles as he notices Jenna throw a ball to Jillian at one end of the pavement. Their faces are tight with concentration as they practice the movements he demonstrated that morning. The two close friends consistently pay close attention to the details of physical activities he teaches. He can visualize them enjoying their developing skill as the summer unfolds. Like the give and take required of a close friendship, throwing and catching are interdependent activities. When an individual releases the ball into the air, it moves in flight toward a target destination, the catcher. Whether the exchange occurs on a ball field, on the beach, or in the back yard, utilizing proper throwing and catching movements makes for more efficient and satisfying play.

Due to the rigorous demands of the workplace, many parents have little time to devote to such leisure activities with their children. Whereas some children spend after-school hours in physical activities with neighborhood peers, many latchkey kids are instructed to remain behind locked doors until the evening return of their parents. Thus, the instruction provided by elementary educators may be integral to the early development of throwing and catching skills for those who have little such activity time after school or in summer.

In a study by Mark Manross (2000, p. 32), 54 children testified to their "thoughts, feelings, and knowledge" about learning to throw. Manross shaped the following three assertions: (1) throwing is an important skill to learn; (2) practicing alone and/or with a friend is the best way to learn to throw; and (3) the children understood what was helpful or not helpful in their physical education classes. One reason the students believed in the significance of skill development was that knowing how to throw opened avenues for them to be able to play a variety of games and sports. They also thought it important because a degree of skill development could prevent their being embarrassed in front of friends and help them to avoid disappointing teammates.

Such information affirms the importance of providing instruction in correct procedures. Students look to those with know-how to aid in developing skills that they are expected to know as part of the youth culture. Thus, classroom and physical activity instruction both contribute to developing early success and confidence in children.

Children can gain valuable throwing and catching practice during free time.

FUNDAMENTALS OF THROWING

Throwing provides momentum to transport an object through the air a desired distance. Whereas throwing a short distance requires little but a flick of the wrist, throwing an extended distance demands a greater physical investment, which is more mechanically efficient. In working with students to develop more mature throwing skills, teachers should design learning experiences that encourage forceful throwing. Repeated throws across a wide activity area demand more forceful throwing than many students may have previously experienced.

Underhand Throwing

In mature underhand throwing, the hand holding the object glides back to an extended position, while the hips face forward and the opposite foot steps ahead. Next the hand bearing the object sweeps down past the supporting knee and releases when it reaches a point in direct line with the target (see Figure 14.1). The amount of momentum required is in proportion to the distance necessary. Working toward increased force empowers students to repeat correct form toward achieving accuracy and distance. Throwing a softball underhanded to a batter or a bowling ball at ten pins requires a similar procedure.

Overhand Throwing

Mature overhand throwing is generally used when a greater force is required. The primary differences from throwing underhand are hip placement and trunk rotation and the additional use of the elbow (see Figure 14.2). Whereas in underhand throwing the body faces forward and the arm flows straight through, in overhand throwing the side of the body faces the target and the elbow leads the arm through the throw.

FIGURE 14.1
Mature underhand throwing.

FIGURE 14.2
Mature overhand throwing.

Developmental Levels

Level One.

Often in the early levels of throwing the child's stance faces forward, limiting the force of the throw. The arm becomes the sole source of power and the feet remain stationary as the ball is released.

Overhand Throwing

Box 14.1

Level I	Level II	Level III
Stance is face forward	Step forward with same foot as throwing arm	Stance sideways to target
Arm sole source of power	Arm follows forward and downward	Non-dominant arm hangs loosely against side of body
Feet stationary on ball release	Bend at waist	Dominant hand grasps ball
		Raise arm until parallel to ground
		Step forward on non-dominant foot and shift weight
		Elbow leads and forearm moves forward to propel ball
		Arm follows through in direction of target

Level Two.

At this level the child steps forward with the same foot as the throwing arm, mistakenly supposing that the force of both together will propel the ball. The arm may follow through forward and downward as the child bends forward at the waist.

Level Three.

In the most advanced level the student stands turned to the side with the non-dominant arm hanging loosely against the side of the body facing the target. The dominant hand grasps the ball and raises the arm until it is parallel to the ground. The student steps forward on the non-dominant foot and shifts weight to that foot as the elbow leads and the forearm then moves forward to propel the ball. As the ball is released the student's arm should follow through in the direction of the target.

See Box 14.1 for additional information on the developmental levels of throwing.

Learning Cues

- Grasp ball with finger pads
- Rotate body away from target
- Elbow leads arm forward
- Step forward with opposite foot
- Follow through

Common Difficulties

- Ball in palm
- Stepping through with same foot as throwing arm
- Lack of hip rotation
- Bending forward at waist
- Downward release

FUNDAMENTALS OF CATCHING

Because children develop at varying rates, their catching skills are rarely predictable. The less mature the child, the more difficult for her or him to determine the distance and speed of an approaching ball. When a child lacks confidence in his or her ability to catch the ball, often the first impulse is to duck or flinch when a ball approaches. Because a peer thrower

FIGURE 14.3
Mature catching.

is also unskilled, the accuracy of the ball's approach is inconsistent, adding to the evasive response such an exchange invites. For this reason the use of foam balls in early development may offer the practice necessary to increase skill levels while increasing confidence.

When catching above the waist, students press the length of their thumbs together with hands open in a receiving position. Below the waist catching differs in that the length of their pinkies should be parallel and touching. By first raising hands as in catching a fly ball and then shifting into position to catch a low ball, they can feel the difference. See Figure 14.3.

Developmental Levels

Level One.

Students in the early levels of catching often demonstrate fear of the approaching ball. Because of their lack of speed and depth perception, they use their entire body to stop the ball, standing up tall rather than bending to meet the ball. They often scoop their arms upward to grasp the ball against themselves before it drops.

Level Two.

In this phase the student displays greater confidence by reaching to catch the ball, yet lacks needed proficiency. Reliance upon scooping to trap the ball may occur. However, stepping into the catch is still not evident. Absorbing the impact with hands stretched forward may result in dropping the ball.

Level Three.

In preparation for the catch the student stands with knees slightly bent and feet comfortably apart. Upper arms hang relaxed at the sides of the body while hands and forearms are held in front. Eyes on the ball, the catcher moves his or her body directly in line with the oncoming ball. If the catch is anticipated above the waist, the thumbs of the hands are

Catching   Box 14.2

Level I

Fear of approaching ball

Whole body used to stop ball

Standing up tall rather than bending to meet ball

Scoop arms upward to trap ball against body

Level II

Reaches to catch ball

Continued reliance upon scooping to trap ball

Stepping to catch not evident

Hand stretched may cause ball to drop

Level III

Stance with knees slightly bent and feet apart

Hands and forearms held in front

Hands and forearms held in front

Eyes focused on ball

Body moves directly in line with oncoming ball

Thumbs together for catch above waist

Pinkies together for catch below waist

Reach to grasp ball

Absorbs force by giving with ball to midline of body

---

together. A low ball requires that pinkies be together. The student reaches to grasp the ball and absorbs the force of the throw by giving with the ball into the midline of the body. See Box 14.2 for additional information on the developmental levels of catching.

Learning Cues

- Reach toward oncoming ball
- Relax fingers, aiming down for low and up for high balls
- Bend knees, feet apart
- Finger pads receive ball and pull it in toward trunk

Common Difficulties

- Fear of ball
- Remaining upright
- Trapping ball at chest
- Catching with palms

MOVEMENT EXPERIENCES

It's a Ringer

Objective

To further develop mature underhand throwing and catching skills

To strive toward underhand throwing for force and accuracy

To appreciate the collaborative nature of underhand throwing

Targeted Age Group

Grades K-2

Equipment

30 beanbags (one for each student)

15 hula hoops (two to a hoop)

Management

1. Each student selects a beanbag.
2. Children pair up.
3. Each pair takes a hoop.

Pre-Activity

Students review mature form of underhand throwing.

Students discuss activities when throwing is used.

Teacher adds directions necessary for this activity.

Activity

1. The hula hoop is placed on the floor approximately 15 feet in front of each pair.
2. Alternating throws, the two practice tossing the beanbags underhand into the hoop.
3. Alternating throws between the two children, they toss the beanbags into the ring of the hoop. After three in a row land inside the hoop, the team takes one step back.
4. Children prop hoops up along the wall, step back ten steps, and throw into the hoop. When three in a row land inside the hoop, the team takes one step back.

Modifications

- Students vary the types of throwing objects for added challenge.
- Children count by fives, tens, and twenties with each throw.
- Students add a point for each throw that is lands in the target and subtract one when there is a miss.
- Children move through the alphabet with each throw, calling, "A-alligator," "B-bar-b-que," etc.

Assessment

Did participants demonstrate mature underhand throwing form?

Did the children work collaboratively?

Were all pairs able to back up for throwing at least five paces?

Oh Beans!

Objective

To further develop mature underhand throwing and catching skills

To strive toward underhand throwing for force and accuracy

To appreciate the collaborative nature of underhand throwing and catching

Targeted Age Group

Grades K-2

Equipment

30 beanbags (one for each student)

yardstick

Management

Each student selects a beanbag.

Students spread out at least ten steps apart from each other over a wide area.

Pre-Activity

Students review mature forms of throwing and catching.

Students discuss activities when throwing and catching are used.

Teacher adds directions necessary for this activity.

Activity

1. The teacher shows the yardstick and then has a student demonstrate a throw of approximately that height. With both hands each participant throws the bean bag upward, keeps their eyes on the bean bag, and catches it.
2. Once students have demonstrated awareness of correct throwing, they then practice mature catching, whereby the hands reach up to catch and upon contact give until the ball is cradled at the waist.
3. Students are challenged to see how many catches in a row they can make.
4. Next the students repeat the process, keeping eyes on the ball as they throw the bean bag two yardstick lengths into the air and catch it.
5. Then the participants throw the bean bag into the air with the dominant hand only and catch it with both hands.
6. When a large percentage of the students have demonstrated mastery, challenge them to catch with one hand.
7. Next children toss the bean bag slightly ahead into the air and step forward until they catch it, absorbing the force with a downward pull.
8. Finally participants stand facing one another 15 feet apart and practice throwing and catching to each other. The teacher calls out, "Oh beans!" signaling students to throw while calling out kinds of beans like "butter beans," "navy beans," "chili beans," "lima beans," "green beans," "French-cut beans," "pinto beans," etc. When they call out a bean type and successfully exchange without dropping the beanbag, they may each take one step back. (Students may need to see a lineup of labeled beans prior to engaging in the game to familiarize themselves with types of beans.)

Modifications

- Students vary the types of throwing objects for added challenge.
- Students count by fives, tens, and twenties with each throw/catch.
- Students add a point for each throw that is caught and subtract one when there is a miss.
- Children throw and catch to the beats of a recorded song or while singing a song.

Assessment

Did the students follow the guidelines for the "Oh Beans" activity?

Did participants demonstrate mature throwing and catching forms?

Did children remain on tasks as described by the teacher?

Were students enthusiastically engaged?

Catch Me If You Can

Objective

To further develop mature overhand and underhand throwing and catching skills

To strive toward overhand and underhand throwing for force and accuracy

To appreciate the collaborative nature of overhand and underhand throwing and catching

Targeted Age Group

Grades 3–5

Equipment

One ball for every two students

Management

Students are paired and each pair selects a ball.

Pre-Activity

Students review correct throwing and catching techniques.

Children pace out a 15-foot distance between them.

Activity

Throwing with a Partner

Maintaining the 15-foot separation, pairs run the length of the extended area, throwing the ball back and forth as they run without stopping.

Upon reaching the other side, they turn and return, throwing and catching as they run.

Throwing with a Group

In groups of four, students form circles at least 10 paces apart.

At a signal from the teacher all students begin to run around their circles. Without stopping one child throws the ball to any other student in the group while running.

Throwing and catching while on the move continues until the teacher indicates that students should widen the circle but not stop the activity. Groups challenge themselves to continue expanding the circle until they are no longer successful throwing and catching while in motion.

Modifications

- The thrower calls out a multiplication problem as she or he throws and the catcher shouts the answer as she or he catches.
- Music starts and stops the activity, and when throwing with a group indicates time for the circle to expand.
- A second ball may be added to the group activity to intensify involvement.

Assessment

Are the students successfully completing the activity as directed?

Are the children demonstrating effective throwing and catching skills on the move without stopping?

Are students demonstrating good sportsmanship with classmates?

Bouncin' off the Walls

Objective

To further develop mature overhand throwing and catching skills

To strive toward throwing for force and accuracy

To appreciate the collaborative nature of throwing and catching

To keep children mindful of safety precautions when throwing and catching balls

Targeted Age Group

Grades 3–5

Equipment

One tennis ball per child

2 polyspots or cones

Management

Polyspots or cones mark an imaginary line approximately ten steps back from long wall

Pre-Activity

Students review mature forms of throwing and catching.

Students discuss activities when throwing and catching are used.

Teacher adds directions necessary for this activity.

Teacher reminds students to be careful not to strike others with balls.

Activity

Throwing Individually

1. Children first catch the ball with one bounce and at a signal from the teacher throw more forcefully and catch with no bounce.
2. Students demonstrate correct catching—entire body behind the catch, stepping to meet the ball, and retrieving the ball to midbody with each catch.
3. Children count each ball caught in a row, challenging themselves to increase the number.

Throwing with a Partner

1. Students pair up, sharing a ball for each pair.
2. One participant throws the ball against the wall and the other catches it and then returns the throw.
3. Children first catch the ball with one bounce and at a signal from the teacher throw more forcefully and catch with no bounce.
4. Students demonstrate correct catching, entire body behind the catch, stepping to meet the ball, and retrieving the ball to midbody with each catch.
5. Children count each ball caught in a row, challenging themselves to increase the number
6. Pairs count the number caught in two minutes, as timed by the teacher, then time again to beat their count.

Modifications

- Before shifting to one bounce before catching, let ball bounce twice before catching.
- Student names a state as she or he throws and the peer names the capitol as she or he catches, moving on to state bird or state flower.
- Students name a former president with each throw or catch.
- Children name a vocabulary word with the throw and the definition with the catch.
- Participants can review math tables with the question on the throw and the answer on the catch.
- Music can accompany as students throw and catch on the beat.

Assessment

Are the students successfully completing the activity as directed?

Are the children demonstrating effective throwing and catching skills?

Are students demonstrating good sportsmanship with classmates?

References

Manross, M. (2000). Learning to throw in physical education class: Part 2. Teaching Elementary Physical Education, 32–34.

Chapter **Fifteen**

Manipulative Skills: Volleying and Dribbling

On the Fourth of July, Phillip's family hosts an annual friend and family get-together at their home. After the barbeque they inevitably team up for a friendly game of volleyball. Players include jolly Mr. Simpson from across the street, Phillip's seven-year-old cousin Nick, and his older sister Susan, who played on the volleyball team in high school. All enjoy the camaraderie and Phillip senses his contribution to the team. Without serious adherence to the rules, the teams focus instead on getting the ball across the net and having a good time.

In August Mr. Landbeck, Phillip's fourthgrade teacher announces, "Today we are going to work on volleying." Phillip smiles at his pleasant memories. His enthusiasm and confidence shine through as he listens, receptive to advice that may improve a game he already enjoys.

Though the sport of volleyball most commonly relies upon volleying, there are other opportunities for using the skill such as heading the ball in soccer or playing hacky sack. Volleying differs from throwing and catching in that rather than grasping the ball and redirecting it, the body meets the ball and the impact sends it in an intended direction. The forearms, the head, the knees, and the finger pads serve as impact points. Because volleying may include participants of all ages, developing mature skills in the early grades can provide a foundation for lifelong enjoyment.

In the early stages of volleying children should use only large soft balls or balloons that negate fear of contact. Also, the advantage of sizable balls is that the flight pattern is

Underhand striking is practiced in this modified volleyball activity.

slowed, allowing the child time to prepare for the impact. With the exception of the use of finger pads to set volleyball, generally a larger body area connects with the ball. Children can enjoy volleying individually, with a partner, or with a group.

FUNDAMENTALS OF VOLLEYING

Volleying provides momentum to transport an object through the air a desired distance. The total body is situated to direct the ball to its target. Though it may appear that the simple passing of a ball to another is effortless, the complex investment required may be difficult for young children, who are generally inexperienced with ball striking. In early stages children need substantial practice simply passing balls to and fro. With experience they grow more adept and are ready to develop specific sports skills. Volleying with the forearms is essential when the ball comes at an angle requiring contact just above the waist. Overhand volleying, however, is necessary when the ball comes in high above the head of the student. Developing the use of the forearms for underhand and finger pads for overhand volleying leads to mature form.

Forearm Volleying

In mature volleying the body must be in position to receive the ball in order to effectively execute a pass. With back posture firm, trunk leaning forward, and knees slightly bent the receiver rivets eyes to the ball. Hands are extended with the dominant hand clutched and clasped in the palm of the non-dominant hand. The forearms should be pressed closely together forming a flat platform to connect with the ball at the broadest point. The legs provide propulsion by rising in tandem with the shoulders to send the ball toward its target. After the ball rebounds the body follows through in the same direction. See Figure 15.1.

Developmental Levels

Level One.   In the early levels of forearm volleying the child is often unable to assume the appropriate position with knees bent to make contact at the correct place on the forearms. Children may eagerly fling their joined arms upward to hit the ball rather than to position their arms lower to meet the ball and allow it to rebound upon impact. They may stand tall without bending their knees.

Level Two.   Here the child continues to have difficulty predicting the ball's descent and positioning to power it upward. Occasional upward arm thrusts preclude the ball's contact with the forearms at a preferred point beneath the chest. Some students may be able to send a ball to an intended target.

Level Three.   In the most advanced level the student is positioned slightly crouched under the ball in its approach with the lead foot slightly forward. Wrists and hands are pressed together. Arm motion is rooted in the shoulder rather than the elbow as the parallel arms rise in conjunction with the legs to meet the ball and send it upward.

See Box 15.1 for additional information on the developmental levels of volleying.

FIGURE 15.1
This photograph shows mature forearm volleying.

Learning Cues
- Position body directly under the predicted contact point of the ball
- Crouch slightly and keep eyes on the ball
- Press wrists and hands together
- Lock elbows
- Lift with legs and poise for ball to meet forearms

Common Difficulties
- Incorrect prediction of ball's path for body positioning
- Raising arms to meet ball rather than waiting for descent

Forearm Volleying   Box 15.1

LEVEL I	LEVEL II	LEVEL III
Feet together Standing tall rather than bending knees	Feet together or apart Slight bending of knees	Lead foot forward Slightly crouched beneath predicted contact point of approaching ball
Flinging joined arms upward to contact ball	Occasional upward thrust of arms Wrist and hands apart	Arm motion rooted at shoulders Wrists and hands pressed together Parallel arms rise in conjunction with legs to meet ball

- Connecting with ball at a place other than the broadest points on the forearms
- Upper rather than whole body upward force to send ball

Overhand Volleying

In overhand volleying the body is crouched directly under the ball with one foot slightly ahead of the other. The face is turned upward toward the approaching ball with hands poised palms up above the hairline and elbows bent outward. Finger pads contact the ball at a point above and in front of the forehead and as it is propelled, the legs and arms extend simultaneously. See Figure 15.2.

Developmental Levels

As a child's abilities mature, she or he passes through the following levels:

Level One.   In the early levels of volleying the child is often unable to position her or himself under the ball or to make contact with both hands simultaneously. She or he also has difficulty predicting the path of the ball in its approach. When attempting a volley, the child often slaps from behind, forcing the ball straight ahead or downward rather than up.

FIGURE 15. 2
These are examples of overhand volleying.

Overhead Volleying   Box 15.2

LEVEL I

Unable to position self beneath predicted contact point

Unable to make contact with both hands

Slaps ball from behind

No centering of movement

LEVEL II

Sometimes positions self beneath approaching ball

Sometimes makes contact with both hands

Slaps ball from behind

Movement centered on upper body, not total body

LEVEL III

Positioned slightly crouched beneath approaching ball

Lead foot slightly forward

Wrists firmly pressed together remain fixed

Finger pads direct ball

Contacts ball close to hairline

Whole body follows through toward target

Level Two. At this level the child continues to have difficulty following the ball's approach, getting under the ball to power it upward and slapping it from behind. Movement still centers upon the upper body rather than the total body investment essential for mature volleying. It also is evident that the student cannot yet predict the return volley's flight path.

Level Three. In the most advanced level the student is positioned slightly crouched under the ball in its approach with the lead foot slightly forward. Upon contact close to the hairline the finger pads direct the ball in an intended pattern, wrists remain firmly fixed, and the student's whole body follows through in the propulsion of the ball toward its target.

See Box 15.2 for additional information on the developmental levels of overhead volleying.

Learning Cues

- Position body directly beneath the predicted contact point of the ball
- Crouch slightly and keep eyes on the ball
- Contact the ball with the finger pads at the hairline
- Extend whole body upward for follow-through

Common Difficulties

- Inability to predict path for body positioning
- Slapping at ball from behind
- Inability to strike simultaneously with hands
- Engaging only upper body for contact and follow-through

FUNDAMENTALS OF DRIBBLING

Dribbling in organized sports is done in basketball and team handball. Whether in a stationary position or while on the move, the player pushes the ball to the floor and it bounces back to the waiting finger pads of the cupped hand. A skilled dribbler is adept at dribbling from one hand to the other. When playing with an opponent, an experienced dribbler can shield the ball to maintain possession. The head is held upright with eyes focused ahead.

One of the advantages of dribbling is that a child does not need a companion in order to enjoy the activity. By dribbling independently she or he develops skill level and confidence that can apply to future group activities. Also, dribbling can be accomplished with a variety of types and sizes of balls, so the equipment limitations are few.

FIGURE 15.3
This illustration shows
a boy dribbling.

When dribbling the body is bent only slightly at the knees and hips with the ball at the side and the opposite foot forward. Finger pads make contact with the center of the ball to push the ball down to bounce off the floor and return. At the end of the push the arm and fingers should be fully extended downward. As the ball rises again the finger pads rest lightly on the ball until waist high and then push down again. See Figure 15.3.

Developmental Levels

Level One.   In the early levels of dribbling the child drops and catches the ball without a rhythmic pattern. Rather than dribbling at the side, the child often slaps from behind with feet together, forcing the ball straight ahead or in an unforeseen direction. She or he is unable to return the ball to a specific point and must often lunge for the ball as it bounds ahead. This level challenges the child's timing and reflexes, but the ball controls the child's actions.

Level Two.   At this level the child may still slap the ball from behind and may flex the elbow slightly but without the full extension downward seen in a mature dribbler. The student may stand with one foot slightly before the other but may still be unable to predict the ball's return to a desired location. At times the ball rebounds to waist level; however, at this stage the child begins to gain some control of the ball and demonstrate some movement confidence.

Level Three.   When the dribbler reaches the most advanced level, she or he stands with one foot before the other and pushes the ball to the floor or ground with full arm extension downward. The child then predicts where to pause the hand to wait for it to reconnect with the fingerpads. She or he bounces the ball at the side and is able to ward off opponents by shielding the ball with the forearm.

See Box 15.3 for additional information on the developmental levels of dribbling.

Learning Cues

- Bend slightly at the knees and the hips
- Contact the center of the ball with finger pads
- Push the ball down to bounce off the floor and return
- Downward full extension of the arm
- Reconnect when the ball rises
- Dribble at waist level or lower

Common Difficulties

- Inability to predict path of ball's bounce
- Slapping at ball from behind
- Failure to extend the arm fully downward
- Follows rather than directs the ball's course

Dribbling   Box 15.3

LEVEL I

Legs upright
Positions feet together

Ball is dropped and caught
Slaps ball from behind
Unable to return ball to specific point

Lunges at ball

LEVEL II

Legs may or may not be bent
Sometimes has one foot before the other
Less slapping at ball

Better able to return ball
May flex elbow without full arm extension downward

Ball sometimes rebounds at waist level

LEVEL III

Slight bend at knees and hips
Positions one foot before the other

Uses fingerpads to control ball

Predicts where to pause the hand to wait for the ball
Pushes ball to ground with full extension downward
Ball rebounds to the side and at waist or lower
Shields ball with forearms

MOVEMENT EXPERIENCES

Keep It Up!

Objectives

To further develop mature forearm volleying and overhand volleying skills

To strive toward volleying for force and accuracy

To appreciate the collaborative nature of volleying

Targeted Age Group

K–2

Equipment

A balloon for each child (with extras in case of popping)

Management

Distribute balloons.

Students spread out at least ten steps apart from each other over a wide area.

Pre-Activity

Review forms of volleying.

Discuss activities using each type of volleying.

Establish directions for this activity.

Activity

1. With feet stationary, students send up their balloons and keep them in the air by volleying alone.
2. Volley off a wall, striving to keep the balloon's momentum controlled.
3. With a partner, volley to each other.
4. With a partner, volley to each other off the wall.

Modifications

Count each volley to see how many hits in a row can keep the balloon aloft.

- Use hits to recite the days of the week, months of the year, mathematic problems, or to count in a different language.
- Play music and volley to the beat. Stop and start with the playing of the music.

Assessment

Are the students successfully completing the activity as directed?

Are the children controlling the balloons?

Are students working well with partners?

Bonkers at the Beach

Objectives

To further develop mature forearm volleying and overhand volleying skills

To strive toward volleying for force and accuracy

To appreciate the collaborative nature of volleying

Targeted Age Group

K-2

Equipment

A beach ball or large plastic ball for each child

Chalk for marking courts

Beach music (such as Beach Boys)

Management

Distribute balloons.

Set up CD player.

Students spread out at least ten steps apart from each other over a wide area.

Pre-Activity

Review mature forms of volleying.

Discuss activities using each type of volleying.

Gives directions for this activity.

Activity

1. While beach music plays, using hands or forearms students "bonk" beach balls in the air as in playing beach volleyball.
2. Students pair up with one beach ball between them and volley to each other, counting the number of bonks in succession without allowing the ball to drop to the floor/ground.
3. Students are next grouped in three to continue the same counting activity.
4. Students in pairs draw a chalk line to separate them and establish sides. To practice underhand hitting, the student lets the ball bounce once off the floor before bonking it back across the line to a partner.

Modifications

- Use music of varied cultures.
- Use jungle music and have students call out a jungle creature each time they bonk the ball.
- Say a letter with each bonk to spell words (i.e., name, spelling list, vocabulary list).

Assessment

Are the students successfully completing the activity as directed?

Are the children controlling the force and developing accuracy?

Are the students cooperating with one another?

Entirely Underhanded

Objectives

To further develop mature underhand volleying skills

To strive toward volleying for force and accuracy

To appreciate the collaborative nature of volleying

Targeted Age Group

Grades 3–5

Equipment

One soft ball volleyball size or larger for each pair of children

Several pieces of chalk

Management

Students pair up.

Each pair has one ball.

Students form two parallel lines approximately 10 feet apart, standing directly across from their partners.

Pre-Activity

Review mature forms of volleying.

Discuss activities using each type of volleying.

Activity

1. One partner tosses the ball to the other, who strives to use mature underhand volleying to return it to the tosser, who catches it. The first partner must toss rather than volley the ball, as this ensures the ball's arrival at the correct spot. The process is repeated ten times in order to help the receiver focus on volleying the ball back to the tosser with an underhand stroke. Then the students switch roles. This procedure can continue for numerous rounds. Students can challenge themselves to see how many good volleys they can make out of ten attempts.

2. This task is similar to activity 1; however, the tosser should pitch the ball so that the volleyer has to move a step or two into a good position to volley.

3. Now students volley with partners, challenging themselves to see how many continuous volleys can be received and returned by the partner.

4. In the gymnasium, pairs use an existing line on the floor; if outside, they draw one on the pavement to separate them. Use chalk to mark a line representing a suspended net and pace off a 15-step square, marking corners to establish boundaries. Lines are then drawn to connect corners and form a square.

5. Partners each pace back four steps from the line and then begin volleying the ball up and over the line.

6. When the ball hits the ground a point is awarded to the last individual who successfully sent the ball up and over the line. If the ball goes out of bounds, however, as indicated by the boundary markings, the last student to touch the ball loses a point. Scoring continues until the teacher indicates that it is time to stop.

Modifications

- Perform activity with three rather than two participants.
- Pairs join another pair to form two teams.
- Use varying sizes of balls.

Assessment

Are the students successfully completing the activity as directed?

Are the students developing mature underhand volleying skills?

Are the students respectful of one another and working in a cooperative manner?

On the Double

Objectives

To further develop mature underhand volleying skills

To strive toward volleying with a partner

To appreciate the collaborative nature of volleying

Targeted Age Group

3–5

Equipment

One ball for every group of four students

One piece of sidewalk chalk per group

Management

Students form groups of four and divide into two teams.

Each group has one ball.

Students draw a line to represent a suspended net and pace off a 15-step square and mark corners to establish boundaries. Lines are then drawn to connect corners and form a square.

Pre-Activity

Review mature forms of volleying.

Discuss respectful rules of play.

Activity

1. The student whose birthday falls first in the year sends the ball up and over the imaginary net.
2. One of the members of the other team uses an overhand or underhand hit to return it or to send it to his or her partner with three hits limited per side.
3. When the ball hits the ground a point is awarded to the last individual who successfully sent the ball up and over the line. If the ball goes out of bounds, however, as indicated by the boundary markings, the last student to touch the ball loses a point. Scoring continues until the teacher indicates that it is time to stop.

Modifications

- After each indicated time break, partners break to form a team with an individual not in the original foursome.
- After five minutes of play the teacher signals stop and partners have to find a new team to challenge.

Assessment

Are students striving toward mature volleying?

Are students competing cooperatively?

Are teams making democratic decisions?

Spell and Count

Objectives

To develop dribbling skills in a stationary position

To work on spelling and math skills

To create rhythm patterns

Targeted Age Group

K-2

Equipment

One ball for each student

Management

1. Each student selects a ball
2. Students spread out at least 10 steps from one another over a wide area

Pre-Activity

Review dribbling form

Discuss respect for others' boundaries

Activity

1. At a signal from the teacher the class counts to 20 or higher slowly, attempting to bounce on each number
2. Count down from 20 to 1
3. Use skip counting to each bounce
4. Each child spells her or his name, saying one letter for each bounce
5. Recite the alphabet with one letter per bounce
6. Create individual patterns, such as "2 2 1, 2 2 1" or "c c g, c c g"

Modifications

- Practice mathematics tables to each bounce
- Rehearse spelling words bouncing on each letter
- Recite rhymes while bouncing to the beat
- Play music and strive to bounce to the rhythm
- Use color patterns like "red red green, blue blue yellow"

Assessment

Are the students successfully completing the activity as directed?

Are students all participating in counting, spelling, or patterning?

Are students developing confidence with dribbling?

Pitter Patter

Objectives

To develop dribbling skills

To create rhythm patterns

Targeted Age Group

K-2

Equipment

30 balls—one ball for each student

30 hula hoops—one hoop for each child

Management

1. Spread out over a wide area
2. Children place their hoops on the ground or floor before them

Pre-Activity

Review dribbling form

Activity

1. At a signal from the teacher, dribble the ball with the dominant hand within the perimeter of the hoop
2. On cue dribble in the hoop with non-dominant hand
3. Create patterns of dribbling whereby the ball hits the ground as the term is spoken, such as "horse horse bird," "cheese cheese cracker"
4. Shift dribbling from one hand to the other
5. Create a pattern that includes ball shifting
6. Bounce inside and outside the hoop in an alternating pattern
7. Create a pattern dribbling inside and outside the hoop
8. Change height of dribbling with a signal from the teacher

Modifications

- Play "Captain, May I" with dribbling commands to the crew
- Move clockwise and then counter-clockwise around the hoops while dribbling

Assessment

Are the students developing dribbling competency?

Are students joining in to create patterns?

Are children developing dribbling skills with the non-dominant hand?

Indy 500 Dribble

Objectives

To develop a positive attitude toward dribbling with feet and hands

To develop dribbling skills

To encourage cooperation among students

Targeted Age Group

Grades 3–5

Equipment

6 cones/polyspots to mark the race track

1 polyspot for every 2 children

1 soccer ball for every 2 children

1 basketball for every 2 children

CD player

Motivating music

Management

1. Arrange the cones so that they form a large rectangular race track.
2. Scatter the polyspots inside the race track.
3. Students pair up.
4. Partners select a basketball and soccer ball and find a polyspot.

Pre-Activity

Discuss races and how drivers have to make pit stops.

Review proper hand and foot dribbling form.

Review safety precautions, especially space awareness.

Activity

1. As the music begins one student from each partnership dribbles the soccer ball with the foot around the outside of the cones. The other student dribbles the basketball anywhere inside the race track, attempting to avoid the polyspots. Practice continues for 4–5 minutes.

2. When the music stops the partners meet at their pit stop (polyspot), exchange equipment, and change roles.

3. As the music begins again, the students dribble in their new roles.

Modifications

• The area may be a path through the jungle with trees, snakes, and lions' dens to avoid.

• The path may be across the United States with polyspots marked with products, state birds, state flags, or famous landmarks to avoid.

• Students may be window shopping for holiday gifts or pets or toys marked by polyspots and move along the street until coming to a shop where they dribble in place.

• Individuals may move in prehistoric times, avoiding carnivorous dinosaurs (indicated by labeled cones/polyspots).

Assessment

Are the students successfully completing the activity as directed?

Are children developing confidence as they gain experience?

Are students safely moving without running into others?

I Got Rhythm

Objectives

To develop dribbling skills

To dribble in a rhythmic pattern

To develop listening skills

Targeted Age Group

3–5

Equipment

One ball for each student (variety of types and sizes)

iPod or CD player

Variety of recorded music (e.g., jazz, country, R&B, hip hop, folk, easy listening, classical, marching band)

Management

1. Scatter polyspots around a large area

2. Each student selects a ball

Pre-Activity

Review proper hand dribbling form.

Review safety precautions, especially space awareness.

Activity

1. At the start of the music all students begin to dribble with the beat.
2. When the music stops each child bounces the held ball to another student and catches a different ball to dribble.
3. With each stop and start a different kind of music sets the pace.

Modifications

- Use a metronome and gradually increase the pace
- Use a tambourine, bongos, or a drum to set the beat
- Students dribble in time with jump rope rhymes

Assessment

Are the students successfully completing keeping pace with the music?

Are students moving and bouncing the balls safely?

Are students following directions in an orderly manner?

Chapter **Sixteen**

Manipulative Skills: Kicking and Punting

Erica, a 4th grader, has played soccer for a local club team since she was five. Her coach works with the team on kicking extended distances and developing accurate passing skills. Because of her years of experience at a young age, she already has become a skillful kicker. Others in her class who have not been exposed to such intense training demonstrate only limited skill at effectively striking a ball with their feet. A wise teacher will depend on those most skilled to aid in instructing those with less experience. Erica would best serve not only as a model for others but also as an aid in teaching others better striking skills.

Kicking is a foundational skill for a variety of sports. Children enjoy playing kickball, football, and soccer, all of which require dexterity of the feet. Kicking involves forcefully striking a stationary or a moving object with the foot. If a child is given a playground ball, she or he is likely to kick it. Kicking for an extended distance, punting, and passing a ball pose delightful challenges for youngsters.

FUNDAMENTALS OF KICKING

Whereas kicking a short distance requires little but a brush with the foot, kicking for an extended distance demands an investment of the whole body, which is more mechanically efficient. In working with students to develop more mature kicking skills, teachers should design learning experiences that encourage forceful kicking. Repeated kicks across a wide activity area demand more forceful kicking than students may have previously

Soccer requires children to manipulate the ball in dynamic environments.

FIGURE 16.1
This illustration shows
mature kicking.

experienced. The size of the ball is a vital component. Using a beach ball, foam ball, or slightly deflated playground ball the size of a soccer ball is best, for it is not too large to kick a long distance but is large enough to allow efficient contact with the ball. Also, because of the softness of such balls, the children's feet are not hurt and balls do not sail so far that the child has difficulty rapidly retrieving them. Students need experience kicking a variety of ball sizes and types; thus, by including footballs and other balls appropriate to their size, opportunities are offered to children to develop more mature ball-kicking skills.

When aiming for distance the kicker contacts the ball behind the center so it soars slightly off the ground. When kicking for height, the kicker makes contact below the center of the ball to lift it upward into an arc. In both cases students should be encouraged to contact the ball with their shoelaces. See Figure 16.1.

Developmental Levels

Children develop at varying rates, dependent upon experience, cognitive development, skill level, and fitness. Because of the time and experience required to reach a mature level of performance, clearly development of skill levels will advance and regress over time. The following three levels define kicking development:

Level One.

In level one kicking movement is limited to a nearly straight kicking leg with only a minimal backswing. The foot may make contact at the toe, along the side, or from the shoelaces, sending the ball in unpredictable paths with irregular distances. Little movement of the trunk is exhibited and arms are used only to aid in balance.

Level Two.

In this level there is a much greater backswing and follow-through with the kicking leg. The child flexes the kicking leg at the knee and steps forward to prepare to kick the ball. Contact with the foot may occur at the shoelaces; however, consistency in direction and distance is unlikely. Arms may move in opposition to the leg, the arm extending forward opposite the foot that strikes.

Level Three.

In level three the child either runs or leaps to the ball with arms swinging in opposition to the kick, adding momentum. As the kicker leans back the hip engages in forming the kick and the length of the backswing and the follow-through increases. At the point of impact the kicker rises on the support toes or even leaves the ground. In order to maximize contact an effective kick is generated from the instep or shoelaces. See Box 16.1 for additional information on the developmental levels of kicking.

Learning Cues
- Run to the ball
- Swing kicking leg way back
- Shift weight to the support foot

Kicking   Box 16.1

LEVEL I	LEVEL II	LEVEL III
Straight leg	Leg flexed at knee	Runs or leaps to ball
Contact ball with toe or side of foot	Contact ball with toe or side of foot	Contact ball with shoelace at the top of the foot
Minimal backswing	Greater backswing and follow-through with kicking leg	Leans back with hip engagement in forming the kick
Little amount of trunk	Trunk moves forward and back	Length of backswing increases
	Steps forward to prepare to kick	On impact kicker rises on support toes or even leaves the ground
Arms used only for balance	Arm forward is opposite of foot that strikes	Arm forward is opposite of foot that strikes

- Swing arms to add force
- Contact ball with shoelaces
- Follow the ball with your leg

Common Difficulties

- Beginning kick from stationary position
- Contacting ball with toes
- Omitting backswing with kicking leg
- Neglecting a high follow-through
- Failing to swing arms

FUNDAMENTALS OF PUNTING

Punting is a difficult form of kicking because the child needs to coordinate forward movement with dropping the ball to be kicked before it reaches the ground. Because of the complexity of this action, it is probably best for children to develop simpler forms of kicking first. To punt the child moves forward rapidly a few steps before leaping to punt the ball. The child holds the ball at arm's length in front of the body, drops it without tossing it upward, then shifts weight to the support leg, leans back, and contacts the ball below the knee before it touches the ground. Upon contact both feet are elevated above the ground for maximum force. See Figure 16.2.

Learning Cues

- Quick approach
- Drop the ball without any uplift
- Swing kicking leg way back
- Shift weight to the support foot
- Move arms in opposition to legs
- Lean back to kick
- Contact ball with shoelaces
- Follow the ball with your leg, both feet off ground

Common Difficulties

- Releasing ball in upward motion
- Contacting the ball with toes

FIGURE 16.2
This football player is demonstrating mature punting.

- Failing to lean back
- Neglecting a high follow-through
- Failing to lift both feet off ground

MOVEMENT EXPERIENCES

A Day at the Beach

Objectives
To enhance awareness of mature kicking form
To develop kicking and punting skills
To increase enthusiasm for kicking

Targeted Age Group
K-2

Equipment
A beach ball for each child
10–15 long jump ropes
CD player
Beach Boys music

Management
1. Jump ropes are stretched into a wavy pattern to indicate the shoreline.
2. Each student is given a ball.

Pre-Activity

Students brainstorm items commonly found at the beach.

Students review proper kicking form.

Students review safety precautions.

Activity

1. Students line up along the beach and kick their beach balls as far into the ocean as they can.
2. Periodically the teacher calls out "seagull," "kite," "parasail," or other item typically found in the sky at the beach, after which the children kick as high as they can to touch the imaginary airborne object.
3. The teacher intersperses watercrafts and sea creatures such as "sailboat," "banana boat," or "buoy," so that students practice kicking for distance over the waves.
4. After kicking the balls far out into the sea, students use a swimming motion to dash to retrieve their balls and then swim back.
5. On occasion during retrieval, the part of this activity emphasizing quick movement, the teacher calls out "tidal wave," "shark," or "sting ray," signaling to the children to race to safety on the shore.

Modifications

- Schedule this activity in tandem with a unit on marine life.
- Have students give themselves a point for each time they kick the ball high or far when signaled by the teacher.

Assessment

Are the children responding to the teacher's signals?

Are the students using good kicking form?

Are the youngsters enjoying the activity?

Kicking That Counts

Objective

To combine kicking, counting, adding, and subtracting activities

To develop a more mature kicking form

To engage in enjoyable partnered activity

Targeted Age Group

K-2

Equipment

Score sheets for each partner pair

Writing utensils

Assortment of balls

Play money

Cones or polyspots

Chalk

Tall ladder to mark goal

Management

1. Students are assigned to four equal-numbered groups.
2. Score sheets are distributed.
3. Partners join and write their names on their score sheets.
4. Each pair selects a ball.

Station One

Parallel restraining lines are situated 25 feet apart.

Partners line up across from each other on the parallel lines.

Station Two

Parallel cones designate a restraining line and a goal line.

Station Three

Chalk marks on a wall or other high target define kicking goal.

Station Four

Cones mark a restraining line 25 feet from a wall.

Pre-Activity

Students review mature form for kicking for height and distance.

Activity

Four groups of paired students will rotate to the next station at a signal from the teacher.

Station One: Counting

1. Standing at their respective restraining lines, partners kick the ball back and forth, stopping the ball before kicking.
2. Children count the number of times they kick the ball to their partners without their having to move more than one or two steps to retrieve the ball.
3. Partners' scores are combined and recorded.

Station Two: Addition and Subtraction

1. With a partner, students kick 20 times to a goal. Count how many times the goal was hit.
2. Participants subtract the number of times the target is missed from total number of attempts.
3. Partners combine scores.

Station Three: Counting Money

1. With a partner, students alternate turns kicking a ball up to a high chalk mark on the side of the school building or another high target.
2. Each time a child hits the mark she or he earns a quarter. Partners combine their winnings.

Station Four: Prediction and < >.

1. Students will each have 10 times to kick the target wall from their restraining line. Partners first predict how many times they think their team will hit the target.
2. Partners combine scores.
3. Participants will determine whether the number of times they hit the target is greater than (>) or less than (<) the number of times they predicted.

Modifications

- Vary the amounts of money to suit skill levels
- Vary mathematics required to match the skills and concepts appropriate to the students' development

Assessment

- Did the students complete the score sheets?
- Did participants demonstrate mature kicking form?
- Did children remain on task as described by the teacher?
- Were students enthusiastically engaged?

Graph That Kick

Objective

To develop kicking for distance skills
To develop graphing skills
To engage in enjoyable partnered activity

Targeted Age Group

3–5

Equipment

Score sheet for each student
Writing utensils
Assortment of balls
Cones or polyspots
Tape measures
Tongue depressors

Management

1. Students quickly choose a partner.
2. Graphing score sheets are distributed.
3. Partners join in pairs and each writes her/his name on graphing score sheets.
4. Each pair selects a ball.

Station One: Pie Graphs

Place or draw several large targets on a wall. These can look like target archery targets, with the bull's-eye in the center in one color and other concentric circles of varying colors around the inner circle. These can be constructed on a variety of surfaces, including large poster board or bed sheets.

Place a cone to indicate the kicking line.

Station Two: Bar Graphs

Parallel restraining lines are marked by cones situated 25 feet apart. Partners line up across from each other on the parallel lines.

Station Three: Line Graphs

Cones mark a restraining line. Tape measures are placed beside cones.

Pre-Activity

Students review mature form of kicking for height and distance.
Students review aspects of different types of graphs.

Activity

Three groups of paired students will rotate to the next station at a signal from the teacher.

Station One: Pie Graphs

1. Standing at their respective restraining lines one student kicks 20 times at the colored target on the wall.

2. A partner keeps a tally of the color that is hit with each of the 20 kicks.
3. Partners switch roles.

Station 2: Bar Graphs

1. Partners kick the ball back and forth, stopping it before kicking. Each partner kicks the ball 25 times.
2. Children count and record on the score sheet the number of times they kick the ball to their partners without having to move more than two steps to retrieve it.

Station 3: Line Graphs

1. One partner kicks the ball ten times as far as s/he can.
2. After each kick the other partner darts out to insert a tongue depressor at the point where the ball stops and retrieve the ball.
3. After one partner has kicked the ball ten times the students use the tape measure to determine the distance each ball has been kicked.
4. Then partners switch roles.

After students have completed the tasks at all three stations they use the totals they have documented to construct each of the three types of graphs noted.

Modifications
- Use these procedures with varied skills, such as punting, jumping, and throwing.
- Use computers to construct the three graphs.
- Use metric measurements.

Assessment
Did the students complete the graphs?

Did participants maintain mature kicking form?

Did children remain on task?

Were students enthusiastic about the activity?

Kicking & Punting Golf

Objective
To further develop mature kicking & punting skills

To strive toward kicking & punting for accuracy and distance

To enjoy competing against a kicking & punting course to improve individual score

Targeted Age Group
3–5 grade

Equipment
30 balls (one for each student)

Cones/polyspots

10 Ropes

5 Hoops

Individual score sheets

Writing utensils

Posters printed with numbers 1-9

Management
1. Course is mapped out over a large area with a hoop as the target for each of the nine "holes." Allowing for a safe distance, a polyspot is situated past each hoop as the starting point for the next hole.

2. Students divide into groups of two to three.
3. Each group is assigned a different number as a starting point as indicated by polyspots. Golfers call this a "shotgun start."
4. Each student writes her/his name on a score card.
5. Students start at beginning polyspot.
6. Jump ropes indicate lines of kicking/punting directions.
7. Hoops are situated at each target point and labeled with a numbered poster.
8. Cones are placed at midpoints between targets.

Pre-Activity

Students review mature forms of kicking and punting.

Students share what they know about golfing procedures.

Teacher adds directions necessary for this activity.

Activity

1. One participant kicks the ball to the target cone. Each kick counts as one.
2. The kicker then punts the ball from the cone toward the target hoop. Each punt counts as one.
3. The kicker totals the number of kicks and punts required to reach the target and records it on the score card.
4. When the first kicker hits the hoop goal, the second kicker begins.
5. When all kickers have taken a turn on the playing area, participants all rotate to the next target's starting polyspot to begin again.

Modifications

* Students vary the types of balls for added challenge.
* Students design the course as an out-of-class assignment.
* Students use nerf balls or heavy duty balloons on a shortened course.
* The same course can be used with different skills, such as throwing or striking with golf clubs, hockey sticks, or rackets.

Assessment

Did the students complete the score sheets?

Did participants demonstrate mature kicking and punting forms?

Did children remain on tasks as described by the teacher?

Were students enthusiastically engaged?

Chapter **Seventeen**

Striking with Hands and Rackets

Diondre peers out the window of her high-rise apartment, watching two children below batting a balloon about with a pair of antiquated rackets. They had invented a game of sorts and were passing the morning with attempts to keep the balloon airborne. She jostled the sleeping child beside her and urged, "Come on, Bubba. Do you want to go see Jonetta and James' new game?" Her brother opened his eyes a slit and nodded. They scrambled down the aging stairs to the exit and joined the children on the barren lawn. "Hey Jonetta, what ya playin'?" Jonetta flashed a grin and replied, "Dunno, but it's fun. Wanna take a turn?" Diondre took the racket as Jonetta took the younger child's hand, and James called, "The rules are to keep the balloon off the ground by hitting it back and forth with the rackets." Jonetta piped, "How about we play, too, just using our hands to hit the b'loon?"

Firing objects against walls or across nets has provided entertainment for centuries. Tennis courts can be seen in parks and on school lots across the nation, and temporary badminton nets are erected at family gatherings and plant picnics to allow for a variety of ages and types to join in the fun of sending a birdie or a ball to a destination on the other side. A brick wall serves as an ideal partner for an individual wishing to play alone, guaranteeing a return from each ball bounced against its surface. This inexpensive pastime is entertaining and can be enhanced with minimal awareness of the principles of the organized sports that call for such skills.

Striking requires a part of the body or a racket, bat, hockey stick, or other implement to give impetus to an object. The propulsion that sends the object sailing determines the distance and

Children love the challenge of making contact with the shuttle.

direction the object travels. Thus, by refining the use of force and targeting, children can improve their skills in underhand and eventually sidearm and overhand striking.

FUNDAMENTALS OF UNDERHAND STRIKING WITH HANDS

Striking provides momentum to transport an object through the air a desired distance in a chosen direction. In working with students to develop more mature skills, teachers should design learning experiences that encourage forceful striking. Repeated hits across a wide activity area demand more forceful striking than many students may have previously experienced.

Underhand striking with the hands is used in handball and volleyball. In volleyball there are several types of serves, but the underhand strike is the least complex for young learners. Children are often challenged by the force and accuracy required to serve a ball over the net; therefore, they should have substantial practice serving to large targets from a short distance.

The serve begins with the child facing the target, the ball held in the non-dominant hand just below waist level. The non-dominant foot is ahead of the dominant foot, and body weight rests primarily on the back foot. The striking arm extends behind the body, then forward in pendulum motion. Simultaneously the body weight shifts from the back foot to the front foot. To maximize the surface of the hand's contact with the balloon or other object, students extend their fingers to expose the palm and strike with the heel of the hand. Following through with the striking hand ensures more accurate direction.

See Box 17.1 for additional information on the developmental levels of striking.

Developmental Levels

Level One.

Often in the early levels of underhand serving the child faces forward, but the feet are planted, limiting level the force of the strike. The arm becomes the sole source of power as the ball is struck. Immature striking may also include a clenched fist and lack of follow-through.

Level Two.

The child recognizes the need for weight transfer but his or her timing to shift in tandem with arm movement is off. Also, occasionally children drop the ball before it is struck so that it meets the palm in midair rather than being held until the moment of impact.

Striking with Hands and Rackets   Box 17.1

LEVEL I	LEVEL II	LEVEL III
Stance faces forward	Partial turn to side	Stance to the side with dominant foot a shoulder width behind non-dominant foot
Arm sole power source as feet remain stationary	Arm power assists minimal weight shift	Dominant arm extends the racket back as weight shifts to back foot
Little or no weight transfer	Minimal weight transfer	As weight transfers to non-dominant foot, torso rotates
	Racket partially extended with inconsistent path	Racket fully extended and parallel to ground
		Racket connects with object at point directly above non-dominant foot
		Arm follows through across body

Level Three.

In the most advanced level the student stands facing the target with the dominant foot positioned behind the non-dominant foot. Weight rests on the dominant foot during the backswing and shifts to the front in the contact and follow-through. The ball rests on the fingers of the non-dominant hand as the dominant hand pulls backward and then sweeps ahead to connect with the ball and send it forward, the hand following through in the direction of the target.

Learning Cues

* Dominant foot positioned behind non-dominant foot facing target
* Rest ball on fingers of non-dominant hand
* Pull dominant arm back
* Swing arm forward until the heel of the dominant hand connects with the ball
* Shift weight to front foot during swing
* Follow through

Common Difficulties

* Dropping ball rather than waiting until the dominant hand makes contact
* Contacting with fist
* Lack of weight transfer
* Lack of follow-through

FUNDAMENTALS OF STRIKING WITH RACKETS

Striking with rackets is used in sports such as badminton, racquetball, paddleball, ping pong, and tennis. Although the underhand strike is the least difficult for young learners, developing skills in forehand and backhand striking is also essential. Children are often challenged by the force and accuracy required to strike a ball or shuttle over the net; therefore, they should have substantial practice.

The child grips the racket in the dominant hand as she or he would hold another's hand to shake in greeting. She or he turns to the side with the dominant foot a shoulder-width behind the non-dominant. Weight is balanced on both feet but shifts to the back foot as the dominant arm fully extends the racket back parallel to the ground. As the stroke begins the student shifts weight forward to the non-dominant foot. Next the student transfers her or his weight as the torso rotates 45 to 90 degrees, racket fully extended and parallel to the ground. Then the racket connects with the object at a point directly above the non-dominant foot, and the student's arm follows through in the direction of the target. See Figure 17.1.

FIGURE 17.1
A boy demonstrates mature striking with a racket.

Developmental Levels

Level One.

Often in the early levels of striking the child faces forward, limiting the force of the strike. The arm becomes the sole source of power and the feet remain stationary as the object is contacted. Transfer of weight may be overlooked.

Level Two.

At this level the child may make the 45–90 degree turn, yet neglect to transfer weight. Students may have difficulty judging the force with which to strike and may not follow through as needed.

Level Three.

In the most advanced level the student grips the racket in the dominant hand with a shake-hands grip and turns to the side with the dominant foot a shoulder-width behind the non-dominant. Weight shifts to the back foot as the dominant arm extends the racket back. Shifting weight forward to the non-dominant foot, the student rotates the torso, racket fully extended and parallel to the ground. The racket connects with the object at a point directly above the non-dominant foot as the arm follows through.

Learning Cues

- Grip racket as if hand shaking
- Rotate body away from target
- Shift weight to back dominant foot, racket extended behind
- Transfer weight to non-dominant foot
- Contact ball directly above non-dominant foot

Common Difficulties

- Insufficient weight transfer
- Failure to rotate body away from target
- Overhand rather than sidearm swing
- Contact other than middle of racket
- Inadequate follow-through

MOVEMENT EXPERIENCES

Strikes Me as Fun

Objectives

To enhance awareness of mature form for striking a ball with the hands

To develop underhand striking skills

To increase enthusiasm for striking

Targeted Age Group

K-2

Equipment

A beach ball for each child

Polyspot for each child

Management

1. Polyspots mark an imaginary line approximately five steps back from a long wall. Each student has a polyspot that serves as a home position.
2. Each student acquires a beach ball.

Pre-Activity

Review mature form for underhand striking with the hands.

Discuss activities that involve striking with the hands.

Activity

1. Students strike the beach ball into the wall, allow the ball to bounce once on the ground, and then catch the ball. They repeat the sequence for adequate practice.
2. As children repeat the strike, bounce, catch sequence, the target height of the bounce rises progressively up the wall.
3. Students see how many times they can repeat the strike, bounce, catch sequence without losing control of the ball.

Modifications

- Vary the equipment. Younger children or those with less experience with underhand striking can use large balloons. Those with more experience can use foam balls.

Assessment

Are the students successfully completing the activity as directed?

Do students use good form for underhand striking?

Are the students appropriately challenged for their skill level?

Do the students come back to their polyspots before each hit?

Partners Go on Strike

Objectives

To enhance awareness of mature form for striking a ball with the hands

To develop underhand striking skills

To increase enthusiasm for striking

Targeted Age Group

K-2

Equipment

One beach ball for each pair of students

Management

1. Students find a partner.
2. Each group of two acquires a beach ball.

Pre-Activity

Review mature form for underhand striking with the hands.

Discuss activities that involve striking with the hands.

Converse about the necessity of partner cooperation.

Activity

1. Partners find a safe work area away from other students.
2. One student begins by bouncing the ball to the partner, who underhand strikes the ball back to the student, who then catches the ball. The first partner has 10 trials in this sequence and then switches roles with second partner. This routine is repeated 5–10 times.
3. Students see how many times they can repeat the bounce, strike, catch sequence without losing control of the ball.
4. Participants underhand strike continuously with their partners. The sequence for this task is bounce, strike, bounce, strike.

Modifications

- Vary the equipment for this activity. Children with more experience can use dense foam balls or large playground balls.

Assessment

Are the students successfully completing the activity as directed?

Do students use good form for underhand striking?

Are the students appropriately challenged for their skill level?

A Strike in Return

Objectives

To enhance awareness of mature form for striking a ball with the paddles

To develop underhand striking skills

To increase enthusiasm for striking

Targeted Age Group

K-2

Equipment

A small beach ball for each child

A ethafoam paddle for each child (also called lollipop paddles, these are lightweight and great for young students)

A polyspot for each child

Management

1. Polyspots mark an imaginary line approximately five steps back from a long wall. Each student has a polyspot that serves as a home position.
2. Each student acquires a beach ball and a paddle.

Pre-Activity

Students review mature form for underhand striking with paddles.

Students discuss activities that involve striking with paddles.

Activity

1. Students will strike the beach ball into the wall, allow the ball to bounce once on the ground, and then catch the ball. Repeat the strike, bounce, catch sequence for adequate practice.
2. Participants will strike the beach balls so that the balls go higher on the wall. Repeat this strike, bounce, catch sequence.
3. Challenge students to see how many times they can repeat the strike, bounce, catch sequence without losing control of the ball.
4. Challenge students to underhand strike continuously against the wall. The sequence for this task is bounce, strike, bounce, strike.

Modifications

- Use different ball types and paddle lengths.
- As a challenge, move polyspots progressively farther away from the wall.

Assessment

Are the students successfully completing the activity as directed?

Do students use good form for underhand striking?

Are the students appropriately challenged for their skill level?

Four Square

Objective

To further develop mature underhand striking skills

To strive toward underhand striking for force and accuracy

To appreciate the collaborative nature of underhand striking

Targeted Age Group

3–5

Equipment

One playground ball for every four students

Chalk

Management

1. Students form groups of four
2. Representatives from each group chalk off boundaries, establishing a large square divided into four smaller squares as the playing area *(see diagram)*
3. Each group selects a ball

Pre-Activity

Students review mature form of underhand striking

Students discuss activities when striking is used

Teacher adds directions for this activity

Activity

1. Individuals from each foursome establish positions in the corners of the group's square.
2. Players identify the numbered ordering of the four internal squares.
3. The player in Square 1 serves the ball to bounce first in the child's own square and then across the division into another of the three remaining squares.
4. The receiving player uses an underhand strike to send the ball into another player's square, where it must bounce once before that receiver strikes it to send it once again to another player's square.
5. If the ball lands directly on the line, if a player does not forward the ball with an underhand strike, or if the receiver fails to send the ball into another square, the player who last fired the ball correctly into a player's square receives a point.
6. When a point is scored the serve shifts to the player in the next square.

Modifications

- Students vary the type of balls used as objects for added challenges
- Students use rackets
- Children move through the week's spelling list with each strike
- If the player who serves makes an error, she or he moves to the fourth square and the player in the second and third squares move up toward the first square to become the server. The object is to remain in Court 1 as long as possible.

Assessment

Did participants demonstrate mature underhand striking form?

Did the children work collaboratively?

Were all groups able to demonstrate some degree of mastery of the game?

Did the students display good sportsmanship?

On Strike

Objective

To further develop mature striking skills with a racket

To strive toward striking for control and accuracy

To work independently on striking with a racket

Targeted Age Group

3–5

Equipment

A racket and ball for every student

Pencil and sheet of paper for each student

Management

1. Each student selects a ball and a racket
2. Students receive pencil and paper

Pre-Activity

Review mature form of striking with a racket

Students spread out over a wide area along an indoor or outdoor wall

Teacher demonstrates an abbreviated striking routine which includes an interesting starting and ending point and a repeatable sequence. *(For example, the routine starts with the ball balanced on the racket, followed by 10 strikes directing the ball upward, 10 strikes downward to bounce off the floor/ground, 1 strike upward followed by 1 strike downward 10 times, 1 strike upward followed by a flip of the wrist to strike 1 time upward again backhanded repeated 10 times, ending with the ball balanced upon the racket.)*

Activity

1. Each student creates a routine using controlled striking skills
2. Routine is recorded on the sheet of paper
3. Routine includes a combination of striking upward, striking downward, striking off the wall, swiveling the wrist to strike backhanded, with a clear starting and ending point

Modifications

- Students vary the type and size of balls used as objects for added challenges
- Students strike balls with increasing intensity, sending them farther from the racket with each strike, and then reduce the distance to a close proximity
- Students use short-handled paddles
- Shuttlecocks are substituted for balls
- Children perform routines to selected music
- Children move through the week's spelling list with each strike
- Students go through multiplication or division tables with each strike
- Students pair up to develop a routine with a partner

Assessment

Did participants demonstrate mature striking forms?

Did the children follow directions to develop a repeatable routine?

Were all groups able to demonstrate some degree of mastery of striking in a pattern?

To the Line

Objective

To further develop mature striking skills with a racket

To strive toward striking for control and accuracy

To work with a partner or small group on striking with a racket

Targeted Age Group

3–5

Equipment

A racket and ball for every pair of students

Cones, polyspots, jump ropes, and/or chalk for establishing boundaries

Management

1. Students team with a partner
2. Each student selects a racket
3. Each pair selects a ball

Pre-Activity

Review mature form of striking with a racket

Partners establish boundaries using cones and polyspots

Jump ropes or chalk define a net across the middle of the space

Activity

1. Partners warm up by striking ball to each other across the virtual net.
2. Peers determine if their practice will be cooperative or competitive.
3. If cooperative, players will strive to strike the ball directly to each other; if competitive, players will work to challenge peer to move to strike the ball. Rules for collaboration or competition will be established by each pair.

Modifications

- Students use short-handled paddles
- Shuttlecocks are substituted for balls
- Children may work in groups of four to set up doubles play
- Students may use a wall to simulate racket ball courts

Assessment

Did participants demonstrate mature striking forms?

Did the children work collaboratively in establishing and executing rules?

Were all students able to demonstrate some degree of mastery of striking?

Chapter **Eighteen**

Striking: Bats, Sticks, & Clubs

"Grace, come on! Let's play baseball!" Cameron shouted. Grace grabbed her bat and sped after the group of children running to the empty ball field. As they approached hot sun streaks bore into the carpet samples that served as bases. Pluto, a local stray mutt, rose from his rest and lumbered off, well aware of the activity about to burst forth on the field. It was Saturday, the best day of the week for the kids from 1st to 5th grade to cast their cares aside and join in the merriment. Jerome fired the ball over home plate into Cassie's mitt. Panos warmed up nearby, smacking an imaginary ball out of the ball park.

Neighborhood pick-up ball games are characteristic of many children's evening, weekend, and summer activities. Rules of baseball and softball are easily modified to accommodate number of players, equipment, and available space. These informal experiences provide students with an opportunity to practice batting, throwing, catching, and base running. Children anticipate their chance to become the batter. Striking with a bat requires the player to track an approaching ball and swing, just in time to connect with the ball and send it into the outfield.

STRIKING WITH BATS

In the early stages of skill development the use of a wiffle or foam ball and a plastic bat offers a safe encounter with striking. Children are often provided a stationary batting tee,

For beginning learners a stationary cone is used to eliminate the challenge of hitting a moving ball.

enabling them to take their time as they attempt to contact a motionless ball. If a commercial tee is not available, plastic orange traffic cones suffice, and if the child is too tall for a cone of standard height, the cone may be positioned on a folding chair as a workable adaptation.

With practice the child may progress to a point where the ball can be softly tossed upward from his or her side, so she or he may swing at a slowly moving target. At the next stage the pitcher may gently toss the ball from a distance with the intention of the child's successfully striking. Then she or he may practice self-tossing the ball upward, grasping the bat, and swinging. With experience the child is ready to receive a rapid pitch from an adversarial pitcher, make contact with the ball, and send it in a targeted direction.

Because children gain skills through repeated practice, the teacher should create practice conditions that maximize batting opportunities for

FIGURE 18.1
This drawing illustrates
mature striking with a bat.

each child. The best means of optimizing batting experience is by pairing children and providing a plastic bat and wiffle or foam ball, so that one may strike from a tee while the other retrieves; then roles can be reversed.

Once a child has some degree of mastery of connecting with the ball, she or he should begin to work on controlling the direction the ball takes and the degree of distance it travels. An advanced batter directs the swing toward an area where no one is standing, thereby affording an advantage in running bases. By hitting the ball just below its center, one can produce a fly ball; when one strikes the ball dead center, she or he may deliver a line drive; connecting with the ball near the top results in a grounder. Likewise, designating the amount of force applied empowers the striker to determine how far the ball will travel and anticipate where it will drop. See Figure 18.1.

Striking skills, as other physical skills, can be categorized as **closed** (in specific unchanging conditions) and **open** (changing and requiring on-the-spot adaptation). Closed skills are predictable with a definite start and finish, whereas open skills require rapid decision making while in action. Often offering opportunities to hone skills in isolation in closed situations leads to successful applications in open settings.

Degrees of batting skill usually vary greatly among a class of elementary students. Time and experience play essential roles in the child's batting mastery, so providing opportunities for closed skill development may offer guidance for those with less experience and enhancement for those at higher mastery levels. The following three levels define batting development.

See Box 18.1 for additional information on the developmental levels of striking with bats.

Striking with Bats   Box 18.1

LEVEL I	LEVEL II	LEVEL III
Faces pitcher	Partial turn toward pitcher	Stance turned with non-dominant side toward pitcher
Feet close together	Moderate extension of feet	Feet spread slightly farther apart than shoulder width
Weight distributed evenly	Some weight transfer occurs	Weight on balls of feet with dominance on back leg
Hands held apart	Hands may or may not touch each other	Grips bat with dominant hand on top and hands touching
Bat resting on shoulder	Bat above dominant shoulder	Bat above dominant shoulder
Bat moves vertically as in chopping wood	Bat movement inconsistent	Elbows extended away from body
		Small steps taken to drive bat horizontally through ball
		Weight shifts to front foot
		Eyes on ball until it contacts bat
		Follow through across body

Developmental Levels

Level 1.

As the batter prepares to swing, the child turns toward the pitcher with little distance separating her or his feet, allowing for little or no weight transfer. As a result it is difficult to follow through with the swing, and direction and force are unpredictable. Hands are often held apart, and the bat moves vertically rather than horizontally.

Level 2.

In a position partially turned toward the pitcher, the batter extends both feet moderately, so that some weight transfer occurs. Frequently a batter at this level rests the bat on the dominant shoulder. Hands may or may not touch each other, and because of the inability to fully shift weight, follow-through is limited.

Level 3.

The mature batter turns sideways with feet spread slightly farther apart than shoulder width. Weight is centered on the balls of the feet with dominance on the back leg. The child grips the bat, right above the left, hands touching, with the shaft positioned above the right shoulder. Elbows extend away from the body. When the striker takes a small step to drive the bat horizontally through the ball, weight shifts to the front foot. Eyes center on the ball until it meets the bat. In the follow-through the top hand rolls over the bottom hand as the bat moves across the body in the direction of the hit.

Learning Cues

* Face the pitcher with the non–dominant side
* Grip bat with dominant hand on top and hands touching
* Position feet shoulder-width apart
* Rest weight on balls of feet
* Situate bat above the right shoulder
* Hold elbows away from body

- Keep eyes on ball
- Rotate hips forward, shifting weight
- Swing bat horizontally
- Follow through across body in direction of the hit

Common Difficulties

- Facing the pitcher
- Situating hands apart
- Standing with feet too close together
- Resting bat on shoulder
- Leaning back on heels
- Keeping elbows close to body
- Chopping down with bat
- Forgetting to follow through

Striking with Hockey Sticks

Striking with hockey sticks is similar to striking with bats as it requires that the lengthy implement swings at a distance from the body. In striking with a hockey stick, however, the puck does not move through the air but along the floor. As a result, the action is centered below the hips, and the swing takes place along the ground. Some children learn to strike with hockey sticks through experiences in ice hockey or roller skate hockey; others acquire their hockey skills from games of street hockey, field hockey, or floor hockey. Floor hockey is most common in the school setting. In order to develop skills in striking with hockey sticks, students may begin with closed-skill efforts and advance to striking while moving in open-skill environments. See Figure 18.2.

Safety is a key concern whenever students hold long-handled implements. A few rules can help ensure well-being for all. First, equipment should be developmentally appropriate. Small pliable balls, wiffle balls, or spongy pucks decrease the likelihood of injury as do short plastic hockey sticks. Second, sticks should be kept on the floor and never lifted higher than waist level. Third, an appropriate distance between students should be maintained so that students are able to shoot or pass the puck without contacting others. Fourth, game-like tasks should be limited to two or three players per team. When a safe environment is cultivated students can focus on gaining skill instead of fearing injury.

Children work on striking with long-handled implements as they move the hockey puck down the floor.

Even early elementary students can develop dribbling and passing skills. When dribbling the student controls the ball/puck as it is tapped with the blade of the stick, whereas in passing the ball/puck is sent to a teammate. Students should learn that play is faster when passing is utilized, and that passing ahead of the receiver allows him/her to proceed without slowing down. To grip the floor hockey stick the hands rest approximately 5–10 inches apart with the non-dominant hand farthest from the floor. The stick is positioned to the right of the body with the blade gliding along the floor (Figure 18.2). Passing requires a forceful contact with the ball/puck and a follow-through in the direction of the target. Dribbling incorporates taps on the ball/puck with either side of the blade.

The levels of skill in passing and dribbling are diverse among elementary students. Practice

FIGURE 18.2
This girl demonstrates mature striking with a hockey stick.

plays a critical role in the child's mastery. The following three levels define passing development:

Developmental Levels

Level 1.

The beginning passer does not turn sideway to the target; the passing action tends to take place in front of the body. Hands are placed close together on the stick. Weight transfer at the point of contacting the ball/puck does not occur since the passer is front facing. Backswing and follow-through are unpredictable, and the stick usually moves higher than waist level. Eyes do not center on the ball/puck until it meets the stick.

Level 2.

In a position partially turned toward the target, the passer extends both feet moderately so that some weight transfer occurs. Hands may be close together, and because of the inability to fully shift weight, follow-through is limited. Backswing and follow-through are more predictable, and the stick usually moves closer to waist level. Eyes may center on the ball/puck until it meets the stick.

Level 3.

The mature passer turns sideways with feet spread slightly farther apart than shoulder width. Weight is centered on the balls of the feet with dominance on the back leg. The stick is positioned on the dominant side of the body with the blade touching the floor. Hands

Passing with Hockey Sticks

Box 18.2

LEVEL I	LEVEL II	LEVEL III
Does not turn sideways to target	Partially turned toward target	Turned sideways with feet spread wider than shoulders
Passing takes place in front of body	Feet spread moderately so some weight transfer occurs	Weight centered on balls of feet with weight on back foot
Hands are close together on stick	Hands may be close together	Strike on dominant side with blade touching floor
No weight transfer	Follow-through is limited	Hands spread on stick 5–10" apart, non-dominant at top of stick
Backswing and follow-through not predictable	Stick moves closer to waist level	Elbows extend away from body
Stick higher than waist level	Eyes usually centered on puck until it meets the stick	Backswing begins as stick is lifted back at a level no higher than waist
Eyes not centered on puck		Weight shifts to front foot as puck is contacted
		Eyes on puck until it meets stick
		Follow-through in direction of hit

spread on the stick 5 to 10 inches apart, with the non-dominant hand at the top of the stick. Elbows extend away from the body. The back swing begins with the stick lifted to the back at a level no higher than the waist. The passer then shifts weight to the front foot as the ball/puck is contacted. Eyes center on the ball/puck until it meets the stick. In the follow-through the stick moves in the direction of the hit.

See Box 18.2 for additional information on the developmental levels of striking with bats.

PASSING WITH A HOCKEY STICK

Learning Cues
- Grip stick with non-dominant hand on top, palm facing away from body, and all fingers wrapped around stick (see Figure 18.3)
- Grip stick with dominant hand 5 to 10 inches below non-dominant hand

FIGURE 18.3
This boy demonstrates mature passing with a hockey stick.

- Hold stick to front and right side of the body (right dominant)
- Face the target with the non–dominant side
- Position feet shoulder-width apart
- Focus eyes on ball/puck
- Situate stick to the rear below waist level
- Contact ball/puck
- Shift weight from back foot to front foot as ball/puck is contacted
- Follow through across body in direction of the hit no higher than waist level

Common Difficulties

- Situating hands too close together on stick
- Standing with feet too close together
- Contacting ball/puck in front of the body instead of to side
- Chopping down with stick
- Failing to transfer weight from back to front foot
- Completing backswing and follow-through higher than waist level

DRIBBLING WITH A HOCKEY STICK

Learning Cues

- Grip stick with dominant hand on top and hands 5 to 10 inches apart
- Hold stick to front and right side of the body (right dominant)
- Position feet shoulder-width apart
- Focus eyes on ball/puck
- Situate stick to the rear below waist level
- Contact the ball/puck with little taps (while walking/jogging)
- Keep ball/puck close to stick

Common Difficulties

- Situating hands too close together on stick
- Contacting ball/puck in front of the body instead of to side
- Tapping the ball/puck too far in front of stick
- Failing to move fast enough to progress the ball/puck
- Keeping head down while watching the ball/puck

STRIKING WITH A PUTTER

Striking with a putter is similar to striking with a hockey stick in that the club strikes the ball so it moves along the ground. In striking with a putter, however, the stroke must be controlled, as the distance is limited and the target is small. The child turns sideways to the hole with feet shoulder-length apart and the ball centered between them and forward 4–6 inches. Hips remain fixed and the body is bent at the waist, hunched up and over the club head. Arms are straight and firm.

The putting grip must stabilize the left wrist so that it does not bend toward the hole during the follow-through of the stroke. A common method is to position the right hand closer to the shaft with the right thumb resting on top of the club. The forefinger of the left hand should cover the little finger of the right. The club is pulled back away from the ball only a few inches and deliberately pressed forward. Throughout the swing and strike eyes should remain fixed on the ball. Follow-through with the club for about six inches after striking safeguards against the loss of control that results when the child pops the ball and immediately pulls the club back (Figure 18.4).

FIGURE 18.4
This boy demonstrates
mature putting.

The strike takes place along the ground. Some children may have learned to strike with putters through experiences with their families at miniature golf courses; others may have enjoyed playing on actual golf courses. Since putting strikes total nearly 50 percent of the hits in a round of golf, efforts toward developing a controlled hit are essential, and these early foundations may develop children's skill and confidence in aiming, striking, and sending the ball toward the hole. Likewise, such experience will enhance enjoyment with miniature golfing.

Level of skill in putting is typically limited for elementary students. Practice plays a critical role in the child's mastery. The following three levels define putting development. See Box 18.3 for additional information on the developmental levels of striking with bats.

Developmental Levels

Level 1.

The beginning putter does not turn fully sideways to the target. Weight may transfer during the swing. Hands are placed apart or clenched together over the stick and elbows are slightly bent. A common difficulty is stabilizing the left wrist to prevent it from breaking down and allowing the right wrist to flip the putter head down the target line. The backswing is too

---

Striking with a Putter   Box 18.3

LEVEL I	LEVEL II	LEVEL III
Not sideways to target	Turns slightly toward target	Stance is sideways
Weight may transfer	Putter weight may shift with swing	Feet slightly father than shoulder width apart with weight evenly distributed
Hands apart or clenched together on club	Hands may be fully overlapped or too far apart	Non-dominant hand at top of club; left forefinger covers right pinkie finger
Elbows bent	Arms straight or slightly bent	Arms straight
Left wrist unstable. Right wrist may flip the putter head down the target line	Swing centered at wrist	Wrists stabilized
Too much backswing making follow-through unpredictable	Backswing more controlled and more follow-through	Club head 6–12" behind ball
Eyes on club rather than ball	Eyes on ball until contact with club	Eyes on ball

great and thus follow- through becomes unpredictable. Rather than focusing on the all, eyes focus on the club as it approaches and taps the ball.

Level 2.

In a position slightly turned toward the target, the putter's weight may shift with the swing. Hands may be fully overlapping or be too far apart on the gripping portion of the club. The action of the swing is centered at the wrist if it is not stabilized. Backswing is more controlled with some follow-through. Eyes may center on the ball until the club taps it forward.

Level 3.

The mature passer turns sideways with feet spread slightly farther apart than shoulder width. Weight is distributed evenly on the feet. Arms are held straight and wrists are stabilized. The club head is poised 6–12 inches behind the ball. Hands are positioned with the non-dominant hand at the top of the stick and the left forefinger covers the right pinkie finger. Eyes center on the ball. The club presses slowly and deliberately toward the ball and after contact continues to follow through a few inches.

MOVEMENT EXPERIENCES

Roll to the Bat

Objectives

To enhance student awareness of striking with a bat

To improve students' skill in striking with a bat

To encourage students to seek batting experience

Targeted Age Group

3–5

Equipment

6 bats

6 balls (wiffle, dense sponge, tennis, soft softball)

6 rubber bases or carpet squares

Management

1. Designate a large activity area.
2. Divide class into groups of 4–5. Have each group appoint a leader to retrieve a bat, ball, and base. This student will also become the first batter for each group.
3. Explain that within the large activity area each group should designate their own playing field, establishing as much distance between groups as possible.
4. Within each small playing field, a rubber base or carpet square will serve as home plate. One student will bat and the other four or five students will serve as fielders.

Pre-Activity

The teacher reviews mature batting form and includes a student demonstration of self-tossing the ball upward, grasping the bat, and swinging.

Activity

1. Within each small game, the batter hits the ball and the others attempt to field that ball.
2. Once a fielder has control of the ball s/he attempts to roll the ball along the ground to make contact with the bat that the batter has laid horizontally on the ground.
3. The bat should be facing or giving the most advantage to the fielder who will roll the ball.
4. If the fielder's rolled ball makes contact with the bat, then s/he is the new batter.

5. The fielder can also become the batter if the ball is caught before it touches the ground, as in a pop fly or a line drive. In this case no rolling the ball to contact the bat is necessary.

Modifications

- Have each student take five turns at self-tossing and striking the ball with the bat. Fielders attempt to follow the rules of "roll to the bat." Each student gets a point every time s/he rolls the ball and contacts the bat.
- Follow the game format using a floor hockey pass (or drive).

Assessment

Are all students striving to bat with mature form?

Are students following rules and safety measures?

Are students enthusiastic about the activity?

T-Ball Blitz

Objectives

To enhance student awareness of striking with a bat

To improve students' skill in striking with a bat

To encourage students to seek batting experience

Targeted Age Group

K-2

Equipment

4 plastic bats

4 balls (wiffle, dense sponge, tennis, soft softball)

4 rubber bases or carpet squares

4 T-ball rubber tee or large safety cones

Management

1. Designate a large activity area.
2. Divide class into groups of 4–5. Have each group appoint a leader to retrieve a bat, ball, cone/tee, and base. This student will also become the first batter for each group.
3. Explain that within the large activity area each group should designate their own playing field, establishing as much distance between groups as possible.
4. Within each small playing field, the rubber tee or large cone will hold the ball and will serve as home plate. Approximately 20 yards away place the rubber bases or carpet squares. One student will bat and the other three or four students will serve as fielders.

Pre-Activity

Students review correct form for striking with bats

Activity

1. Within each small game, the batter hits the ball and the others attempt to field that ball.
2. The goal of the batter is to hit the ball, safely drop the bat, run around the base (rubber base or carpet square) and back to the tee before the fielders are able to field the ball and throw it to each other.

Assessment

Are the students successfully completing the activity as directed?

Are batters dropping their bats safely?

Are students improving form and stroke?

Cup It

Objectives

To learn proper form of putting

To develop skills with putting

To enjoy working independently

Targeted Age Group

K-5

Equipment

Putter for every child

2–3 balls for each child

Large plastic cup for each child

Management

1. Distribute equipment.
2. Direct students to spread out over a large area and place cups on their sides.
3. Remind children to keep clubs pointed at the ground at all times for safety.

Pre-Activity

Students review correct form for putting

Activity

1. Each child will assume the correct position, place the balls in a row outward directly in front of her/himself, and press the ball toward the open end of the cup.
2. Then the child will move forward to the next ball and do the same.
3. After all three balls are struck the child with gather them and replace them in a row before her/him.
4. Each time a child taps the ball into the cup, she or he says, "Cup it!"

Modifications

- A series of numbered cups can be spread in progression around a large area—red, blue, green and yellow routes, according to the color of the cups. Students are divided into four groups and each group is assigned a color. Each group progresses from one numbered cup to the next until completing the course. Older students may count strokes for each cup and add them up to determine their "golf score."
- Children start two feet from the cup. Once a child taps two of the three balls into the cup on the first attempt, she/he moves away one step from the cup, and again strikes the balls until two of the three hit the target on a first attempt. This continues increasing the distance from the cup and thereby improving skill and accuracy.
- Each child is given a 10-foot string to extend in a straight line from the ball to the target. She/he taps the ball to trace along the line.

Assessment

Are the students successfully completing the activity as directed?

Are students keeping their clubs safely lowered?

Are students improving form and stroke?

Chapter **Nineteen**

Creative Movement: Concepts, Dance, and Imagery

Jennifer, a first year fourth-grade teacher, bounced into the teachers' lounge beaming. "I just love teaching dance to these kids. Their creativity keeps surprising me." Jack, a twenty-year veteran, rolled his eyes and replied, "You must be kidding." Dance has nothing to do with athletics. It's for ballerinas." Jenny stopped and looked at him. "Are you saying that dance has no value for physical education?" Silence. Jenny continued, "Dance is one place where children get to put ideas into motion. They work with one another rather than trying to compete. It's a shame all children can't have more opportunities to develop self-confidence with body movement."

The term "dance" may make some teachers cringe. Often they recall their unsuccessful attempts to mimic the movements of others on the dance floor as they tangoed, waltzed, or even line danced. However, teaching dance does not require the mentor to move with the grace and polish of Fred Astaire and Ginger Rogers. In working with traditional dance the teacher needs only to be willing to join in the learning, while striving to replicate traditional dance steps to music. In addition, all forms of dance do not follow a culturally established routine. In many cases dance steps are movements that are self-generated to express ideas and feelings creatively, while contributing to physical fitness.

BENEFITS OF DANCE

Establishing a specified time for students to learn structured dance or to explore creative rhythmic movements affords them an opportunity to use movement both functionally and creatively. When students strive to learn dance routines, they watch the model who demonstrates the desired action, commit to memory the movement as they move repeatedly through the process, and self-assess as they measure their own movements against those of the model, making adjustments when needed. For instance, a fifth-grade boy watches carefully as a peer moves through the steps in a waltz. He gets a sense of the rhythm, takes tentative steps, and repeats the action until it becomes comfortable and almost routine. If the added dimension of a partner is required, a social component is added. As the youth turns to claim a partner, he realizes that his own properly executed movements are no longer adequate. He must now move in sync with another, whose movements may be equally proficient, far more skillful, or out of rhythm. Likewise, incorporating dance movements into classroom activities provides a means for students to reflect upon what they are studying, translate the content into movement, and elaborate through gesture. A first-grade class studying the habits of African wildlife may divide into groups representing varied animals and assume roles of predator and prey, demonstrating movements characteristic of their animals while jungle music plays in the background. Finally, individually created expressive dance invites children to formulate a sequence of movements in reaction to their thoughts. The teacher may, for example, use tone of voice, selection of words, and volume as indicators of expected changes in movement.

FUNDAMENTALS OF TRADITIONAL DANCE

In striving to meet public demands, studios typically cater to tiny ballerinas and lively tap dancers. Competitive young gymnasts are also taught to integrate dance in their routines. Later, when children move into adolescence, they are often drawn to try out for pom dance or flag teams that also rely upon prescribed movements. Also, at high school dances bodies gyrate as boom boxes roar, releasing the pent-up energies of youth. During the college years and in their 20s and 30s, young men and women enjoy dancing while DJs play music in clubs. Finally, in adulthood, couples join square dance clubs or sign up for ballroom or Latin or swing dancing lessons to enjoy the social benefits of dance.

These experiences require established disciplined movements, varied only by the individual's personal style. Despite the costs incurred by such structured dance experiences, those who have had the opportunity develop poise before an audience, confidence in physical movement, and awareness of definitive movement patterns. However, not all children have had parents capable of funding these opportunities and willing to sacrifice the time and energy needed to ferry their offspring to and from frequent practices and performances. In order for all children to enjoy such experiences, time devoted to teaching the kinds of structured dances that provide such social contexts is essential. Those children already adept in specific dance steps can learn new forms of dance and aid in teaching their own areas of expertise to peers.

FUNDAMENTALS OF CREATIVE DANCE

Another form of dancing that offers opportunities for creative expression coupled with physical activity is creative dance. Integrating creative movement with information from other disciplines such as science or mathematics can extend learning and add to the pleasure. If, for example, the class is studying the movement of a storm front, children can demonstrate the way moisture accumulates, swirls, and spills onto the earth. Lightning bolts and rolling thunder can invoke even more vigorous movements. In order to enhance the experience, CDs that include sounds of nature can contribute to rhythmical movements and spark additional ideas.

Using streamers helps children communicate ideas.

Another means of inviting such expression is by reading a piece of literature while music of a similar tone is played in the background. As students listen to the teacher reading while they interpret the story or poem through dance, their focus rests not on the effectiveness of others' performances but upon their own subsequent physical movement, thereby decreasing self-consciousness and encouraging free reign of expression. For an added twist the students may be divided into small groups to represent varied characters calling for unique movements.

ELEMENTS OF CREATIVE DANCE MOVEMENT

In order for creative dance to be cohesive a number of factors are essential. Most significant is the body, for it is the element that creates and demonstrates the movement. Whether the focus is upon the body as a whole, upon the movements of its many parts, or upon the body's shape, body awareness is elemental. Also, the movement of the body is limited to a given space, and a child's awareness of the body's movement in that limited area is a key contributor to skill development (see Box 19.1). Each of the movements of the body is dependent upon effort. How the body moves is determined by the expended force, flow, and time. Finally, the relationships between partners and among a group of dancers or objects are key elements in dance.

Elements of Creative Movement   Box 19.1

THE BODY	SPACE AWARENESS	EFFORT AWARENESS	RELATIONSHIP AWARENESS
Body Parts	Location	Time	Objects or others
Head, trunk, arms, legs, etc.	Self-space, general space	Fast, slow	Between, inside, outside
		Force	Around, through
Shapes	Directions	Strong, light	In front of, behind, beside
Curved	Forward, backward		Under, over
Twisted	Up, down	Flow	On, off, across
Narrow	Right, left	Bound, free	Above, below
Wide	Clockwise, counter-		
Symmetrical	clockwise		Partners
Asymmetrical			Leading
	Levels		Following
Locomotor	Low, middle, high		Meeting
Walk			Parting
Jump	Pathways		Matching
Hop	Straight, curved, zigzag		Mirroring
Slide			
Gallop	Extensions		
Skip	Far, near		
Nonlocomotor			
Sway			
Swing			
Twist			
Turn			
Bend/curl			
Stretch			
Sink			
Push			
Pull			
Shake			

The Body

In dance the body becomes an instrument to be moved as a means of expression. The activities the body performs vary from subtle, flowing movements to vigorous, definitive expressions. The dancer moves along the floor using leaping, spinning, rising, and falling motions, or may extend the arms in a broad stretch or draw them inward, folding into the self.

Body Parts

Usually children take for granted the relationships among their body parts. When marching, for example, they do not concern themselves with the awareness that when the right elbow bends to raise the right arm, the left arm simultaneously extends downward. Likewise, in sync with the right arm the left knee bends to lift the leg, while the right leg is extended in opposition. However, when marching becomes a part of a dance, it is essential for children to be made aware of the role played by each body part as it moves through its planned pattern. In less structured dance movements body parts may move in harmony or in asymmetrical motions.

Body As a Whole

As the body engages in dance, a variety of whole body activities offer means of creative expression. **Locomotor** movements, such as stepping, sliding, skipping, running, jumping, rolling, and leaping, can play an integral role as the dancer travels around the dance area. Non-locomotor actions, including stretching, swaying, and twisting, may interrupt traveling movements in a dance sequence. Such combinations allow for movement interpretations of a variety of events or emotions, inviting students to create, define, and rehearse novel ways of moving.

For any dance movement body parts may lead, be isolated, or serve as support for a movement. For example, if a child extends a hand in a reaching motion as if to pluck a daisy, the hand leads the movement. If the child stands motionless except for her/his head nodding up and down as if watching snowflakes fall, that movement is in isolation. Finally, if the child stands on one foot as she or he bends at the waist, hands outstretched as a figure skater, the foot and leg serve as support.

Shape of the Body

The body has a shape that shifts with movement. The shape also changes when you view the body from the front, the side, the back, or from the top down. Common body shapes are

Children express themselves as they engage in creative dance.

curved, twisted, and narrow. Children can use their bodies to make specific shapes, such as a box or a pear or an arrow. Their awareness of body shape can be even more enhanced when they work collaboratively toward constructing a shape.

Space Awareness

Space is where the body moves. The emotion or mood of the dance is demonstrated through the use of space. As children explore the use of space, their awareness of space is enhanced. Subtle alterations in pathways, levels, and extensions add to the color of the dance and challenge dancers to use their creativity.

General Space and Self-Space

General space includes all of the area in the arena of activity. Students can penetrate any of the general space within the physical or teacher-established imaginary boundaries. Self-space, on the other hand, is limited to the area around the body of each child, governed by the distance her/his extremities can stretch from a stationary position. In order for children to fully understand safety, it is essential for them to first have a clear awareness of self-space that can eventually be expanded as they begin to explore general space.

Pathways

Floor and air patterns are formed as students create pathways though movement. If a child were to step in paint before entering the house, footprints would designate the child's pathways along floor patterns. Also, when a child traces a pattern in the air with a sparkler, often the air pattern lingers after the sparkler has moved on. Though such paths are invisible in dance, the patterns are there nonetheless. Typical patterns are straight, curved, and zigzagged. As a golfer visualizes the pathway the ball will travel before taking a swing, a child can visualize her or his pathway when planning a dance pattern.

Levels

Three levels of space can be utilized when a child dances. The area above the shoulders is labeled a high level, whereby movements such as jumping, leaping, pressing up on tiptoe, hopping, or reaching overhead occur. When the waist becomes elevated above its usual position, a high level of space is being penetrated. The middle level of body space is the area between a child's shoulders and knees. In bending from the waist and dropping or extending arms forward, backward, or sideways, the student can explore the self-space at this level. Finally, the low level of space is the area from the knees to the ground. When asked to demonstrate a movement from that level, a child's first response may be simply to collapse to the floor. However, the student should also be encouraged to explore the myriad of other possibilities such as crouching with arms grasped around the knees while balanced on toes to support the body.

Directions

Dance is comprised of a series of motions in a combination of potential directions, like forward/backward, side-to-side, or up and down. Change of direction is critical in dance, as the ongoing motion is what provides the experienced as well as the viewed esthetic expression. Younger children can be reminded that in a movement forward the belly button leads, in shifting to the side the hip leads, and in backing up the heels lead. They can also remember that pushing upward is toward the ceiling and downward is toward the floor. In developing a dance the direction of movement must become routine so that students are able to anticipate their next move.

Extensions

Two kinds of movements characterize the extensions of the body during dance. Those that are close to the body and less dynamic are considered small movements. Children delight in closing their bodies into a tightly drawn self-space. In contrast, when body parts extend widely throughout the self-space, they are labeled large movements. To use

Children enjoy the challenge of curling themselves into a tight ball.

boundless gestures, broadening self-space to the maximum, releases pent-up tensions and energies. Again, a combination of small and large movements are what give the dance style and shape.

Effort Awareness

Three kinds of movements exemplify the dynamics or effort expended: force, flow, and time. Varying the power, shift and motion, and pace provides the artistry of the dance. Such efforts serve to interpret the thoughts and emotions given themes evoke in young dancers.

Force

The energy expended to begin, sustain, and complete a movement is described as force. When the movement is weighty and firm the force is deemed strong, such as tromping like an elephant through the general space. Light movement, on the other hand, is airy and buoyant, demonstrating a leaf on the wind or a dragonfly on a lake. Force plays a key role in communicating the mood of the dance.

Flow

The two kinds of flow are bound and free. When a child springs from one point to another, regroups, and then springs again, these movements are deemed bounding. We commonly see such actions after a rainstorm when one attempts to cross a street scattered with deep puddles, moving like the grasshopper, who gathers himself up, leaps, lands, and then retracts to gather momentum to spring again. Free flow differs in that movement is fluid and continuous with any pause in the flow so subtle as not to be noticed. The dancer moves with seeming abandon, even if the basic structure of the dance is planned. Bounding interspersed with free flowing movements can blend into an intriguing dance.

Time

The speed of a dance may be slow and deliberate with sustained emphasis on each motion or fast with quick, light or zesty, sharp actions. When the teacher selects musical compositions to underscore dance, it is important to expose students to a variety of tempos in order to develop awareness of pace in dance. If the students are to express excitement in anticipation of the county fair, for instance, a lively air invites them to race, skip, spin, and leap with the thrill of what's in store. However, when the mood is heavy with foreboding, the music should have a deep resonance, telling of gloomy or fearful possibilities. Students may be dancing their way out of dark, unfamiliar woods and the music can convey their wary watchfulness. To strike a blend of both paces the music must range from vigorous to serene.

Relationship Awareness

Because young children are focused primarily on themselves, it seems only natural to offer them opportunities to center on the self in dance. By having students move specific body parts, these young dancers can develop an awareness and an understanding of their bodies' coordination of movements. Likewise, when children join in pairs to coordinate movements, attention to specific body actions is needed. Whether they mirror one another's actions or move asymmetrically, their awareness of others' movements in relationship to their movements is significant. Finally, when dancers have reached a degree of relationship sophistication, they are ready to join as a group of three or more to dance in a collaborative effort.

With Partners

Some individual dancers may readily grasp concepts of meeting and parting actions, whereas others may feel bewildered. Often it is easier for a child to further develop her/his awareness of body parts through mimicking or contrasting movements with a partner. As a child dances with another to express an idea, she or he is reassured by the presence of a collaborator. The advantage of dancing with a partner results not only in psychological support, but also in physical support. Students may come together with hands joined and then rapidly stretch apart. One may rise as the other drops. They may stand side-by-side and lean in parallel directions or join the connecting hand and pull outward from joined hips. One's outstretched reach toward the sky is further enhanced by a partner's contrasting thrust toward the floor. Such exploration of movement with the awareness of responsibility not only to oneself but also to another can be a valuable experience.

With Others

Before students can explore creative dance in groups, they need to be mature enough to negotiate the movements needed to choreograph a given theme or story. When the collaborative effort extends to include a group of dancers, the planning grows more complex. Perhaps two of the children want to bound through the space with arms extended like an airplane, while the other two want to fold arms inward. Blending the participants' movement may make the dance even more interesting.

If the teacher notes a group like this floundering, she or he needs only to assure members that all ideas are worthy. By suggesting that students simply intersperse gentle confined movements within a framework of broad sweeping movements like a snowstorm bursting forth and a flower folding inward against the first snow, both ideas are acknowledged as valuable.

Children must adjust their movements to others when dancing with partners or in groups.

The benefits of group dance include building social relationships, developing skills in compromising, and combining ideas to make a plan. The movement concepts applied in creative movement and dance are applicable in a wide range of skills and activities. Developing abilities to utilize pathways enhances movement in open skill use. Relying on rhythm in movement contributes to effective timing. Space awareness is essential in sport, gymnastic, dance, and fitness activities. It also contributes to a safe moving environment. Likewise, if children have a clear sense of the importance of relationships in physical activities, they are more likely to thrive in situations where they rely on partners or teams.

Jennifer's efforts to introduce dance to her classes in her first year may have lasting benefits for her fourth graders. As they romp across the playground mimicking a band of wild mustangs, Jenny recognizes their unique interpretations of the movement. She recognizes their growing ability to make their movements in rhythm with the beat of the music. Through dance they gain confidence as they use their bodies to express themselves and develop awareness of their bodies, space, effort, and relationships in ways that cannot be generated elsewhere.

MOVEMENT EXPERIENCES

Spellchecker

Objective

To be aware of what it means to isolate body parts

To review the week's spelling list

To work collaboratively to spell

Targeted Age Group

2–5

Equipment

Weekly spelling list

Management

1. Direct students to spread out in a scattered formation.
2. Teacher has list of the week's spelling words.

Pre-Activity

Students review spelling list in class. Students talk about the use of sparklers to spell out their names in the night sky, remembering the way the pathway of the light through the darkness. Each student spells her or his name in the air with one finger.

Activity

1. Students are in a scattered formation. The teacher calls out, "Point to your rib cage. Now spell your first name in the air three times with your rib cage."
2. Next she or he declares, "Lift up your ankle. Spell your last name in the air three times with your ankle."
3. After a few such efforts the students will choose a different body part to spell each of the spelling words three times. The teacher calls out one of the spelling words and the students all spell it with a body part.
4. Then the teacher asks the students to spell the word in unison. Two more times the students move to write the letters with two new body parts as the teacher and class spell the words.

Modifications

- Join a partner and use body parts to make the letters to spell out the words, going through the list three times.
- Using a body part or the whole body, with a partner write out a full sentence using one of the spelling words.
- In a group use body parts or whole bodies to spell out the words.
- Listen to music and shape letters in rhythm with the beat.

Assessment

Is there an improvement in spelling scores?

Are students moving creatively as they choose different body parts to spell out words?

When performing partner or group tasks are children working cooperatively?

Flash Dance

Objective

To move creatively as inspired by picture cards

To move safely in general space and self-space

Targeted Age Group

K-5

Equipment

Stack of cards with pictures of colors, numbers, objects, animals, machines, vehicles, etc.

Management

1. Direct students to spread out in a scattered formation.
2. Teacher has stack of cards displaying pictures.

Pre-Activity

Students are to dance in ways they choose to represent what the card suggests to them.

To demonstrate several students create movements inspired by selected cards, such as "peacock," or "train whistle," or "lavender."

Activity

1. Teacher lifts the top card, announces what is on the card, and displays it for all to see. Students perform single movements.
2. Teacher turns and announces a series of cards (e.g., turkey, pink, sewing machine, soda pop) as children move in ways they choose to depict the cards.
3. Students choose a sequence of three or four of the movements they have created and work toward developing smooth transitions from one to the next.
4. Dancers create a personal introductory movement and a concluding movement to frame the sequence.
5. Next dancers begin with the introductory movement, repeat the rehearsed sequences three times, and conclude.
6. One-third of the students performs their dance sequences simultaneously as the other students watch. Then another third performs and finally the last group performs.

Modifications

- Students are divided into groups of three or four dancers. Each dancer draws a card and the group works together to choreograph a dance with the three or four movements interpreted from the cards. Two groups at a time perform their routines for the rest of the class.
- Cards can be created to reflect a lesson from another discipline (e.g., mathematics, science, language arts).
- Cards can reflect specific holidays or themes.
- Students can each be given three index cards and assigned to draw or cut out and paste on a picture to be included in the dancing.
- In groups students can act out mathematics story problems.
- Music may be used describing animals (such as "Itsy Bitsy Spider" or "Old MacDonald," for instance, and children move with rhythm as the animal in the music moves. If a form of transportation is in the music, such as the train in "Chattanooga Choo Choo," children fall into place as a train and move in sync depicting the turning wheels.
- Using music to accompany routines may aid in developing their sense of rhythm.

Assessment

Are all dances reflective of the cards they represent?

Do the sequences flow together with smooth transitions?

Are the dances imaginative?

In group dancing are all children cooperative and respectful of others?

Take Five

Objective

To apply elements of space, relationships, and effort

To create a travel movement sequence

To develop confidence with creative movement

Targeted Age Group

3–5

Equipment

CD player

A variety of CDs with varying tempos

Management

1. Direct students to spread out in a scattered formation.
2. Distribute equipment after rehearsal.

Pre-Activity

Teacher explains that students are to dance in ways they choose to include five basic traveling movements.

Teacher demonstrates possible travel movements the children might create.

Activity

1. Students choose a specific travel movement to perform.
2. The teacher directs the students to shift to a new form of travel and practice the first two in sequence.
3. Subsequently the students add a third means of travel, then a fourth, and finally a fifth. (Repetition of the type of travel movement is fine.)
4. Children develop smooth transitions to shift from one movement to the next.
5. Students create an introduction and a conclusion.
6. Students rehearse dance with introduction, five travel movements repeated twice, and a conclusion.
7. Musical selections change during rehearsal so students first perform the entire segment at a moderate pace until they have it mastered, then repeat it at a faster tempo, and finally at a slow speed while performing their dances. (It is best not to change pace mid-dance as it may be confusing for the students.)

Modifications

- Use beanbags, wands with streamers, hula hoops, or other objects to enhance the dance.
- Vary levels, speed, direction, or force while performing the created dance.
- Prepare the dance with a partner or a group.

Assessment

Are the students successfully combining travel movements into a creative dance?

Are the introductions, transitions, and conclusions smooth and appropriate?

When asked to change speeds do the students comfortably adapt?

Do the students gain confidence with repetition of the dance?

I Got Rhythm

Objective

To shape dances based on varied types of music

To develop creativity and enhance confidence in movement

To work collaboratively and develop social skills

Targeted Age Group

K-5

Equipment

CD player

In advance the teacher should tape a combination of brief segments of a variety of types of music, such as classical, country, jazz, rock, rap, and tango strung together without interruption (e.g., 30 seconds of rap followed by 30 seconds of country followed by 30 seconds of jazz).

Streamers

Management

1. Direct students to spread out in a scattered formation.
2. Distribute streamers.

Pre-Activity

Teacher explains that students are to dance in ways that reflect the music.

Teacher explains the way streamers can emphasize movement.

Teacher demonstrates possible movements the children might create.

Activity

1. Students listen for a moment to the first piece of music.
2. Then the teacher directs them to use only the hand with the streamer to demonstrate movements inspired by the music.
3. After a few moments students begin to dance using the streamers in sweeping motions.
4. Another type of music is introduced and the students once again begin by listening, then using the streamers only, then by creating dances.
5. Children dance to the CD with a combination of music types, developing smooth transitions.

Modifications

- Older children can be separated into groups and sent to stations where each group has a specific type of music. They can prepare dances as groups and perform for the rest of the class.
- Art work, photographs, or poetry can be used to inspire the dancing.
- Nature sounds can be substituted for music.
- Students can be paired or separated into small groups to prepare dances collaboratively.

Assessment

Are the students successfully creating dances that simulate the music?

Are the transitions of the final combined dance smooth?

When the music changes do the students comfortably adapt?

Do the students gain confidence with repetition of the dance?

Chapter **Twenty**

Educational Gymnastics: Balancing, Weight Transfer, and Rolling

Shavon cries, "Follow me," flops to the ground, and rolls down the hill. Lisa giggles and merrily rolls after her, followed by Madeline and then Grace. As each girl in the playful foursome slows to a stop at the bottom, she springs up and darts back up the hill to begin again. This kind of gaiety, requiring no equipment, no rules, and no competition, engages the girls as they delight in their own ingenuity. As children choose tumbling and body control as entertainment, they enjoy self-paced opportunities to develop agility and strength.

The kinds of activities children choose to enjoy outside the classroom offer opportunities for classroom teachers to encourage balance, weight transfer, rolling, and self-expression as viable components of the curriculum. Such investments result in a variety of wellness outcomes, including body control, social development, and self-esteem. Because students are empowered to set personal goals and to self-assess, the teacher's role is to plan and monitor activities and ensure safety.

America's love for Olympic gymnastics stars has prompted thousands of parents to enroll their children in afternoon and evening classes to replicate the dynamic gyrations of these champions. In order to direct such activities, equipment such as balance beams, parallel bars, and floor mats is essential. Since access to these apparatus is unlikely and most teachers lack the expertise to teach or even supervise such activities, fundamental balancing, weight-transfer, and rolling activities provide a simple foundation for elementary children. Most of the creative movement concepts described in the previous chapter are threaded throughout these elements as well. At a glance you can see the ways in which body space, effort, and relationship awareness also enhance performance in educational gymnastics.

DEFINING SPACE

A key consideration in educational gymnastics is the space each individual is granted for movement. Once that space is defined the individual must gauge the extent of movement allowable within those conditions, an awareness that develops through experience. Emphasizing use of space and control of extension within that space can be a key contributor to skill development.

When developing balance, weight transfer, and rolling skills, it is vital for students to limit their use of space to a defined parameter. Many families are riveted to the television during Olympic gymnastic competitions. Part of the audience's fascination lies in acknowledging the competitors' ability to constrict movement, regardless of how elaborate, to a defined area.

FUNDAMENTALS OF BALANCING

From a child's first steps the importance of balance is recognized. With growth children may learn to ice skate, skateboard, and water ski, all individual skills that are dependent upon balance. When children rely upon a partner or group for balance, such as riding on a seesaw or building a pyramid, cooperative movement is required. In order to maintain stability an individual needs to keep the body's gravity centered above the body parts used for support. With static balance a child moves into a position and freezes, for example, with head down and feet skyward on the monkey bars. Dynamic balance is the ability to maintain balance while engaged in movement, as one does while snow skiing. A boy standing on one foot demonstrates an example of static balance, whereas a girl riding a bicycle portrays dynamic balance.

Developing Balancing Skills

Balancing is successful when it can be sustained for an extended time. A boy uses balancing skills when he springs from one spot to another on the street to avoid puddles or when stepping on stones to cross a brook. If he reaches his destination with dry feet, he has balanced successfully. By repeatedly relying upon balancing skills, a child's balance improves.

Mechanical Principles of Balance

Three principles describe factors that contribute to the development of balancing skills: support base, center of gravity, and use of extensions. Typically a child's balance develops in daily living; however, by using specific applications of the mechanical principles of balance, skill levels may be markedly improved. A clear understanding of ways in which these elements intersect may aid in shaping curriculum aimed at improving balance.

Support Base

An individual's support base is the area of the body that is touching the floor. If one is standing on tiptoes, for instance, the toes are serving as the base of support. Difficulty of balance is relative to the breadth of the base of support. If feet are spread two feet apart, balancing an egg on one's shoulder is much easier than if heels are touching. Balance becomes even more difficult if the point of balance is reduced to one foot.

Children enjoy the challenge of maintaining balance.

Center of Gravity

An individual's center of gravity, typically located in the stomach area, serves a primary function in defining balance. The closer one's center of gravity is to the ground, the more stable is one's stance. Body tension, the tightening of the muscles, sustains balance. One's balance is dependent upon her or his base of support and center of gravity. Therefore, if the center of gravity is shifted outside the support base, balance is challenged.

Use of Extensions

Although arms or legs may aid in balancing, they may also serve to counterbalance the body. When an extension reaches in one direction, a counterbalancing extension is required of another body part in the opposite direction. When a child bends to the right, extending the right arm, the left leg may be extended to counterbalance the action.

Children are motivated to use counterbalance to maintain their balances.

One way for a teacher to aid students in improving their balance is to ask them to balance objects on specific parts of the body. When a girl walks along a line on the floor with a Frisbee on her head, her ability to balance is demonstrated. Likewise, if a student is able to repeatedly stand storklike for periods of time, balance typically improves. One's balance is dependent upon the base of support, the center of gravity shifts, and counterbalance to maintain stability.

FUNDAMENTALS OF WEIGHT TRANSFER

In order to move from one place or position to another, a transfer of weight must occur. Tightening muscles creates a force necessary to transfer weight, while countering with a force in the opposite direction. Despite the resulting momentum, it is essential to continue to maintain balance by shifting the center of gravity as needed.

Common ways children use to transfer weight is by performing cartwheels and handsprings, executing routines on parallel bars, or using vaults. These highly athletic activities demonstrate advanced levels of transferring weight. However, for elementary children to develop rudimentary levels of weight transfer, less intensive challenges are equally as valid. Because students need experience with varied forms of weight transfer, the classroom teacher can offer a myriad of opportunities for growth.

Locomotion

One of the earliest experiences of weight transfer for a child is locomotion. In the early months of a child's life she or he learns to lift the head and eventually to roll over. By the time a baby is six months old parents are beaming at their child's ability to crawl. Then, when she or he reaches a year old, first steps delight witnesses. These forms of locomotion require the constriction of muscle to alter the center of gravity and allow weight transfer. Later the same skills are refined when children bound to catch a football, play leapfrog during recess, twirl until disoriented, and jump to avoid a crack that may "break your mother's back."

Transferring Weight to Other Body Parts

At elementary school age children unconsciously use weight transfer to pull themselves forward by their hands on a horizontal ladder, fling feet skyward and walk on their hands, perform a forward roll, or engage in a crabwalk. As children develop movement skills they work toward a smooth transition from one base of support to another, as seen when an Olympic gymnast moves through a series of weight transfers without any abrupt shifts in the routine.

Fundamentals of Rolling

A use of weight transfer that children enjoy is rolling. The ability to defy gravity by constricting muscles to roll the body in a chosen direction demonstrates the use of the back as a base of support. Even partial rolls offer positive experiences with weight transfer.

Side Rolling

Children are tireless when opportunities for rolling down an incline occur. Once they set the roll in motion, the incline serves to intensify the momentum and set them spinning toward the bottom. Log rolling does not require a tilt, however, as students can also propel themselves rolling across a plane. The child begins by lying flat on her or his back with arms extended above the head, thighs pressed together to ensure a minimum of resistance, and feet joined with toes pointed. The body then rolls to the side making 360-degree rotations. The egg roll is similar, but the body begins in a crouched position, hands clasped behind knees. The child leans to the side and rolls a complete rotation, arriving on the knees, then rising.

Learning Cues

Log Roll

- Body lies stiffly in a straight position
- Arms press firmly against sides as the child log rolls to the side in a straight path
- Arms fully and firmly extended overhead
- Rolls to the side in a straight path

Common Difficulties

- Body loose without firm control
- Arms loosely held and moving with the roll

Egg Roll

- In couched position with hands behind the knees
- Leans to the side and rolls
- Arrives on the knees and rises to a standing position

Common Difficulties

- Hands coming unclasped
- Struggle to roll from back to position on knees
- Trouble rising easily to standing position

Side rolls are especially appropriate for children who fear forward or backward rolling.

FIGURE 20.1
This boy demonstrates mature forward rolling.

Forward Rolling

When toddlers work to perform a forward roll, the vision is comic. Because of their lack of balance and body control, they often roll to the side rather than forward or backward. It is much easier for young children to learn to do a forward roll down an incline than on a flat surface, because the slant contributes momentum. Teachers can aid in a child's attempts by centering on the steps toward roll completion. The child starts with hands on the floor in a crouching position with back bent into a "C" and chin pressed to the chest. With elbows bent the child pushes off with hands and feet, hoisting the seat into the air and forcing weight transfer from the feet to the arched back while maintaining a curled body. The roll ends with weight returning to the feet. See Figure 20.1.

Learning Cues

- Hands on floor, crouching with back bent into a "C"
- Chin presses against chest
- Elbows bent, pushes off with hands and feet
- Seat is hoisted into the air
- Weight transfers from feet to arched back in tight tuck
- Arrive on seat and feet and rise to a standing position

Common Difficulties

- Hands not comfortably reaching floor
- Maintaining balance while crouching
- Back too upright
- Chin up
- Falls rather than pushing off
- Momentum insufficient to carry over to seat
- Recovering balance to rise with ease

FIGURE 20.2
This girl is demonstrating mature backward rolling.

Backward Rolling

As children develop rolling skills they often strive to propel themselves backward. Such actions transfer weight from the seat to the back to the shoulders. For most children, rolling backward is much more difficult than forward and some may not have the upper-body or abdominal strength or body control necessary. Thus, a child should never be required to perform a backward roll. Children who are developing skills and do not seem ready to complete backward rolls should sit with arms around knees and knees drawn to chest and roll onto back and shoulders. After mastering this stage of development they may clasp hands behind the head and again rock to the shoulders and back as a rocking horse does.

When encouraging students to work toward mature backward rolling, teachers should offer guidelines dependent upon participant readiness. First students should connect fingers behind the neck with elbows jutting outward. Next they must assume a crouching stance with knees tucked against the chest. By dropping their seats to the floor and rocking backward, they propel their bodies back and follow through with a backward roll onto the knees again. Then backs are raised to a perpendicular position and hands are released. See Figure 20.2.

Learning Cues

- Connect fingers behind neck, elbows jutting outward
- Crouch, knees tucked against chest
- Drop seat to floor and rock backward
- Propel body back and over
- Arrive on knees and rise to standing position

Common Difficulties

- Maintaining balance while crouching
- Failure to stay tucked
- Tipping to side during roll
- Momentum insufficient to complete back roll
- Recovering balance while rising

Considerations when opting to focus on balancing, weight transfer, and rolling include simple safety measures. No spotters are needed for these activities as students moderate their own movement, so there is little likelihood of injury. By individualizing expectations by encouraging students to decide the extent to which they are willing to take risks with these activities, teachers establish an environment free of competition that is challenging for the less skilled students, while offering advanced strategies for more mature movers.

Such agency draws upon students' resourcefulness, willingness to take risks, independence, creativity and self confidence. As students perform self-paced movements in tandem with others, they may choose to join in cooperative efforts toward accomplishing a task. Support for one another that such applications encourage contributes to the children's social development.

During physical education, centering on balance, weight transfer, and rolling offers opportunities to develop social skills and self esteem as skill levels improve. Also, by setting personal goals and striving to self-assess, students are encouraged to reflect on their own development and create new goals. Since fundamental balancing, weight-transfer, and rolling are simple procedures requiring a minimum of space, children can engage in foundational activities without the need for elaborate equipment.

MOVEMENT EXPERIENCES

Under the Big Top

Objectives

To develop children's balance, weight transfer, and rolling

To encourage students to self-pace and self-assess their readiness for multiple degrees of difficulty for balance, weight transfer, and rolling tasks

Targeted Age Group

K-2

Equipment

5 ropes

Circus music

CD player or MP3 + speakers

Microphone (optional)

Index cards or poster/pictures at each station to designate expectations

Management

1. Big Top boundaries are established
2. Circus participants divide into groups of five and gather in three indicated rings in the area designated as the Big Top.

Pre-Activity

Students brainstorm what performances might be included in a circus.

The students are told they are all circus performers and are about to present the day's show.

Activity

The Ringleader [teacher] is centered in the middle of the children with a hand-held speaker.

The Ringleader calls out a start and stop time for experience at each ring (station), reinforced by the starting and stopping of circus music.

Examples

Ring I   "And now, ladies and gentlemen, in Ring I the 2nd-grade tightrope artists will demonstrate their feats while defying gravity."
In turn children will

- With arms extended walk heel to toe along a marked line, an extended rope or jump rope, or balance beam
- At midpoint on the tightrope balance on one foot extending the other straight ahead or upward with bended knee to a count of three
- Use counterbalance to touch the rope with the right hand while extending the left foot backward
- Develop a four-step repeatable routine that each will practice until the Ringleader signals the time to change rings

Ring II   "Children and grandparents, see the antics of the circus clowns tumbling in Ring II."
Simultaneously children choose which of the following activities

- Perform side rolls with five rotations
- Execute forward rolls in succession

- Present backward rolls or shoulder rolls
- Rock back and forth on the back in crunched position

"Puppies and parakeets, direct your attention to Ring III where the terrific trick riders perform amazing feats!"

Ring III

1. On fixed benches or sturdy chairs children simulate riders whose acts are performed on the backs of horses or elephants. (Note: each chair should be stabilized by a partner who holds the back.) Any of the following movements or any created by the students are appropriate.

   - While poised on one foot, grasp the calf of the opposite leg and raise it as high as they safely can
   - Crouch and then spring upward and return to the original standing position
   - Bend a knee and lift the foot behind the body and hold to a count of three while maintaining balance. Do the same with the opposite foot.
   - Create four repeatable feats while perched on the saddle of the steed chosen

2. At a signal from the Ringleader all children perform the routines they have rehearsed at their current station as if performing before a crowd at the circus.
3. Each group of children moves to the next ring, and after performances at the second ring they move to the third.

Modifications

- Vary activities so that the Big Top can be performed multiple times (e.g., juggling, trapeze acts on the monkey bars, acrobats, etc.)
- Connect this lesson to a drawing, painting, or coloring activity.
- Study circus life and the varied kinds of talents required.
- Use mathematics or maps to chart the distance and direction the circus travels on its circuit.

Assessment

Have the students maximized the activity possibilities?

Are students demonstrating correct form?

Are all students enthusiastically engaged?

Swamped

Objectives

To join in an adventure while centering on balance and weight transfer

To develop body control and choose appropriate challenges for the child's capability

Targeted Age Group

K-2

Equipment

30 polyspots

6 short cones

10 ropes

12 hula hoops

Management

1. Arrange hula hoops in two groups of six in one corner of the activity area.
2. Scatter polyspots as stepping stones in two columns spaced apart a distance children can navigate.
3. Line ropes in two rows, narrow at one end and widening to a distance that would challenge students to jump across.

Pre-Activity

Students review their awareness of the principles of balance and transferring weight.

Students break into three groups and each group positions near one of the obstacle areas.

Activity

At a signal from the teacher groups simultaneously begin their challenges and continue until another signal.

Stepping Stones   Polyspots represent stones offering support for crossing a swampy area.

1. In two rows children leap from one stone to the next, shifting their center of gravity to transfer weight.
2. When weight is transferred from one stone to another, the child stops to regroup and jump again.
3. Upon reaching the end of one series of stones they proceed to the next.

   Cones may be interspersed in the area to require jumping over a cone to get to the next stone.

Crossing Quicksand

Hula hoops indicate solid ground surrounded by quicksand

1. Children form two groups, each of which will leap from one patch of land to the next, transferring weight, stopping, and turning to regroup and leap in a new direction.
2. When they all have crossed the quicksand, they switch to the other trail to return again to their starting position in the swamp.

Raging River

1. Because the river narrows at one end and broadens at the other, children may choose the most desirable place to cross, transferring weight to hands or feet.
2. Children may choose to start at the most narrow point and continue to the most challenging point they can master or may repeat a comfortable crossing indefinitely.

   It is important for them to note that alligators swim in this river and may surface at any time, creating the need for a more rapid crossing.

3. Children who are waiting to cross or who have already crossed and are waiting to cross back may take turns crying, "Alligator!!!," calling for a higher, faster leap.

Swinging Vines (optional)

If this activity occurs on the playground, a fourth activity area may be designated.

1. Children simulate swinging from vines as they swing on or cross the horizontal ladder.
2. When members of their group cry "Snake!," students swing more quickly or to the side to avoid the snake on a nearby branch.

Modifications

- Monkey bars may be used to denote tree climbing to transfer weight using the arms.
- A slide may be used for transferring weight while climbing the ladder before riding down the waterfall.
- Students would enjoy this activity in conjunction with some study of swampland characteristics, locations, wildlife.
- The teacher reads "The Elephant Child" by Rudyard Kipling and children assume the characters of the animals in the story.

Assessment

Are the students successfully and safely maintaining balance and transferring weight?

Do students challenge themselves appropriately when self-selecting levels of difficulty?

Wax Museum

Objectives

To develop balance

To sustain a pose using body control

To represent a key figure through body positioning

Targeted Age Group

K-2

Equipment

None

Management

Museum boundaries are established

Students spread out in a scattered formation

Pre-Activity

Students review their awareness of the principles of balance and transferring weight

Pre-Activity

Students discuss what a wax museum is

Students brainstorm what characters might be seen in a wax museum

Students are told they are about to pose in the wax museum and will need to use balance to remain totally still to the count of five

Activity

1. The teacher calls out a model and each child strikes a pose.

Examples

"Principal Johansen discovers one of the toilets is overflowing!"

"Your favorite baseball pitcher releases the ball!"

"A baseball fielder springs up to catch a fly ball."

"A baseball star is up at bat."

"A rock star plays the guitar at a big concert."

"One singer wails into the microphone."

"The drummer plays a solo."

"A soldier marches in a parade."

"A band member marches in the parade."

"The Mardi Gras queen waves to the crowd as she rides along the parade route."

"A ghost frightens your friend."

"Witch Wanda flies by on her broom."

"A firecracker explodes."

"A climber scales a mountain."

"A stork pauses in the water."

"A peacock struts his stuff."

"A lion roars at a panther."

"A frog poises to leap."

"The elastic man fits in a tiny box."

"The policeman directs traffic."

"A postman is chased by a dog."

"A gorilla beats his chest."

"A turtle hides in his shell."

"An eagle soars."

"A kicker punts the football."

"A lightning bolt strikes."

2. Children pair up or gather in threesomes for group poses.

Examples

"Movers carrying a piano"

"Window washers"

"Player balances a football for the kicker"

"Frogs in a pond"

"Bears waking from hibernation"

"Kids sledding"

"Rowing a boat"

"Disco dancing"

"Floating on melting ice"

"Rafting over rapids"

"Slipping in a mudslide"

"Fireman fighting fire"

"Three kids make a pyramid"

"Spacemen emerge from the spaceship"

Modifications

* Couple this lesson with a unit on jungle life, insects, sports, professions, punctuation, shapes, numbers
* For holidays use representative figures
* Read a story and pose as the characters in actions depicted
* Strike poses that correspond to music
* Have students create a scene for others to guess

Assessment

Have the students maximized the activity possibilities?

Are students demonstrating effective balance?

Do all students recognize the prompts?

Moon Walk

Objectives

To develop balance, weight transfer, and rolling skills

To use imagination and creativity to enact the adventure

Targeted Age Group

3–5

Equipment

Playground equipment

Cones

Polyspots

Ropes

Hula hoops

Management

1. Children break into groups of four to create an expedition on the moon for others in the class to follow
2. Each group is given three cones, three polyspots, three hula hoops, and three ropes to use in constructing their moonwalk
3. A designated area is assigned to each group

Pre-Activity

Students discuss the principles of balance, weight transfer, and rolling

Students review class discussion on moon features, astronauts' movements, effects of the lack of gravity

Activity

Each group maps out a moonwalk using distributed equipment to represent

- craters
- mountains
- regolith (ground-up rock)
- paths of lava flow
- giant rocks

Areas depicting the Maria and the Highlands on the moon are identified

Students are reminded that movement is slow and deliberate due to the lack of gravity and their cumbersome apparel.

Because of previous explorers parts of the moon's surface are covered with footprints. Perhaps students would want to include a segment of stepping into those imaginary steps.

Groups create a repeatable path, incorporating balance (holding precarious positions while preparing for following movements, weight transfer (e.g., leaping across craters, climbing mountains, moving sideways along a mountainside, hurdling rocks), and rolling (e.g., tumbling down a mountain, falling into a crater).

Three groups unify to lead one another through their created paths.

Modifications

- The same kind of path can be constructed

    1. through a jungle, using vines to transfer weight, struggling with thick foliage and quicksand as obstacles, using balance to cross gorges on fallen logs, and acting fast to transfer weight as creatures attack unexpectedly
    2. across dunes, maintaining balance while fighting a sandstorm, transferring weight to maintain balance while riding camels, finding an oasis, and crouching to avoid burning sun
    3. on a ship venturing through a storm at sea, maintaining their sea legs (balance) as the ship is tossed, ropes are maneuvered, equipment is secured, and sailors need rescuing from the water
    4. prehistoric times, climbing up to ride a brontosaurus, crouching to avoid teradactyls, running from a predator

Assessment

Are the students working cooperatively without conflict?

Are all students engaged?

Are students considering balance, weight transfer, and rolling as they plot their courses?

Chapter **Twenty One**

Health-Related Fitness: Muscular Strength and Endurance and Flexibility

Stephanie, a first-year teacher, joined Grace, a seasoned veteran, for recess duty. Children surged out of the building onto the playground, racing to the equipment they most enjoyed. "I wish I had their energy!" Grace chuckled. "There's Austin climbing up the ladder of the slide," Stephanie noted. "I wish I could get him that excited about math facts." "I know," Grace replied, "Hannah resists reading but is always the first one to the swings."

All fifty states require recess time to allow a break in the intensity of classroom learning and to promote physical activity. Most children are charged with energy when set free on the playground. Those children who pump little legs to gain momentum on the swings, who dangle from monkey bars, or who climb ladder slides in order to whoosh down to the ground are all engaging in activities that promote physical strength and endurance and flexibility. However, even though we see evidence of children heartily engaged in physical activities, we also see Jason idly propped against a tree talking to Morgan and Mariah sitting cross-legged on the ground sorting rocks.

Clearly time needs to be structured into each day for organized physical activity to ensure that every child maximizes opportunities for developing and maintaining physical fitness. Health-related physical fitness denotes areas of fitness that affect a child's health, energy, and ability to engage in daily activities. Contemporary physical education targets health-related fitness. Certainly a primary goal is for children to become competent movers by developing motor skills. Five components comprise health-related fitness: muscular strength and endurance, flexibility, cardiovascular endurance, and body composition. The combination of muscular strength and endurance and flexibility determine musculoskeletal fitness. Strides to establish musculoskeletal fitness must be maintained to ensure the overall health and well-being of each child.

A debate continues as to whether developing competency with specific skills or concentrating on overall physical fitness development is most critical. Both approaches endeavor to provide physical education programs that will help individuals lead physically active lifestyles. Some argue that a focus on fitness will prompt fitness activity outside of school, while others believe that as individuals develop motor skills, they are more likely to be active participants, thereby increasing fitness levels. Stodden, Lagendorfer, and Roberton (2009) examined the relationship between competence in three fundamental motor skills (throwing, kicking, and jumping) and six measures of health-related physical fitness in young adults and found the that performance in only three motor skills can account for 79 percent of the changes in physical fitness, making the argument that motor skill competence is highly related to physical fitness. Thus, a focus on motor skill competency can indirectly impact physical fitness. Regardless of philosophical stance, however, ongoing devotion to physical activity is essential in maximizing opportunities for children to develop good health.

MUSCULAR STRENGTH AND ENDURANCE

Muscular strength is the ability of the body to exert force against resistance, measured by determining the greatest amount one can lift, push, or pull in one all-out effort. Muscular endurance, however, is one's ability to exert force against resistance repeatedly. Because most skills require endurance rather than strength, developing muscular endurance is desirable. When a child does pull-ups, strikes a ball with a racquet, or performs an educational gymnastics routine, muscular endurance is required. Muscular strength and endurance are similar in that a child who is strong is capable of exerting a muscular effort for a more extended time period than a weaker child.

Benefits

In order to aid students in working to improve their physical performance, efforts toward increasing strength and endurance are vital. Most of the skills included in a physical education curriculum require a degree of strength. Activities such as serving a ball underhanded, swinging a hockey stick, and performing a cartwheel rely upon upper body strength, whereas bicycle riding, jogging, and kicking demand lower body strength. Even slightly increased strength will result in less fatigue and increased pleasure during such activities. Elementary students, however, should comprehend that working until their muscles feel tired is beneficial. Some physical education teachers say, "Tired today means stronger tomorrow."

Health-related benefits of increased muscular strength and endurance include an increased metabolic rate, insurance against premature loss of bone density and mass, prevention of potential back problems, and reduced cardiovascular disease risks. Such awareness may seem far removed from difficulties experienced by an elementary child, but developing a health-related fitness routine and sustaining such activities may have far-reaching results. In addition, an improved sense of well-being can result as a child sets strength and endurance fitness goals and achieves them.

Training Principles

Until puberty girls and boys have nearly equal potential for developing their strength and endurance, but after puberty males enjoy a greater increase in muscle sizes due to testosterone, whereas girls' fat increases. Factors that may influence a child's efforts toward developing strength and endurance, however, include the child's confidence and enthusiasm regarding physical activity. Achieving strength and endurance goals requires persistence. Four important principles govern training for physical strength and endurance: individuality, specificity, overload, and reversibility.

Individuality.
Individuality addresses the same kind of desirable tailoring a teacher should consider for any content area. In developing fitness within the curriculum a teacher must reflect on the varied abilities and level of fitness of each student. Some younger children can recognize improvement in strength and endurance quickly, whereas others require a longer duration of training before achieving goals. Much of this is due to their genetic composites, their previous efforts toward muscular strength and endurance, and their enthusiasm.

Specificity.
Certainly overall strength and endurance is beneficial. However, the teacher must consider the significance of developing particular muscle areas. For instance, to increase students'

Backbends are an example of static stretching.

leg strength, repeated leg use, such as rope jumping, jogging, and bicycling, is desirable. This continued focus on a particular muscle area should result in increased muscular strength and endurance of leg muscles.

Overload.

The overload principle requires increasing the level of difficulty of a fitness activity. If the goal is for students to increase chest muscle and arm strength and endurance, for example, increasing the number of push-ups daily can play a key factor in working toward overload. Through prolonged use the size of the chest muscles increase. Once a level of proficiency is demonstrated, however, the activity must be sustained in order to retain the desired status of chest muscle strength and endurance.

Reversibility.

Unfortunately the benefits of muscular strength and endurance enjoyed after a persistent program of fitness exercise can be reversed, resulting in a shrinking of the very muscles one has worked to develop. The expression "use it or lose it" is commonly used to describe reversibility. Improvements in strength and endurance levels can decline quickly and may even be lost in as early as six weeks. Therefore, a commitment to develop this fitness component carries with it a demand to sustain ongoing activities.

Application of the principles of training is essential in planning fitness activities for students. Activities targeting specific skills can certainly contribute to increased muscular strength and endurance. However, the principles of training should undergird the goals a teacher sets for her or his students. By combining muscular strength and endurance with flexibility development, students can maximize opportunities for fitness.

FLEXIBILITY

Another form of musculoskeletal fitness is demonstrated through range of motion of a joint. One can have a wide range of motion in one joint but not in another. One child may be able to bend at the waist and touch the floor without bending her knees yet be incapable of sitting cross-legged with knees parallel to the floor. Historically flexibility has been the most neglected of the five components of health-related fitness. However, many individuals have turned to activities aimed at increasing flexibility as a means of contributing to overall fitness.

Activities that increase flexibility can help to overcome factors that cannot be controlled, such as age, gender, and genetics. Children grow increasingly flexible until puberty, when their flexibility declines. Females are typically more flexible than males in the early years. Although children usually burst out onto the playground without any kind of warm-up, it would be advantageous for them to do some light activity, such as walking or jogging and stretching, before plunging into a higher intensity physical activity. As students grow older and lose flexibility, established patterns of stretching before and after an activity are beneficial. Flexibility differs from other fitness components in that no equipment is necessary and stretching can take place almost anywhere, including the classroom.

Benefits

In addition to strength and endurance, flexibility definitely gives students an advantage.

Enhanced Performance.

Though some of the students in a class may regularly participate in gymnastics, karate, or ballet and have increased flexibility, all children should develop their flexibility. In order to swim, throw a ball, perform a cartwheel, or complete a forward roll a child needs flexibility of specific joints. By developing flexibility a child's prowess as well as her or his enjoyment can be enhanced.

Pain Prevention.

Though the primary benefit of stretching is to increase flexibility, stretching *before* an activity is found to cause injuries. For this reason children should develop a routine of stretching *after* strenuous activity, when the body is warmed up. Although the threat of injury through stretching before vigorous activity is rare for children, developing an awareness of the importance of stretching after the body completes strenuous activity may be essential for lifelong safety. Stretching exercises may also reduce back pain and muscle cramping. For example, by stretching the hip and pelvic joints gnawing menstruation pains can be alleviated. Increased flexibility also results in improved posture.

Types of Stretching

To capitalize on the flexibility of elementary children, goals should be established to increase the distance they can stretch, the duration they can hold the stretch, and the number of stretches they perform. Two common ways to increase flexibility through stretching are static and dynamic stretching.

Static Stretching

For children the most recommended kind of stretching is static, whereby the stretch is pressed slowly to the limit and is held in position for 20 to 30 seconds and then repeated. When performing the butterfly stretch, for instance, the child sits on the floor and presses the soles of both feet together close to the body. Arms rest on the thighs and gradually press the thighs toward the floor. The child should be able to feel the pressure of the stretch upon the inner thigh without feeling pain.

In the butterfly stretch children wiggle their legs to simulate moving butterfly wings.

Dynamic Stretching

Bouncing or bobbing as a form of stretching can be harmful; thus experts agree that this kind of stretching is not advisable. Though alternating toe touches and bouncing stretches were once a common fitness activity, such movements may stretch the muscle too far and result in injury. The best time to work on stretching of any kind is after the children have been engaged in activities and are warmed up. Dynamic stretching uses speed, momentum, and muscular involvement. Children may sweep their arms in large circle stretches, kick imaginary balls into the air, and lunge ahead taking giant steps, affording opportunities to stretch in more fluid motions without a stop at the end.

MOVEMENT EXPERIENCES

Mighty Muscles and Fabulous Flexibility

Objective

To develop muscular strength and endurance and flexibility

To recognize valuable lifetime activities for enhancing muscular strength and endurance and flexibility

To enjoy working toward improved fitness

Targeted Age Group

K-5

Equipment

Disc player

Lively music

Pictures of children performing each activity

Jump ropes

Step aerobic bench

Exercise mats

Management

1. Establish six areas for a variety of stations.
2. Post pictures at each station to indicate the expected activities.
3. Divide the class into six small groups and assign each to a starting station.

Pre-Activity

Students review the importance of developing muscular strength and endurance and flexibility.

Activity in the Gymnasium or Outside or in the Classroom

Students begin the assigned activity when the music starts to play. Students can perform any or all of the suggested possibilities for each station. After 3–4 minutes the music stops, indicating that groups should rotate to the next station. This is repeated until all participants have progressed through all the stations. If time remains they can begin again.

Station I *Push-ups to develop upper body strength and endurance. (Note: Students should choose from the following four options the form of push-up appropriate for their fitness level.)*

1. Assume push-up position on knees or toes and hold the position until she or he chooses to relax. Repeat the action.
2. Perform push-ups from the knees until a rest is needed. After a short pause repeat the action. (Be careful not to mistakenly refer to these as "girl push-ups," as they are a valid form of push-up for both genders.)
3. Perform push-ups from the toes.
4. Push up from either the knees or the toes, and when moving into the elevated position thrust upward, clap hands, and then return to lower the body again.

Station II *Partner stretches to develop flexibility and establish collaboration.*

1. Two children stand side by side, each with hands clasped above the head. In sync they lean first to the right and count slowly to 10 and then to the left and repeat.
2. Students stand side by side, each bending the knee to lift the right leg behind the body and holding her or his shin near the ankle with the right hand. After a slow count to

10 each child returns the right foot to the ground and repeats the process with the left foot.

3. Standing side by side children rest the outside of one foot against the outside of a partner's foot, then join their hands between them and lean outward, counting slowly to 10. Repeat on the other side.

4. Children sit on ground with legs extended into a V and soles of feet touching the soles of a partner's feet. First each child leans to reach toward the right foot with hands traveling along the shin to the slow count of 10. Then each switches the stretch to the left for the slow count of 10.

Station III   *Line-straddling for lower-body and cardiovascular endurance.*

1. Children begin with one foot on either side of an imaginary line on the floor/ground. Next they jump on both feet and cross feet in midair. They land with feet crossed and then bounce back to the starting position. Repeat the action for 20–30 seconds. Rest briefly and then repeat the action.

2. Students jump on one foot back and forth across the imaginary line for 20–30 seconds and then repeat the action on the other foot.

3. Children begin with one foot on either side of the imaginary line and spin 180 degrees and then spin back. Repeat the action for 20–30 seconds.

4. Students begin with both feet on one side of the line and hop back and forth across the line with both feet.

Station IV   *Step-it-up is an activity to develop lower-body muscular and cardiovascular endurance.*

Students position themselves facing the bleachers or step aerobic benches. If the bleachers are too high, it would be better to use a shorter step to avoid knee strain. They begin by stepping up with one foot and then placing the other beside it. Then they lower one foot and follow with the other (i.e., step-up [right], step-beside [left], step-down [left], step beside [right]).

Station V   *Stretch-it-out is an activity that targets flexibility.*

1. Children sit on the floor/ground with knees extended outward and the soles of their feet pressed together. Hands press down simultaneously on both knees and hold in stretched position for 20–30 seconds.

2. Student sits on the floor/ground with right leg extended and the left leg crossed over the right with the left foot planted on the floor/ground. She or he twists upright upper trunk to the left over the bent knee and rests both hands on the floor/ground. Hold for 20–30 seconds and then reverse the position with left leg extended.

3. Children stand with one foot crossed over the other and planted. Then they bend at the waist and stretch down toward the toes and hold for 20–30 seconds. Then rise, relax briefly, and repeat the action.

4. Student sits on the floor/ground, extends the right leg, and presses the sole of the left foot against the right knee with the left knee pressed to the floor/ground. Then she or he bends from the waist with arms fully extended toward the right toe. Hold in position for 20–30 seconds and then relax briefly before repeating the action.

Station VI   *Awesome abs is an activity aimed at strengthening abdominal muscles.*

1. Children lie on the floor/mat with legs bent at the knees and feet flat on the floor/mat. They slowly raise their upper bodies, sliding their hands up their thighs to the knees, and hold 20–30 seconds.

2. Students lie on the floor/mat with legs bent at the knees and heels planted. They cross arms across their chests and slowly raise themselves upright, then return slowly to an outstretched position on the floor/mat.

Modifications

- Students spend only two minutes at each station so they can move through the rotation quickly two times.
- Variations may include jumping rope, jumping on a pogo stick, leg lifts, or crab walk. Older students may create their own static stretches.
- One student can select one of the above activities while a partner copycats the action. Each time the music stops, the other child becomes the leader.

Assessment

Are the students successfully completing the activity as directed?

Are the students making brisk transitions from one activity to the next?

Is their action sustained enough to develop muscular strength and endurance or flexibility?

Are the students enthusiastic about participating?

Pick a Card, Any Card

Objective

To develop muscular strength and endurance and flexibility

To recognize valuable lifetime activities for enhancing muscular strength and endurance and flexibility

To enjoy playing a game while working toward improved fitness

Targeted Age Group

3–5

Equipment

Deck of cards

Section of newspaper for each student

Carpet square for each student

Jump ropes

Management

1. Direct students to spread out in a scattered formation.
2. Ask for volunteers to lead each of the activities. Each volunteer is responsible to demonstrate the activity when the number corresponding to that activity is drawn.

Pre-Activity

Students review the benefits of developing muscular strength and endurance and flexibility. *Pick a card, any card* is intended to demonstrate for the children a variety of activities to produce these benefits.

Activity

Students are in a scattered formation. One at a time their names are called by the teacher to step to the deck of cards, pick a card, and lead the others through the activity. If the card drawn is a diamond or a heart the activity targets muscular endurance (diamonds are upper body; hearts are lower body). If the card drawn is a spade or a club, the activity targets flexibility (clubs are upper body; spades are lower body).

1. *Inch Worm (upper-body muscular endurance)*

   Children bend at the hips with hands outstretched until they are resting upon the floor. Hands reach ahead; feet follow up the stretch. The action is repeated as students make their way across the activity area.

2. *Push-ups (upper body muscular endurance) (Note: Students should choose from the following four options the form of push-up appropriate for their fitness level.)*
   - Student assumes push-up position on knees (using a carpet square) or toes and holds the position until she or he chooses to relax. Then repeat the action.
   - Student places a carpet square on the area beneath her/his knees and performs push-ups from the knees until a rest is needed. After a short pause the action is repeated. (Be careful not to mistakenly refer to these as "girl push-ups," as they are a valid form of push-up for both genders.)
   - Student performs push-ups from the toes.
   - Students push up from either the knees (using carpet squares for protection) or the toes, and when moving into the elevated position thrust upward, clap hands, and then return to lower the body again.

3. *Crab Walk (upper- or lower-body muscular endurance)*

   Children sit and press hands against the floor behind them, lifting their torsos. Using their heels and the palms of their hands, they travel across the activity area.

4. *Newsflash (upper or lower muscular endurance)*

   Children bend from the hips and rest hands on a section of newspaper before them. Then they slide the paper ahead with their hands and follow with their feet.

5. *Rope Jump (lower-body muscular endurance)*

   Each child takes a jump rope by the handles and flips it forward or backward over her/his head, using any variety of stepping that s/he chooses.

6. *Frog Jump (lower-body muscular endurance)*

   Students crouch on their haunches like frogs and then spring forward repeatedly.

7. *Mountain Climber (lower-body muscular endurance)*

   Facing the floor children prop themselves up with hands together and arms extended. Then they bend first one knee and then the other, springing off alternating feet while hands remain stationary.

8. *Monkey Reach (upper-body flexibility)*

   Children reach up like monkeys and jump to grab a banana out of a tree, maximizing the reach by dropping one shoulder to elevate the other.

9. *Side Stretch (upper-body flexibility)*

   Leaning to one side each child stretches one arm straight up, while the other slides down the other side of the body. Alternate sides.

10. *Butterfly Stretch (lower-body flexibility)*

    Each child sits on the floor and presses the soles of both feet together close to the body. Arms rest on the thighs and gradually press the thighs toward the floor.

11. *Toe Touch (lower-body flexibility)*

    Children cross one foot over the other and bend from their hips toward their toes. Alternate foot crosses.

12. *Line Straddle (lower-body muscular endurance)*

    Children begin with one foot on either side of an imaginary line on the floor/ground. Next they jump on both feet and cross feet in midair. They land with feet crossed and then bounce back to the starting position. Repeat the action for 20–30 seconds. Rest briefly and then repeat the action.

Modifications

- Instructions can be more complex for upper-level students, using odd and even numbers for specific activities or identifying specific activities for face cards.
- Any variety of activities to develop muscular strength and endurance and/or flexibility may be substituted.

Assessment

Are the students successfully completing the activity as directed?

Are the students moving quickly to turn over a card and choose an activity?

Is their action sustained enough to develop muscular strength and endurance or flexibility?

Are the students enthusiastic about participating?

"The Elephant's Child"

Objectives

To use cross-disciplinary activities to enhance learning

To develop a positive attitude toward physical fitness

To build muscular strength and endurance and flexibility

To increase awareness of the kinds of activity appropriate for developing strength and endurance on their own

Targeted Age Group

K-3

Equipment

CD player

CD of Simon and Garfunkel's Bookends, featuring "At the Zoo"

Typed lyrics of "At the Zoo" (Found at http://www.medialab.chalmers.se/guitar/at.the.zoo.lyr.html)

Management

Direct students to scatter around a large activity area.

Pre-Activity

Students review the benefits of muscular strength and endurance and flexibility. "At the Zoo" is an activity intended to increase muscular strength and endurance and flexibility.

Activity

1. During language arts students read the lyrics, listen to the song, and discuss Paul Simon's "At the Zoo" as a poetry selection. Inform students that they will be using this song as they work to develop muscular strength and endurance and flexibility.

2. Students may also enjoy reading Kipling's "The Elephant's Child" or any number of stories, plays, and poems about animals.

3. As the music is played the teacher calls out the name of an animal (e.g., elephant) and demonstrates or has a student demonstrate the physical animal activity of one of the following:

Zebra Kicks (flexibility)   Zebras all run three steps and then jump up, fling their arms down and back, and arch their backs. Repeat until a new animal is called.

Wart Hog Waggle (upper- and lower-body muscular strength and endurance)   Wart hogs rest hands on the floor before them. Creatures lean forward and poke their buttocks into the air as feet and hands move them forward

Elephant March (lower body muscular strength and endurance)   Using one arm to represent their trunks, elephants bend forward allowing trunk to drop nearly to the ground. Trunks swing from side to side as elephants move around the activity area.

Giraffe Stretch (flexibility)   Giraffes reach high over their heads, interlocking thumbs, stretching to finger some tasty leaves.

Wildebeest Walk (upper- and lower-body muscular strength and endurance)   Wildebeests move as quickly as they can, bending at the waist and resting on hands and feet.

Monkey Swing (flexibility)   Monkeys reach up and grab a vine, keeping arm tautly stretched. They bend their knees and swing to the next tree, then use the opposite arm to grab the next vine and swing.

Seal Waddle (upper-body muscular strength and endurance)   Seals lie with hands resting on the ground, pressing the upper body up, arching the back, and stretching the neck. Arms drag legs around the activity area.

Penguin Strut (lower-body muscular strength and endurance)   Penguins hold bodies rigidly upright with arms rigidly at the sides, wrists bent tightly upward, and fingers extended. Back and head are arched as they take tiny repeated tight steps.

Kangaroo Jump (lower-body muscular strength and endurance)   Kangaroos bend elbows to 45 degrees and drop paws. Knees are bent enough to add momentum as they jump around the activity area.

Ostrich Stretch (flexibility)   Ostriches drop at the waist and lower their heads as far as they can to hide their faces from view.

Polar Bear Fishing (flexibility)   Bears stand at the imaginary water's edge and drop at the waist. One arm is raised above the shoulder and then a huge paw sweeps down through the air and into water after a fish. Alternate arms.

Modifications

* Farm animals or sea life can be substituted.
* Students can sing along for pleasure and other animal songs can be alternated.
* This could be combined with a unit on Africa.
* A trip to the zoo would be an added delight.

Assessment

Are the students successfully completing the activity as directed?

Are the students performing the activities with intensity?

Is their action sustained enough to provide muscular strength and endurance and flexibility benefits?

Are the students enthusiastic about participating?

Simon Says, "Let's Go Tubin'"

Objectives

To personalize strength and endurance building by using creative movement against resistance

To isolate muscle groups for development

To promote good listening skills

Targeted Age Group

Grades K-2

Equipment

A bicycle tube or exercise band for each student

Management

1. Ask each child to secure a bicycle tube or exercise band.
2. Direct students to find an area broad enough for them to stretch out with the bands.

Pre-Activity

Students discuss the benefits of working against resistance to build strength and endurance.

Students should be reminded to keep movements slow and deliberate with a slight pause at the outstretched position before returning to the starting point.

Activity

1. Teacher calls out "Simon Says" activities such as the following:

   Lower both knees onto the band and repeatedly
   - stretch as high as you can reach over your head
   - bend forward stretching the band in front of you
   - arch backward
   - lean to the right/left
   - start with the band at your waist and curl arms up to your shoulders and back
   - hold the band waist high and rotate from side to side
   - bend at the waist and press the band out to your sides

   Stand and repeat the process with both feet on the band

   Sit on the band and repeat again

   Sit on the floor and stretch the band across the bottom of your feet, hold the band in your hands and repeatedly

   - keep hands at the waist while you stretch shoulders back to the floor and then rise again
   - hold band steady at your waist and alternate bending knees and pulling feet up toward your buttocks
   - pull right arm up and across the body until both arms are outstretched to the left; return the right arm to the floor on the right and lift the left up and over to meet the right

2. After repeating several of these activities, the teacher can name a student to lead the activity.

Modifications

Students can
- count as they do ten of each movement
- count by fives
- recite a poem
- move to a beat established by the teacher
- stretch into shapes defined by the teacher (animals, letters, fruits, numbers, geometric shapes)

Assessment

Are the students successfully completing the activity as directed?

Are students able to keep their balance while performing the activity?

Are students shifting gradually with a pause before returning to the initial position?

References

Stodden, D., Langendorfer, S. & Roberton, M. A. (2009). The association between motor skill competence and physical fitness in young adults. *Research Quarterly for Exercise and Sport, 80*(2), 223.

Chapter **Twenty Two**

Health-Related Fitness: Cardiovascular Endurance

Each morning buses, cars, minivans, and SUVs stream by school entrances dropping off children laden with backpacks and lunch boxes. The vision of students walking or riding bicycles to school with neighborhood friends is a sight of the past. Parents arrange work schedules and organize car pools to ensure that their children will arrive safely at school. At the end of the school day the procedure is reversed, assuring that youths clamber back into vehicles and are carried safely home without incident.

Unfortunately the activities following the school day may also not involve physical activity. Unless children are fortunate enough to be enrolled in gymnastics, dance, or club sports, they are often left to their own devices to find entertainment. Many young people immerse themselves in television programs or video games, while others flock to communicate online. The effect is the same. Such sedentary endeavors have led to increased incidents of obesity. Today 40 percent of children between the ages of 5 and 8 are obese and have elevated blood pressure and cholesterol, and only one of three between the ages of 6 and 17 meet minimal standards for cardiovascular fitness, flexibility, and abdominal and upper-body strength (Kalish, 1996). In recent decades children have become so physically inactive that they expend approximately 600 calories a day less than did children 50 years ago (Boreham, C., & Riddoch, C. 2001).

Rope jumping is an excellent activity for academic integration.

In order to ensure that this sedentary lifestyle is interrupted, it is vital for young people to see the pleasure they can derive from fitness activities. The National Association for Sport and Physical Education (NASPE) Outcomes Project identifies a physically active person as one who (1) is active, (2) values physical activity, and (3) knows the health benefits of physical activity. Certainly it is clear that an active lifestyle is a healthy one. Thus, introducing young people to fitness activities is a desirable goal. However, it is essential for children to associate a positive social experience with the activity in order to develop a positive attitude toward such movement. Therefore, by encouraging children to join in the merriment of jumping rope, running, climbing, or cartwheeling, we offer the opportunity to develop habits that can aerobically benefit participants throughout their lives.

Children ages 10 to 16 in the United States spend three-quarters of their waking hours inactive and only roughly 13 minutes every day in vigorous physical activity (Strauss, Rodzilsky, Burack, & Colin, 2001). Because today's young people tend to be rooted in a sedentary lifestyle, it is paramount that they be afforded physical education at school. Unfortunately there is generally not enough time allotted during the school day for students to meet even the minimal daily physical activity guidelines established by the Council on Physical Education for Children (1998). Clearly physical education class is the primary physical activity for most students (Sallis & McKenzie, 1991); therefore, it is imperative that no activity time be wasted on lengthy explanations by the teacher or on waiting for a turn to participate. The teacher responsible in part for children's physical education should construct plans that devote the maximum amount of time to movement.

HEALTH-RELATED PHYSICAL FITNESS

Fitness activities ward off diseases typical to those who maintain a sedentary lifestyle. Body composition, flexibility, strength and endurance, and cardiovascular fitness are considered the primary components determining health-related fitness. When one is fit, she or he can sustain strenuous activities long enough to benefit the cardiovascular system.

Body Composition

The ratio of body fat to leanness determines one's body composition. By measuring the thickness of folds of skin with its underlying layer of fat, the total percent of body fat can be determined. The more dense one's body fat, the more difficult the challenge to attain fitness. However, frequent, sustained activity leads to a more balanced body composition.

Flexibility

Flexibility is the ability to move joints freely through a wide range of motion. Children are extremely limber but lose flexibility if they are not spurred to maintain such motions as they mature. Flexibility is at least in part genetically determined; however, stretching can aid in developing elasticity in muscles, tendons, and ligaments and thereby contribute to fitness. Serving a volleyball, passing a soccer ball, and completing a forward roll are activities that develop flexibility. Simply touching one's toes reflects the flexibility of one's hips and lower back, and repetition of this activity can increase that suppleness.

Strength and Endurance

Strength is the muscles' ability to exert force over a short time period; endurance is the ability to sustain that exertion. Most sport activities require endurance, but fitness activities that repeat a taxing activity without quickly resulting in fatigue are also desirable. For example, completing a succession of cartwheels can result in increased muscular endurance as can repeated throwing and kicking. Typically elementary physical educators do not work on developing children's muscular strength but rather on their endurance. An added benefit results because generally muscular endurance activities also strengthen cardiovascular endurance.

Cardiovascular/Endurance Fitness

The most significant element of health-related fitness is one's cardiovascular fitness, since a healthy heart is the key to a healthy existence. The heart is a pear-shaped muscle requiring regular exercise as any other muscle in order to increase and maintain strength. A large powerful heart can pump more blood more efficiently with each stroke. Endurance determines the sustained ability of the respiratory system, the heart, and the supporting blood vessels to efficiently process oxygen over an extended time period. Thus, fitness activities that benefit the cardiovascular system are generally aerobic. If an activity that dramatically increases one's heart rate is sustained for more than three minutes, the endurance of the cardiovascular system is improved. For example, if a child jumps rope for a period of five minutes without interruption, she or he has accelerated the heart rate, taxed the respiratory system, and strengthened endurance.

Monitoring children's heart rates affords clearer insights regarding the degree of stress an activity exerts on the heart. Since each person's body reacts differently to varying degrees of stress, using heart rate monitors can offer increased awareness and even serve as a basis for assessment of a child's fitness accomplishments. Establishing targets after measuring resting and maximum rates aids in individualizing goals. By this means improvement rather than performance can be measured.

PRINCIPLES OF PHYSICAL FITNESS

The acronym FITT serves as an easy framework for developing a fitness plan. *F* stands for frequency, denoting the number of times per week the activity will be scheduled. Fitness activity is recommended three times per week for minimal fitness, despite the failure of many school systems to build that amount of time into the curriculum. Therefore, a classroom teacher's devotion to aid her or his students in striving toward fitness goals can reap evident benefits. *I* represents intensity and clarifies the amount of exertion necessary to measurably recognize gains in health-related fitness. For cardiovascular improvement sustained elevation of the heart rate is essential, whereas muscle development results from increasing the resistance against movement. Intensity in flexibility occurs when muscles are stretched to new lengths. The next element in the FITT process is type, designating the kind of exercise chosen to achieve a desired goal. To improve the cardiovascular system's functions cardio respiratory activity is most effective. This includes running, cycling, swimming, and other exercise that is continuous and uses large muscle groups. Resistance training, on the other hand, improves muscular strength and endurance, focusing instead on the neuromuscular system. Such activities for young children include weight transfer from feet to hands or climbing a rock wall. The final element, *T,* indicates the time or duration of the activity. In order to enjoy cardiovascular benefits the duration should be a minimum of 15 minutes. Time and intensity are interrelated in that if intensity is increased, duration can be decreased. For example, a child may skip for 5 minutes at a fast speed or for 8 minutes at a leisurely pace and the cardiovascular benefits are parallel. Whereas you may enjoy a strenuous 20-minute workout on the Stairclimber at the YMCA, your students tend to shy

Physically active teachers are positive role models.

away from such high-intensity activity in favor of a 30-minute game of tag, and either offers similar benefits. In designing lesson plans for fitness activities you will want to keep the FITT format in mind.

ESTABLISHING A POSITIVE FITNESS LEARNING ENVIRONMENT

In order to ensure that children will join in fitness activities by choice, it is essential to provide opportunities for enjoyed success. When a positive attitude toward fitness activities is nurtured, children are more likely to not only engage in the activity at school but also possibly outside of school as well. If students develop a positive self-esteem regarding their roles in fitness activities, they may encourage others to join in, thereby stimulating increased and ongoing devotion to fitness.

Model Fitness

As in all forms of instruction, it is important that you practice what you teach. In order for students to see the importance of fitness in your own life, it is vital for you to share with them the fitness activities you enjoy. For instance, if you make it a habit to walk for 30 minutes each evening, seize the opportunity to share with your students a constellation you observed on your walk. If you play racquetball three mornings a week before school, mention that activity to your class. At the lunchroom at midday, let them see you enjoying a healthy lunch. Also, as they work at fitness activities at school, join in on occasion so they may see you as a vibrant fitness enthusiast. Take care, however, not to be so engaged in the activity that you are unable to continue in your role as orchestrator. Through such endeavors your students will be able to recognize the value of fitness throughout one's lifetime.

Encourage Social Interaction

If students are to enjoy fitness activities, they need to recognize that such participation is clearly a social event. Solomon (1997) maintains that a primary human drive is to socialize through play. Structure activities so that students are able to maximize contacts with the other participants. For example, students can do a partner run and on a signal from you quickly change partners to run again. Small groups can be established as teams to work toward improving their own scores rather than competing with others in completing a fitness obstacle course. Don't expect silent participation, for one of the goals is for the students to recognize the activity as a desirable social outlet.

Most students enjoy the opportunity to be active during the school day.

Offer Choices for Fitness Activities

Individualizing activities to suit the abilities and attitudes of a group of children is the best means of encouraging a positive perspective on fitness activities. No longer is the military style of calisthenics acceptable, whereby rigid rows of young people complete jumping jacks in unison at the command of the teacher. Instead of such drills children should be provided a variety of activity choices. Options should include both competitive and non-competitive activities. Though many children perform at superior levels when asked to compete, others shut down and actually lose motivation to participate. If children have choices regarding the type and level of difficulty of the activity, they establish ownership of their own fitness. Inviting them to determine how much time is spent on each activity is also vital. Thus, if you have allotted 30 minutes for fitness development and have afforded a variety of options they may pursue, they should determine the activities. Setting specific time measures is better than expecting all students to complete the same number of repetitions. If you wish students to improve abdominal strength, for instance, rather than defining 25 sit-ups, instead have them do a variety of self-selected abdominal exercises for three minutes. This investment in determining their fitness development may be integral to their opting to continue such activities outside of school.

Provide Music to Accompany Activity

Playing music when students are moving can serve as a powerful motivator. A variety of music types may be effective in intensifying or slowing movement. To enhance the social aspect further students may bring in music they enjoy that is appropriate to specific activities. One way of integrating music is to tape record a combination of classical, country, and rock 'n' roll music. When the children hear classical music, their mission is to walk; when the music shifts to country, they jog; when rock and roll, they run. The duration of each type also may differ, as one song may be quickly cut short to shift to another.

Use Pedometers

Pedometers are devices that count steps. They are easily worn on the child's hip to document the distance traveled or steps taken. Using pedometers and specific step-count goals is more effective than walking interventions that use time-based goals, because the individual is motivated by the opportunity to see her or his progress and track accomplishments. Hultquist et al. (2005) found that sedentary women who were given pedometers and

Measuring distance with the use of pedometers is quite motivating for students.

who were instructed to walk 10,000 steps a day walked almost 2,000 steps per day more than women who were instructed to go for a brisk 30-minute walk each day.

An analysis of studies conducted using pedometers suggests that 8-10-year-old children accumulate 12,000-16,000 steps per day (Tudor-Locke &Myers, 2001), and that 10,000 steps per day is not high enough for children (Tudor-Locke, 2002).Because the cost and needed storage space are minimal, pedometers have gained popularity with teachers pressing for student engagement with building personal cardiovascular endurance.

The benefits of using pedometers is the accurate tabulation of step counts. It takes a child approximately 3,000 steps to go one mile. If students use mathematics skills to add the number of steps taken by each individual and multiply times the number of miles they wish to travel, they can plot journeys to various points they are studying in social studies. Likewise they can step to music characteristic of the area where they are traveling, thus enhancing the experience. During language arts studies they can explore literature of the region. Such integration of learning encounters offers students interrelated practical applications and heightens enthusiasm for learning.

Establish a Practice of Goal Setting

When students establish achievable goals for their own fitness, they become stakeholders in their personal wellness. Taking a few moments to compose a brief list of individual goals makes the quest more concrete. Maintaining a daily journal to chronicle the activities enjoyed in working toward those goals also aids in productivity. As students review the measures they have taken toward achieving their goals, they are able to reflect on their accomplishments and establish additional challenges. Ongoing feedback from the teacher regarding the students' achievements can fuel enthusiasm and improve self-concept. All students, not just those with the highest achievement records, need such affirmation.

Exercise as Reward

Rewards for a lifetime of fitness are recognized and appreciated only by older adults. However, positive feedback from the teacher can serve as a powerful motivator to children. If your intention is for students to adopt and maintain an informal fitness plan, reinforcement toward that end is appropriate. Activities that lead to elimination from participation lead to a lowered self-esteem and indeed reduced activity. Clearly, those most in need of the activity are often the first eliminated.

Exercise as punishment also defeats your purpose, as it carries a negative connotation. Just as an English teacher would protest the assigning of an essay as punishment, so does a physical educator recognize the detrimental effects of assigning exercise as punishment. The reverse is also true; it is not acceptable to punish a student who has misbehaved by denying her or him participation in a period devoted to physical activity. By maintaining a positive class climate the teacher encourages enthusiastic participation. Rewards in such an environment are profuse. All students deserve a victory lap at the close of the activities.

Promote Lifetime Fitness

One goal of every teacher eager to aid students in achieving fitness is for the students to recognize the importance of maintaining an active fitness program throughout their lives. If the time spent on fitness at school is pleasurable, the children recognize exercise as a positive choice when determining outside-of-school activities. Heightening their health awareness can be achieved by emphasizing the role physical activity plays in strengthening the cardiovascular system. Perhaps students will be able to spark physical activities among family members if the teacher requests a one-week log of physical activities enjoyed by the students' families. At the very least this will afford the teacher insights into the children's motivation or lack of motivation to join in physical activities. Awarding certificates or other forms of recognition for physical activities in which the children are engaged outside of school may also serve as a valuable motivator.

Consider Climate Conditions

Whether the time you set aside for physical activity is spent indoors or outside, temperature is a vital component. If the heat is high enough to provoke body temperature to elevate to dangerous levels, hyperthermia can result. The American College of Sports Medicine (1987) identifies symptoms to watch for as clumsiness, stumbling, profuse sweating, headache, nausea, dizziness, apathy, and any gradual impairment of consciousness. In order to prevent hyperthermia, limit the intensity and duration of fitness exercise, strive to schedule physical activities during the coolest time of the day, and be careful to assure that students drink a generous amount of water prior to and at intermittent points during the activities.

Cooldown offers children a time to relax before heading to the next challenge in the school day.

ACTIVITIES TO PROMOTE CARDIOVASCULAR ENDURANCE

As the classroom teacher in charge of planning and conducting at least a portion of your students' physical education, it is your prerogative to determine when fitness will be addressed. Either the students will allot a small portion of each physical activity period to health-related fitness, or they will spend a more focused and sustained period centering only on activities devoted to developing cardiovascular endurance.

Setting the Stage for the Activity

It is not imperative that young children perform warm-up activities. In fact, valuable activity time can be wasted in pointless repetition of unnecessary actions. Instead, children can begin the activity at a less intense pace than they will be expected to achieve as the lesson progresses. If students are typically keyed up at the outset of the activity period, to prepare them to focus on the objectives for the lesson, ask them to spend a few moments in vigorous activity before presenting the plan for the day.

Closing the Activity Period

In order to ensure that the students do not return to the classroom charged with unbridled energy, devote a brief period for them to cool down. This is a good time for them to exercise at a slower pace and also to review what has been covered. You may want to play soft music and direct the students to continue the activity they have been doing in slow motion while questioning them on the components of fitness they have addressed that day. To impress upon them the impact of health-related fitness activities, identify the cardiovascular benefits they have enjoyed as a result of the activity.

MOVEMENT EXPERIENCES

Rainbow Run

Objectives

To develop a positive attitude toward physical fitness

To build cardiovascular endurance

To increase awareness of the kind of activity appropriate for strengthening the cardiovascular system

Targeted Age Group
K-5

Equipment
Index cards with varied colors displayed in lines drawn with magic markers; colors can be repeated; each card should have colors arranged in an order different from other cards

Traffic cones

Multiple magic markers that match the colors on the index cards

Hula hoop

Management
1. Place a hula hoop at the starting position and scatter cones at varied locations approximately 100 yards away.
2. Set three different-colored markers next to the cone of the same color.
3. Distribute index cards bearing rainbow colors to each student.

Pre-Activity
Discuss the cardiovascular benefits to be gained by running for an extended period of time. Rainbow run is an activity intended to increase heart rate and ensure oxygen is delivered efficiently by the respiratory system.

Activity
1. Students will run to the cone that is the color of the first stripe on their cards, grab the corresponding marker, and swipe a mark next to that first color.
2. Next the children race back to step inside the hoop, and then dart to the next cone matching the second stripe on the card.
3. Students repeat the process, returning to the hula hoop after reaching each cone and marking the card, until all the colors have been marked.

Modifications
- Each cone can be marked with a square of construction paper indicating the color it represents.
- To increase the pace the activity can be competitive.
- In order to build a collaborative spirit, students can be paired.
- For an interdisciplinary approach, when students reach the cone they can work a quick mathematics problem or answer a science question related to a lesson taught earlier in the day.
- To expand the activity students may jump rope 10 times at the red cone, for instance, complete 10 sit-ups at the yellow cone, and execute other similar activities.

Assessment
Are the students successfully completing the activity as directed?

Are the students running, jogging, or fitness walking (brisk pace) during the activity?

Is their action sustained enough to provide cardiovascular benefits?

Are the students enthusiastic about participating?

Traffic Signals

Objectives
To maximize the use of locomotor skills toward developing cardiovascular endurance

To react to signals to stimulate motion

Targeted Age Group
K-2

Equipment

Three sheets (green, yellow, and red) of construction paper
Five cones

Management

1. Cones are placed in a wide circle.
2. Students are directed to remain on the outside of the cones or to scatter in a wide area.

Pre-Activity

Question students about the role running plays in increasing cardiovascular endurance. Ask students what green, yellow, and red traffic signals mean.

Activity for Gymnasium or Outside

1. Students will run or jog in a wide circle or in a scattered formation when you hold up a green piece of paper.
2. Students will then fitness walk (brisk pace) when you lift up the yellow paper.
3. When you raise the red sheet, students will walk in place.

Activity for Classroom

Students will move in place beside their desks/chairs (e.g., running in place for green, walking in place for yellow, and jumping in place for red).

Modifications

- Students can choose from a variety of locomotor movements, but the intensity should remain the same (i.e., green light = high intensity; yellow light = moderate intensity; and red light = low intensity).
- For interdisciplinary practices students can use this activity during a unit on transportation or traffic safety.
- Students can be taught to use hand signals to indicate the direction in which they are going to turn.
- Students may make the sound of a horn when coming close to another participant.
- Students can move like they are a sports car when they see a green light, a minivan when they see yellow, and an old jalopy when they see red.
- Play a tape with traffic sound effects to add to the pleasure.

Assessment

Are all students remaining in motion throughout the activity?
Are students' movements in keeping with the color-motivated motion?
If students are running in a scattered formation, is safety ensured for each participant?
Are the students enthusiastic about the activity?

Shopping Spree

Objectives

To sustain ongoing movement to contribute to cardiovascular endurance
To stimulate imaginative thinking

Targeted Age Group

3–5

Equipment

Jump ropes
Carpet squares

Index cards/Note tablet
Writing utensils

Management

1. Announce to students that today they are each winners of a shopping spree at their favorite store. Every child will have 10 minutes to gather up as many items as possible in that time.
2. Jump ropes can be extended on the ground in long rows to indicate store aisles. Be certain to place them far enough apart to ensure safety for students clamoring for similar items.
3. Make-believe automobile trunks represented by carpet squares should be situated approximately 100 yards from the aisles.
4. Next to each square should be placed an index card or notebook and a writing utensil for each student.
5. Label aisles with categories likely to appeal to the age group, such as "Toys," "Camping Equipment," "Games," "Books," "Sporting Goods," "Clothing," "Electronics," "Jewelry," or "Candy."

Pre-Activity

Review with the students the cardiovascular benefits of running.

This is your opportunity to enhance your students' enthusiasm toward the Shopping Spree activity. Remind them that they will want to rush in order to acquire as many free gifts as possible. Also, prompt students to lift their "heavy" items carefully, bending at the hips and knees and using the strong muscles in the legs and buttocks.

Activity for Gymnasium or Outside

1. Students will run from their carpet squares to the aisles that interest them.
2. After miming the securing of the item from an imaginary shelf, the student will then turn and dash back to the carpet square as quickly as she or he could conceivably move if carrying the actual item.
3. Upon reaching the "trunk," the student will place the object there.
4. Next the participant will pick up the index card and pen and draw a picture of or write the name of the item that was selected.
5. The process is repeated for 10 minutes or until each student has gathered 10 items.

Activity for Classroom

Product names will be paired on the black/white boards with the numbers of rungs up the imaginary ladder the student will need to climb in place to reach the items (e.g., if the child desires a game of "Monopoly" or "Twister," she or he will look to the board, see that games are up 25 rungs, and begin counting each rung as she or he climbs in place. Upon reaching the 25th rung, she or he will stop, pick up the card from her or his desk, and write the name of or draw the box holding the Monopoly game). The activity continues until 10 items are acquired.

Modifications

* If time and space allow, actual boxes of varied sizes labeled as products by the students may enhance enthusiasm.
* The students can do a follow-up mathematics activity to use the Internet to determine prices of the items won and to total the amount of their prizes.
* Students can develop individual spelling lists based upon the names of the products.
* Participants may be paired and told they are to buy whatever is needed to go on a trip to the place of their choice.
* Participants may be told they are gathering animals to go on an ark.
* Children may gather varied leaves to develop a leaf or bug collection.

Assessment

Did the students maximize the movement time while on the shopping spree?

Did writing the item delay movement unnecessarily?

Did students maintain a safe distance from other participants?

Did the students enjoy the activity?

Import/Export

Objectives

To improve cardiovascular endurance through movement

To heighten enthusiasm for fitness activities

Targeted Age Group

K-5

Equipment

One hula hoop for every student

Two beanbags for every student

Management

1. Scatter hula hoops over a wide area. The farther the hoops are spread, the greater the students' energy expenditure will be.
2. Place two beanbags in each hoop.

Pre-Activity

Inform students that this activity will aid in developing their fitness.

Explain that the activity represents the importation and exportation of products among continents.

Clarify for students that their objective is to accumulate as many beanbags in their hoop as they can in the allotted time.

Remind participants to move safely, avoiding collisions with others.

Activity for Gymnasium or Outside

1. Students stand inside their hoops to start.
2. On signal each student dashes to another child's hoop and retrieves a beanbag.
3. The participant then races back to her or his home hoop, touches the hoop with her or his foot, and deposits the new beanbag there. (The emphasis is on placing the beanbag inside their hoop rather than simply throwing it to the hoop from a distance.)
4. This process is repeated until the teacher signals for them to stop.
5. No student can return to a hoop from which she or he has previously taken a beanbag.
6. No participant can guard her or his hoop.
7. The student with the most beanbags wins, though of course it is the process rather than the outcome that should be emphasized.

Modifications

- Additional beanbags can be assigned to each hoop.
- The locomotor skills can be altered for subsequent rounds to include hopping, jumping, or skipping.
- This activity may introduce or follow a class discussion on the process of importation and exportation. Beanbags can represent food products, electronic equipment, tools, or other common commodities.

Assessment

Did the students engage in continuous movement to enhance fitness?

Did the students adhere to the rules?

Did all students participate enthusiastically?

Walk across America

Objectives

To maintain cardiovascular endurance while continuing this activity over the course of the semester.

To encourage students to adopt a fitness activity that can be lifelong.

To enhance participants' awareness of geography.

Targeted Age Group

K-5

Equipment

Map of America

Pedometer

Management

1. Choose a route across America beginning from your hometown to a selected location, such as Disneyworld, the White House, or the Grand Canyon.
2. Allot specific time periods each week to devote to walking/jogging, multiplying the distance times the number of walkers, and documenting that distance.

Pre-Activity

Invite students to continue the activity at home, at recess, and before or after school, and to keep a record of the distance traveled.

Notify parents about the activity and invite them to participate as a family.

Emphasize the health benefits of extending the movement beyond the limited class experience.

Display a map in the classroom with the route highlighted.

Activity for Gymnasium or Outside

1. Participants will walk or jog for a predetermined distance or time.
2. At the end of the activity the teacher or the students can record the distance covered multiplied by the number of participants.
3. Students can then trace that distance on the map and mark the distance they have covered.
4. Subsequent miles will continue the trek to the desired location.

Activity in Classroom

Students walk/run/hop in place at one minute equaling one mile to reach desired destination.

Row/swim in place across the English Channel, the Bering Straits, the Erie Canal, the Guadacanal, the Panama Canal.

Modifications

- Choose a location based upon an event or a site you are studying (e.g., a battlefield, a chocolate factory, a hot air balloon race).
- This can be the center for an interdisciplinary unit incorporating distance measurements, maintaining a log, researching varied locales/events, exploring history, engaging in art activities, or enjoying music native to the culture of sites visited.

- Substitute rollerblading, biking, swimming, ice skating, climbing, or other locomotor movement.
- Travel from one coast to the other.
- Travel across Europe or any other country.
- Travel from site to site within your own state.
- Climb the steps of the Statue of Liberty, the Sears Tower, the Empire State Building, the Eiffel Tower, or the Great Pyramid.
- Brochures from varied stopping points can be obtained from each community's local Chamber of Commerce free of charge and will enhance the experience for the students.
- If a pedometer is unavailable, the teacher can chart out a half mile or mile course using her or his vehicle.
- Use the walls of the classroom to serve as a map with pictures of sites along the way to the final destination.
- Use travel videos to bring imagined journeys to life.
- Set destinations from different time periods, such as the Crusades, the Midnight Ride of Paul Revere, the Oregon Trail, the California Gold Rush.

Assessment

- Were all students able to travel the designated distance?
- Was water available at stopping points on hot days?
- Were students enthusiastic enough about the activity to accumulate additional distances outside of class?

Ups and Downs

Objectives

- To improve cardiovascular endurance through movement
- To heighten enthusiasm for fitness activities

Targeted Age Group

K-5

Equipment

One cone for each participant

Management

1. Distribute one cone to each student.
2. Assign every participant to either the *up* or the *down* team. Strive to divide the number of students equally between teams. Because the time invested in standing up the cone may be longer than to knock one over, if there are an odd number of participants, it may be wise to assign the extra person to the *up* team.
3. Instruct participants to scatter over a wide area and place their cones beside them in either the up or the down position, dependent upon what they have been assigned.

Pre-Activity

Discuss the ways in which running benefits the heart.

Explain that Ups and Downs is intended to increase their cardiovascular endurance.

Activity for Gymnasium or Outside

1. On a signal from the teacher students whose cones are up each rush to one of the cones that is down to set it upright. Likewise, students whose cones are down dash to put down a cone that is up.

2. Participants must use their hands to change the position of the cone; they may not tip the cones over with their feet. This is simply a safety issue to prevent children from being kicked.

3. Students must progress to a new cone and may not directly return to a previous cone.

4. Children continue from cone to cone, the *up* team continuing to set cones that are down up and the *down* team continuing to put upright cones down.

5. When the teacher signals that the time is ended, the team with the most cones up or down wins.

Modifications

* If the number of cones is limited children can be paired.
* Other equipment can be easily substituted, such as milk jugs, Indian clubs, or boxes.
* If there is a decidedly larger number of either up or down cones, you will want to redistribute team numbers.

Assessment

Were all students actively engaged?

Did students follow the rules?

Were the up and down cones approximately equal at the culmination of the activity?

Were the students enthusiastic about participating?

Rope Jumping

Objectives

To improve cardiovascular endurance through vigorous movement

To develop a skill that can be done at home

To heighten enthusiasm for independent fitness activities

Targeted Age Group

3–5

Equipment

One jump rope for each student

Management

1. Have each student step on a jump rope with both feet and pull the ends up to her or his armpits. If the rope fits, the length is appropriate for that individual; if the rope is too long, the child will need a shorter rope.

2. Apportion enough space for each child so that ropes will not overlap while jumping.

Pre-Activity

Explain that jumping rope is an excellent cardiovascular activity. Football players, boxers, and tennis players use jump roping to build and maintain endurance.

Remind participants to remain in their own space while jumping.

Activity in Gymnasium or Outside

1. At the outset ask students simply to jump while you observe their varied skills. Invite them to show you what steps they can do. When you recognize students performing the particular steps, call upon them to demonstrate how they have done them in order for the rest of the class to try. Be sure to call upon both genders to teach in order to counter the misconception that rope jumping is for girls only. Watch for the following steps being performed either forward or backward:

   Both feet together

   Switching feet

     Jumping on one foot

     Shifting both feet together from side to side or forward and backward (skier)

     Crossing feet while jumping

     Crossing the rope as it passes under the body and uncrossing it as it passes over the head

     Double jump, where the rope passes under the feet twice before the feet hit the ground

     Leap step, where one leg leaps ahead to step over the rope and the body springs back onto the other leg as the rope passes over the head

2. If some children cannot follow the leads set by their classmates, they can simply continue jumping steps that are comfortable for them.

3. Students can also learn chants to accompany their jumping. Some examples follow:

     Old Man Lazy

     Drives me crazy

     Up the ladder,

     Down the ladder

     H-O-T spells *hot!* (when they say "hot" they begin jumping at top speed)

     Cinderella dressed in yellow

     Went downstairs to kiss her fellow

     How many kisses did she get?

     One, two, three, four . . .

     Peanuts, popcorn, soda pop,

     How many jumps before you stop?

     Close your eyes and you will see

     How many jumps that this will be.

     Pease porridge hot, pease porridge cold,

     Pease porridge in a pot, nine days old.

     Some like it hot, some like it cold

     Some like it in the pot, nine days old.

     I'm a little Dutch girl dressed in blue.

     Here are the things that I can do:

     Salute to the captain,

     Bow to the queen,

     Turn my back on the submarine.

     I can do a tap dance,

     I can do a split,

     I can do the holka polka

     Just like this.

4. When some degree of mastery of basic jumping principles has been established, students can choose a partner for jumping. The children may face each other and jump while one student swings the rope, or each child may hold one end as they jump hip to hip facing the same direction.

5. Long rope jumping includes two students who turn the rope, while another or a group of others jump. This builds a collaborative spirit; however, the reduced activities of the rope turners make it less desirable as a cardiovascular activity than individual or paired jumping.

6. Jump rope routines have a starting step, a middle repetitive step segment, and a closing step, all of which is repeatable. After learning a variety of steps students create routines according to the predefined criteria (i.e., four different steps). For instance, a student

may begin with the skier step, proceed to the cross-over step, shift to the leap step, and end with the double-jump step. As students' proficiency improves, they can create more complex combinations. For an additional movement, students can pair up and teach their partners their routines.

7. Using music makes jumping more enjoyable. It provides a tempo for their jumping and can be intensified if you wish them to jump faster. When students grow more adept at jumping, they can eventually shape routines according to strands of music.

Activity in Classroom

Students use imaginary jump ropes to carry out the above activities.

A strip of tape for each student is adhered beside each desk or in a central area and students jump across the strip and back as they would while jumping rope.

Modifications

* Students can search the Internet for chants.
* Students can practice multiplication or division tables as chants while jumping.
* The history of jump roping can be researched.
* Children can create their own steps and chants.

Assessment

Are the students sufficiently skillful at rope jumping to be active enough to reap cardiovascular benefits?

Are all students attaining some level of skill?

Are the students enthusiastic about rope jumping?

Double Digits

Objectives

To improve cardiovascular endurance through vigorous movement

To develop a skill that can be done at home

To heighten enthusiasm for independent fitness activities

To apply mathematics skills

Targeted Age Group

3–5

Equipment

Pedometer for each child

4 cones or polyspots

Pencils and score sheets

Step benches for each pair

Management

Place cones or polyspots in a square over a large area.

Pre-Activity

Discuss cardiovascular benefits gained by running/jumping for an extended time.

Review how to operate pedometers.

Students team with a partner.

Activity in Gymnasium or Outside

1. Partners take A or B position.
   * All A partners take a position inside the square to jump rope.
   * All B partners divide into four groups and each group begins at a different cone to run around the square.

2. At a signal from the teacher A partners start their pedometers as they begin to jump rope and B partners start theirs as they begin to jog around the square.

3. After five minutes the teacher signals the students to stop.

4. Partners join to tabulate the number of steps they have taken as a team.

5. Students switch roles with their partners and repeat the process.

6. Activities change and after each activity steps are tabulated.

7. At the close of the session students determine (a) the total number of steps of each individual, (b) the total number of steps of each team, and (c) the total number of steps of the entire class.

Activity in Classroom

1. Partners perform all activities in place.

2. For classroom activities students use step benches in varying assigned patterns.

Modifications

- A locomotor movements may include jumping Jacks and Jills, push-ups, sit-ups, squats, and crab kicks (from a seated position students lean back, lift their weight off the floor/ground resting on hands and feet, and alternate kicking each foot toward the ceiling).
- B locomotor movements may include walking, skipping, and jumping.

Assessment

Are the students following directions correctly?

Are students correctly applying computation skills?

Are all students maximizing movement toward cardiovascular fitness?

Are students cooperating with partners and other classmates?

Tag Activities

Objectives

To increase cardiovascular endurance

To introduce students to the kind of activity that promotes cardiovascular fitness

To demonstrate ways in which students can enjoy fitness activities

Targeted Age Group

K-5

Equipment

Colored cones or polyspots

Management

1. Scatter cones or polyspots over a wide area.

2. Group students as a whole class, divide into two groups, or divide into smaller groups.

3. Identify those students who will be the chasers ("Its").

Pre-Activity

Review principles of cardiovascular fitness.

Discuss importance of safety in tagging gently and controlling movement.

Activity in Gymnasium or Outside

1. Cones or polyspots are safety zones for those being chased. By touching a foot against a cone or by standing on the polyspot one cannot be tagged.

2. A maximum of two participants may share a cone or polyspot. One can remain in the safety zone only through the count of five.

3. When a participant is tagged, she or he must freeze in the position held when tagged and perform a task defined by the teacher, such as recounting a specific multiplication table, identifying the colors in the spectrum, or reciting a previously assigned poem.

4. Every two minutes the "Its" are reassigned.

Modifications

- *Shark tag:* At the far end of the area students form two parallel lines with an equal number of participants in each line. At a signal from the teacher the "sharks," who form the line farthest away, move their fins in a swimming motion as they chase the "swimmers" to the "shore," a stopping point designated by the teacher. All then turn back and the swimmers move their arms in a swimming motion as they chase the sharks back out into the ocean.

- *Tummy tag:* Once tagged the children can be asked to perform other abdominal strengthening activities, such as sit-ups or curl-ups for a specified number of repetitions before rejoining the activity. If players are performing jumping jacks they are safe from tagging.

- *Flag tag:* Each student tucks a strip of cloth into a pocket, the back of her or his pants, or a belt loop. The assigned Its' task is to gather as many flags as possible in the designated time. If the child stops and sings "Yankee Doodle Dandy" or another American classic, she or he is considered safe from tagging.

- *Square dance tag:* Students join in this tag game while square dance music reverberates in the background. A player cannot be tagged if she or he is performing an elbow swing or a do-si-do with a partner. Once tagged the participant does a hoe-down stomp clap for 20 beats.

Assessment

Are all students maximizing movement toward cardiovascular fitness?

Are all students following the directions and safety rules?

Do students demonstrate a positive demeanor as they participate?

Rodeo

Objectives

To enthuse students about cardiovascular fitness activities

To increase/maintain cardiovascular endurance

To engage children in entertaining yet beneficial fitness activity

Targeted Age Group

K-3

Equipment

30 cones and/or polyspots

5 small hoops or rings

10 jump ropes

CD player

Country Western CDs

Management

1. Divide the activity area into quarters, defining parameters with polyspots. Designate the following areas:

Barrel Races   In one activity area place four cones 10 feet apart in a straight line. Form five parallel lines 10 feet from each other. If there are more than five students per group, adjust according to that number.

Calf Roping   Situate five (or the number of students per group) cones in lines at each end of three activity arenas. Place five additional cones at the opposite ends.

Establish restraining lines 5–7 feet from the cones at either end.

2. Assign each student to one of four groups.

3. Designate a starting station for each group.

4. Play country western music for the duration of each activity.

5. Each group will continue the activity until the teacher stops the music, signaling them to end the activity and change stations.

Pre-Activity

Describe the kinds of activities that contribute to cardiovascular endurance.

Brainstorm rodeo activities and discuss specific criteria for these events at a rodeo.

Participants demonstrate ways in which they can replicate those movements.

Activity for Gymnasium or Outside

1. *Barrel racing*

One students will stand at the start of one of the five rows. At a signal from the teacher they will begin to weave down the row of four cones. When they reach the fourth cone they will circle around it and then weave back toward the starting position. This will be repeated until the teacher signals a halt.

2. *Calf roping*

Students will each carry a ring/hoop as they run to the jump rope placed before a cone opposite their starting point. Students will stop, toss the ring/hoop over the cone, and then retrieve it to dart back to the jump rope separating them from the cones at the opposite end and once again toss the ring/hoop. They continue at their own pace, keeping track of how many calves they have roped.

3. *Saddle bronc riding*

All of the students in each group will run three steps in a scattered formation and then buck as a bronc before running three more steps and repeating the action.

4. *Bareback riding*

All of the students in the group will gallop in a scattered formation in the area designated. If available they may enjoy using stick horses.

Modifications

- Ask students what their favorite rodeo events are and have them create actions that simulate those events while ensuring cardiovascular activity.
- Establish barnyard areas paralleling activities of active farm animals.
- Develop jungle activities replicating movements of active jungle animals.
- Brainstorm and create circus acts requiring cardiovascular activities.

Assessment

Have students followed directions for the activities and maintained safety measures?

Have students been in constant motion except for when they are changing stations?

Is it evident that students are enjoying the activity?

Fitness Stations

Objectives

To encourage children to develop a positive attitude toward exercise

To develop cardiovascular endurance

To increase students' understanding of appropriate activities to improve cardiovascular endurance

Targeted Age Group

K-5

Equipment

CD player and lively *music*

Cardiovascular exercises written on *poster board*

Cones or *polyspots* to mark the station areas

Boxes, benches, or *bleacher* steps

Individual *jump ropes*

Management

1. Prepare each station and mark off each station area.
2. Divide the class into smaller groups according to the number of stations available. For five stations divide students into five groups.
3. Display the poster board with the designated exercise at each station.
4. Designate a starting station for each group.
5. When the students hear the music they begin the activity and continue until the music stops. They then rush to the next station. Children should be challenged to work for a minimum of five minutes at each station.

Pre-Activity

Review the benefits of cardiovascular endurance. Explain that activities at the fitness stations will promote healthy hearts and lungs.

Activity in Gymnasium or Outside

Stepping Station

1. Students step up and down on wooden boxes/benches, step aerobic boxes, or bleacher steps.
2. They begin stepping by facing their equipment.
3. First one foot goes up on the bench/box and then the other foot.
4. Next the initial foot is returned to the ground, followed by the other foot. Students step to the music in a rhythmical "up, up, down, down" pattern.
5. Students continue stepping until the music stops.

Jump Rope Station

Students jump rope individually. They can choose their own jumping style, suggested by a posted list.

Jogging with a Kick Station

Students jog in the designated area. For variety encourage students to lift their knees high in front and then kick their own backsides.

Jumping Jacks and Jills Station

Students perform traditional Jumping Jacks or can change the legs and arm movements to create their own versions of Jumping Jills, such as scissor kicks or two bounces out, two bounces in, or other varieties.

Locomotor Movements Station   Place four cones in a large square. One or two students stand beside each cone with all students facing the same direction. Students move from cone to cone, changing to the locomotor movements of their choices at each cone. For example, a student may move to the second cone with a skip, change the skip to a leap as she or he passes the third cone, and perform a sliding crossover step to the next cone. Encourage children to be creative.

Activities in the Classroom

The same stations may be modified for the classroom by limiting rope jumping to imaginary ropes, jogging in place, jogging with a kick in place, and locomotor movements in place.

Modifications

- *Partner Circle Station*

Students work with a partner or in a group of three. Partners join hands and place their feet close together. Next they lean back and begin to move in a circle. Students should stop if they feel dizzy and recover before they begin again.

- *Parroting*

Students work with a partner or in small groups. A leader is designated and the partner lines up behind her or him. The leader chooses the locomotor movements and the partner must parrot the movement as they snake around the station area. Then roles are reversed so that everyone gets a chance to lead.

- *Monkey See, Monkey Do*

Partners face each other and mirror movements. The leader must choose the locomotor movements, and the follower moves in the same direction. Easy movements for this activity are the slide and the grapevine.

Assessment

- Are the students following directions to complete the activities?
- Do the students move quickly from station to station?
- Are their actions continuous and vigorous enough to provide cardiovascular benefits?
- Are the students enthusiastic about the activity?

References

American College of Sports Medicine (ACSM). 1987. Position stand on the prevention of thermal injuries during distance running. *Medicine and Science in Sports and Exercise, 19,* 529–533.

Boreham, C., & Riddoch, C. (2001). The physical activity, fitness and health of children. *Journal of Sports Sciences, 19*(12).

Council on Physical Education for Children. (1998). *Physical activity for children: A statement of guidelines.* Reston, VA: National Association for Sport and Physical Education.

Hultquist, C. N., Albright C., & Thompson D. L. (2005). Comparison of walking recommendations in previously inactive women. *Medicine and Science in Sports and Exercise, 37*(4), 676–683.

Kalish, S. (1996). *Your child's fitness: Practical advice for Parents.* Champaign, IL: Human Kinetics.

Sallis, J., & McKenzie, T. L. (1991). Physical education's role in public health. *Research Quarterly for Exercise and Sport, 62,* 124–137.

Solomon, G. (1997). Fair play in the gym. *Journal of Physical Education, Recreation & Dance, 68*(5), 22–25.

Strauss, R. S., Rodzilsky, D., Burack, G., & Colin, M. (2001). Psychosocial correlates of physical activity in healthy children. *Archives of Pediatric and Adolescent Medicine, 155,* 897–902.

Tudor-Locke, C. (2002). Taking steps toward increased physical activity: Using pedometers to measure and motivate. Bloomington, IN: President's Council on Physical Fitness and Sports.

Tudor-Locke, C. E., & Myers, A. M. (2001). Methodological considerations for researchers and practitioners using pedometers to measure physical (ambulatory) activity. *Research Quarterly for Exercise and Sport, 72(1),* 1–12.

Chapter **Twenty Three**

Educational Games: Cooperative and Student-Designed

Natalia swung around the corner of the school building and called out to the 4th graders gathered there, "Who's ready to play a game?" To her surprise only about half of the students piped, "Me!" "I am!" "Yeah!" Others looked at one another and rolled their eyes or cast their gaze to the wood floor. As she outlined the day's game and set it in motion, she pondered the lack of enthusiasm among a large number of the class members. Studying the degree to which some students flung themselves into the activity while others hung back, she noted that the most athletic and confident participants shone with excitement as they easily maneuvered the steps required. Those with less dexterity and limited success with competitive victories, however, held back and exerted only the required amount of energy.

Debates on whether physical educational goals should center on competitive or cooperative activities often arose in her pre-service pedagogy classes. Those who were proponents of competition relied upon the demands of the public. Henkel (1997, p. 22) identified four assumptions about competitive games: (1) competition prepares an individual for nonsport life experiences; (2) competition results in greater productivity and achievement; (3) children prefer competitive activities; and (4) "participating in competitive sports enhances moral development and character building." However, such reasoning has proven inconclusive.

Those who believe competition is learned and has a negative effect cite problems with self-esteem in some students and aggressive and unfair play in others. No one is naïve enough to believe that children can go through life without competition and failure; however, it is the task of educators to *limit* the amount of repeated failure their students encounter. One means of balancing the notion of competition with motor skill improvement is to engage children in activities requiring that they compete with their own previous performances.

GAMES

Certainly one means of ensuring that students enhance essential team-building skills is through collaboration. Fletcher and Kunst (2003, p. 3) describe such activities as "fun, cooperative, and challenging games in which the group is confronted with a specific problem to solve." They assert that initiative games can teach leadership skills and demonstrate reflection on experiences that offer opportunities for practicing responsibility. In these circumstances competition may be incorporated, but in order to ensure experiences with success are not exclusive, students can switch teams.

Fun is considered a crucial motivator for participation in games and other physical activities. For this reason they advocate games that increase participation levels, increase awareness of the benefits of an active lifestyle, develop leadership and social skills,

Children are provided an excellent opportunity to cooperate as they work together in educational games.

enhance school spirit, and result in physical skill development. They believe that students who establish a positive appreciation of physical activity in the school arena are more likely to engage in similar activities at home. Some of the factors they suggest that hamper enthusiasm are lack of self-confidence, hesitancy to take risks, limited skills, and lack of opportunity.

In examining cooperative games promoting physical activities, both teacher- and student-created games merit consideration. In keeping with theories on cooperative learning across the curriculum, as advocated by Johnson and Johnson (1984), positive goal interdependence exists in tandem with individual accountability. It is imperative that the group understands that they sink or swim together. Likewise, Butler (2006, p. 243) advocates that using games to develop physical skills is in essence a democratic approach, focusing on "creating play as a shared experience, not just on being winners." Because cooperative games may take a variety of forms, both cooperative and student-designed games provide opportunities for students to develop independent and interdependent skills.

Games may serve as tools to further enhance instruction already inherent in the curriculum. By using them as a preliminary event, student interest in the information is piqued. If integrated as the unit evolves, greater clarity may be achieved. Certainly, cooperative games centering on physical activities make endeavors that may be threatening in other circumstances more comfortable.

Cooperative Games

The teacher's role in establishing a cooperative game is to arrange equipment, assign groups, establish rules, and monitor play. Although cooperative games typically require little equipment, advance organization of needed materials allows for more time in activity engagement. In assigning groups, consideration should be given to the number of participants that will maximize individual opportunities and ensure interdependence. When children are being introduced to cooperative games, smaller group sizes may more easily facilitate learning. With practice, increased numbers may enhance team-building skills.

Types of Games

In competitive games children in one group oppose children in another group in efforts toward a goal attainable by only one group. Such games often rely on the skills of the best competitors and sometimes leave some students sitting on the sidelines or standing off to one side while others vie for victory. In individualized games, however, children set goals only with themselves, such as in gymnastics, swimming, golf, and other events. Cooperative games, on the other hand, depend on participants working collectively. All should contribute to achieve the goal, competing only with personally set goals.

Student-Designed Games

Certainly the teacher's involvement is integral in establishing the framework within which students create their own cooperative or competitive games. However, student engagement is increased when they are entrusted to design games intended to develop specific skills. Rovegno and Bandhauer (1994) maintain that child-designed games may help children to develop a deeper understanding of skills and strategy, think critically about playing games, learn how to solve problems collaboratively, and create games that are meaningful to them. Since not all children are developmentally ready for competitive games, such frameworks should not be required. Certainly for many children the time comes when cooperative games are no longer challenging, and thus they are ready to move to a competitive venue.

When students are asked to design games targeting a specific skill, such as varying pace when striking foam balls with paddles across a net, they gather in small groups, brainstorm possible rules and boundaries, and begin to practice. When unforeseen problems arise with the established criteria, they halt, discuss alternatives, and try again. In this way the use of games may strengthen communication skills and aid in building rapport among students. If an additional goal is to apply this activity to other subjects in the curriculum, the students may explain the rules in written form to share with classmates. This may be taken a step further by drawing the position of the paddle when approaching and striking the ball. Likewise, the experience may fall within the parameters of social studies, as students discuss what makes effective team efforts or leadership traits.

MOVEMENT EXPERIENCES

Snowballing

Objectives
To develop cooperative skills
To learn how to solve problems collaboratively
To generate a positive attitude toward cooperative movement

Targeted Age Group
K-3

Equipment
CD of "Let It Snow" or any snow-themed recording
CD player

Management
Direct students to scatter around a large activity area.

Pre-Activity
Discuss the factors that make good team building.
Discuss rules of safety.

Activity
1. As the music begins students twirl like a snowflake in the wind.
2. When the teacher stops the music, children join both hands in pairs as a bigger snowball and spin together.
3. The music stops again and pairs join another pair and the four join hands and spin together as an even larger snowball.

4. The next time the music stops groups of four join other groups of four to form groups of eight, and all spin together in a giant snowball.

5. This continues until one huge snowball is formed and everyone spins together.

Modifications

- Corn popping and sticking together with caramel
- Cotton candy swirling around a stick
- Rice Krispies and marshmallows joining to make Krispie treats
- Add $1 + 1, 2 + 2, 4 + 4, 8 + 8$
- After shaping one huge snowball students divide by numbers called out by the teacher
- Show how one voter joins with another and another to elect a candidate

Assessment

Are the students cooperatively completing the game as directed?

Are the students demonstrating teamwork?

Are the students performing the activities safely?

Are the students enthusiastic about participating?

Team Tightrope

Objectives

To develop cooperative skills

To work together toward a solution

Targeted Age Group

K-5

Equipment

One jump rope for every team of 3

Management

1. Divide into groups of three.
2. Each team gets one jump rope.
3. Situate cones or polyspots in two lines at least 50 feet apart.

Pre-Activity

Discuss elements of teamwork.

Discuss safety precautions.

Activity

1. Teams spread out ropes like tightropes and walk the distance together on the ropes.
2. Feet must remain on the ropes (see possible strategies below).
   - Team may work together to move along the rope to one end, then reach back and fling it forward to proceed.
   - Team may slide the rope along under their feet.

Modifications

- Students may measure the rope and determine distance from one line to the other by determining how many rope lengths it takes and multiplying it by the length.
- Children may balance a yardstick, broom handle, umbrella, or other object in their hands or a book on their heads as they trek the distance.
- One foot must remain on the rope at all times.
- Use five polyspots rather than the ropes and step only in the spot to move forward.

Assessment

Are students working cooperatively to cross the divide?

Are students respectful of teammates?

Why Knot?

Objectives

To develop cooperative skills through games

To work together to solve a dilemma

Targeted Age Group

3–5

Equipment

None

Management

1. Divide class into groups of seven or eight.
2. Have groups situated far enough apart so as not to disturb other groups.

Pre-Activity

Discuss characteristics of effective cooperative effort.

Activity

1. Students join hands in a tight circle. All hands remain joined throughout the activity.
2. One student leads those holding her/his hands under or over a pair of joined hands somewhere else in the group.
3. Another student leads those beside him/her under or over another pair.
4. This continues until the group is untangled and can no longer move.
5. At a signal from the teacher groups begin to untangle without letting go of hands.

Modifications

- Join entire class in one huge, tangled group
- Right hands to right hands; left hands to left hands
- Remain silent during the entire activity
- When each tangle is woven, all stand on one foot while one team member counts to 20

Assessment

Are the students successfully completing the activity as directed?

Are children working collaboratively?

Mix it Up

Objectives

To work cooperatively toward a goal

To move safely

Targeted Age Group

K-5

Equipment

Drum and drumsticks

Management

1. Establish a position in the center of the area

Pre-Activity

Students spread out over a wide area

Activity

1. At the beat of the drum students group according to the number of beats (e.g., if the teacher beats the drum four times, students gather in groups of four).
2. One person in the group calls out "knee" or "wrist" or "elbow" or any body part, and all group members connect those parts at the center of the circle.
3. At the next series of drum beats children leave the group, moving at least 20 feet into a new group of students; a body part is called out.

Modifications

- Students may call out a vocabulary word and spell it in unison.
- Teacher may call out a math problem and the groups call out the answer.
- Use the scientific name for the bone or muscle to be joined.
- Group creates a limerick centered on the body parts joined.

Assessment

Are newly formed teams working cooperatively?
Are the students successfully completing the activity as directed?

Spill the Beans

Objectives

To work collaboratively toward a goal
To develop communication skills

Targeted Age Group

3–5

Equipment

Package of dried navy beans
One wooden clothespin for every two students

Management

1. Along a line scatter at least 25 beans in a small area for each pair.
2. Use one polyspot for each pair to mark another parallel line 50 feet away from the first line.
3. Each pair gets one clothespin.

Activity

Students pair up, join hands or lock elbows, and assume a position beside their polyspots.
While waiting children practice maneuvering the clothespin.

Activity

1. Each child holds one leg of the clothespin throughout this activity.
2. At a signal from the teacher each pair dashes to its pile of spilled beans.
3. Together a pair picks up one bean by closing the clothespin over it and carries it together to the polyspot.
4. This procedure is repeated until 20 beans are collected in their polyspot.

Modifications

- One leg of each team member is tied with a scarf to the opposite leg of her or his partner as they go through the above process.

- Pairs take one crayon or colored marker across and draw/color a picture together, returning to the starting point for each additional color.
- Students work a math problem together alternating writing each number.
- At one side students pick up a folded paper with the name of a state written in a unique color. At the other side they alternate turns coloring in each state on an unmarked map of the United States.
- One at a time from a collection of 20 blocks on one line, students carry each block to the polyspot and construct a sculpture.

Assessment

Are students successfully completing the activity as directed?

Have students worked cooperatively?

Student-Designed Cooperative Games

1. Using three balls, five students collaboratively create rules, scoring, and boundaries for a game demonstrating correct dribbling form while shielding the ball.
2. Using jump ropes, basketballs, or playground balls, students design rules, scoring, and boundaries for a game utilizing jumping and catching simultaneously.
3. In small groups, students create rules, scoring, and boundaries for a game that combines dribbling and kicking and a target.
4. In groups of four, children design rules, scoring, and boundaries for a game that incorporates punting, receiving, and throwing.
5. In groups of five, students propose the rules, scoring, and boundaries for a game that involves throwing and catching tennis balls, bean bags, and/or footballs while on the move.
6. In groups of four, plan the rules, scoring, and boundaries for a game of soccer for your group.
7. In a small group, prepare rules, scoring, and targets for a game of Frisbee golf.
8. In groups of six, use a plastic bat, wiffle ball, and four polyspots to design a game that emphasizes base running.
9. Employing underhand striking with hands, three players create rules, scoring, and boundaries for a game using balloons, beach balls, or foam balls.
10. With badminton rackets and two shuttles, groups of four propose rules, scoring, and boundaries for a game.

References

Butler, J. (2006). Curriculum constructions of ability: Enhancing learning through Teaching Games for Understanding (TGfU) as a curriculum model. *Sport, Education and Society, 11*(3), 243–258.

Fletcher, A., and Kunst, K. (2003). *So, you wanna be a playa? A guide to cooperative games for social change.* Olympia, WA: The Freechild Project.

Henkel, S. (1997). Monitoring competition for success. *The Journal of Physical Education, Recreation and Dance, 68*(2), 21–28.

Johnson, D., & Johnson, R. (1984). *Circles of Learning.* Washington, DC: Association for Supervision and Curriculum Development.

Rovegno, I., & Bandhauer, D. (1994). Child-designed games: Experience changes teachers' conceptions. *The Journal of Physical Education, Recreation and Dance, 65*(6), 60–64.

Chapter Twenty Four

Quality Recess

Green doors fling outward and children spill onto the playground toward specific destinations. In one grassy corner neon cones serve as soccer goals, and players scrimmage with a ball even before reaching the field. On the blacktop, hands sweep ropes, inviting friends to jump to double-Dutch rhythms. The repetitive screech of swings in motion as seesaws drop to earth signal that many children are maximizing their time of limited liberty.

Recess, a cherished part of the school day for many children, provides time to socialize with friends and freedom to choose preferred activities. Though inconsistent from school to school, recess periods typically occur once or twice a day lasting 10 to 20 minutes each. Despite the relaxation and revitalization intended by including recess in the schedule, surprisingly "nearly forty percent of the nation's 16,000 school districts have either modified, deleted, or are considering deleting recess" (NAECS/SDE, 2001, p. 1). Rationale for omitting these programs stems primarily from a desire to devote more time to academics and a concern for the liability potential with playground activities. Quality recesses, however, play significant roles in students' social, emotional, physical, and cognitive development.

One rationale for eliminating recess is that students have scheduled physical education. However, whereas physical education follows a sequential standards-based curriculum and provides students with the skills and knowledge to lead a physically active lifestyle, recess invites children to assume agency for their actions. They may gravitate to playground equipment, engage in a game of baseball, or simply meander with a friend around the play area. The goals of recess and physical education are different, but the two in tandem apply toward the recommended minimum of 60 minutes of physical activity each day. This is also problematic in that many schools have eliminated multiple PE sessions in order to accommodate increasing academic standards for children.

Recess is the highlight of most children's days.

The percentage of children 6–11 years of age who are overweight has more than tripled in three decades, as physical activity levels continue to decline. Using the Youth Media Campaign Longitudinal Survey of more than 3,000 children aged 9–13, Howe and Freedson (2008) found that "less than 40 percent reported participating in organized physical activity while more than 20 percent reported no free-play activity outside of school hours." The National Association for Sport and Physical Education recommends at least 150 minutes per week of instructional physical education for elementary school children." However, the 2006 CDC's School Health Policies and Programs Study revealed that "only 4 percent of elementary schools provide daily physical education

The children who miss recess because of poor behavior are generally the children who really benefit from recess activity.

throughout the school year. These factors provide a dilemma leaving the classroom teacher in the crossfire. Clearly students are better ready to learn after periodic breaks of physical activity. However, if schools make conscious decisions to eliminate scheduled recess periods, how can teachers be assured their students are maximizing opportunities for better physical and mental health?

Some educators may be annoyed at the interruption to classwork that recess sometimes causes. However, if students are encouraged to engage in physical activities or social inter-action for brief segments of the day, they usually return refreshed and ready to attack more heady issues, thus serving to enhance learning. Since schools are responsible to develop students' awareness and skills not only on academic subjects but also on wellness and ap-propriate social behavior, commitment of teachers to support recess periods is essential.

Unfortunately some educators utilize recess time for students to make up late work or as punishment for classroom transgressions, thereby limiting their students' chance to engage in necessary physical activity. Recess is not a reward for good behavior but a vital compo-nent of students' education. Certainly the benefits enjoyed by children make the time allot-ted worthwhile.

BENEFITS OF RECESS

The American Association of a Child's Right to Play advocates the importance of recess for children, allowing a break from studies and a chance to enjoy physical activity. In fact recess is the single most effective strategy for increasing physical activity among children (Recess Rules, 2007). Recess can contribute to the development of children's social, emo-tional, physical, and cognitive skills.

According to Miller (2009), reducing the amount of unstructured time for students did not result in improved student learning due to more time spent in the classroom. He sug-gests that without play, students are less attentive during class hours; also children need recess activity to develop social skills. In addition, he advocates recess as an opportunity to promote creativity, imagination, and resilience.

According to Clements (2000), recess is one time during the day that children engage in experiences that contribute to meaningful development in all these domains.

Recess Provides a Forum for Developing Social Skills.

Persistent efforts toward maintaining silence or near silence in classrooms and hallways and even in the lunchroom reinforce the need for release that recess provides. Likewise,

Hopscotch is a classic physical activity.

many children scurry off to after-school agendas managed by adults, such as day care, athletics, dance or music lessons, or clubs such as Girl Scouts, 4-H, or church organizations. Others return to their homes as latchkey kids, expected to fend for themselves in solitude or with siblings until parents return from work or other commitments. Neither venue affords children opportunities simply to play with other children—negotiating activity planning, building trust, working toward conflict resolution, and establishing leadership roles—all skills needed for social growth.

Recess invites interaction, such as two boys meandering across the field chattering, a cluster of girls hammering out the rules to their kickball game, or players taunting the tagger in a game of chase. Such student-driven involvements are fodder for role taking in structured arenas. Four 3rd graders gather on the blacktop at the start of recess. Maria poses, "Should we play four square?" "Nah," Chris shrugs, "we always play that." "What about hopscotch?" Alexis suggests. "That's fine," replies Janet. "If we don't get going we will be out of time! You draw the squares, Shin Yung, and you the numbers, Chris." "I'll get the rocks," pipes Alexis. "Great!" nods Janet. "When we get it drawn, you start, Alexis, since your name starts with 'A.'" This kind of collaboration requires leadership, negotiation, and consensus, life skills essential to any cooperative activity. Due to the unsupervised nature of the discussion, students initiate negotiation for a plan of action, developing their social skills.

Recess Enhances Emotional Development.

Many students live in areas in the community that have no sidewalks, unsafe roadways in front of homes, and threatening crime potential. Because of the number of latchkey kids across the nation, many children are under strict orders to forego afterschool play time with friends and go immediately home after school and lock the doors. In his testimony before the House Government Reform Committee, Dr. William Dietz of the Center for Disease Control announced that 61.5 percent of all children "do not participate in any organized physical activity outside of school hours." This awareness helps to verify the essential role recess holds in children's lives. Not only can recess aid in managing stress, but it also encourages students to interact on a social level, self-assess as they learn what is acceptable behavior with peers, and develop confidence in themselves as independent thinkers.

In the regulated confines of the rest of the school day students are discouraged from creating excess noise for fear of disrupting learning. Thus, social development and therefore self-esteem can be stifled. The importance of developing childhood friendships through school encounters should not be overlooked. In many schools recess is the only opportunity children have to forge such relationships.

Recess Enhances Physical Development.

Physically active recesses promote wellness. The U.S. Department of Health and Human Services (2004) reports that in the last 10 years, obesity rates in adults have increased by more than 60 percent. Approximately 45 million adults, or 25 percent of the population, are obese. These figures are jarring, but even more frightening are the implications for today's youth. Obesity rates have doubled among children and tripled among teens in 10 years, resulting in nearly 8 million overweight young people. Because obesity contributes significantly to cardiovascular disease, these data are particularly alarming. Gordon-Larson, Nelson, and Popkin (2004) document increasing evidence that the inactivity of America's youth continues into adulthood. Current predictions warn that today's children will be the first generation whose life expectancies will be shorter than their parents' (Olshansky et al., 2005).

Recess serves as a catalyst for movement. According to the publication Recess Rules (2007), recess offers about half of the existing opportunity to promote physical activity among kids during the school year. Therefore, "trying to improve children's health without focusing on recess forfeits our best chance for reaching students with the greatest need" (p. 2). Although not all young people are engaged in vigorous physical activity during recess, most do choose to be active. Also, if the usual time for recess is delayed, a benchmark study by Pellegrini, Huberty, and Jones (1995) determined that children became progressively inattentive resulting in more active play when recess occurred. Likewise, the balance between classroom attentiveness and playground activity is puzzling. Students who are least attentive in the classroom engage in higher activity levels when at recess (Pellegrini and Smith, 1993). The same phenomenon extends to after-school behavior. On those days when children do not have physical education or recess, they are less active at home. Such discoveries attest to the importance of physical activity in sparking alertness and promoting well-being.

Cognitive Advantages.

Breaks in the rigor of classroom learning improve cognitive skills. Though the desirability of recess as an opportunity for increasing physical activity is obvious, the significance of these breaks in the days is far reaching because students return to the classroom refreshed and ready to learn. Caterino and Polak's (1999) determination that physical activity has a positive influence on concentration and memory and on classroom behavior provides added support for celebrating recess. Clearly, alertness corresponds with the number of cognitive breaks afforded learners. When children must focus for extended periods, they grow increasingly inattentive. Thus, students who do not participate in recess may have difficulty with concentration and grow restless (National Association for Sport and Physical Education, 2006).

- Recess provides a valuable strategy for reducing stress incurred due to academic demands, family issues, and peer pressures.
- Research shows 4th graders were more on task and less fidgety in the classroom on days when they had recess, with hyperactive children among those who benefited the most.
- Allocating more curricular time to physical activity positively effects academic achievement (Hillman et al., 2009).

These findings cannot be ignored. If recess reduces stress and relieves fidgeting without negatively affecting academic performance, clearly these designated breaks are worthwhile.

Not only students benefit from the release time, but teachers, too, recognize advantages. With increasing class sizes and legal requirements of supervision, teachers often have no opportunities to use the restroom, get a drink, or collect their thoughts until students are gone for recess. Likewise, it offers time to organize, disseminate materials, and make needed office contacts. Also, teachers benefit from opportunities to reflect on the day's events or connect with colleagues.

Multiple benefits result from a commitment to allotting time for recess. During this time period students develop social, emotional, physical, and cognitive skills. Also, scheduled breaks from the daily vigor of seatwork provide a needed respite for students and teachers alike. However, not only should recess and physical education play an integral role for children, but periodic physical activity during cognitive applications is also vital to good performance.

Teachers enjoy interacting with other adults during recess.

QUALITY RECESS TIME

Most educators agree that recess is essential, providing release time for social, physical, and cognitive experiences . Consideration for the times when recess is scheduled, the expectations for time use, and the significance of safe habits all contribute to the overall quality of recess.

Scheduling Recess.

Although children celebrate the freedom typically enjoyed during the recess period, a number of factors may contribute to ensuring quality recess time. When nutritional needs are met students enjoy increased attention and ability to learn. Unfortunately children are often so anxious to rush to the playground for noon recess that they bolt away from the lunch table leaving heaps of plate waste. The National Food Service Management Institute (2004) avers that recess should be scheduled before the lunch hour. In a recent study they found that whereas students wasted more than 40 percent of their meals when recess was scheduled at noontime, the food waste dropped to 27 percent when recess was scheduled before lunch. To encourage appropriate food consumption, recess should not directly follow the lunch period.

Use of Recess Time.

Despite the freedom children are generally offered during recess, some children are lost without specific directions. If simple activity equipment is provided along with ideas for involvement, many children can spring into action delighted with a sense of direction. For those teachers whose school budgets are stretched thin, requesting donations from parents or local organizations can reap a variety of equipment to lure children into activity.

Opportunities for Integrated Learning.

In order to promote integrated learning, teachers may wish to have students write a recess plan before charging onto the playground or perhaps a goal setting paper or a narrative when they come indoors. Likewise, they may be assigned to count the number of elm, oak, and maple trees in sight for science, to add up steps to determine the distance around the perimeter of the play area for mathematics, or write a poem on the sounds that can be heard during recess for English. If early American history is being taught in social studies, students can practice the Virginia Reel; in studies of Mexico perhaps salsa music can be played so children can rehearse Spanish dances for class presentations. Any of these activities

Dance offers unique opportunities for children.

requires only minimal effort from the teacher but may result in ongoing positive experiences for students. Also, when students return to the classroom, calming activities relating to recess may provide a transition to their daily school work.

Playground Safety.

In order for students to maximize opportunities for physical, social, and cognitive growth it is vital for rules to be established and enforced. If children know, for instance, that they must wait outside the designated area until it is their turn, respect for others is demonstrated and safety is ensured. Not only is it vital to rely upon school-wide playground expectations, but independent classes should be invited to develop several rules they deem appropriate. Such investment in determining rules may increase student investment in playground safety.

Of course, teachers should periodically examine playground equipment in attempts to guarantee that children will not suffer injuries due to rusty chains or merry-go-rounds, sharp edges, or tight spaces where a child's arm, leg, or foot could be caught. Because some students are less respectful during turn taking, teachers on playground duty need to monitor equipment use to prevent monopoly. Likewise, separation of students of different ages from other grade levels results in greater harmony and safety.

According to the Academy of Orthopaedic Surgeons more than 500,000 injuries related to playground equipment appear in annual hospital and doctor's records. Climbing equipment is responsible for most of these injuries, but swings, slides, and seesaws are also culprits. The National Program for Playground Safety attests that approximately 40 percent of all playground-related injuries are the result of inadequate supervision. They also note that through safety training of recess supervisors those numbers can be drastically reduced. For effective supervision the pupil-to-teacher ratio should be limited. If more than twenty-five students are on the playground at one time, more than one educator should be present to supervise.

Providing quality recess time for students requires attention to scheduling, so that students can enjoy maximum benefits. Teacher input on activities and provisions for equipment helps to spark student involvement. If teachers wish to promote a whole-learning experience, integrating recess activities with classroom learning is effective. Also, ensuring student safety while on the playground is paramount in maintaining quality recess time.

Quality recess time provides essential opportunities for social, emotional, physical, and cognitive growth. A break from the confines of daily seatwork and the freedom to choose activities refresh and energize children, so they may return more focused and less fidgety. When considering the benefits of a safe and well-supervised recess, the development of the whole child is affected.

References

American Academy of Orthopedic Surgeons. (2004). Playground safety. http://orthoinfo. aaos.org/fact/thr_report.cfm?Thread_ID=95&topcategory=Children

Caterino, M. C., & Polak, E. D. (1999). Effects of two types of activity on the performance of second-, third-, and fourth-grade students on a test of concentration. *Perceptual Motor Skills, 89,* 245–248.

Clements, R. (Ed). (2000). *Elementary school recess: Selected readings, games, and activities for teachers and parents.* Boston: American Press.

Gordon-Larson, P., Nelson, M., & Popkin, B. M. (2004). Longitudinal physical activity and sedentary behavior trends: Adolescence to adulthood. *American Journal of Preventive Medicine, 27*(4), 277–283.

Hillman, C. H., Pontifex, M. B., Raine, L. B., Castelli, D. M., Hall, E. E., and Kramer, A. F. (2009). The effect of acute treadmill walking on cognitive control and academic achievement in preadolescent children. *Neuroscience, 159*(3), 1044–1054.

Howe, C. A., and P. S. Freedson. (2008). Physical activity and academic performance. *President's Council on Physical Fitness and Sports Newsletter.*

Miller, M. C. (2009). The importance of recess. *Harvard Mental Health Letter, 26*(2), 8.

National Association for Sport and Physical Education & American Heart Association. (2006) In: *Shape of the nation report: Status of physical education in the USA.* Reston, VA: National Association for Sport and Physical Education.

National Association of Early Childhood Specialists in State Departments of Education (NAECS/SDE). (2001). Recess and the importance of play: A position statement on young children and recess [Online]. Available:http://www.naecs-sde.org/recessplay.pdf?attredirects=0. (ERIC Document No. ED463047)

National Food Service Management Institute. (2004, Spring). Relationships of meal and recess schedules to plate waste in elementary schools.

Olshansky, S. J., Passaro, D. J., Hershow, R. C., Layden, J., Carnes, B. A., & Bordy, J. (2005). A potential decline in life expectancy in the United States in the 21st century. *New England Journal of Medicine, 352*(11), 1138–1145.

Pellegrini, A.D., Huberty, P., & Jones, I. (1995). The effects of recess timing on children's playground and classroom behaviors. American Educational Research Journal, 32, 845–864.

Pellegrini, A. D., & Smith, P. K. (1993). School recess: Implications for education and development. Review of Educational Research, 63(1), 51–67.

Recess Rules: Why the undervalued playtime may be America's best investment for healthy kids and healthy schools. (September 2007) Robert Wood Johnson Foundation, Princeton, NJ. Retrieved November 30, 2007, from http://www.rwjf.org/pr/product.jsp?id=20591&catid=15&typeid=136

2006 CDC School Health Policies and Programs Study—Below is the requested reference CDC School Health Policies and Programs Study (SHPPS) 2006. Journal of School Health. 2007; 27(8).

U.S. Department of Health and Human Services. (2004). Steps to Healthier Women.

Photo Credits

Chapter 1

Page 4: Sean Justice/Corbis; p. 5: Image 100/PunchStock; p. 9: (a) Digital Vision/Getty Images; p. 10: Jon Dessen/Illini Studio, Champaign, IL.

Chapter 2

Page 12: Jon Dessen/Illini Studio, Champaign, IL; p. 15: © Lars Niki; p. 15, 18, and 21: Jon Dessen/Illini Studio, Champaign, IL; p. 23: A. Chederros/Getty Images.

Chapter 3

Page 27: Jon Dessen/Illini Studio, Champaign, IL; p. 29: © Lars Niki; p. 39: Jon Dessen/Illini Studio, Champaign, IL.

Chapter 4

Pages 42, 45, 46, and 48: Jon Dessen/Illini Studio, Champaign, IL; p. 52: © Lars Niki; p. 54: Jon Dessen/Illini Studio, Champaign, IL; p. 56: © Lars Niki.

Chapter 5

Page 59: © Lars Niki; p. 60: Royalty-Free/Corbis; p. 64 and 71: Jon Dessen/Illini Studio, Champaign, IL.

Chapter 6

Pages 76 and 79: Jon Dessen/Illini Studio, Champaign, IL; p. 81: Photographer's Choice/Getty Images; p. 82, 83, and 86: Jon Dessen/Illini Studio, Champaign, IL; p. 88: © Lars Niki; p. 89 and 91: Jon Dessen/Illini Studio, Champaign, IL; p. 92: © Lars Niki.

Chapter 7

Page 95: © Lars Niki; p. 96: Jon Dessen/Illini Studio, Champaign, IL; p. 97: Ingram Publishing; p. 99, 101, 102, 103 and 104: Jon Dessen/Illini Studio, Champaign, IL.

Chapter 8

Page 108: © Photodisc Collection/Getty Images; p. 109: Jon Dessen/Illini Studio, Champaign, IL; p. 111 and 115: © Lars Niki.

Chapter 9

Page 122: Jon Dessen/Illini Studio, Champaign, IL; p. 125: Dynamic Graphics Group/Creatas/Alamy; p. 126 and 129: © Lars Niki; p. 132: Jon Dessen/Illini Studio, Champaign, IL; p. 133: Image Source/Getty Images.

Chapter 10

Pages 136 and 139: © Lars Niki; p. 141 and 144: Jon Dessen/Illini Studio, Champaign, IL; p. 146: Comstock/PictureQuest; p. 148: Jon Dessen/Illini Studio, Champaign, IL.

Chapter 11

Page 153: © Image Source/Corbis; p. 157: Jon Dessen/Illini Studio, Champaign, IL; p. 158 and 159: © BananaStock/PunchStock; p. 163: Jose Luis Pelaez Inc/Blend Images LLC.

Chapter 12

Page 168: David Ashley/Corbis. All Rights Reserved; p. 168: Ingram Publishing; p. 170: Jon Dessen/Illini Studio, Champaign, IL; p. 172 and 174: © BananaStock/PunchStock.

Chapter 13

Page 177: © Lars Niki.

Chapter 14

Page 187: © BananaStock/PunchStock.

Chapter 15

Page 197: Jon Dessen/Illini Studio, Champaign, IL.

Chapter 16

Page 210: Ingram Publishing.

Chapter 17

Page 219: Jon Dessen/Illini Studio, Champaign, IL.

Chapter 18

Page 228: Jon Dessen/Illini Studio, Champaign, IL; p. 231: © Lars Niki.

Chapter 19

Page 240: Jon Dessen/Illini Studio, Champaign, IL; p. 242: Image Source/Getty Images; p. 244: Jon Dessen/Illini Studio, Champaign, IL; p. 245: © Lars Niki.

Chapter 20

Page 251: © Comstock/PunchStock; p. 252 and 253: Jon Dessen/Illini Studio, Champaign, IL.

Chapter 21

Page 264: LWA/Dann Tardif/Blend Images LLC; p. 265: D. Berry/PhotoLink/Getty Images.

Chapter 22

Pages 273, 275, 276, 277, and 279: Jon Dessen/Illini Studio, Champaign, IL.

Chapter 23

Page 295: Blend Images/ SuperStock.

Chapter 24

Pages 301 and 302: Jon Dessen/Illini Studio, Champaign, IL; p. 303: © Lars Niki; p. 305: Jon Dessen/Illini Studio, Champaign, IL; p. 306: © Lars Niki.

Index

Page numbers followed by *f* indicate figures; *b*, boxes.

How Does
Government
Work?

Getting
Elected

A Look at Running for Office

Robin Nelson and Sandy Donovan

Lerner Publications Company
Minneapolis

Lerner Publications Company
A division of Lerner Publishing Group, Inc.
241 First Avenue North
Minneapolis, MN 55401 U.S.A.

Website address: www.lernerbooks.com

Library of Congress Cataloging-in-Publication Data

Nelson, Robin, 1971–
     Getting elected: a look at running for office / by Robin Nelson and Sandy Donovan.
          p.   cm. — (Searchlight books™—How does government work?)
     Includes index.
     ISBN 978-0-7613-6519-8 (lib. bdg. : alk. paper)
     1. Political campaigns—United States—Juvenile literature. 2. Campaign management—United States—Juvenile literature. 3. Elections—United States— Juvenile literature. I. Donovan, Sandra, 1967– II. Title
JK2281.N45 2012
324.70973—dc22   2010041859

Manufactured in the United States of America
1 – DP – 12/31/11

Contents

ELECTIONS IN A DEMOCRACY

The United States is a democracy. In a democracy, the government is run for the people and by the people. But people don't do all the work. They choose representatives to make decisions for them. These people help the government do its job.

Government representatives take the oath of office. This is a promise to do their jobs well. What do representatives do?

Two children look on as their mother casts her vote.

People elect representatives. That means they pick them by voting. In the United States, we elect presidents, members of Congress (the Senate and the House of Representatives), and governors. We also elect school board members and judges.

Who Can Vote?

Voting is a right and a duty of people in a democracy. All U.S. citizens over the age of eighteen can vote.

THESE HIGH SCHOOL SENIORS IN UTAH ARE REGISTERING TO VOTE.

Who Can Run for Office?

A person running for office is called a candidate. To be elected to most offices, candidates must be a certain age. They must be U.S. citizens. Running for office also takes hard work.

We're going to follow Kate Brown (a fictional character) as she runs for the U.S. Senate. As we'll see, Brown finds that running for office is hard but rewarding. Elected officials get to help decide how to make a town, a state, or even the whole country a better place to live.

Carol Moseley Braun of Illinois talks to reporters. She hopes to be elected mayor of Chicago.

Chapter 2

BROWN FOR SENATE

Brown has been the mayor of Hillville for six years. Her main job has been to listen to the people of Hillville. She helps solve their problems. She also makes sure that city departments, such as the fire department, are running smoothly.

Brown likes being mayor. She feels she's made a difference in people's lives. Most people say she's done a good job.

Mayor Richard M. Daley visits a school in Chicago. Do you know what a mayor's main job is?

Brown feels ready for a bigger challenge. She'd like to help improve the rest of the state and the country. She wants to be one of the two senators her state sends to Washington, D.C. That's where Congress meets. If elected, Brown can help make laws in Congress that will improve more people's lives.

Ned Lamont of Connecticut announces that he will run for U.S. Senate in 2006.

Hard Work

Brown knows running for office is hard. But she's used to working long hours. When she ran for mayor, she often slept just four hours a night. During the day, she campaigned. Campaigning includes all the work of running for office. It includes meeting voters and giving speeches.

But running for the Senate will be tougher than running for mayor. Brown will need to win votes across the state, not just in Hillville. Many people don't know who Brown is.

When Barack Obama ran for president in 2008, he met with voters across the country.

Brown will have to spend money on her campaign. Most voters get information about a candidate from advertising. Brown will have to spend money on TV, radio, and Internet ads.

AN AD FOR U.S. SENATE CANDIDATE SHARRON ANGLE IS ON THE SIDE OF THIS TRUCK.

Parties

The United States has two main political parties. They are the Democratic Party and the Republican Party. Other parties are called third parties. The Green Party is a third party. Political parties are groups of people who join together to gain control over government. Members of a party have similar beliefs about the way government should work. Brown belongs to the Democratic Party.

This artwork shows the symbols for the Republican Party (TOP) and the Democratic Party (BOTTOM).

VOTE

Democratic Party leaders told Brown this is the right time for her to run for the Senate. They like her ideas about how to improve the government.

It's Official

Brown has decided to run next year. Her family and friends said they would support her. They'll work hard to help her win.

Family support is important to candidates. Baltimore, Maryland, governor Martin O'Malley stands with his wife, daughters, and sons after announcing his reelection campaign.

Florida governor Charlie Crist announced his plans to run for the U.S. Senate in 2010.

It's time to get to work. Brown calls a press conference to announce her candidacy. At press conferences, people answer questions from reporters. Reporters from around the state come to hear Brown's announcement and to report what she has to say.

Vice presidential candidate Dick Cheney thanks volunteers and staff who worked on his 2000 election campaign.

Finding Good Help

Brown's press conference is in March. The election will be in November of next year. Brown has almost two years of campaigning ahead of her.

Brown is ready to work. But she knows she can't win this election by herself. She'll need a staff to run her campaign.

The first person Brown looks for is a campaign manager. He or she will manage the details of the campaign. The next person Brown finds is a fund-raiser. This person will be in charge of raising money to pay for the campaign. Finally, Brown picks her treasurer. The treasurer keeps track of campaign money and pays the bills.

AL GORE RAN FOR PRESIDENT IN 2000. HERE HE INTRODUCES HIS CAMPAIGN MANAGER, DONNA BRAZILE.

Chapter 3

CAMPAIGNING

The work of campaigning is just beginning. On Election Day, Brown will face two opponents for the Senate seat. One is Senator Charles Howe. He is running for reelection. He's a Republican. The other is a Green Party member named Ryan Hu.

South Carolina candidate for governor Nikki Haley watches election results with her family and supporters. What are some things candidates do to try to get elected?

During a 1992 debate, presidential candidates (FROM LEFT TO RIGHT) **Ross Perot, Bill Clinton, and George H. W. Bush discuss issues of importance to voters.**

The Issues

For the next several months, the candidates will discuss issues that affect voters. Each candidate will try to convince voters that his or her beliefs about the issues are what's best for the state and the country. Brown tells voters her beliefs on health care, jobs, and the environment.

On the Campaign Trail

Brown knows she can't waste time. Her campaign has to tell voters why she should be the next senator. To do this, her staff members plan campaign activities. They run TV and radio ads. The ads talk about Brown's success as mayor. They explain how Brown will be a better senator than Howe has been.

Staff members of Colin Wong hand out information about Wong's ideas. He ran for state senator of Hawaii in 2004.

Candidates meet with voters out in public. U.S. Senator Barbara Boxer of California holds a baby in 2010.

Brown's days are full. Every morning, she gets up early and meets with her staff. As mayor of Hillville, Brown has city business to take care of during the day. She wants to make sure she's still doing a good job as mayor.

In the evenings, Brown campaigns. She travels to meet voters. She gives several speeches a week.

Raising Money

Brown's fund-raiser works on raising money for her campaign. Fund-raising events are one way to get money. Brown's campaign raises lots of money by holding fancy dinners for wealthy Democrats.

Sometimes politicians attend fund-raisers for candidates in their own parties. In 1995 Vice President Al Gore (RIGHT) went to a fund-raiser for Jerry Estruth, who was running for U.S. Senator of California.

Brown's campaign also gets smaller donations from others. Staff members call people and send letters asking for donations.

Volunteers make phone calls asking supporters of presidential candidate John McCain to donate money for the campaign.

Chapter 4

THE FINISH LINE

In the days before the election, Brown is busier than ever. She attends meetings called rallies.

Senator Paul Wellstone (LEFT) of Minnesota greets supporters at a rally in 1996. Why do voters go to rallies?

At a rally in California, supporters cheer candidate for governor Meg Whitman.

Rallies take place in malls, town halls, and other spots. Voters go to rallies to show support for a candidate. Brown gives a speech, and the crowd cheers.

Election Day

After a blur of speeches and rallies, Election Day arrives. Election Day is Brown's last chance to convince people to vote for her.

In some places, campaigning on Election Day is illegal. But it's not illegal in Hillville. So Brown wakes early and meets with her campaign manager. They discuss their campaign plans for the day.

Campaign volunteer Charlie Warner (RIGHT) of Nevada calls voters on Election Day.

At seven in the morning, Brown goes to her polling place. This is where people vote. News cameras film her walking in. When she comes out, she smiles at the cameras.

Barack Obama's daughters Malia (LEFT) and Sasha (RIGHT) watch as their father casts his vote in the 2008 presidential election.

New York mayor
Michael Bloomberg
shakes hands with
voters on Election Day.

Next, Brown goes to a rally outside Hillville City Hall. Hundreds of supporters there cheer for her. After the rally, Brown talks to as many people as possible. She walks down the streets and asks people to support her. Many people want to shake her hand. They wish her luck in the election.

Meanwhile, Brown's staff is hard at work. Staff members will try to get as many of Brown's supporters to the polling places as they can.

CAMPAIGN WORKERS GIVE THEIR
CANDIDATES ONE LAST SHOW OF SUPPORT
AS VOTERS HEAD INTO POLLING PLACES.

Election Night

Brown spends the day going to rallies and giving speeches. At eight in the evening, the polling places close. Brown waits for the results. Voting areas across the state report their results slowly. By eight thirty, just a few areas have reported their votes. Senator Howe is winning. Brown is in second place. The Green Party candidate is in third. But it's too early for Brown to be worried. Results have just begun to come in.

Voters can watch the election results on TV. The red places on this map from the 1984 presidential election show states in which Ronald Reagan won the most votes.

Candidate Michael Bennett and his wife and daughters watch election results to see if Bennett will be the next senator from Colorado.

By ten, half the voting areas have reported their votes. Howe and Brown are tied. Soon Brown begins to take a lead. By the time most of the votes are counted, reporters are saying Brown will win.

Brown hugs her family. But it isn't time to announce her victory yet. Friends and staff members call to congratulate her. She tells them it isn't over, but she knows she has won.

PEOPLE WATCH ELECTION RESULTS IN TIMES SQUARE IN NEW YORK CITY TO SEE WHO WILL WIN THE 2008 PRESIDENTIAL ELECTION.

At ten thirty, an important phone call comes. It's Senator Howe. He's calling to concede. This means he'll publicly announce that he has lost the election. He too knows Brown has won. Howe congratulates Brown. He tells her she ran a good campaign.

Sharron Angle of Nevada speaks to supporters after learning that her opponent in the race for U.S. Senator has won.

Victory Party

By quarter of eleven, supporters have gathered to celebrate Brown's victory. Brown and her family enter the victory party. They wave to the crowd. The crowd cheers wildly.

Ronald Reagan celebrates his victory in the 1980 presidential election.

Brown gives her victory speech. She thanks her family and her staff for their work. She says she couldn't have won without them.

Barack Obama speaks to his supporters in Chicago's Grant Park after he was elected president in 2008.

U.S. Senator Elizabeth Dole takes the oath of office in 1993. Her husband, Bob Dole (CENTER), looks on.

What Happens Next?

After almost two years of campaigning, Kate Brown has won the election. In January, she'll go to Washington, D.C. She will begin her term as Senator Brown. She will have offices in Washington and in Hillville.

Before long, Brown will think about running for reelection. She knows firsthand that campaigning is hard. She'll have to decide if she'll do it all again.

Norm Coleman of Minnesota ran for reelection as senator in 2008.

Glossary

campaign: a series of actions organized over a period of time to win an election

candidate: a person who runs for office

citizen: a person who lives in a city, a state, or a country

concede: to publicly admit defeat in an election

Congress: a group of elected officials who write, talk about, and make laws. The U.S. Congress is made up of the Senate and the House of Representatives.

democracy: a political system in which government is run for the people and by the people

donation: money given to a person or a cause

elect: to pick by voting

fund-raiser: a person whose job is to raise money for a candidate. A fund-raiser is also an event set up by a fund-raiser.

political party: a group of people who join together to gain political power. Members of political parties have similar beliefs about the way the government should be run.

polling place: the official place where people vote in their neighborhood

press conference: a meeting where people answer questions from TV and newspaper reporters

representative: a person who is elected to help the government do its job

staff: a group of people who do paid work for an organization

Learn More about Government

Books

Goodman, Susan E. *See How They Run: Campaign Dreams, Election Schemes, and the Race to the White House.* New York: Bloomsbury, 2008. This fun title includes lots of information about elections.

Nelson, Robin, and Sandy Donovan. *The Congress: A Look at the Legislative Branch.* Minneapolis: Lerner Publications Company, 2012. Read all about the Congress, the part of government that character Kate Brown joined when she got elected.

Stier, Catherine. *If I Ran for President.* Morton Grove, IL: Albert Whitman, 2007. In this lively book, six children explain the election process.

Sutcliffe, Jane. *Barack Obama.* Minneapolis: Lerner Publications Company, 2010. Read the life story of Barack Obama, from his childhood in Hawaii and Indonesia to his election as president of the United States.

Websites

Ben's Guide to U.S. Government for Kids

http://bensguide.gpo.gov/3-5/election/index.html

This guide to the U.S. government includes details about the election process.

Kids in the House

http://kids.clerk.house.gov

This website from the U.S. House of Representatives provides educational and entertaining information about the legislative branch of the U.S. government to students of all age levels.

Kids Voting USA

https://netforum.avectra.com/eWeb/StartPage.aspx?Site=KVUSA

This website features information on how kids can get involved in elections around the country.

Index

Photo Acknowledgments

The images in this book are used with the permission of: AP Photo/Charles Dharapak, p. 4; © Jewel Samad/AFP/Getty Images, p. 5; AP Photo/The Salt Lake Tribune, Scott Sommerdorf, p. 6; © Scott Olson/Getty Images, p. 7; © Barry Brecheisen/Getty Images, p. 8; © Darren McCollester/Getty Images, p. 9; © Chip Somodevilla/Getty Images, p. 10; © Ethan Miller/Getty Images, pp. 11, 23; © Matthew Trommer/Dreamstime.com, p. 12; © Timothy A. Clary/AFP/Getty Images, p. 13; AP Photo/Gail Burton, p. 14; © Joe Raedle/Getty Images, pp. 15, 27; © Paul Buck/AFP/Getty Images, p. 16; © Luke Frazza/AFP/Getty Images, p. 17; AP Photo/David Goldman, p. 18; © Eugene Garcia/AFP/Getty Images, p. 19; AP Photo/Lucy Pemoni, p. 20; © Kevork Djansezian/Getty Images, p. 21; AP Photo/Susan Ragan, p. 22; AP Photo/Andy King, p. 24; AP Photo/Lenny Ignelzi, p. 25; © Melina Mara/The Washington Post via Getty Images, p. 26; © Craig Warga/NY Daily News Archive via Getty Images, p. 28; © Christopher Capozziello/Getty Images, p. 29; © Robert Maass/CORBIS, p. 30; © Matt McClain/Getty Images, p. 31; © Jemal Countess/Getty Images, p. 32; © Robyn Beck/AFP/Getty Images, p. 33; AP Photo, p. 34; © Anthony Jacobs/Getty Images, p. 35; © Mark Wilson/Getty Images, p. 36; AP Photo/Winona Daily News, Melissa Carlo, p. 37.

Front cover: AP Photo/David Goldman (top); © Ken Skalski/CORBIS (bottom).

Main body text set in Adrianna Regular 14/20
Typeface provided by Chank